To Have and Have Not

Wisconsin/Warner Bros. Screenplay Series

To Have
and Have Not

Edited with an introduction by

Bruce F. Kawin

Published for the Wisconsin Center for Film and Theater Research by
The University of Wisconsin Press

Published 1980

The University of Wisconsin Press
114 North Murray Street
Madison, Wisconsin 53715

The University of Wisconsin Press, Ltd.
1 Gower Street
London WC1E HA, England

First printing

Printed in the United States of America

For LC CIP information see the colophon

ISBN 0-299-08090-0 cloth; 0-299-08094-3 paper

Publication of this volume has been assisted by a grant from
The Brittingham Fund, Inc.

Contents

Foreword

In donating the Warner Film Library to the Wisconsin Center for Film and Theater Research in 1969, along with the RKO and Monogram film libraries and UA corporate records, United Artists created a truly great resource for the study of American film. Acquired by United Artists in 1957, during the period when the major studios sold off their films for use on television, the Warner library is by far the richest portion of the gift, containing eight hundred sound features, fifteen hundred short subjects, nineteen thousand still negatives, legal files, and press books, in addition to screenplays for the bulk of the Warner Brothers product from 1930 to 1950. For the purposes of this project, the company has granted the Center whatever publication rights it holds to the Warner films. In so doing, UA has provided the Center another opportunity to advance the cause of film scholarship.

Our goal in publishing these screenplays is to explicate the art of screenwriting during the thirties and forties, the so-called Golden Age of Hollywood. In preparing a critical introduction and annotating the screenplay, the editor of each volume is asked to cover such topics as the development of the screenplay from its source to the final shooting script, differences between the final shooting script and the release print, production information, exploitation and critical reception of the film, its historical importance, its directorial style, and its position within the genre. He is also encouraged to go beyond these guidelines to incorporate supplemental information concerning the studio system of motion picture production.

We could set such an ambitious goal because of the richness of the script files in the Warner Film Library. For many film titles, the files might contain the property (novel, play, short story, or original story idea), research materials, variant drafts and scripts (from story outline to treatment to shooting script), post-production items such as press books and dialogue continuities, and legal records (details of the acquisition of the property, copyright registration, and contracts with actors and directors). Editors of the Wisconsin/Warner Bros. Screenplay Series receive copies of all the materials, along with prints of the films (the most authoritative ones available for reference purposes), to use in preparing the introductions and annotating the final shooting scripts.

In the process of preparing the screenplays for publication, typographical errors were corrected, punctuation and capitalization were modernized, and the format was redesigned to facilitate readability.

Unless otherwise specified, the photographs are frame enlargements taken from a 35-mm print of the film provided by United Artists.

In theory, the Center should have received the extant scripts of all pre-1951 Warner Brothers productions when the United Artists Collection was established. Recent events, however, have created at least some doubt in this area. Late in 1977, Warners donated collections consisting of the company's production records and distribution records to the University of Southern California and Princeton University respectively. The precise contents of the collections are not known, since at the present time they are not generally open to scholars. To the best of our knowledge, all extant scripts have been considered in the preparation of these volumes. Should any other versions be discovered at a later date, we will recognize them in future printings of any volumes so affected.

Tino Balio
General Editor

Introduction: *No Man Alone*

Bruce F. Kawin

The story of the making of *To Have and Have Not* is an exciting and complex one, ranging from the well-known romance between its stars, Humphrey Bogart and Lauren Bacall, to one of the subtler developments of the alliance between the U.S. government and the Batista regime in Cuba. It is also the story of a collaboration among four very fine writers: Ernest Hemingway, Howard Hawks, Jules Furthman, and William Faulkner. Although the film builds on the contributions of two Nobel Prize winners, a scenarist of the first rank, a masterful cinematographer, a skillful editor, and such creative actors as Walter Brennan, Marcel Dalio, Hoagy Carmichael, and of course Bogart and Bacall, it is also that auteur critic's dream, a film that clearly reveals the guiding influence and personal vision of a single artist, Howard Hawks, who conceived, produced, rewrote, and directed this tough-edged, sexy, comic melodrama. "I can make a picture out of your worst story," Hawks once told Hemingway. It was not Hemingway's worst story, and Hawks did not make a picture out of it; what he made instead is an entertaining and unpretentious masterpiece.

The Novel

With the exception of *For Whom the Bell Tolls*, *To Have and Have Not* is Hemingway's only deliberate and sustained attempt at political commentary. In part, it was a response to such critics as Wyndham Lewis who had come, in the light of the Depression, to disparage Hemingway's fiction for being "entirely closed to politics."[1] It was also, and more crucially, a response to the conditions Hemingway observed during a layover in Havana in 1933, on the first leg of a trip to Madrid, Paris, and Africa.

Brigadier General Gerardo Machado y Morales had been elected president of Cuba in 1924 and enjoyed great popular support until 1929. The sugar industry prospered, relations with government and banking forces in the United States were mutually satisfactory, and a large public works project improved the roads, the public buildings, the hospitals, and the schools. By 1929, however, Machado had decided to emulate Mussolini. At just the time he was coming to seem like a brutal megalomaniac, the Depression hit Cuba, and it became impossible for Machado to silence his critics by pointing to a solid economy. On September 30, 1930, the Havana police killed a student demonstrator, and from then until 1933, Cuba was in turmoil, mostly in the form of battles between terrorist student groups and the army and police. In July 1933, Machado temporarily restored constitutional rights and found that he had unwittingly sanctioned a public protest against his regime.[2] During the first days of August there was a general strike. Hemingway, who was in Havana between August 4 and 7, privately endorsed the cause of the people and referred to Machado as a "lousy tyrant."[3] The day he sailed for Europe there were false rumors of Machado's resignation; cheering crowds were massacred in the streets. On August 12 Machado fled the country. Within five months Colonel Fulgencio Batista y Zaldívar had taken control.

When Hemingway arrived in Madrid, he found the Spanish Republic in a shaky condition. An inefficient bureaucracy appeared to have absorbed the liberal idealists, and it was Hemingway's guess that another revolution was on the way. He was coming to feel that the process of revolution and the interests of the indi-

1. Carlos Baker, *Hemingway: The Writer as Artist* (Princeton: Princeton University Press, 1963), p. 203.

2. John Edwin Fagg, *Cuba, Haiti, and the Dominican Republic* (Englewood Cliffs, N.J.: Prentice-Hall, 1965), pp. 74–82.

3. Carlos Baker, *Ernest Hemingway: A Life Story* (New York: Scribner's, 1969), p. 245.

vidual were opposed. While in Madrid, in September 1933, he wrote a story that became Part One of *To Have and Have Not*; called "One Trip Across," it celebrated the virtues of a tough, independent fisherman, Harry Morgan, who becomes a smuggler rather than let his family go hungry. When he returned to his Key West home in 1935, Hemingway wrote the second part of the novel, a story called "The Tradesman's Return." In July 1936, he decided to rework these stories into a novel about the nature of revolution and the decline of the individual.[4] At that point the Spanish Civil War broke out, intensely focusing Hemingway's political consciousness.

He wanted to be in Spain but felt he had to finish the novel. The first draft of *To Have and Have Not* was completed in January 1937. Hemingway then went to Spain, where he wrote the voice-over narration for Joris Ivens's film *The Spanish Earth* (1937).[5] Back in America during the late summer, he spent two weeks revising the proof sheets of the novel, which was as close as he got to doing a second draft.

To Have and Have Not was published by Scribner's in October 1937 and became a best-seller. The critics tended generally not to like it; although they patted Hemingway on the back for showing "social consciousness," many considered the book structurally flawed, confused, preachy, and even sloppy. In his typical fashion Hemingway—who was never able to accept criticism gracefully— assumed that the critics had ganged up on him and became bitter about the whole matter.[6] His rejecting attitude, his angry and self-pitying isolationism, is ironically appropriate, since the basic theme of the novel is that one man alone has no chance against large, hostile forces. I say "ironically" since it is just this theme that Hawks, Furthman, and Faulkner reversed, and it is

4. Baker, *Hemingway*, pp. 203–204.

5. This commentary was first recorded by Orson Welles, but Ivens soon substituted Hemingway's own reading of the text. Apparently both versions are now in circulation.

6. Baker, *Ernest Hemingway*, pp. 320–21. Compare Hemingway's response to the critics of *Across the River and into the Trees*, who were later cast as the sharks in *The Old Man and the Sea*.

their celebration of the *power* of the individual and the momentum of the anti-Fascist cause that has accounted for much of the film's success. In emphasizing what he saw as the positive elements of Hemingway's vision, Hawks also rejected that current of self-pity (or perhaps it should be called an embattled defeatism) that wears down many of the novel's characters and that was a consistent feature of Hemingway's imagination and of his personal life.

Hemingway, Furthman, Faulkner, and Hawks all had different versions of Harry Morgan, and it is interesting to observe how well Humphrey Bogart could have played any of them. Furthman's was a tough adventurer, Faulkner's a sometime misogynist on the verge of political commitment, and Hawks's a witty and self-confident professional—but Hemingway's was a family man, an ex-cop, a desperate planner, an unsentimental killer, an individualist ground to death by giant forces, a loser.

The novel opens in a bar in Havana, where Morgan refuses to carry three Cuban terrorists to the States and then watches them get shot up in the streets. He goes to his charter-fishing boat and meets his friend Eddy, a rummy who "used to be a good man." They take the client, Mr. Johnson, out for a day of fishing; Johnson hooks two huge fish and loses them both, along with Morgan's expensive rod and reel. Johnson says he'll pay Morgan the next day, but instead flies to Florida. Unable to pay for new equipment, and needing money to support his wife, Marie, and their three daughters (who live in Key West), Morgan agrees to smuggle some Chinese out of Cuba. The man who hires him, Mr. Sing, clearly expects him to drown the cargo. On his way to pick up the Chinese, Morgan discovers that Eddy has stowed away on the boat and decides he will have to kill him. After loading the men, Morgan strangles Mr. Sing, puts the furious cargo more or less ashore, and heads home to Key West, having decided not to kill Eddy after all.

The second part of the novel finds Morgan smuggling liquor from Cuba to Florida. It is about six months later, and the implication is that he was never able to finance a return to the charter-fishing business. He is in his boat with a Negro named Wesley, and both have been shot—Wesley in the leg and Morgan in the arm. They are spotted again, and Morgan dumps the liquor overboard.

The third and longest part of the novel is set a few months later in Key West. Morgan's boat has been impounded (thanks to the man who spotted him) and his arm has been amputated. Robert Simmons, a lawyer Morgan refers to as Bee-lips, hires him to take four Cubans to Havana after they rob a bank (to finance the anti-Machado terrorists). Morgan hires Albert Tracy, a workman on relief, to be his mate. After an unsuccessful attempt to steal back his own boat, Morgan gets Simmons to rent the boat belonging to Freddy, the proprietor of the bar where much of the action of this part of the novel takes place. Then he spends the night with Marie.[7]

At this point Hemingway introduces a whole new set of characters: rich writers and businessmen who hang around Freddy's bar or loll in their yachts. The central figure is Richard Gordon, a writer apparently based in part on John Dos Passos, who is trying to write a proletarian novel and who is both conceited and insensitive. While his long-suffering wife, Helen, explores her friendship with a Professor MacWalsey, Gordon goes to bed with a rich bitch named Helène Bradley, who "collected writers as well as their books." When Gordon gets home, he and Helen have a brilliantly written fight and realize their marriage is over. Back at Freddy's, Gordon gets drunk with a large group of workers on relief,[8] picks a fight with MacWalsey, gets knocked out by the bouncer, and stumbles home.

7. Marie is forty-five (two years Morgan's senior), a bleached blonde with an extensive sexual past. She might be described as a Molly Bloom metamorphosed by suffering and compassion.

8. These workers are based on a real community that was wiped out in a 1935 hurricane. Hemingway helped collect the two hundred bodies and wrote about that experience for *New Masses*. One of Morgan's central compulsions is not to go on welfare. Hemingway's reference to these workers, and Albert's fate in the novel, help show the reader why Morgan's tragic position makes sense.

The story of the Gordons is told in parallel with that of Morgan's final voyage.[9] This parallel montage is the source of most critics' objections to the novel.

Morgan prepares Freddy's boat, the *Queen Conch*, for the voyage, hiding a gun near the engine. The bank is robbed, and one of the terrorists (Roberto) kills Simmons. The four Cubans pile aboard, and Roberto horribly and suddenly kills Albert. Morgan buys time by setting a course that will miss Cuba, engages in a discussion of revolutionary tactics and priorities with the youngest of the radicals, and decides to himself that no one with real sympathy for the working man could have killed Albert. Late that night he kills all four of them with the hidden gun, but is mortally gut-shot in the process. The boat drifts till late the next day, when it is found by the Coast Guard. Before losing consciousness, Morgan tells the men who have found him, "No matter how a man alone ain't got no bloody fucking chance."[10] Hemingway felt this was the message of his book[11] and observes in the narrative that this is what it had taken Morgan his whole life to learn. As the boat is towed into the harbor, Hemingway surveys the bedrooms of the various yachts and with them the failures of the upper classes; it is a bitter chapter. Morgan dies in the hospital without regaining consciousness, and Marie prepares herself for a life without meaning, hoping that it will be easier if she dies inside. The last sentence of the novel describes a yacht "hugging the reef as she made to the westward to keep from wasting fuel against the stream."

9. One of the intersections of these plots, chapter 19, is a high point of the novel. The day before his affair with Hélène, Gordon passes Marie on the street; she is returning from the sheriff's office, presumably having reported Morgan missing. Gordon is convinced he understands her—her ugliness, her sexual unresponsiveness, her lack of sympathy for her husband, and a number of other qualities he invents—and rushes home to write a chapter about her. Toward the end of the novel Marie drives past Gordon as he heads home after his fight in the bar and dismisses him as a poor rummy. She is, of course, a better judge of character than he is.

10. Ernest Hemingway, *To Have and Have Not* (New York: Scribner's, 1937), p. 225.

11. Baker, *Ernest Hemingway*, p. 383.

Wasting fuel against the stream is what most of the people in this novel have been doing, and the stream is not just an image of malevolent Fate but also one of the Depression (and the government's manner of handling it). A man alone has little chance against such forces, and even men banded together for revolution are presented as having lost sight of their goals. (The only exception appears to be a radical Gordon meets in the bar, who tells him his books are "shit.") The solo artist, at least one like Gordon, has fewer moral resources and less real success even than Morgan, who at least never quits. This is the key to the novel's title, which refers to two sets of haves and have-nots: those with or without life and money, and those with or without guts and moral power. The function of the parallel plotting in Part Three of the novel is to orchestrate these social, economic, and psychological disparities; no solution is suggested.

The points of contact between this novel and the film that uses its name are slight. Walter Brennan's Eddy is related to the novel's rummy Eddy and also to Albert Tracy. The fishing scene with Johnson is hardly changed, and in both stories Morgan's financial hardship leads to his having to deal with radicals. The Gordons undergo several metamorphoses until Helen and Helène show up as Helene de Bursac and Gordon is lost in the shuffle. Wesley becomes Horatio, and the *Queen Conch* keeps her name but changes ownership. And that's about it.

Fishing for a Writer

So one day Ernest Hemingway and Howard Hawks went off on a ten-day fishing trip.

Hawks had been trying to get Hemingway to write scripts for some time, but Hemingway had said he was good at what he was already doing and didn't want to go to Hollywood. "You don't have to go to Hollywood." said Hawks. "We can meet just the way we're doing now. You don't even have to write down the story—I'll dictate it." Hemingway remained adamant, and Hawks said, "Ernest, you're a damn fool. You need money, you know. You can't do all the things you'd like to do. If I make three dollars in a picture, you get one of them. I can make a picture out of your worst story."[12] "What's my worst story?" asked Hemingway. "That god damned bunch of junk called *To Have and To Have Not* [sic]." "You can't make anything out of that," said Hemingway, and Hawks said, "Yes I can. You've got the character of Harry Morgan; I think I can give you the wife. All you have to do is make a story about how they met."

They planned a story during the next several days, on Hemingway's boat; all this probably occurred early in 1939. In May 1939, Hemingway sold all movie, radio, and TV rights in his novel to the Hughes Tool Co. (with which Hawks had connections) for $10,000. In October 1943, Hawks bought these rights from Hughes for $92,500 and sold them to Warner Brothers for $92,500 plus a quarter interest in the picture. "When I told [Hemingway] how much that picture made," Hawks later said, "and I said, 'You only got $10,000,' he wouldn't talk to me for six months."

Hawks was a great teaser, and one of the things he told Hemingway in a last-ditch attempt to get him to write this script probably struck a nerve. "Okay," he said, "I'll get Faulkner to do it; he can write better than you can anyway." (The story may, of course, have been invented years later, long after the events of 1944 had in fact brought Faulker onto the picture.)[13] Hemingway is on record as having admitted twice—to James T. Farrell in 1936 and to Jean-Paul Sartre in 1944—that Faulkner was a better writer than he, but he could hardly have enjoyed anyone else's pointing this out. In 1947, when Faulkner made his statement that the best

12. Much of this information and all Hawks quotations come from an unpublished interview between Hawks and myself on May 24, 1976. For further background on Hawks and Faulkner, see Bruce Kawin, *Faulkner and Film* (New York: Ungar, 1977) and Meta Carpenter Wilde and Orin Borsten, *A Loving Gentleman* (New York: Simon and Schuster, 1976).

13. Hawks's stories were often unreliable. One has to distrust especially those stories that contain ironic coincidences—a completely unfounded one, for instance, of Faulkner's working in a bookstore and selling *The Sound and the Fury* to unsuspecting customers. Lauren Bacall says this of her own first experiences with Hawks's stories: "He took me to lunch and told me about his directing experiences with various actresses. It was always what he said to them, or to Howard Hughes, to Jack Warner—he always came out on top, he always won. He was mesmerizing and I believed every story he told me." (Lauren Bacall, *Lauren Bacall by Myself* [New York: Knopf, 1979], p. 79.)

modern novelists were Wolfe, Dos Passos, Caldwell, Hemingway, and himself, and that of the five Wolfe had the most experimental courage and Hemingway the least, Hemingway was furious; feeling his courage in general had been maligned, he got a friend to write Faulkner about his war record! Faulkner apologized, but that apparently didn't do much good. When in 1952 Faulkner praised Hemingway's independence as a writer, Hemingway decided he had been insulted again; he apparently never saw a review Faulkner wrote shortly thereafter, to the effect that *The Old Man and the Sea* was perhaps "the best single piece of any of us—I mean his and my contemporaries." By 1955 Hemingway was referring to Faulkner as "Old Corndrinking Mellifluous," and by 1956 as "a no-good son of a bitch."[14] Although Hawks continually urged Faulkner and Hemingway to meet, they always refused—something Hawks considered amusing.

Faulkner's attitudes toward Hemingway were less motivated by egotism. In 1955 he explained his "courage" ranking as follows: "I rated Wolfe first, myself second. I put Hemingway last. I said we were all failures. All of us had failed to match the dream of perfection and I rated the authors on the basis of their splendid failure to do the impossible. . . . I rated Hemingway last because he stayed with what he knew. He did it fine, but he didn't try for the impossible."[15] There is no record of his judgment on *To Have and Have Not*, but in his 1942 original screenplay, "The De Gaulle Story" (Warner Brothers, unproduced), he had one of his characters praise *For Whom the Bell Tolls* as a source of political and personal inspiration:

EMILIE: But after we reached Paris, and they overtook us again, and it was no use to flee again, because now nothing remained that we could be despoiled of, another musician, a Frenchman, a young man who knew Father, would come to see us. And one night he brought a book, an American book written by a Mr. Hemingway. He would read it to us at night and translate it. It told about a young girl to whom that [i.e., rape by soldiers] had happened also, and about an older woman who was very

14. Baker, *Ernest Hemingway*, pp. 297, 439, 461, 503–504, 532, 534.
15. Harvey Breit, "A Walk with Faulkner," *New York Times Book Review*, January 30, 1955, p. 4, quoted in Baker, *Ernest Hemingway*, p. 647.

wise about people anyway, who said how, if you refused to accept something, it could not happen to you. And I was comforted.[16]

Hemingway, of course, never saw this screenplay.

By the time Hawks sold the rights on *To Have and Have Not* to Warner Brothers in October 1943, the project was well underway. Its first stage had been the working-out of that basic story line in 1939, and it is worth remembering that Hemingway and Hawks had agreed to throw out most of the novel and instead to tell the story of how Marie and Morgan might have met, with Hawks creating the character of Marie. Warners had assigned Humphrey Bogart to the picture early in 1943, but Hawks had been unable to cast Marie, and said so to his wife, Nancy "Slim" Hawks, one morning at breakfast. Slim, a former model and a prominent socialite, pointed to the photo on the cover of the current issue of *Harper's Bazaar* and suggested Hawks try out that model, one Betty Bacal. (Slim also discovered Joanne Dru and Ella Raines—each of whom, like Bacal, bore some physical resemblance to herself.)[17]

Hawks sent for the eighteen-year-old Bacal in April 1943 and spent several months training her. He was especially struck by the deep voice he was encouraging her to develop, and felt she might become another Dietrich. With that in mind, he told Jules Furthman—who had already begun work on the screenplay and who had written for Dietrich herself—to change the character of Marie, whom they were already calling Slim, into a sultry, almost masculine Dietrich type. When Bogart heard about these plans, Hawks told him he was "going to try and make a girl as insolent as you are." "Fat chance of that," said Bogart, and Hawks replied, "I've got a better than fat chance. . . . In every scene you play with her, she's going to walk out and leave you with egg on your face."[18] Shortly after she turned nineteen, Hawks changed her name to Lauren Bacall and wrote a scene for her screen test, which

16. George Sidney, "Faulkner in Hollywood: A Study of His Career as a Scenarist" (Ph.D. dissertation, University of New Mexico, 1959), p. 189.

17. "'Slim' Hawks," *Life*, January 20, 1947.

18. Joe Hyams, *Bogart and Bacall: A Love Story* (New York: Warner Books, 1976), pp. 60–68.

he shot early in January 1944. She leans against a door and says, "You know how to whistle, don't you? You just put your lips together and blow."[19] The rest, as they say, is history. Bacall so successfully dealt with the major challenge the role presented her (which was, as she later wrote, that of "trying to figure out how the hell a girl who was totally without sexual experience could convey experience, worldliness, and knowledge of men")[20] that Hawks told Furthman he could stop writing the script in two versions—one of which had a lesser role for Marie, in case the actress should prove too weak—and start working on a Final Screenplay. As matters between Bacall and Bogart developed, not even the Final allowed sufficient room for the romantic interest between Morgan and Marie to be dealt with. It is almost possible to organize all the versions of the script in terms of the gradually larger and more daring roles they offer Marie. But before we get too far ahead of ourselves, we should examine the story as Furthman originally wrote it.

The initial or Temporary Screenplay was completed by October 14, 1943.[21] It is both long (208 pages) and entertaining, and might even be called an adaptation of Hemingway's novel. It indicates how Hawks first conceived the project (there is no record of the Hemingway-Hawks treatment) and what Furthman contributed to the final product. For these reasons the plot line will be given below in some detail. First, however, a story that shows how Hawks and Furthman worked together, as well as some of the process that led to the character of Marie. This is the way Hawks told it:

Furthman could only work with Joe Sternberg, Vic Fleming, and myself. Everybody hated him so, but we sort of liked him because everybody hated him. . . . He was just obnoxious, [and] he had a strange life. He was married to a beautiful girl. They had a baby—turned out to be a moron—great *big* moron, didn't recognize anybody . . . and it would yell

19. Hyams, *Bogart and Bacall*, p. 73, and Bacall, *Lauren Bacall by Myself*, p. 90.
20. Bacall, *Lauren Bacall by Myself*, p. 91.
21. This is the date on which the script department finished copying the screenplay. The screenplay completion dates in the Inventory and throughout this Introduction should be taken in the same sense.

and everything. They had to move from a beautiful home in Bel Air, and he went down and bought some property outside Culver City. It turned out to be the most valuable manufacturing property there was. So he had a couple of million dollars worth of property. And if he didn't think anybody had any talent, Christ Almighty, he was a bad person to work for! He and Faulkner got on OK, but the average writer . . .

In *To Have and To Have Not* he wrote a story where Lauren Bacall has her purse stolen. He wrote a good scene about it and brought it in—very pleased with himself. "What do you think?" I said, "Well, Jules, there's a thing I always get a hard-on about—I get a complete erection for a little girl who's had her purse stolen." "You big son of a *bitch*," he said, and he stalked out and he came back the next day and wrote a scene where she stole a wallet. It was eight times as good. And I used to treat him that way, you know, to get him to work, because he did such damned fine work.

For the record, that "damned fine work" includes the screenplays for *Treasure Island* (1918), *Underworld* (1927), *The Drag Net* (1928), *The Docks of New York* (1928), *Morocco* (1930), *Shanghai Express* (1932), *Blonde Venus* (1932), *China Seas* (1935), *Mutiny on the Bounty* (1935), *Only Angels Have Wings* (1939), *The Shanghai Gesture* (1941), *The Outlaw* (1943), *The Big Sleep* (1946), *Nightmare Alley* (1947), *Rio Bravo* (1959), and more than eighty other films, either solo or in collaboration. Richard Corliss has described Furthman's recurring preoccupation as "the story of a grizzled adventurer who, with great exertions of will and the love of an equally adventurous woman, finds salvation for himself and those around him."[22] That is as good a description as any of *To Have and Have Not*, even though the film bears only occasional resemblance to Furthman's scripts for it.

Furthman's First Version

The Temporary Screenplay opens with Johnson's fishing scene. Apart from their being just outside the *Havana* harbor, Johnson's losing the two marlins and Morgan's tackle is played in the film

---

22. Richard Corliss, *Talking Pictures: Screenwriters in the American Cinema* (Baltimore: Penguin Books, 1975), p. 268.

basically as written here. Morgan's only crew member is Rummy (later Eddy), already endowed with his enigmatic line, "Was you ever bit by a dead bee?"

Back on the dock, Johnson reluctantly agrees to having the question of how much money he owes Morgan decided by Decimo and Benicia, the proprietors of the Pearl of San Francisco Cafe (Decimo becomes Frenchy/Gerard in the film; his wife, Benicia, an old flame of Morgan's, is dropped). They side with Morgan, and Johnson says he'll go to the bank the next day. Corinne (later Marie), a young woman who has been playing the cafe's piano and ordering rum swizzles while waiting for a nonexistent gentleman, picks up Johnson when Benicia threatens her with kitchen duty.

Later, Johnson collapses from too much liquor, and Corinne steals his wallet. Morgan corners her; they sarcastically call each other Steve and Slim, names neither of them likes. He has to slap her before she'll produce the wallet. They are interrupted (in a private dining room) by three Cuban students—Coyo, Florencio, and Pancho—who offer Morgan five thousand dollars to take them to Cienfuegos in his boat, apparently to rob a bank. Rummy comes in to tell Morgan that the boat has been attached until Morgan pays his local debts; he and the students go through the "drinking don't bother my memory" exchange. After Rummy leaves, the students ask Morgan whether he supports Machado, and he says, "It's nothing to do with me one way or another," but rejects the offer in the interests of personal safety and fear of losing his boat.

Morgan takes Corinne back to Johnson, intending to watch her return the wallet, but finds she has planted it in his own coat. Angry at Morgan, Johnson splits the wallet's contents with Corinne, then goes off with her to call the police. Outside the cafe, Pancho guns them down, having mistaken Johnson for Morgan. Johnson is killed, and Corinne's head is grazed. The killing is investigated by Lieutenant Caesar of the Havana police (Captain Renard in the film, although here he is "very slick and natty, carrying a brief case under his arm," and a friend of Morgan's). Because Corinne has a criminal record, Morgan hides her from Caesar; he also doesn't implicate the students. After Caesar leaves there is some business about the students' wanting to silence Corinne and Benicia's hoping they kill her.

Instead it turns out that the students have kidnapped Rummy. Morgan offers to trade them Corinne for his friend.[23] They say they'll keep Rummy and Corinne until Morgan drops them in Key West after the robbery. Florencio pulls a gun, and Morgan shoots him through the drawer of the table (more or less as in the film). Although uncontrollably angry at being pushed around, Morgan is convinced by Corinne and Benicia to let the others go, rather than kill them, so they can return Rummy.[24] By now Corinne and Benicia are friends.

The next day Mr. Kato (Mr. Sing in the novel) hires Morgan to smuggle a load of liquor to Florida that night. Rummy shows up; to get rid of him Morgan hits him hard and says, "You're poison to me." Morgan shoves off with a Negro crewman. Near dawn they are fired on by a Coast Guard cutter; the Negro is hit in the leg and Morgan in the arm. They are spotted again and not pursued (as in the novel—the other boat is captained by Morgan's friend). They decide to have a drink from the cargo and discover that they are actually carrying bottles filled with dope. Saying "what do I care about money? I got principle—" Morgan dumps the load overboard.

That night, in Morgan's bedroom, Corinne bandages his not-too-serious wound. Decimo brings in Kato; Morgan gives Kato the last bottle of morphine and arranges for Caesar to capture him with the evidence. Morgan goes downstairs and meets an American with his own set of tackle, Sam Essex, who charters his boat.

The next day, Sylvia ("a sleek, beautiful New Yorker"—later

23. Florencio observes that Morgan's decision proves that "A man who forms a tie is lost. No matter how great his courage. For he is no stronger than the thing he ties himself to." Decimo counters that such a man is "not lost, but safe. For no man is strong enough to look at life alone." This is the nearest Hawks and Furthman come to the sense of Morgan's dying words in the novel, and a bridge to the film's theme of the importance of personal and political commitment. It shows up in the film as the "no strings" exchange.

24. This ends the first of seven days. The film has a three-day plot, the novel three seasons.

Helene de Bursac, more or less) enters the cafe and recognizes Morgan. She turns out to be the "dame" in Morgan's past who soured him on women, the first woman who ever walked out on him—and married his best friend, Turner (now dead). Corinne and Benicia walk in; Morgan tells Sylvia that Corinne reminds him of her. "Where?" asks Sylvia. "Through the knees," says Morgan. There is a great deal of sparring until it is revealed that Essex is Sylvia's husband.[25] Essex comes in and announces that he has to fly to Key West on business, which postpones the fishing and incidentally gives Morgan and Sylvia the chance to have dinner and talk about old times, while the jealous Corinne gets drunk.

In the morning Corinne tries to explain to Rummy what a hangover is, then goes downstairs and makes friends with Sylvia. Essex shows up and Morgan arranges to take him fishing the next day. The students again kidnap Rummy, and Caesar indirectly helps Morgan free him—but the point has been made. To insure the safety of Rummy and Corinne, Morgan agrees to take the five revolutionaries (Pancho, Coyo, Enrico, Juan, and Esteban) on his boat. They apologize for applying such pressure, but insist that "the end justifies the means." Morgan observes that Machado said the same thing just the other day; as far as he's concerned, they should be fighting against the principle that "might is right." Juan

25. Not realizing that Turner has died, Morgan downplays the fact that he had left New York and become a fisherman in order to forget Sylvia, and pretends to be married and the father of two daughters. When he finds out that Turner is dead (of bleeding ulcers: "He insisted on keeping them for pets," says Sylvia. "He loved them and they loved him, I guess. Because one day they bled until he died for them"), Morgan admits he's single, kisses her roughly, and tries to leave with her. However, it seems that Sylvia herself was only playing "rich widow," for she is forced by Essex's entrance at this point to reveal that he is her husband. When Essex goes off to buy an antique fishing reel (he collects them), Sylvia gives Morgan enough information for him to figure out that Essex was *Turner's* best friend and that she was, therefore, basically responsible for her husband's death. She says Essex was the only man who could help her forget Morgan. Morgan realizes in a fury that she had tried to make *him* feel responsible for what she had done (contributed to the death of Turner, Morgan's best friend). Sylvia calms him down by suggesting they get together sometime. Corinne, who is as jealous as Benicia by now, tells Morgan he won't get any more credit at the cafe; Sylvia pays Morgan's sixty-five-dollar bill, giving Corinne a five-dollar tip. Corinne throws the money in her face, fights with Morgan, and is led off by Benicia. Enter Essex.

is moved by this argument ("If that is true, what have we to offer the people? Nothing but a change of masters"), but they all decide they'll have time to talk on the boat. Morgan tells them to seize his boat the next morning so that Essex can testify to Morgan's innocence.

The Cubans hijack Essex along with the boat. Morgan is surprised and angry to find that Rummy has stowed aboard too. Around noon they dock at Cienfuegos; four of the Cubans rob the bank while Juan keeps the boat covered. Morgan reassures Essex, who has been belowdecks vomiting from fear, that his reaction is normal (source of Morgan's fear-dialogue with the de Bursacs). The robbery is a success, but as they shove off Morgan needles Juan for allowing so much killing in the process.[26] Despite a passing impulse to shoot Morgan at this point, Juan says, "I wish you were on our side. You could go far with us. You have the quality to lead." "No thanks," says Morgan, "I haven't got the stomach for it." This exchange is significant as the climax of the political-involvement theme; it is very different from the film, since Morgan is asserting his moral convictions and abandoning his neutrality, and thereby *not* joining the anti-Fascists.[27]

Pancho goes belowdecks and finds that Rummy has drunk his special bottle of Fundador, so he grabs a machine gun and kills him at point-blank range (as with Albert in the novel).

Morgan and Essex make a plan. When Morgan goes up on deck to talk with the Cubans, Essex chokes the motor. To get Morgan to fix it, the Cubans pretend they will let Morgan kill Pancho. Morgan gets Coyo to help him throw Rummy's body overboard;

26. Juan explains, laughing, "They always get a little drunk when they kill so much. You know how it is." "I know how sharks get," says Morgan. Juan says that the other four are "good revolutionaries but very bad men" and admits that "when we come into power we will liquidate" the bad men whom they now need. Morgan laughs, and Juan draws a gun on him, saying he doesn't care what happens, Morgan can't laugh at his sacred cause (they need Morgan to run the boat). "Well," says Morgan, "that's different. When a man doesn't care about anything he's pretty hard to handle. I get that way myself sometimes." Juan smiles in admiration at Morgan's skillful reply.

27. In fact, the politics of the whole screenplay project a right-wing integration of imperialism and individualism, even though Machado is condemned throughout.

at the same time, Morgan kicks the machine gun into the sea (just as in the novel). This is noticed, but they still need him to fix the motor. In the engine room he signals the hidden Essex to open a valve, then gets out the small machine gun he had hidden. He returns to the deck and, asked whether everything's all right, says, "Everything is perfect." There is a fade out as he starts to fire.

The next morning Caesar lectures Morgan about trying to do everything on his own, tells him that the entire revolutionary group has been arrested or killed, and forgives Morgan's having taken the $825 Johnson owed him out of the bankroll.

Morgan then goes to the cafe, where he had sent advance word that he especially wants to see Slim (at the news, Corinne had cried for joy). Corinne tells him it was her fault Rummy died: she hadn't stopped him from sneaking off to the boat, because she knew how it felt to want to be with Morgan. Morgan goes upstairs for some sleep, but finds Sylvia in his room.

She tells him Essex will give him a job in New York and that she'll leave Essex to be with Morgan there. Morgan refuses, saying he really likes Essex now, but Sylvia realizes "it's that blonde inebriate." After she says this, she hits him in the face, then explains, "I had a feeling you were going to do it to me" and kisses the place. Then she suggests Morgan marry Corinne and bring her along, but he won't do that either, so Sylvia has Morgan unfasten her pearl necklace and tells him to give it to Corinne. "What's the idea?" asks Morgan, and Sylvia closes the script with these splendid lines: "I don't know. (Kissing him, she looks into his eyes, gay and insolent as ever.) 'The robbed who smiles steals something from the thief.' (Then, turning and picking up her hat.) Shakespeare."[28]

The most important difference between the Temporary Screenplay and the novel is that here, whatever losses Morgan suffers are reversible, whereas what Hemingway showed was an inexorable process of one loss's leading to another until Morgan was destroyed. In the novel Morgan's being cheated by Johnson makes it impossible for him to earn his living as a fisherman; his

28. *Othello* act 1, sc. 3, l. 208.

smuggling run results in the loss of his arm and boat; reduced at last to dealing with revolutionaries, he gets killed. Of course Hawks wanted to tell a story of how Morgan and Marie might have met, and would hardly have felt it appropriate to kill off the hero—but even beyond that, Hawks had a temperamental objection to stories about, as he put it, losers. So in the first screenplay Morgan goes through the same basic sequence of situations (Johnson, smuggling, revolutionaries) and ends up with a wife, a healed arm, and the money Johnson owed him—his only loss being Rummy. (Hawks followed this same principle of adaptation on *The Big Sleep*.) By the same token, the theme of the isolated hero is redeemed by reversal: Hawks and Furthman show how Morgan discovers that men must fight together in order to win (i.e., he needs Essex and Caesar to beat the revolutionaries, and the revolutionaries falter because they distrust each other), but on the other hand they present Morgan as doing a pretty good job on his own anyway.

A number of other basic transitions from the novel to the film are begun or established here. The character of Eddy/Rummy is hardly changed from here on, though he is of course not killed in the film. Marie/Corinne is an odd mix of drunk, tramp, and insolent princess. Morgan has been recast for Bogart. Decimo and Juan are ready to be melded into Frenchy/Gerard. A cafe/hotel/bar has been made the major location of off-seas action. And there is an attempt at retaining the novel's double focus (Cuba and the eastern U.S. establishment) via Essex and Sylvia; this doubleness, however, is well on the way to being the simple love triangle (Morgan, Marie, and Helene) that dominates Furthman's later scripts as well as the press releases for the film (which made much of Bogart's being chased by two blondes—Bacall and Dolores Moran). In the film, Sylvia survives only in Marie's lines, "Who was the girl, Steve . . . ? The one who left you with such a high opinion of women." Sylvia's sexy wit is transferred to Marie (or dropped), and Helene gets the pearl necklace.

The good cop becomes a bad cop when the film takes on a different set of Fascists. There is little focus to the Temporary Screenplay's politics beyond a distrust of terrorist priorities. Morgan doesn't care one way or the other about Machado, but he has sufficient "principle" to dump the load of morphine and turn Kato over to the police. Despite Caesar's lectures on political change and solidarity, the important ties Morgan discovers are those of love (Corinne) and friendship (Rummy). This most problematic area of the adaptation is resolved by the later decision to model much of *To Have and Have Not* on *Casablanca* (1942)—not just because it raised no political ambivalence to oppose the Vichy during wartime, but also because *Casablanca* had shown how the Bogart persona could be led into a clear political stance by considerations of love and friendship. All this is a further side effect of the change of story locale from Cuba to Martinique, from Machado to Vichy.

Furthman's Revisions

Furthman's Revised Temporary Screenplay, which was generated in case Bacall should turn out to be unable to handle a starring role,[29] was left unfinished (at 111 pages) before January 5, 1944. In this version the character and functions of Corinne are split between Marie and Amelia, who is Morgan's American girlfriend. Sylvia is renamed Helen Gordon and has no husband. Rummy is Eddy, and the Negro bait cutter, Wesley (later Horatio), is introduced. There is a piano player, Chuck (later Cricket), working for Decimo and Benicia. Johnson is killed accidentally during a street battle between two revolutionary factions. Lieutenant Caesar, who is now a chubby fellow in charge of the secret police, and not Morgan's friend, is still full of theories about what it takes to make "an honest revolution." Morgan has two smuggling scenes (basically as in the novel): in the first he kills Kato and sets the Japanese—not Chinese—ashore; in the second he receives a serious arm wound and dumps the load of liquor overboard.

Furthman wrote the Final Screenplay in January and early February, and completed it before February 14, 1944. It is 151 pages long, and may have been the direct source for Faulkner's shooting script (the Second Revised Final, printed in this volume). There was a Revised Final, signed by Furthman and dated February 18, 1944 (discovered in the University of Southern California Library

29. Hyams, *Bogart and Bacall*, p. 70.

by Holly Yasui), but for reasons explained in the Foreword, page 8, I haven't been allowed to examine it. Other materials that are undoubtedly relevant but unavailable at this time include extensive notes and drafts of scenes written for Hawks during January and February of 1944 by the mystery writer Cleve F. Adams. In one letter I did see, Adams asks Hawks whether he ought to keep writing independently of someone named Chambers, or begin to collaborate with him. These materials are on deposit at the USC Library.

The account of the Cuba-to-Martinique change that is presented in this introduction is a reconstruction based on more than a year of research. My basic conclusion is that Faulkner was responsible for many of these changes and is the sole author of the Second Revised Final. I am especially indebted to Meta Carpenter Wilde, who was script girl on the picture, for her clear memory of Faulkner's contribution to the project. Hawks took credit for the change to an anti-Vichy story, though he says the censors suggested the Martinique location. The Second Revised Final bears the names of Furthman (typed) and Faulkner (in a bold handwriting that is not Faulkner's). The Adams scenes were apparently generated as alternatives to some of Furthman's before the locale was changed; no one seems to know anything about Chambers. It seems likely that Furthman's Revised Final was the actual script from which Faulkner worked, and that since Furthman worked on that Revised Final for only four days, it did not differ considerably from the Final discussed here. So it is proper to say that Furthman and Faulkner wrote the screenplay of *To Have and Have Not*, so long as one remembers that they did not work together. Furthman remained on the payroll but did no writing after Faulkner was brought on the job.

The Final is full of interesting and significant changes; it is still a complex and somewhat redundant story, however, and I offer some of it in detail as a way of showing both what Faulkner had to work with and how economically he restructured and clarified that material. (It is of course no secret that Faulkner was a great writer and a master of construction, but it is good to have evidence of his having applied those skills in Hollywood.)

Although Amelia and Benicia are still present in the Final, they play relatively minor roles, and it is clear that by this time "that kid from New York" had the role of Marie and that Furthman and Hawks were writing whole scenes for her. Helen Gordon is an important figure, but the Dietrich-like Marie is for the first time her match. The screen test Hawks had written for Bacall ("You know how to whistle") here appears for the first time, and Marie is even given a line lifted directly from *Shanghai Express* (1932; directed by Von Sternberg, written by Furthman, and starring Dietrich). In that film, when Shanghai Lily is interrogated as to her reasons for going to Shanghai, she answers, "To buy a new hat"; Marie here says this to Captain Renardo, Lieutenant Caesar's nasty assistant, during the investigation of Johnson's death (much as in the film). Other changes:

The Final begins with a dock scene rather than with the catching of the first marlin. When Morgan and Johnson go to the cafe, they find Cricket at the piano and Marie humming along. Morgan is established as a man who refuses to borrow money and will not even accept a free meal. Later that night, when Morgan examines the wallet Marie has stolen from Johnson, he finds a plane ticket and nine hundred dollars in traveler's checks. The student revolutionaries are friends of Decimo's, and when Morgan refuses to take them to Cienfuegos he does wish them luck. Marie does not frame Morgan when he makes her return the wallet. Johnson is killed during a battle between the students who have just left Morgan and the police (Renardo and Coyo); the only student to escape is Pancho. Renardo interrogates Morgan and Marie and slaps them both; Caesar (Morgan's friend again) intervenes and insults Renardo for killing a tourist during racing season; for the first time, Caesar keeps the contents of Johnson's wallet for evidence. Leaving Eddy with Amelia, Morgan escorts Marie to her hotel (only in Faulkner's version do they stay in the same hotel), where they decide to have a drink in the basement cafe and Marie has to hustle a bottle. In her room they go through what will become the most famous scene in the film, from "You're sore, aren't you?" to the whistle line, with the difference that Morgan does accept her cash reserve (which he uses the next day to buy her a ticket home); also, the whistle line is intended to be bitter, as the climax to Marie's developing feeling of cheapness.

29

Morgan agrees to take Kato's Japanese cargo. He gives Marie her ticket and goes to his room, where he finds Eddy asleep and Helen Gordon taking a shower. Helen's current husband is divorcing her in Reno; it is established that Helen married two fishermen on Morgan's account and that Morgan was with Benicia before he was with Helen. Marie gets a job singing in the cafe. That night Morgan kills Kato and gets the Japanese ashore; Eddy has stowed aboard despite Morgan's hitting and insulting him. Morgan uses Kato's money to buy a load of liquor, which he dumps after he and Wesley are shot.

Recuperating in Marie's room, Morgan calls her his "Jonah"; in his delirium he speaks his dying lines from the novel (slightly censored). Pancho brings a leftist physician, and in a few days Morgan recovers; by that time Helen and Marie are friends. Marie urges Morgan to help Pancho rather than fly off to New York with Helen like a quitter. What convinces him is her saying *she's* not leaving Havana until she's licked, and that it was Pancho and not Decimo (as Morgan had assumed) who brought the doctor.

Pancho insists that he and Morgan carry Eddy along with them to Cienfuegos (where they will pick up the four bank robbers), since he knows so much about their plans. One of the robbers kills Eddy when he makes a fuss about picking them up. Pancho realizes that now they will have to kill Morgan too, but Morgan stalls and that night kills all of them with his hidden gun. The next day Morgan turns the money (from "Machado's private bank") over to Caesar and says the revolution needs not "crooks or fanatics" but men like Caesar who have cool heads and love Cuba; otherwise "they're going to end up with something just as bad as the thing they're trying to bust."

Morgan returns to the cafe, where Helen is packing his things; they are going to fly to New York, where Helen intends to sell her property so that she and Morgan can marry and live in Havana. Just before they get on the seaplane Morgan changes his mind, and Helen gives him the pearl necklace to give to Marie.

So by the middle of February 1944, Hawks and Furthman had put together a witty and elaborate script, telling the story of how Morgan and Marie might have met, and retaining from the novel

Johnson's fishing trip, Mr. Sing/Kato's alien-smuggling operation, Morgan's arm wound, and the bank robbery, together with some commentary on Machado and the coming revolution. Then came what Hawks described to the *New York Times* as "a modern Hollywood version of a Tinker-to-Evers-to-Chance triple play."[30]

Enter Faulkner

The Office of the Coordinator of Inter-American Affairs suddenly objected to Warner Brothers' plans to film a novel that might embarrass the Batista regime in Cuba. Although *To Have and Have Not* concerns the Machado regime, it was felt that the project featured smuggling and insurrection in a way that would reflect badly on Cuba no matter when the story was set. It seems clear from this distance that what really motivated that cleverly reasoned objection was the Batista regime's recognizing its kinship with the Machado regime (not its fear that it would be mistaken for Machado's kin, in other words, but the true and undiscussable contemporaneity of the story).

The specific way that Office applied pressure was to predict that the picture would not receive an export license from the Office of Censorship. Without such a license, it would be almost impossible for the picture to earn much money, since it could not be shown overseas. The United States and Cuba were allies in the current war effort, and the United States was at this point interested more in supporting and receiving the sugar crop than in implying that Cuba could stand another revolution.

Since the Cuban setting was ruled out, Jack Warner told Hawks they could not do the picture, even though some of the sets had been built, second-unit photography had already started, and close to a million dollars had been invested. Hawks asked the Inter-American Affairs Office whether it could suggest another location (much as he later asked the censors to come up with an acceptable ending for *The Big Sleep*), and it told him that the French territory of Martinique was outside its sphere of concern.

30. Fred Stanley, "Hollywood Report," *New York Times*, April 2, 1944.

At that point Hawks asked his friend Faulkner for advice, as he often did when he was having trouble with a scene or story.[31] Faulkner had been on the payroll at Warner Brothers since 1942 (when he helped Hawks with two scenes for *Air Force*) and in 1942–43 had written an anti-Vichy screenplay—"The De Gaulle Story," excerpted above—which Warners had decided not to produce. Faulkner suggested that *To Have and Have Not* be rewritten so that the political interest would be the conflict between the Free French and the Vichy government, and Hawks hired him to do the job on February 22, 1944. Although Hawks himself took credit for thinking of this change, Meta Carpenter Wilde (Hawks's script girl and, intermittently, Faulkner's lover) has emphatically vouched that the idea was Faulkner's.[32] By saving this picture, Faulkner markedly advanced his reputation as a professional screenwriter.

The government, however, was not through yet. As the *New York Times* put it, "Since the new treatment involved Europe and the present war, the picture immediately became the concern of the Overseas Branch of the Office of War Information. Furthermore, because of the over-all character of the subject and the possibility of Production Code infraction in regard to the treatment of foreigners, the Hays office was brought into the picture. Now, as the script is being written, just ahead of production, individual scenes are sent to all three offices for review and suggestions."[33] Faulkner's scenes were written, on an average, three days before being shot. For such a shy and autonomous artist, this ought to have been an impossible working situation, but Faulkner managed to please everyone concerned and still write a good script, one that does, thirty-six years later, merit publication on its own.

The first cast reading took place on March 6, 1944, and the last script changes are dated April 22; shooting was completed on May 10. Although this last-minute writing gave Faulkner an unusual

31. See Bruce Kawin, "Faulkner's Film Career: The Years with Hawks," in Evans Harrington and Ann J. Abadie, eds., *Faulkner, Modernism, and Film* (Jackson: University Press of Mississippi, 1979), for details of their relationship, most of it from Hawks's point of view. For a list of Faulkner's screenplays, see Bruce Kawin, "A Faulkner Filmography," *Film Quarterly* 30 (Summer 1977): 12–21.

32. Unpublished interview between Mrs. Wilde and myself on June 20, 1978.

33. *New York Times*, April 2, 1944.

amount of control over the final product—it would have been virtually impossible for Hawks to *restructure* his script under these
conditions—there were a great many changes *within* the scenes,
as the Notes section of this volume demonstrates. In an interview
Bogart gave late that April, he said that Faulkner, Hawks, and
himself were devising new scenes, dialogue, and gags as they
went along, on the set; he made no mention of Furthman, who
was still on the payroll but—according to Mrs. Wilde and others—
not doing any writing.[34] In her autobiography Bacall says that Bogart and Hawks revised much of the dialogue and that Faulkner
preferred to remain in Hawks's office.[35] Most of these on-the-set
changes had the effect of making the characters less "literary" in
feel, more in harmony with their established screen personalities—
but there were substantial changes too, particularly in the treatment of women. These will be discussed shortly.

Hawks said that Faulkner enjoyed changing Hemingway's material just because it was Hemingway's. In fact, Faulkner seems to
have had little interest in that aspect of the project, and was more
interested in the political aspects of the script; his personal interest
was in helping his friend Hawks out of a jam. His anti-Vichy sentiments are evident in the comic tone of the opening scene and the
serious tone of the closing, as well as in his treatment of the de
Bursacs and Captain Renard (who are not simply lifted from *Casablanca*, although it might seem that way at first). In a letter written to his agent, Faulkner revealed no enthusiasm for the script he
was writing, did not even mention Hemingway, and concentrated
on the difficulty of doing good work while there was anything as
serious as a war going on:

As soon as I got here, Howard Hawks asked for me. He is making a
picture at our shop. As usual, he had a script, threw it away and asked
for me. I went to work helping to rewrite it about Feb. 22. He started
shooting about Mar. 1. Since then I have been trying to keep ahead of
him with a day's script. I should be through about May 10–15.

I dont know when I shall get back at it [i.e., his novel, *A Fable*]. . . .
War is bad for writing, though why I should tell you. This sublimation

34. *New York Herald Tribune*, April 30, 1944.
35. Bacall, *Lauren Bacall by Myself*, pp. 95–96.

and glorification of all the cave instincts which man had hopes that he had lived down, dragged back into daylight, usurping pre-empting a place, all the room in fact, in the reality and constancy and solidity of art, writing. Something must give way; let it be the writing, art, it has happened before, will happen again. . . .

When and if I get at it again, I will write you. After being present for a while at the frantic striving of motion pictures to justify their existence in a time of strife and terror, I have about come to the conclusion which they dare not admit: that the printed word and all its ramifications and photographications is nihil nisi fui; in a word, a dollar mark striving frantically not to DISSOLVE into the symbol 1A.[36]

This is hardly an inspiring mood, and the closing joke reflects badly on the studio's pious propaganda efforts. It seems that Faulkner put his anti-Vichy sentiments into the script and saved his antiwar sentiments for *A Fable*; he was also evidently still upset about never having been in combat himself.

Despite all this ambivalence, Faulkner did a solid and professional job on the Second Revised Final. Most of his changes will be evident to the reader, but a few of them merit mention here. He developed Helen Gordon into Helene de Bursac, Caesar and Renardo into Captain Renard, Decimo into Gerard, Pancho into Beauclerc, and the Cuban revolutionaries into the supporters of de Gaulle. He turned Morgan from patient to physician. He let Eddy survive. He dropped Benicia and Amelia, Frankie (a go-between) and Mr. Kato, the bank robbery, both smuggling scenes, all of Morgan's immoral actions, and the whole question of the legitimacy of the anti-Fascist cause. He made the relationship between Morgan and Eddy more tender. He took aspects of the de Bursacs (agitators in hiding, male-oriented wife) from *Casablanca*. He left Marie as Morgan's only love-interest—although he apparently could not resist turning Morgan into something of a misogynist; Morgan's washing off Helene's perfume in scene 45, for ex-

36. Joseph Blotner, ed., *Selected Letters of William Faulkner* (New York: Random House, 1977), pp. 180–81. The letter is dated April 22, so my guess is that between then and May 10 he expected to work mostly on last-minute, on-the-set changes. © 1977 by Jill Faulkner Summers. Reprinted by permission of Random House, Inc.

ample, is similar to Marlowe's reaction to Carmen Sternwood in a scene Faulkner wrote for *The Big Sleep*,[37] and Morgan is given numerous lines hostile to women. (He behaves this way neither in Furthman's scripts nor in the film.) Faulkner also played down the theme of Morgan's compulsive independence (whose only vestige in the film is Morgan's refusing Marie's offer of her safety money), made Marie less of a drinker, shortened the story to three days (a major improvement), and firmed up both the plot and its logistics by having Morgan and Marie take rooms in the same hotel. This is, on the whole, the most serious in tone and purpose of all the scripts, as well as the most economically constructed.

Faulkner was apparently not upset at Hawks's changing it, line by line, into a more sexually affirmative, upbeat comedy. Since both the shooting script and a list of significant alterations in the dialogue are available in this volume, I will cite here only a few examples of Hawks's revisions, which may clarify the logic of the others.

The most general rule Hawks followed, besides that of springing a new scene on his actors for the fun of it, was to let a line-change stand if the new version sounded more natural for that actor. In scene 12, for instance, Morgan's "Don't make me feel bad" becomes "Well, boys, don't make me feel bad." If he felt the rhythm of a scene falling, Hawks would rearrange the dialogue into his own "three-cushion" style, full of interruptions and overlapping lines. Here is part of Faulkner's scene 46:

EDDY: Listen, Harry. Could I—?
MORGAN: You've had enough to last you a week. (To Marie.) Don't buy him nothing but beer.
(As he turns to go Frenchy enters.)
MORGAN: Have any trouble getting them ashore?
FRENCHY: No. But Madame refused to let us take them to that place in the country. She said it was too far. He would die before he got there.
MORGAN: What does she know?
FRENCHY: He is very badly wounded, Harry. Anybody can see that.

37. Kawin, *Faulkner and Film*, p. 118.

Here is the Hawks version:

EDDY: Harry, we can use—
MORGAN: She'll buy it for you. Nothin' but beer for him, Slim.
MARIE: I'll remember. We'll be all right, Steve. I've got a job.
MORGAN: Doin' what?
MARIE: Frenchy seems to think I can sing.
MORGAN: Well, it's his place.
MARIE: Sometimes you make me so mad I could—
GERARD: Harry!
MORGAN: You could do what?
MARIE: I could—
GERARD: Harry, I need your help.
MORGAN: Well, what is it now?
GERARD: That— (indicating Marie—an "is she one of us?" look.)
MORGAN: That's all right. Go ahead.
GERARD: That man is very badly wounded, Harry.

The reader will note also the deletion of Morgan's "What does she know?"

There are changes in tone throughout. When Marie exits on her whistle line (after Hawks has rearranged the elements of the scene so that it is less moody and more tongue-in-cheek), Morgan whistles. Or in scene 53, when Marie says, "Give her my love" (meaning Helene), Morgan answers, "I'd give her my own if she had that on" (meaning Marie and her dress), rather than simply looking at her over his shoulder. There is considerable toning-down of Faulkner's longer passages on patriotism and fear (especially in scene 54), and nearly all of Helene's serious lines and erratic behavior are cut out—in favor of a new scene where she offers Morgan her jewels (a holdover from Sylvia/Helen Gordon and her pearl necklace). There is a great deal of downright good-naturedness written in, too, as when Morgan tells Frenchy's cashier that he'll still owe her the hotel bill even after he's fixed Paul's wound (this might have been played as an indication of Morgan's refusal to accept help, but that was clearly neither its intention nor its effect). But the simplest way to conceptualize these changes is to compare Faulkner's and Hawks's closing scenes. Faulkner makes it clear that the theme he announced in his opening—resistance to Vichy—is the major one in the picture, and closes with Frenchy's going upstairs to kill the policemen while Cricket makes enough racket to cover the shooting. (It is common for Faulkner's scripts to end at some tense moment that precedes a resolution.) Hawks, on the other hand, ends with Marie and Eddy's bebopping out of the cafe with Morgan while Cricket strikes up a jazzy exit (that seques into "How Little We Know," the main romantic theme, played by a studio orchestra under the final title card).[38]

Fun on the Set

During the fairly leisurely nine weeks of shooting (March 6 to May 10) the mood on the set ranged from the congenial to the electric, with most of the electricity being generated by and around Bogart and Bacall. Both of them were under stress much of the time. In addition to the predictable anxieties associated with playing a major role in her first film, Bacall felt it necessary to conceal from both Hawks and Bogart, until well after the picture was completed, the fact that she was a Jew (both men made casual anti-Semitic remarks);[39] it seems, in fact, that she kept this secret long after it was not a secret. Bogart had more serious problems: he was married to a wildly violent alcoholic, and his own drinking was entirely out of control. His home life consisted mainly of intense arguments; his wife, Mayo, often threw lamps, etc., once even knifed him in the back, and resented his professional success whenever her own acting career was doing poorly.[40] They were known as the Battling Bogarts, and it was Hawks's opinion as well as that of some of their friends that they were well matched.

The working day was usually divided in three: first, rewriting and blocking the scene; second, lunch—usually a chance for Hawks and Furthman to confer on horses and place their bets; third, shooting. This is Bacall's account of the process:

Howard had a brilliantly creative work method. Each morning when we got to the set, he, Bogie, and I and whoever else might be in the scene,

38. In addition, Hawks has Frenchy decide not to kill the policemen; see note 120.

39. Hyams, *Bogart and Bacall*, p. 95; Bacall, *Lauren Bacall by Myself*, p. 95.

40. Hyams, *Bogart and Bacall*, pp. 75–82; Bacall, *Lauren Bacall by Myself*, p. 98.

and the script girl would sit in a circle in canvas chairs with our names on them and read the scene. Almost unfailingly Howard would bring in additional dialogue for the scenes of sex and innuendo between Bogie and me. After we'd gone over the words several times and changed whatever Bogie or Howard thought should be changed, Howard would ask an electrician for a work light—one light on the set—and we'd go through the scene on the set to see how it felt. Howard said, "Move around—see where it feels most comfortable." Only after all that had been worked out did he call Sid Hickox and talk about camera set-ups. It is the perfect way for movie actors to work, but of course it takes time.[41]

There were exceptions to this process, and not all shooting was done after lunch, but the general rule was that Hawks shot his films at a leisurely (and therefore expensive) pace. He kept a yellow pad on his lap throughout the working day so that he could write new scenes—"to upset the actors," as he put it. This both amused him and increased his control over the actors. But the developing romance between his stars proved a serious challenge to that control.

He was later to claim that he exploited the attraction between Bogart and Bacall, using it to improve the scenes rather than fighting it. He said that his problem was that he couldn't "get them to pay attention." It is certainly true that he decided in midstream to reduce the script's emphasis on Dolores Moran (Helene), realizing that there was no point in trying to work a love triangle into the story since the audience would never take it seriously.[42] In her autobiography, however, Bacall reveals another side to this story.[43] Apparently Hawks had always wanted to play Svengali to some ingenue actress, and he became furious—perhaps even jealous—at Bacall's refusal to make work the focus of her life. He told her Bogart was simply toying with her and that her concentration was suffering. "I'm not going to put up with it," he told her one night at his house. "I tell you I'll just send you to Monogram. I'll wash my hands of you." (Monogram was Hawks's idea of a bottom-of-the-barrel studio; although it is dear to the hearts of many

41. Bacall, *Lauren Bacall by Myself*, p. 96.
42. Bacall, *Lauren Bacall by Myself*, p. 104.
43. Bacall, *Lauren Bacall by Myself*, pp. 77–129, esp. pp. 99 and 123.

B-movie fans, Bacall seems to have regarded it as an outer chamber of Hell.) This threat so upset her that she and Bogart hid the relationship from Hawks until they were well into *The Big Sleep*; once the story did come out, Hawks never again worked with either of them.

Another aspect of Hawks's controlling behavior is that he refused to work while Jack Warner was on the set; this practice was all to the good, since Warner was by all accounts a hostile, meddling, and at times downright stupid person. There's a wonderful story about Warner's sending Hawks a telegram during the shooting of *The Big Sleep*: "Word has reached me that you are having fun on the set. This must stop."[44] They apparently had fun on the set of *To Have and Have Not* as well. On the slapstick side, Dolores Moran got lost in the fog during the shooting of the scene where Morgan first picks up the de Bursacs; she walked off a jetty into the waist-deep studio lake. Hoagy Carmichael, the composer of "Stardust," kept a match in his mouth during most of his scenes; he had never acted before, and this prop, everyone assured him, helped make his characterization "distinctive." The way a press release told the story, Carmichael "came on the set one day to see Humphrey Bogart rehearsing a scene—and nonchalantly chewing on a match. Bogart is the star of the film, so Carmichael suffered in silence and finally left before the scene was shot. He returned an hour later. Walter Brennan was rehearsing a scene. At its most dramatic moment, he took a large kitchen match from his pocket, and casually put it between his lips." Later Bogart explained it was all a hoax.

Hawks and Bogart served as their own technical advisers for much of the picture. Hawks was a champion game-fisherman, and Bogart, who loved the sea, was devoted to sailing, so the scenes on Morgan's boat were carefully and naturally played (despite some obvious rear-projection work in Johnson's fishing scene). One press release describes Hawks and Bogart's examining a shotgun to be used in one of the scenes: "'It's a beauty,' commented Hawks, who rates as one of Hollywood's top shotgun and rifle marksmen. 'Yeah,' agreed Bogart, 'it looks all right, but I

44. Bacall, *Lauren Bacall by Myself*, p. 121.

really wouldn't know about it. I'm a machine-gun man, myself.'" To establish the proper angle of the bullet-effect during the scene where Morgan shoots one of Renard's men through the drawer of a table, Bogart insisted on going outside and shooting "a real slug through the thing."[45] (The publicity for the picture emphasized this sort of "man's man" aspect of Hawks and especially Bogart. Not only was Bacall touted—in advance—as a major discovery, but her and Moran's screen interest in Bogart/Morgan was described as the "Battle of the Blondes.")

Bogart and Hawks worked closely on dialogue changes, as has been said before, and it is worth calling attention to two further aspects of their working relationship: they agreed on matters of "good taste," and trusted each other's judgment. One Warner Brothers press release quotes Bogart to the effect that he felt comfortable in making suggestions to Hawks about how to play a certain scene, that "a good director is like a good psychiatrist; he builds up the confidence of his players until they forget their fears and inhibitions," and that he trusted Hawks to "correct" him if he was "off the beam." He went on to say that "whether a scene calls for you to kiss a girl or kill a man, the element of good taste is vital. The killing scene may be shocking to sensibilities without being offensive to good taste. That goes double for kiss scenes."

This issue of tastefulness has a great deal to do with the excellence of Hawks's style as both producer and director, from his choice of camera angles and wardrobes to his guiding concepts of professionalism and love. He had clear ideas of how things ought to be done, and the people he worked with trusted him.

Hawks described a good director as "somebody who doesn't annoy you."[46] He felt he put the camera in the obvious place it should be. He lit to clarify rather than overstate mood. All this makes his pictures so classical that they are nearly impossible to analyze—they are simply done "correctly." Bogart's comment re-

45. This and other press releases referred to in this section are undated and come from the press book file on the picture.

46. Robin Wood, *Howard Hawks* (Garden City, N.Y.: Doubleday, 1968), p. 11. When I asked Hawks what he considered the best book written about him, he singled out Robin Wood's; it is, unfortunately, out of print. (It is vol. 7 in the *Cinema World* series.) On the unanalyzability of Hawks's work, see pp. 10–11.

veals that actors relied on Hawks to "correct" them—in other words, to bring out the *right* performance; this is a very different matter from that of making sure one is doing whatever the director, who may be capricious or on a very private track, happens to have in mind. And this is an important aspect of what Hawks meant by "professional": not just a skillful or efficient manner of proceeding, but the obviously proper way to get the job done (an attitude that usually carries with it a set of ethics).

Hawks did not intellectualize his approach to cinema. His way of explaining what he did was that he and his actors and writers simply "had fun," tried things out to see what was "comfortable," behaved "professionally," didn't "annoy" the audience. His ethics were similarly unexamined: pride led to a fall, love healed, good work prospered—in *Red River*, for instance—not because Hawks got these concepts out of a manual on Greek and Latin literature but because he was himself a classical artist and a man with a secure world view.

He never did understand what the French critics saw in his work; he was convinced they were reading in meanings he never intended, and so on. (Not that he was modest—he was more than willing to take credit for the things he had done. He recognized, for instance, that no matter how often Orson Welles said he learned directing from screening *Stagecoach*, *Citizen Kane* was much more closely modeled on *His Girl Friday*—and furthermore, said Welles had told him so in 1941.)[47] But one can be a master without being self-conscious about it; one can achieve brilliant results while setting out simply to have fun and do a good job, without being dismissed as a lucky innocent. Perhaps the preceding discussion of his working methods on *To Have and Have Not* may help to clarify the personal and professional sources of Hawks's uniquely clean, efficient, entertaining, and classical style. His assured sense of control, his relative independence from Jack Warner (at least in matters not involving the government), his ability to work with the censors, his manner of dealing with writers (goading Hemingway, teasing Furthman, respecting Faulk-

47. This was the story with which Hawks ended our 1976 interview.

ner), his encouraging his actors to trust him and to feel comfortable coupled with his insistence that they pay careful attention to
his demands, his taking a firm hand in everything from setting
the camera angles and approving all production details to design-
ing the plot and revising the script day by day—certainly all this
contributed to the excellence of the final product as well as to its
coherence. In the case of a work as capriciously conceived and
continually interfered with as *To Have and Have Not*, that coherence
may be its most remarkable feature. Such apparent seamlessness
as the final work manifests is one of the marks of great art, and it
seems proper at this point to introduce a judgment by one of the
cinema's most literate and intense observers.

When he was just starting out as a critic for *Cahiers* (in 1952),
Jean-Luc Godard pronounced Hawks the greatest American artist,
and although that has to be considered an overstatement, Godard
does make a good case:

There is a famous legend which has it that Griffith, moved by the beauty
of his leading lady, invented the close-up in order to capture it in greater
detail. Paradoxically, therefore, the simplest close-up is also the most
moving. Here our art reveals its transcendence most strongly, making the
beauty of the object signified burst forth in the sign. . . . Where Premin-
ger uses a crane, Hawks is apt to use an axial cut: the means of expression
change only because the subjects change, and the sign draws its signifi-
cation not from itself but from what it represents, from the scene enacted. . . . All I mean to claim is that the *mise en scène* of *To Have and Have
Not* is better suited than that of *The Best Years of Our Lives* to convey aber-
rations of heart and mind, that this is its purpose, whereas the object of
the latter is rather the external relationships between people. . . . Certainly one has only to consider the development of the greatest American
artist—I mean Howard Hawks—to see how relative this idea of classicism
is. From the art of *Only Angels Have Wings* to that of *His Girl Friday*, *The
Big Sleep* and indeed, of *To Have and Have Not*, what does one see? An
increasingly precise taste for analysis, a love for this artificial grandeur
connected to movements of the eyes, to a way of walking, in short, a
greater awareness than anyone else of what the cinema can glory in, and
a refusal to profit from this (as I would accuse Orson Welles of doing in
Macbeth, and Robert Bresson in *Journal d'un curé de campagne*) to create anti-

cinema, but instead, through a more rigorous knowledge of its limits, fixing its basic laws.[48]

The only sense in which Godard and I differ here is in our uses of the term "classical": he is referring to a set of conventions within the history of narrative film, and I am referring to a set of structural and ethical assumptions that date back to ancient times. I consider it no accident that Hawks was able to work well with authors of Faulkner's stature, nor that he was the first producer to select a Conrad work for adaptation;[49] his work does demand to be set in the largest possible artistic context. So although I consider Faulkner, Melville, Whitman, Keaton, Gertrude Stein, and a few others to be more likely candidates for the no doubt pointless distinction "greatest American artist," I believe Godard is right to put Hawks in the company of our major creative figures.

The Film and Its Reception

The most accomplished characteristic of Hawks's films is their rhythm, and *To Have and Have Not* shows this aspect of his work at its best. It marks the balance point of his range, which extends from the rapid-fire overlapping dialogue of *His Girl Friday* to the more slow and elegant structural repetitions of *Hatari!* It is not just a matter of the meter and pace of dialogue, but of the way dialogue, music, camera position, and actor movement are gracefully coordinated. There are times when it seems as if Hawks invented the sound film, or at least brought it to perfection—particularly in his first two pictures with Faulkner, *Today We Live* (1933) and *The Road to Glory* (1936). One elegant, easy-to-take example of Hawks's mastery is the script's scene 10 (notes 25 and 26). In its two and a half minutes of screen time, Hawks establishes the attraction be-

48. Jean-Luc Godard, "Defence and Illustration of Classical Construction," in *Godard on Godard*, ed. Jean Narboni and Tom Milne (New York: Viking, 1972), pp. 28–30.

49. When he was a fledgling producer at Famous Players–Lasky, around 1924, Hawks prepared approximately forty pictures a year. During one of those years he produced two Zane Greys and two Joseph Conrads. He didn't tell me the titles, but he did say he was the first person in pictures to have read so widely. One of those Conrads has to have been *Lord Jim* (1925), directed by Victor Fleming.

tween Morgan and Marie, shows Johnson's pawing Marie and her stealing his wallet, takes care of the script's basic business between Morgan and Frenchy, and has Cricket sing an entire song—all of this done so fluidly, so assuredly, with each event swinging its partner as if in a Virginia reel, that the sequence does not even feel fast. What goes before is that Morgan, in his room, tells Frenchy he will not help the radicals (a few seconds after Marie has exited with her lit cigarette). As Morgan closes the door, there is a dissolve to:

[Shot 1] Mid-shot of the bar; two men talking; a waitress walks between the men, holding her tray; the camera follows her to one of the tables and stops panning as we see Morgan sitting alone at a table in the background. The camera tracks forward until Morgan is in close-up in the center of the screen. He strikes a match to light his cigarette, and the music starts.

[Shot 2] Long shot, Morgan's point-of-view; Cricket and his piano are in the center of the screen; Johnson and Marie are at a table, screen left, drinking. (In context this is almost an extreme long shot.)

[Shot 3] Close-up of Johnson and Marie drinking; Johnson is drinking faster and gets ready to pour another; Marie looks screen right.

[Shot 4] Long shot, Marie's point-of-view. Evidently she is looking at Morgan, who is center screen, looking in her direction (perhaps at Cricket).

[Shot 5] Mid-shot (almost a close-up) of Marie and Johnson, favoring Marie. She turns to look at Cricket, and the camera moves with her gaze. Cricket (in mid-shot) finishes the opening lines of the song: "Am I blue? Am I blue? Ain't these tears in my eyes telling you?" (The first "Am I blue" was sung in shot 3; the second begins in shot 4 and continues into shot 5; this subtly motivates our sense that Marie identifies with the persona of the song.)

[Shot 6] Close-up of Cricket at the piano, singing the next three lines of the song: "Am I blue? You'd be, too, If each plan with your man done fell—"

[Shot 7] "—through." Close-up of drummer, who folds up his newspaper and starts brushing the drums. As Cricket sings ("Was a time, I was his only one, but now I'm—") the camera pulls back to reveal the ensemble (in mid-shot).

[Shot 8] (figure 6) Long shot, Morgan's point-of-view, but closer-in than shot 2. Johnson at screen left; a diagonal line runs down from Johnson's head to Marie's head to Cricket's head, which is at center screen; the right side of the screen is taken up by the piano and various elements of the audience. Johnson puts his hand on Marie's arm; she turns to take it off, then gets up to walk to the piano. Cricket sings, "the sad and lonely one, So lonely. Was I gay? 'til—" (It becomes clear in this shot that Marie is driven to the piano to escape Johnson's attentions rather than by a need to hog the audience's interest; by the next shot it is clear that she decides to use her position at the piano to attract Morgan.) So far the sequence has lasted exactly one minute.

[Shot 9] Close-up, from over Cricket's shoulder, as Marie leans on the piano and glances to the side, apparently in Morgan's direction. Cricket finishes the first verse: "—today. Now he's gone and we're through, Am I blue?"

[Shot 10] (figure 7) Mid-shot, from over Marie's shoulder; the camera is at standing height. Cricket, without missing a beat, tells Marie, "Take over," and starts singing "Was a time—". She picks up the line, "I was his only one—". Cricket is struck by her deep voice[50] and mugs his appreciation, then sings, "But now I'm—." She sings, "The sad and lonely one," looking over her shoulder, pointedly in Morgan's direction.

[Shot 11] Close-up of Morgan at his table, as at the end of shot 1. Cricket sings, "So lonely. Was I gay?"

[Shot 12] Same set-up as shot 9. Marie: "Was I gay?" Cricket: "til today—" Marie: "til today—"

[Shot 13] Same set-up as shot 10. Cricket: "Now she's gone and we're through, Baby oh—" and then Marie and Cricket finish the song together: "Am I blue? Am I blue?" There is a cut just after the end of the last chord.

50. Contrary to a widespread story that her songs were dubbed by Andy Williams, Bacall implies in *Lauren Bacall by Myself* (p. 100) that she did her own singing. It is of course possible that she sang for the camera *and* that Williams's track is the one used in the film's soundtrack; Bacall does not address that question.

[Shot 14] Same set-up as shot 8. (By repeating these set-ups Hawks and his excellent editor, Christian Nyby, are giving the song a sense of visual completion, working their way back to the conventional dramatic space as well as establishing, through repetition, that Marie and Cricket are comfortable with each other; they also create a back-and-forth pattern that matches the interchanges and rhythm of the song itself as well as clarifies the relationships among the characters. This particular set-up signifies Morgan's point-of-view and—since it is closer-in than shot 2 and an echo of shot 8—his concentrating his attention on Marie.) Johnson gets up, then gestures to Marie that he's going to the men's room. Someone requests another song; the audience is clapping and talking throughout the shot, and calls of "Bravo!" are distinct. Cricket tells his group to start up the song, and begins to plink-plink his way in, as Marie walks back to her table.

[Shot 15] Mid-shot: Frenchy comes in, agitated; camera tracks with him through the crowd and dips down to sitting level (and close-up) as he sits down at Morgan's table; by now the composition is like that at the end of shot 1, but set off at a slight angle. Frenchy explains that he couldn't get in touch with the radicals to stop them from coming (basically as in Faulkner's script); Morgan says that's not his problem; Frenchy gets up and leaves, but the camera remains on Morgan, shifting slightly to put him center screen.

[Shot 16] Long shot, Morgan's point-of-view; same set-up as shots 8 and 14. Marie steals Johnson's wallet from the table and waves broadly to Cricket as she starts walking screen right.

[Shot 17] Mid-shot: Marie walks through the crowd, and the camera tracks with her. She makes a very brief glance, apparently in Morgan's direction.

[Shot 18] Close-up of Morgan at his table; he thinks, then gets up to follow Marie; the camera does a short pan and tilt to follow him, as he follows her up the staircase (in what is by now a long shot).

It would be possible to go through the entire film this way, but the point has, I hope, been demonstrated. A few more general

observations on the finished picture will be offered here, and beyond these the reader is referred to the Illustrations section with
its captions on lighting and shot composition, as well as, naturally, to the film itself.

To Have and Have Not is a film that makes its audience happy.
There is a completely satisfying balance between good and evil,
fun and melodrama, light wit and tough words, healthy sexuality
and clear politics, and even between impotence (Eddy, a double-
crosser without a stinger) and the redeeming power of love (Eddy
again). The acting ranges from nonacting (Hoagy Carmichael
playing himself with such ease that he achieves the most realistic
mimesis, entirely in tone with the clean rhythm of the whole film
and its no-nonsense, almost stoical clarity) to overacting (Dan Seymour playing Captain Renard with far too much melodramatics
and an unfortunate accent, clearly a creature of the movies rather
than of life, redeeming his performance only marginally in the last
reel), as the interaction between the director and his co-creators
ranges from the spontaneous (taking advantage of the developing
emotion between Bogart and Bacall, which was made simpler by
the necessity—thanks to the government and to Faulkner's being
only a few days ahead of shooting—to shoot the film in sequence)
to the entirely controlled (the lighting, for instance).

The originality of the film has an equally wide range: although
there is simply no other film quite like *To Have and Have Not*, none
so diverse yet so single-minded, so apparently meandering yet on
reflection so efficient, so rich yet so spare—on the other hand, it
is hard to think of a film that appears at first so derivative, not just
of Hawks's earlier films but of Warners' most recent love-and-pol-
itics-and-Bogart-in-a-cafe romantic hit, *Casablanca*. In fact, one of
the unique aspects of *To Have and Have Not* is that it is so superfi-
cially similar to and so profoundly different from the earlier melodrama.

This raises two quick literary comparisons: as Robin Wood has
demonstrated, the writer whose attitudes Hawks most closely
shares is Conrad (the theme of surrounding darkness, the importance of personal and ethical integrity, "the assertion of basic human qualities of courage and endurance, the stoical insistence on

innate human dignity"),[51] but there is also a close connection with Shakespeare (who stole most of his plots, whose seamless work was addressed to a witty and regular audience, who neatly balanced comedy and tragedy, and who appears—to great advantage—not to have taken his dramatic work [as opposed to his poems] too "seriously"). I think the clearest way to point out how little it matters that Hawks "stole" much of this film from *Casablanca* is to draw on another of Wood's allusions: "*Only Angels Have Wings* is no more an imitation of Ford's *Air Mail* (for instance) than *Hamlet* is an imitation of *The Spanish Tragedy*."[52] Of course *Casablanca* offered a way of resolving what became the main problem in the script—the change of Fascists—and that led quite naturally to the reconception of Harry Morgan in terms of *Casablanca*'s Rick. To imitate *Casablanca*, it should by now be more than obvious, was not at all Hawks's original intention.

A quick comparing of the two melodramas reveals a difference, not so much of quality as of tone. *Casablanca* is romantic, but *To Have and Have Not* is a romance. *Casablanca* is centrifugal and compelling, a real gut-wrencher and tearjerker full of gauze shots and "big scenes" such as the singing of the "Marseillaise" and the magnificent conclusion. *To Have and Have Not* is more disciplined, open-handed, airy, elegant, cool, straight. It is almost the difference between Greek and Latin, or between Chaplin and Keaton. Even the songs point to this categorical difference. The romantic beauty of Ingrid Bergman and her Bogart is dreamily focused and intensified in "As Time Goes By," one of the most irresistible pieces of nostalgia in all sound film. The lithe sexiness of Lauren Bacall and her Bogart is sharpened, highlighted, and directed into action by "Am I Blue" and "How Little We Know," which range from the breezy to the honky-tonk. Carmichael's songs comment on the action in a light manner rather than drench it in emotion—for instance, in the "story of the very unfortunate colored man who got arrested down in old Hong Kong: he got twenty years' privilege taken away from him when he kicked old Buddha's gong," an upbeat allusion to Morgan's risky involvement with "lo-

51. Wood, *Howard Hawks*, p. 23.
52. Wood, *Howard Hawks*, p. 12.

cal politics." So that even if these films deal with many of the same issues (love and political commitment in particular), *Casablanca* is heavy where *To Have and Have Not* is light. One leans toward overstatement and the other toward understatement, but both involve real danger, real action, real love, real friendship, and a current world war in which some of the actors were deeply involved—Marcel Dalio in particular.[53] My point is that preference for one film or the other is a matter of personal taste, and that both films are equally serious.

The same could hardly be said of the Warner Brothers publicity campaign for this picture. As has already been mentioned, those elements of the film that were given most emphasis were the macho ones: Hawks the sportsman, Bogart the tough guy, Bacall the blonde, Moran the blonde . . . It was in fact a publicity avalanche, most of it centered on Bacall. Warners' head of publicity, Charles Einfeld, sent the following memo to his staff, and it may serve as an indication of the tone of the campaign as well as of the studio's enthusiasm for the picture:

Polish up the picks, shovels and pans for the gold mine on the way in Howard Hawks' production of Ernest Hemingway's *To Have and Have Not*, which we sneaked last night and which is not only a second *Casablanca* but two and a half times what *Casablanca* was. Here is a story of adventure and basic sex appeal the likes of which we have not seen since *Morocco* and *Algiers*. Bogart terrific, never was seen like this before. Lauren Bacall, new find of ours playing opposite Bogart, distinct personality who positively will be star overnight. Nothing like Bacall has been seen on the screen since Garbo and Dietrich. This is one of the biggest and hottest attractions we have ever had. If this sounds like I'm overboard, well I am.[54]

Many of the early reviews of the picture reflect this campaign rather than a careful response to the picture; this may of course be an occupational hazard of reviewing, press kit in lap, but there is

53. Best remembered for the two great roles he played for Jean Renoir—Rosenthal in *Grand Illusion* and the Marquis de la Chesnaye in *Rules of the Game*—Dalio (Frenchy/Gerard) was the son of Rumanian Jews living in France. He was forced to flee France, and while he was playing minor roles in the United States his parents were killed in a concentration camp.

54. Bacall, *Lauren Bacall by Myself*, p. 107.

little evidence that *To Have and Have Not* received during its first release anything like the intelligent attention it should have. Most of the reviews are of Bacall rather than of the film; some of them praise her, while the others give the impression of resisting her as if she were a gag to help sell a weak picture. Almost all of them point out that the film has little or nothing to do with the novel, but appear not to be upset about that; most of them assume that the source of the story, of the character of Morgan, and of the political attitudes in the film was simply *Casablanca*. If the film was praised, it was as a fast, witty romance; these reviewers, in other words, played into Hawks's cagey self-description as a director who considered plot "an excuse for some good scenes," and assumed there was nothing else going on. *Time* (October 23, 1944) called it a "tinny romantic melodrama which millions of cinemaddicts have been waiting for ever since *Casablanca*." *New York Variety* (October 14, 1944) said it was "not up to Warner's melodramatic story standards," an obvious attempt to follow up *Casablanca*'s "lucrative box-office," characterized by "nifty productional accoutrements" but a "too unsteady" story line. Louella Parsons thought it was "definitely swell entertainment" (*Los Angeles Examiner*, January 20, 1945). The *Chicago Daily Tribune* (March 1, 1945) singled out Carmichael as the best actor in the film. Bosley Crowther (*New York Times*, October 12, 1944) considered it an enjoyable remake of *Casablanca*. Manny Farber (*The New Republic*, October 23, 1944) praised the complexity of Morgan's character, Bogart as a "Hemingway hero," and the fact that some of the dialogue "sounds as if it could have been thought up by the characters"; on the whole, however, he considered the film "spiritless," "half-hearted and slight," with "no more structure or unified effect than a string of familiar but unrelated beads." The *Daily Variety* (October 11, 1944) said the film "fails to materialize as any more than average, somewhat measuredly-paced melodrama where exciting action was rightfully anticipated" and felt Hawks "was handicapped by [a] meandering screenplay," which it called "too leisurely" and "entirely undistinctive." Other reviewers felt the movie's patriotism was too half-hearted, that Morgan was just out for himself. James Agee (*The Nation*, November 4, 1944) enjoyed it but thought *Going My Way* was better; he said, "It gets along on a mere thin excuse for a story, takes its time without trying to brag about its budget or to reel up footage for footage's sake, is an unusually happy exhibition of teamwork, and concentrates on character and atmosphere rather than plot. The best of the picture has no plot at all, but is a leisurely series of mating duels between Humphrey Bogart at his most proficient and the very entertaining, nervy, adolescent new blonde, Lauren Bacall. Whether or not you like the film will depend I believe almost entirely on whether you like Miss Bacall. I am no judge. I can hardly look at her . . . without getting caught in a dilemma between a low whistle and a bellylaugh. It has been years since I have seen such amusing pseudo-toughness on the screen. . . . I enjoyed watching something that obviously involved relaxed, improvising fun for those who worked on it, instead of the customary tight-lipped and hammer-hearted professional anxiety." It should come as no surprise that Agee was the most sensitive and articulate film critic of his time, but in this case even he could have done better.

The film went on to become one of the thirty top-grossing pictures of 1944. It received an award from the National Board of Review (and an export license!), but not even a nomination for an Academy Award. It was the year of *Going My Way, Double Indemnity, Laura, Gaslight, Since You Went Away, Meet Me in St. Louis, Lifeboat, The Uninvited, Thirty Seconds over Tokyo, Mr. Skeffington, Lady in the Dark,* and *Wilson.*

The first critics to pay serious attention to Hawks and to this film were those at *Cahiers*—most notably Godard, whose 1952 critique is the first to put the film in its proper rank and the only one I have seen that mentions Hawks's "increasingly precise taste for analysis" and his attempt to fix the "basic laws" of cinema "through a more rigorous knowledge of its limits." Not very much has been written about *To Have and Have Not* since then, except in the context of larger studies of Hawks.

The best of these one-man studies, in my judgment, is Robin Wood's, and some of his comments on the film deserve mention here. He does a good job on the "I like you and I don't like them" theme, for instance:

Hawks and Bogart give us a man who exists exclusively from his own centre, his actions stemming from the immediate perceptions and impulses of his consciousness. Here the term "individual" really means something: not merely "Someone who is different from other people," but "a conscious being who lives from his own feeling centre of identity." It is not a question of egotism: Morgan is never self-indulgent, or self-seeking beyond what he defines as his rights. He is a man whose sense of essential responsibility has been remarkably uncorrupted by either materialism or idealism.[55]

Calling it "one of the most basic anti-Fascist statements the cinema has given us," Wood recognizes in *To Have and Have Not* "all of Hawks's belief in the individual need for integrity and self-respect." He finds the film's "flexible and empirical morality" (Johnson's thieving is worse than Marie's, etc.) to be founded on the solid ground of Morgan's character, and calls Bogart's Morgan "the most perfect embodiment of the Hawks hero."

Hawks used to say that his first response to any new property was to try to make it into a comedy, and that only if that turned out to be absolutely impossible would he get serious. One of the interesting things about the making of *To Have and Have Not* is that although Hawks did succeed in turning Hemingway's pessimistic novel into a comedy (in the sense that from the outset it was intended that the story end on the note of Marie's and Morgan's impending marriage), he actually began with a series of scripts that were much more violent, negative, and dark than the final product. The story's lighter elements discovered themselves as Hawks and his collaborators worked along.

It is also ironic that *To Have and Have Not* should have emerged as so clearly "a Hawks film" when so many different people took a hand in its creation, some of them well outside Hawks's sphere of control. As a footnote to twentieth-century literature this film is even more of a paradox—or if you prefer, a red herring: Hemingway and Faulkner (with significant contributions from Furthman and Bogart) yield virtually pure Hawks. Still, "no man alone" could have created it. The film both addresses (via its story) and manifests (as a graceful collaboration) the importance of team-

55. Wood, *Howard Hawks*, p. 27.

work, of community. It is anti-Fascist not just in its theme of individualism but, more importantly, in this achieved sense of people's enjoying each other and working together well. Hawks is not the author but the auteur, the crest of the creative wave.

Hawks said he liked everything Hemingway wrote, and once even bought the rights to *The Sun Also Rises*, but sold them when he realized the censorship problems would be insurmountable. He had much the same reaction to Faulkner's *Sanctuary*, except that he didn't buy the rights. (One can only imagine what he might have done with a novel he did not consider Hemingway's worst.) In *To Have and Have Not* he managed in his characteristically cagey and subtle way to get his two hunting companions, Hemingway and Faulkner, to meet, although not in person and in such Hawksian terms that the casual viewer of the film would hardly recognize any trace of the two great novelists. Despite all the reverses and reconsiderations that went into it, then—the professional rivalries, the governmental interference, the pressures of time and money and love and war—*To Have and Have Not*, incredibly enough, fulfilled its original project: "You've got the character of Harry Morgan. I think I can give you the wife."

I am grateful to the people who helped me in the course of this project: the late Howard Hawks, Jorjana Kellaway, James Powers, Carole Raphalian, Anne Schlosser, Meta Carpenter Wilde, and Holly Yasui.

1. *Harry Morgan (Humphrey Bogart) examines the bottle of rum he found on Eddy. A poster of Pétain (the only prominent one in the film) hangs behind him.*

2. *Johnson (Walter Sande) gets his first strike as Morgan and Horatio (Sir Lancelot) watch. An example of Hawks's dynamic yet classically balanced composition—and the only scene in the film that appears in the novel.*

3. *Downtown Martinique. A Vichy agent approaches Morgan and Johnson from behind. These excellent sets have some of the flavor of Havana.*

4. *Morgan takes Frenchy/Gerard (Marcel Dalio) up to his room as Marie (Lauren Bacall) leaves hers. Faulkner's decision to have these rooms face each other facilitated their encounters and simplified the script.*

5. *"Anybody got a match?"* asks Marie; Morgan throws her a box.

6. *Johnson reaches for Marie as Cricket (Hoagy Carmichael) sings "Am I Blue"* *in the cafe of the Marquis Hotel.*

7. Cricket reacts in mid-note to Marie's husky singing voice.

8. Eddy (Walter Brennan) explains to Beauclerc how drinking doesn't bother his memory. "If it did, I'd forget how good it was. Then where'd I be?" Morgan laughs affectionately in the background.

9. *Sound/image rhythm: Marie stops Morgan from losing his temper by striking a match at the instant Morgan says, "and the bank opens at* ten."

10. *Frenchy, Morgan, and Marie size up the "Gestapo." A classical composition emphasizing Morgan's strength and centrality.*

11. *Marie tells the police she got off in Martinique "to buy a new hat" and gets slapped. Note the rich use of low-key lighting and composition in depth.*

12. *"The other times, you're just a stinker," says Marie, just before she kisses Morgan for the second time (and he "helps").*

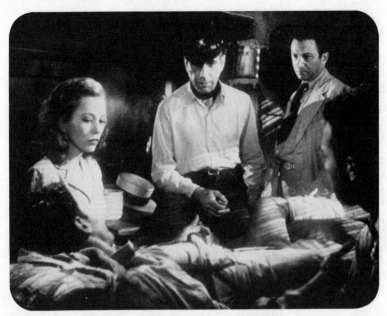

13. *Beauclerc (Paul Marion) tells Morgan how to pick up Paul de Bursac. As in figure 4, windowblind-light contributes greatly to the sense of place.*

14. *Eddy realizes that the reason Morgan didn't want to carry him on the "job" was to protect him. The night-sea fog motivates a rich range of grays.*

15. *Dolores Moran as Helene de Bursac. Morgan, who is in the middle of asking why anyone brought "a dame" along, is stopped by this smile.*

16. *Another remarkable integration of composition, lighting, and set design. Frenchy has just taken Morgan down to the cellar to tend Paul's wound; they are met by Helene, who will try to stop them.*

17. *Renard (Dan Seymour) tries to get Eddy drunk but gets a fish story for his pains.*

18. *In the cellar, Paul (Walter Molnar) explains his mission.*

19. *"How long will it take you to pack?" says Morgan, and Marie moves to kiss him.*

20. *Renard enters Morgan's room for the final interrogation.*

21. *Morgan shoots Renard's bodyguard (Aldo Nadi) through the drawer of the table.*

22. *Marie goes through the "dead bee" routine, and Eddy gets the feeling he's talking to himself.*

23. *Marie shimmies up to Morgan, and they leave the cafe.*

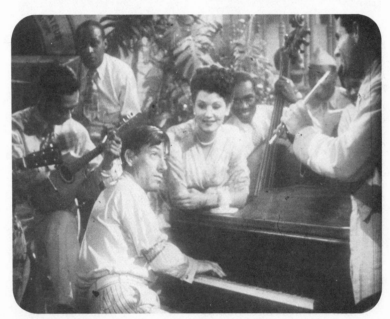

24. *Cricket signals for the last note, ending the film.*

To Have and Have Not

Screenplay

by

JULES FURTHMAN

and

WILLIAM FAULKNER

Based on the novel by

ERNEST HEMINGWAY

To Have and Have Not

Foreword

It is in Fort de France, the metropolis of Martinique, in the French West Indies, a few months after the signing of the Armistice between France and Germany.[1]

FADE IN

1. FORT DE FRANCE DOCK CLOSE SHOT EARLY MORNING
[Large poster of Marshal Pétain on side of military hut. Somebody has neatly torn a large V out of it. CAMERA, DRAWING BACK, shows Chef de Poste, a quartermaster in the uniform of the French navy, dozing in chair tipped back underneath poster. Two Negro urchins, passing by, see what has happened to poster and pause to remark upon it in their soft patois. The quartermaster sits up, turns to see what they are laughing at, and notes V torn out of poster in great consternation. Furiously bidding the two urchins to be gone, he rushes into hut, returns with a new poster. Tearing down the old one, he quickly replaces it with the new one, fastening it in place with thumbtacks. Stepping back to survey his handiwork, he sees—to his amazement—that a large V still appears dimly in poster. Bewilderedly, he examines surface of poster and becomes aware that it is unmarked. Puzzled, he removes poster and looks at back of it. The V has been painted on the back. Crumpling up the poster in horror and rage, he rushes into hut, returning this time with a large framed portrait of Marshal Pétain, which he hangs upon rusty nail to cover the place occupied by poster. As he steps back to look at it, Morgan enters from street.][2]

[QUARTERMASTER:
>   Good morning, Captain Morgan. What can I do for
>   you today?

MORGAN:
>   Same thing you did yesterday.

QUARTERMASTER:
>   You and your client wish to make a temporary exit
>   from the port?

MORGAN:
>   Any objection?

Quartermaster looks very thoughtful and dubious, goes
into hut, opens window, clears throat importantly, prepares to fill out form.

QUARTERMASTER:
>   Name?

MORGAN (patiently):
>   Harry Morgan.

QUARTERMASTER:
>   Nationality?

MORGAN:
>   American.

QUARTERMASTER:
>   Name of ship?

MORGAN:
>   *Queen Conch*, Key West, Florida.

QUARTERMASTER:
>   Purpose of excursion?

MORGAN:
>   Game fishing.

QUARTERMASTER:
>   Period of sojourn?

MORGAN:
   We'll be back tonight.

QUARTERMASTER:
   Length of trip?

MORGAN:
   I don't think we'll go more than thirty miles off
   shore.

Quartermaster, writing this into form, signs it with a
flourish, stamps it, and holds it out to Morgan.

QUARTERMASTER:
   Five francs, please. (As Morgan pays money.) One
   thing more. You must return by sunset.

MORGAN (surprised):
   Is that a new order?

QUARTERMASTER:
   Yes. The decree was issued last night by His Excel-
   lency, Admiral Robert, governor general of the French
   West Indies. (Sharply.) Any complaints?

Morgan shakes head, raises hand holding pass in Nazi
salute to portrait of Pétain.

MORGAN:
   Vive l'empereur!

Then, as he walks out on dock, rusty nail gives way and
portrait falls to ground. Quartermaster hurries out in
alarm. As he starts to pick up picture, he sees a large cross
of Lorraine (the de Gaulle emblem) painted on the back.][3]

2.   FORT DE FRANCE   DOCK
     The *Queen Conch*, of Key West, Florida, a thirty-eight-foot
     fishing cruiser, is moored to the dock. The harbor in the
     background is alive with early morning traffic. Morgan
     enters on the dock [and sees that the Queen Conch has

slipped her stern line and is swinging, well away from the dock, by her bow line. Eddy is asleep in the fishing chair, one leg up over the stern. Morgan jumps down on the deck and goes down toward Eddy. He sees half a dozen empty beer bottles lying nearby. Eddy clutches another empty one to his chest. Morgan pulls the ship into the dock and secures the stern line properly. Then, he lifts Eddy by the scruff of the neck, lowers him over the side, dunks him briefly, and then sits him in the fishing chair again.

EDDY (grinning as he blinks water out of his eyes):
Hello, Harry. How's everything?

MORGAN:
Fine. Do you know the ship almost drifted away?

EDDY (looking around):
No, it never, Harry. All the lines are fast.

MORGAN:
They are now.

He goes amidships and Eddy follows him.

EDDY:
Where you been, Harry? Did you bring me a drink?

Morgan lifts the lid of the icebox, sees all the beer gone but one bottle. He picks that up, opens it. Eddy beams, reaches for it.

EDDY:
I was saving that.

MORGAN:
For me? (Puts bottle to his lips.) Thanks.

Eddy's face falls, and he watches Morgan with thirsty absorption. Morgan looks at him standing there, tall and hollow cheeked, with his mouth loose and that white stuff in the corners of his eyes and his scant hair all faded from the sun. Morgan knows he is dead for a drink.

MORGAN (handing him the bottle):
Here.

EDDY (beaming again):
Harry, you're my pal. I sure got them this morning.

MORGAN:
You have them every morning.

EDDY (draining bottle):
You're sure swell, Harry. Sometimes I wonder why
you're so good to me.

MORGAN:
I wonder all the time. (Nodding toward dock.) Give
Horatio a hand.]⁴

Horatio, the Negro bait cutter, enters on dock carrying a
case of beer on his head. Horatio is a real black Martinique
Negro, smart and gloomy, with blue voodoo beads
around his neck under his shirt and an old straw hat,
which he now carries in his hand. What he likes to do
ashore at night is to rhumba, and aboard ship he likes to
sleep and read the papers. Aided by Eddy, he comes
aboard and rests the case of beer on the side of the icebox.

[HORATIO:
Good morning, Captain. That chef de hoste took a
bottle of our beer.]⁵

MORGAN:
That's all right, Mr. Johnson can afford it.

[EDDY (looking at the sun):
He's almost an hour late, Harry. Maybe he isn't
going out today.

MORGAN:
He'll be here.

HORATIO (looking toward street):
Here he comes now.

Johnson enters on the dock. Johnson is a plump, pursy-faced businessman of forty-five, clad in the sporting-goods-store conception of a practical fishing costume for the tropics: pith helmet, etc.

EDDY:
    Good morning, Mr. Johnson. How's everything?

Johnson nods sourly. It is evident he doesn't think much of Eddy.

JOHNSON (jumping down on deck):
    Morning. (To Morgan.) Well, are we going out?

MORGAN:
    That's up to you, Mr. Johnson.

JOHNSON (looking at the sky):
    What sort of a day will it be?

MORGAN:
    Just about like yesterday. Maybe better.][6]

JOHNSON (lighting a cigar):
    Let's go out then.

MORGAN (to Horatio):
    Cast off those lines.

HORATIO:
    All right, Captain.

Eddy goes astern and starts throwing empty beer bottles over the side.

MORGAN:
    I've got to put some gas in her, Mr. Johnson.

JOHNSON:
    All right.

MORGAN (starting motors):
    [I'll need some money for that.][7]

JOHNSON (taking out wallet):
How much?

MORGAN:
It's twenty-eight cents a gallon. I ought to put in forty gallons anyway. That's eleven dollars and twenty cents.

JOHNSON (taking some bills out of wallet):
Here's fifteen dollars.

MORGAN (taking money):
I'll get change for you at the gas dock.

JOHNSON:
Never mind. Just put it down against what I owe you.

He goes astern and sits down in fishing chair. Horatio casts off stern line and jumps aboard. As Morgan takes ship away from the dock and heads out into the stream,

FADE OUT

FADE IN

3. EXT. OCEAN NEAR MARTINIQUE COASTLINE LATER THAT DAY
Big marlin leaping out of water and making vain attempt to free itself from hook.

4. EXT. MORGAN'S FISHING BOAT NEARBY
Johnson in stern holding rod. Horatio, the Negro bait cutter, folds up newspaper and sits up to watch. Eddy, the rummy, is sleeping on deck. Harry Morgan at wheel yells:

[MORGAN:
Sock him again. Stick it into him. Hit him three-four times—][8]

Johnson obeys and hits fish pretty hard a couple of times more. Then the rod bends double, the reel screeches, and out jumps the marlin—boom—in a long straight jump, shining silver in the sun and making a splash like throwing a horse off a cliff.

JOHNSON:
I've got him—

MORGAN:
Ease up on the drag.

JOHNSON (as line goes slack):
He's gone—

[MORGAN:
No, he's not. Ease up on the drag quick— (To Horatio.) Get those teasers in—

Horatio goes and pulls in teasers, while the fish jumps again and heads out to sea.

JOHNSON (as line slacks again):
He's gone—

Morgan shakes his head.

MORGAN (spinning wheel to follow fish):
Reel in on him. He's hooked good—][9]

HORATIO:
He sure is.

Then once, twice, the big fish comes out stiff as a post, the whole length of him jumping toward the boat, throwing the water high each time he lands.

[JOHNSON (as line slacks once more):
He's gone.

MORGAN:
I'll tell you when he's gone. Reel in fast and keep the drag light—][10]

Johnson (all thumbs) works at reel and all of a sudden his rod jerks and the line goes slack.

MORGAN (in disgust):
Well, he's gone now—

HORATIO:
> Yes, sir—he's gone now.

JOHNSON:
> No, he's not—turn around and chase him—

But Morgan merely stares after marlin, which is still jumping and keeps on jumping until he is out of sight.

MORGAN:
> Reel in your line—

JOHNSON:
> I tell you I can still feel him pull—

MORGAN (leaving the wheel):
> That's the weight of the line—

JOHNSON:
> You're crazy. I can hardly reel it. Maybe he's dead—

MORGAN:
> Maybe—but he's still jumping.

[He feels the drag. Johnson has screwed it down tight. You couldn't pull out any line. It had to break.

MORGAN (angrily):
> Didn't I tell you to keep your drag light?

JOHNSON:
> But he kept taking out line.

MORGAN:
> So what?

JOHNSON:
> So I tightened the drag.

MORGAN (patiently):
> Listen, if you don't give them line when they hook up like that, they break it.

JOHNSON:
> Then you ought to get stronger line—

MORGAN:

> There isn't any line will hold them. When they want it, you've got to give it to them. And you have to keep the drag light as a feather—

JOHNSON:

> I know—I know—you don't have to rub it in—][11] (To Horatio, the Negro bait cutter, who is fixing up a couple of fresh mackerel.) Come on, you—hurry up.

HORATIO (cheerfully):

> I'm hurrying, Mr. Johnson.

He deftly passes the hook through the mouth of the mackerel, out the gills, slitting the side and then putting the hook through the other side and out, tying the mouth shut on the wire leader and tying the hook good so it can't slip and so the bait will troll smooth without spinning.

JOHNSON (to Morgan):

> Can't you put on a bait like that, captain?

MORGAN:

> Yes—sure I can.

JOHNSON:

> Then why do you carry this fellow to do it?

MORGAN:

> When the big fish run you'll see why.

JOHNSON:

> What's the idea?

MORGAN:

> Horatio can do it faster than I can.

[JOHNSON (nodding toward the sleeping Eddy):

> Can't Eddy do it?

MORGAN:

> No, he can't.

JOHNSON:
> A dollar a day. It seems an unnecessary expense to me.

MORGAN:
> He's necessary—aren't you, Horatio?

HORATIO:
> I hope so.

Eddy wakes up, comes back astern.

EDDY:
> What's the matter?

Morgan knows he woke up dead for a drink.

MORGAN:
> You'd better drink a bottle of beer.][12]

Eddy goes to the icebox.

JOHNSON (sourly, reeling in line):
> I don't see why you want that rummy around for.

MORGAN:
> Eddy was a good man on a boat once, before he got to be a rummy.

JOHNSON:
> Well, he isn't any good now. Is he related to you or something?

MORGAN:
> Nope.

JOHNSON:
> Then why d'you look after him?

Morgan looks out toward Eddy and grins.

MORGAN:
> He thinks he's looking after me.

Eddy comes astern, polishing off bottle of beer with deep relish.

EDDY:
> Mr. Johnson, d'you care if I ask you a question?

He tosses empty bottle into sea, and Johnson sourly looks after it.

JOHNSON:
> Listen, mister, it might interest you to know that I not only paid for that beer, but I also put a deposit on the bottles.

EDDY:
> Was you ever bit by a dead bee?

JOHNSON:
> A dead what?

EDDY:
> A dead honeybee?

[JOHNSON (turning his back):
> I never was bit by any kind of a bee.][13]

EDDY (winking at Morgan):
> Well, in that case, I'll just finish my nap. Thanks for the beer, Mr. Johnson.

As Johnson turns to glare at him, Horatio lets out a warning yip and Morgan yells at Johnson.

MORGAN:
> Watch your line!

Johnson turns and sees a big marlin burst head and shoulders out of the water and smash at mackerel with his sword.

[MORGAN (returning to wheel):
> Slack it to him—

JOHNSON:
He hasn't got it—

MORGAN:
Yes, he has. And he's a big one. I'll bet he'll go a thousand pounds—

JOHNSON:
I tell you he hasn't got it—][14]

In reply, the marlin jumps straight up beside the boat, and Johnson rises up in his chair as though he was being derricked, and he stands there clinging to the rod for a second and the rod bending like a bow, and then the butt catches him in the belly and the whole works goes overboard, rod, reel, tackle, and all.

MORGAN (shutting off engine):
Well, I guess that's enough for one day—

Johnson sits down, holding onto his belly where the rod butt had hit him.

JOHNSON (dazedly):
What happened?

MORGAN:
[Nothing. You just had the drag screwed down tight again, that's all, and when the fish struck, it just naturally lifted you right out of your chair and you couldn't hold it.

HORATIO (chuckling):
You had the harness on, that fish'd've taken you along with him.

EDDY (slapping Johnson on the back):
Mr. Johnson, you're just unlucky. Now, maybe you're lucky with women. Mr. Johnson, what d'you say we go out tonight?][15]

JOHNSON (rising enragedly and hitting Eddy in the face):
I'll lucky you, you dirty rummy—

MORGAN (grabbing him as he makes a rush toward Eddy):
Mr. Johnson, are you a good swimmer?

JOHNSON (struggling to get at Eddy):
I've stood all I'm going to—

MORGAN:
So have I—so be careful you don't slip out of my hand.

EDDY (interposing):
Take it easy, Harry—that guy owes you for sixteen days.

[JOHNSON:
Fifteen!][16]

DISSOLVE TO:

5.   EXT. MARTINIQUE DOCK   SUNSET
[Quartermaster dozing in chair tipped back under portrait of Pétain. Morgan, coming up from dock with Johnson, stops and leaves pass in quartermaster's lap. Johnson does the same. As they start on, Johnson indicates tricolor hanging from mast on quartermaster's hut.

JOHNSON:
I thought everybody took down their flag after sunset.

MORGAN:
Most people do.][17]

JOHNSON:
That's Vichy for you.

MORGAN (indifferently):
It's their flag.

[A slit-eyed civilian, leaning against kiosk, lowers newspaper and looks after them.][18]

6.   EXT. FORT DE FRANCE   WATERFRONT STREET
Morgan enters with Johnson. Negro beggar drinking out

of fountain. Slit-eyed civilian, entering and hurrying after them, lifts his hat and speaks to them.

CIVILIAN:
Pardon me, gentlemen.

Morgan and Johnson stop.

CIVILIAN (taking out notebook):
May I have your names?

MORGAN:
What for?

CIVILIAN:
I heard this gentleman make a disparaging reference to Vichy.

He nods toward Johnson.

JOHNSON:
Me? I never said a word about Vichy. (To Morgan.) Did I?

MORGAN:
I wasn't paying much attention.

[JOHNSON:
I was just talking about the attitude of the American government. I said it was very wishy-washy.

CIVILIAN:
You are both Americans?

JOHNSON:
Yes.

CIVILIAN (raising hat):
Pardon me. I thought you were English.][19]

He turns and leaves. Morgan and Johnson continue down the street toward entrance of combination cafe and hotel.

7.   INT. CAFE

Morgan and Johnson enter and pause at bar, behind which hangs usual large portrait of Pétain. At the piano in far corner sits Cricket, the piano player, working on song. Two waiters on. Gerard, the French proprietor, is checking cash register behind bar, and as Morgan and Johnson give order to bartender:

[GERARD:

Well, gentlemen—what luck today? (To bartender.) That's Captain Morgan's bottle. How many times do I have to tell you?][20]

MORGAN:

Not so good, Frenchy.

JOHNSON:

We lost the biggest fish I ever saw.

GERARD (in sympathy):

Well, maybe tomorrow you hook him again.

[JOHNSON:

I give up. I'm through. I'm fed up with this kind of fishing.

MORGAN:

I don't blame you. You fish for sixteen days, hook into a couple of fish any good fisherman would give a year to tie into—

JOHNSON:

All right—all right. Don't rub it in. (Taking out wallet.) I haven't got enough here to pay you off. I'll go to the bank in the morning.

MORGAN:

Okay. (Finishes drink.) See you later.

He starts toward rear. Gerard follows him, overtaking him as he ascends stairway, which leads toward landing, thence into hotel section.

GERARD:

Harry, there were some people asking for you to-day.][21]

MORGAN (pausing):
Fishermen?

GERARD:

No. Some friends of— (looking around cautiously) of friends of mine.

[Morgan looks at him, smiles shrewdly, and shakes his head. Gerard takes his arm and starts down hallway in hotel section.

8.   INT. HALLWAY   HOTEL SECTION
Gerard walking with Morgan.

GERARD:

They only want to use your ship for one night. They will pay you very well, too. Of course, nothing like you would get from Americans.

MORGAN (shaking head):
I'd like to oblige you, Frenchy, but I can't afford to get mixed up in local politics.

GERARD:

It is a very urgent matter. Afterwards, when things are different, it would be very good for you, Harry.][22]

As Morgan stops by door of room and starts to unlock it, the door on opposite side of hall is opened, and Marie comes out with unlighted cigarette in her hand.

[MARIE (seeing Gerard):
Have you got a match?

Gerard searches his pockets and turns to Morgan, who has been doing the same.

MORGAN (opening door):
  I think I've got some in here.

He goes in, followed by Gerard.

9. INT. MORGAN'S SITTING ROOM
Morgan enters, followed by Gerard. Marie pauses in doorway, looking into room. Morgan, opening drawer of table, looks at her as he takes out box of matches. He has placed her in this gaze, and his next movement confirms it.

MORGAN (tossing box to Marie):
  Here you are.]²³

She catches it, extracts a match, lights cigarette, then, closing box, she tosses it back to him.

MARIE:
  Thanks.

Closing door, she exits.

[MORGAN:
  When did she get in?

GERARD:
  This afternoon.

MORGAN:
  On the plane from the south? (As Gerard nods.) What's her racket?

GERARD:
  What makes you think she has one?

Morgan shrugs, and pushes up the transom.

MORGAN:
  Look, Frenchy. About this other thing. The Vichy crowd is on top here and if they catch me fooling around with the de Gaullist bunch, I'll be cooked. Probably lose my ship to boot.

GERARD (resignedly):
> You know best, Harry.

MORGAN:
> I'm all for you, Frenchy—you know that.

GERARD:
> Let's have dinner together.

He opens door to leave.

MORGAN (starting to remove shirt):
> Soon as I have a shower.][24]

FADE OUT

FADE IN

10.   INT. CAFE   THAT NIGHT
[Intimate group around piano, where Cricket is playing some nostalgic song. Marie, sitting at nearby table with Johnson, is singing. They have just finished dinner, and it is evident Johnson is making a play for her. Morgan, dining with Gerard at table across the room, is studying Marie.][25] A colored boy enters and whispers something to Gerard. Latter, dismissing boy, utters an exclamation of concern. Morgan turns and looks at him.

GERARD:
> I tried to head those fellows off, but I can't get in contact with them.

MORGAN (looking out at Marie again):
> The ones that wanted to hire my ship?

GERARD:
> It is dangerous enough for them to come here at all— but to come here for nothing—

Morgan is watching Marie as she finishes song.

[MORGAN:
> Why don't you go outside and keep an eye open for them?

GERARD (nodding toward Marie):
    You like her voice?

MORGAN:
    Not bad.

Gerard finishes his coffee, rises, and goes out toward rear.
As he exits, Morgan sees Johnson excuse himself to Marie
and start unsteadily across floor toward men's room in
hallway behind her. As he exits, Marie finishes brandy,
picks up bag, and starts toward stairway in rear. Morgan
watches her as she approaches. She sees him, and as she
passes she says pleasantly:

MARIE:
    Good evening.

MORGAN (same tone):
    How are you?][26]

Marie looks at him over shoulder as she ascends stairway,
and Morgan, finishing his coffee, rises and follows her.

11.   INT. HALLWAY   HOTEL SECTION
       Marie enters and comes down hall, taking key out of bag.
       Morgan enters, and Marie sees him as she pauses to un-
       lock door. He walks up to her and holds out his hand.

[MORGAN:
    Let's have it, Slim.

MARIE:
    What do you want?

MORGAN:
    Johnson's wallet.

MARIE:
    Are you drunk?

In reply he takes her by the arm, leads her across hall,
opens door of his room, and shoves her inside.

12.   INT. MORGAN'S SITTING ROOM
        Morgan, entering with Marie, closes door.

MARIE:
    Say, mister, what's got into you?

MORGAN (holding out hand):
    Come on, Slim.

MARIE:
    Listen—nobody calls me Slim. I'm too skinny to take
    it kindly.

MORGAN:
    All right—if you want it that way.

He starts toward her; Marie backs away from him.

MARIE:
    What are you going to do?

MORGAN:
    Quit that baby talk.

Marie stares at him for a moment, then smiles.

MARIE:
    You know, Steve—I wouldn't put it past you.

She takes wallet out of bosom of dress and looks at Morgan.

MARIE:
    I thought you were a fisherman—not a hotel detec-
    tive.][27]

MORGAN:
    Johnson's my client.

MARIE:
    He doesn't speak so well of you.

[MORGAN:
    He's still my client. Another thing, I don't care for
    small crooks.

89

MARIE:
> I didn't take it from him. He dropped it and I picked it up.][28]

MORGAN:
> Oh, you were going to give it back to him?

MARIE:
> No, I wasn't. I don't like him.

MORGAN:
> That's a good reason.

[MARIE:
> Besides, I've got to have some money to get out of here.

MORGAN:
> That's another good reason—but you'll have to pick on somebody else.][29]

Morgan takes wallet out of her hand, opens it on table and examines contents.

MORGAN (in disgust):
> Humph! How d'you like that? [Sixty dollars in cash and fourteen hundred dollars in traveler's checks!

MARIE:
> I'll settle for the sixty bucks.

MORGAN:
> That bird owes me eight hundred and twenty-five. "I haven't got that much on me," he says. "I'll go to the bank and pay you off tomorrow," he says. (Looking at airline ticket.) And all the time he's got this reservation in his kick for a plane that leaves here at daylight.

MARIE:
> He was going to slip out on you?][30]

MORGAN (nodding):
Good thing you didn't give it back to him.

MARIE:
Then I did you a favor?

[MORGAN:
Sure did. (Picks up one of the bills.) Here.

Marie takes bill and looks at it.

MARIE (as if amazed at his generosity):
Twenty dollars!

MORGAN:
You can use it, can't you?

MARIE:
Sure I could. But I wouldn't dream of taking it. I couldn't. I only saved you eight hundred and twenty-five.

Morgan, staring at her, snatches the bill out of her hand.

MORGAN:
You saved it for me?

MARIE:
Well, you'd never known Johnson was going if it hadn't been for me, would you?

Morgan stares at her for a moment, then grins, starting to replace bills and things in wallet.

MORGAN:
That's right. What d'you think is fair?

MARIE:
I'll leave it to you.

MORGAN:
What d'you say to fifty-fifty?

MARIE (startled):
Fifty-fifty?

MORGAN:

> Sure. If I hadn't stopped you, you'd have got away with the whole works, wouldn't you? After all, I'm entitled to something.

Marie grins.

MARIE:

> Forget it. If I don't owe *you* anything I'm satisfied.

She starts toward door, but pauses as somebody knocks.

MORGAN:

> Who is it?][31]

Door is opened, and Gerard enters with three young Frenchmen in civilian clothes.

[GERARD:

> Harry, these are friends of mine who wanted to charter your boat.

Marie starts toward door again.

MARIE:

> See you later.

MORGAN:

> Sit down. We're not through yet. (To Gerard.) I told you I wasn't interested.

GERARD:

> That's what I told them—but Beauclerc wants to talk to you.

MORGAN:

> You fellows better clear out of here.

BEAUCLERC:

> We're not afraid.

MORGAN:

> Well, I am.

Beauclerc shrugs resignedly and turns to one of the others.

BEAUCLERC:
Go and see if the street is clear.

GERARD:
I'll go.

He exits and the three young Frenchmen stand there looking sad.

MORGAN:
I'm sorry, boys—but I can't do it.]³²

BEAUCLERC:
We will give you twenty-five hundred francs.

MORGAN:
That's fifty dollars in American money. [I can't do it.

DE GAULLIST NO. 1:
A thousand francs a piece. (Morgan shakes his head.) It is only a little voyage to a place about forty kilometers from here.]³³

BEAUCLERC:
We would give you more money—but we haven't got it.

[MORGAN:
Don't make me feel bad. I tell you true I can't do it.]³⁴

DE GAULLIST NO. 2:
Afterwards, when things are changed, it would mean a good deal to you.

[MORGAN:
I know. But I can't do it.

BEAUCLERC:
I thought all Americans were friendly to our side.

MORGAN:
    Look—they send you fellows to Devil's Island. I'm not that friendly to anybody.

BEAUCLERC:
    They wouldn't dare do that to an American.

MORGAN:
    They would if I was caught with you fellows.

There is a moment of silence. Beauclerc looks at Marie.

BEAUCLERC:
    Is she your sweetheart?

MORGAN:
    No.

Then the door opens and Eddy breezes in.][35]

EDDY (brightly):
    Hello, Harry—how you been keeping?

[BEAUCLERC (unbuttoning his coat):
    Who is he?

MORGAN:
    A friend of mine—

EDDY:
    How'd you come out with Mr. Johnson?

MORGAN:
    Fine. Who's looking after the ship?

EDDY (smiling):
    I am. But I got a little thirsty waiting by myself.

MORGAN:
    Go on back. There's a bottle in the tool chest.

EDDY:
    Thanks, Harry. You're a good boy. You're a credit to me. Who are these guys?

MORGAN:
>I don't know.

EDDY (pointing to Beauclerc):
>He was hanging around the dock for a while after you left—

BEAUCLERC:
>You've got a good memory for a drunk—][36]

EDDY:
>Drinking don't bother my memory. If it did I wouldn't drink. I couldn't. You see, I'd forget how good it was. Then where would I be? I'd start drinking water again.

BEAUCLERC:
>Maybe you'd forget about water, too.

EDDY:
>No, I wouldn't. I see too much of it. Was you ever bit by a dead bee?

The three young Frenchmen laugh.

BEAUCLERC (after a moment):
>I have no memory of being bit by any kind of a bee—

MARIE: (to Eddy):
>Were you?

Eddy beams at her in great delight.

EDDY:
>Say, lady, you're all right. You and Harry are the only ones that ever—

MORGAN:
>Don't forget Frenchy.

EDDY:
>That's right. You and Harry and Frenchy. You've got to be careful of dead bees when you're going around barefooted. If you step on them they can sting you

just as bad as if they were alive. Especially if they were kind of mad when they got killed. I bet I've been bit a hundred times that way—

MARIE:
You have? Why don't you bite them back?

[EDDY (grinning at her):
That's what Harry always says. But I haven't got a stinger—

DE GAULLIST NO. 1 (to Morgan):
Does he always talk so much?

MORGAN:
Always— (To Eddy.) I'll be down to the dock in a little while—

EDDY:
Okay. So long.][37]

Eddy gives them a wave and exits.

[MORGAN:
Sorry, gentlemen. Where were we?

DE GAULLIST NO. 2:
You would have three thousand francs and it could mean a great deal to you later. All this will not last, you know.

BEAUCLERC:
If you take us on this small journey I can almost promise it will not last.

MORGAN:
Listen, I don't care who runs France or Martinique. Or who wants to. Please get somebody else. (To Marie.) Come on—we've got some unfinished business of our own.

Morgan nods to Marie and starts toward the door. Beauclerc bows courteously to Marie as she passes.

BEAUCLERC:
Good night.

MARIE:
Good night.][38]

Morgan opens door and they exit.

13.   HOTEL HALLWAY   OUTSIDE OF MORGAN'S ROOM
Morgan and Marie come out of his room.

[MARIE:
Do you have to take me along?

MORGAN:
Wouldn't you rather do your own lying?

MARIE:
Let's go.

They exit.][39]

14.   INT. THE CAFE
Morgan and Marie come down the steps and meet Johnson near the bar.

JOHNSON (to Marie):
Where have you been? I've been looking all over for
you. (To Morgan.) You're a fine one—running off
with my girl.

MORGAN:
She's got something she wants to tell you. (He leans
against the bar.) Go ahead, Slim.

MARIE (extending the wallet):
Here's your wallet.

JOHNSON (missing the wallet for the first time):
Where did you get it?

97

MARIE (with a look at Morgan):
  I stole it.

JOHNSON:
  Well—that's a fine thing. (He is a little confused.)
  What are you going to do about it?

MORGAN (who has been watching this):
  The question is, what are you going to do, Mr. Johnson?

Johnson looks at Morgan, realizing for the first time that
maybe Morgan has examined the wallet.

MORGAN (continuing):
  Maybe you had better take a look and see if it's all
  there.

JOHNSON (stuttering):
  Oh, I'm sure it's—it's all right.

MORGAN:
  Check it over. She might want a receipt for it.

Johnson gives contents of wallet a hasty, perfunctory
glance.

JOHNSON:
  It's all right. Nothing missing.

MORGAN:
  You sure?

JOHNSON (trying to change the subject):
  Yes. Now, young lady, I don't—

MORGAN (interrupting):
  You had better count those traveler's checks.

[JOHNSON (reluctantly obeying):
  Fourteen hundred.][40]

MORGAN (getting quiet and taking out a cigarette):
  But you had to go to the bank tomorrow.

Johnson is scared.

MORGAN:
>   What's the time on that plane ticket you've got there?
>   (He is starting to move.)

JOHNSON:
>   Six-thirty.

MORGAN (on the move):
>   In the morning. And the bank opens at ten.

Just then, Marie strikes a match and holds it in front of
Morgan and lights his cigarette. He pauses and after a
moment grins at her.

MORGAN:
>   I don't like him any better than you do.

JOHNSON:
>   Look, Mr. Morgan. I was going to—

MORGAN (interrupting):
>   Going to sign some of those checks, weren't you?

[JOHNSON:
>   Why, surely. I—

MORGAN (to the bartender):
>   Got a fountain pen?

As the bartender looks for the fountain pen, the three de
Gaullists come down the stairs headed for the door.

MORGAN (waving to them):
>   Good luck.][41]

Morgan hands the fountain pen to Johnson, and as the
latter starts to sign the first of the checks, Morgan, glanc-
ing toward the front door, grabs Marie and shoves her
out of the way.

15.   INT. CAFE   SHOOTING TOWARD FRONT DOOR AND WINDOWS
Three young de Gaullists, standing on sidewalk, are drawing revolvers and ducking behind ice wagon as big sedan lurches by with a machine gun spitting fire through open window in back. The staccato blast riddles cafe windows breast high on that side and smashes bottles all along wall behind bar and knocks chips of ice out of ice wagon. Beauclerc, climbing up on wheel of ice wagon, fires over driver's seat at sedan.

16.   EXT. STREET IN FRONT OF CAFE
Sedan, swinging sharply to right, jumps over curb, crashes into colonnade, and stops in shop window. Two big fellows crawl out of rear door. One has a Thompson gun and the other has a sawed-off shotgun.

   The one with the machine gun is Captain Renard of the Sûreté Nationale. The one with the sawed-off shotgun is Lieutenant Coyo. Driver of ice wagon runs out of Cunard Bar and goes to heads of plunging horses. Coyo knocks him over with a blast from sawed-off shotgun. De Gaullist No. 1 behind rear of ice wagon fires, and bullet ricochets off street and hits rear tire of car. You can see dust blowing up from street as the air comes out. Renard gets down almost on face and starts to fire a burst under ice wagon.

17.   INT. CAFE
Morgan, on floor, is dragging Marie behind bar.

[MARIE (dazedly):
   Say, what on earth—?

MORGAN:
   Lie down.][42]

He puts both arms around her and holds her close to him as bullets whiz behind to riddle cabinets and bar fixtures just above their heads.

18. EXT. STREET IN FRONT OF CAFE

De Gaullist No. 2, shot, is lying on sidewalk behind ice wagon. De Gaullist No. 1 stoops to lift him up and is cut down himself. Beauclerc, standing on wheel and firing over driver's seat, sees this, grabs reins, and climbs inside wagon, driving horses down the street. Renard and Coyo run after wagon, firing into rear filled with ice. Chips fly and huge hunks fall out as horses break into a gallop and wagon lumbers around distant corner with Renard and Coyo following on foot.

19. EXT. HAVANA SIDE STREET

Ice wagon enters and Beauclerc pulls up horses by alley. He climbs out and dives down alley as Renard and Coyo run around corner, pausing cautiously as they see abandoned ice wagon.

20. INT. CAFE

Gerard, who has been near the door watching what is going on in the street, comes running back to Morgan and Marie.

[MORGAN:
Did they get them all?

GERARD (excitedly):
One got away at least. I think it was Beauclerc. Look, Harry, this is bad. But no one but me knows that you two saw them. And Eddy.

MORGAN:
He probably won't remember.][43]

GERARD (continuing):
When the police come, you know nothing. (Turning to Marie.) Nothing. Do you realize, mademoiselle?

MARIE:
Yes.

[MORGAN:
  She won't talk.][44]

They are interrupted by the bartender's voice.

BARTENDER:
  Monsieur Gerard! Monsieur Gerard!

They turn and see the bartender bending over the body of Johnson. Morgan comes in and rolls him over. Johnson has been shot neatly through the head. Marie stares at Morgan. Morgan takes the traveler's checks and the wallet out of Johnson's hands. He removes the bank notes from the wallet, puts the checks into the wallet, and puts the wallet into Johnson's pocket and the money into his own pocket.

[MORGAN:
  He couldn't write any faster than he could duck. (Marie stares at him.) Too bad they couldn't have put off saving France for a while. Another minute and those checks would have been good.][45]

There is the sound of a police whistle, and they turn toward the door. A sergeant of the gendarmes comes in followed by half a dozen French sailors.

GENDARME:
  Keep quiet everyone. Stay right where you are.

(NOTE: Do this two ways, in English and in French.)

In the silence that follows, we see three menacing-looking men in plain clothes come quietly in, stopping in the center of the open space and looking over the people. They are Renard, Coyo, and Renard's bodyguard. At the bar, Morgan whispers to Gerard.

[MORGAN:
  Who are they?

GERARD (alarmed):
Sûreté Nationale.

MORGAN:
The Gestapo, huh?][46]

They look back at the men, who then start to move around staring at the faces.

RENARD (followed by his bodyguard; sees Johnson):
What happened to this man?

GERARD:
A stray bullet. His name is Johnson—an American.

RENARD (speaking quietly):
Unfortunate. (To a couple of sailors.) Take him away.

He leans against the bar and takes his time and speaks softly to the entire group.

[RENARD:
All this is regrettable. There is no cause for alarm. We are only interested in those persons who have broken the rules laid down for their behavior. I will pick out certain individuals. Those I do not designate will leave immediately. This place will then remain closed for tonight.][47]

Renard then commences walking, pointing out various people, among them Gerard, Morgan, Marie, etc. As Renard points to Marie and passes on, she whispers to Morgan.

MARIE:
Was you ever bit by a dead bee?

At this point, past the sailors guarding the door, we see Eddy sailing serenely in. Suddenly, he stops, takes note of the bristling military situation, turns around, and leaves with the same enthusiasm that brought him in.

FADE OUT

21. INT. POLICE OFFICE   NIGHT

     Morgan, Marie, and Gerard are being questioned. Renard
     sits behind the desk and the bodyguard stands beside
     him. Coyo questions Gerard first.

GERARD:
     I tell you again. I didn't know those men. They came
     in for a drink. That's all I know.

COYO:
     You never saw them before?

GERARD:
     No.

[COYO:
     That's all. You may go.]⁴⁸

As Gerard turns to exit, Renard speaks.

RENARD:
     What are your sympathies, Monsieur Gerard?

GERARD:
     I am for France.

RENARD:
     That is well. Try to remain so.

Gerard moves on again. As Renard speaks to Coyo, Gerard pauses to listen.

RENARD:
     Let us suggest to Monsieur Gerard that the next time
     suspicious characters enter his place that he notify
     us. By that means, he may prevent bloodshed at his
     doorstep.

GERARD:
     I run a public place. How am I to know who is sus-
     picious and who is not?

RENARD:
     I think you will know. Good night.

[Gerard exits. Renard speaks to Coyo.

RENARD (to Coyo):
Continue.]⁴⁹

COYO (to Morgan):
And you did not see these men at all while they were in the cafe?

MORGAN:
That's right.

COYO:
What was your connection with the dead man?

MORGAN:
He rented my boat to fish from.

COYO:
You mean he had rented it. According to this ticket in his wallet, he was to have left Martinique at daylight.

RENARD:
There was no money on him or in his wallet, only some American traveler's checks. Was that customary with him, Captain Morgan?

MORGAN:
He had sixty bucks in it.

RENARD:
What became of it?

MORGAN:
I took it.

RENARD:
Why?

[MORGAN:
Because he owed me eight hundred and forty dollars.

RENARD:
> So at least you didn't kill him, did you?][30]

MORGAN:
> So it would seem.

RENARD:
> But unfortunately for you, someone did. As a result
> of which, you took it on yourself to collect a part of
> the debt. You have this money now?

MORGAN:
> Yes.

RENARD (extending his hand):
> If you please.

Morgan takes his whole roll from his pocket, not only the
money he took out of Johnson's wallet, but his own roll
too. He begins to count the sixty dollars onto the desk.
Renard continues to hold his hand out.

RENARD (with more emphasis):
> If you please, Captain.

MORGAN:
> Some of this is mine.

RENARD:
> How do we know that?

Morgan stares at him a moment, shrugs, tosses the
money across the desk. Renard takes it and puts it into
the drawer.

RENARD:
> Thank you. Do not be concerned. This money is im-
> pounded by a government which, like your own, is
> at peace with the world. If your claim is just, it will
> be discharged.

He turns to Marie.

[RENARD:
   Miss—?][51]

COYO (opening Marie's passport and comparing Marie
with it):
   Browning, Marie. American, age twenty-two. How
   long have you been in Fort de France?

[MARIE:
   Since this—this afternoon.][52]

COYO:
   Residence?

MARIE:
   The Hotel Marquis.

COYO:
   You come from where?

MARIE:
   Trinidad. Port of Spain.

RENARD:
   And before that, from where, mademoiselle? From
   home, perhaps?

MARIE:
   No. From Rio.

RENARD:
   Alone?

MARIE (hesitates):
   Yes.

RENARD:
   Why did you get off here?

MARIE:
   To buy a new hat.

Coyo steps forward and slaps Marie. Morgan is watching all this. He sees Marie take the slap without turning a hair. She is smoking a cigarette. She turns and puts the cigarette into an ashtray on the desk, takes her hat off, and holds it out for Renard to see the label.

[MARIE:
> Maybe you'll believe me now.]⁵³

RENARD:
> I have never doubted you, mademoiselle. It is only your tone that was objectionable. I'll ask you again. Why did you get off here?

MARIE:
> I didn't have money enough to go any further.

RENARD:
> That's better. Where were you when the shooting occurred?

[MORGAN (to Marie):
> You don't have to answer this stuff.

COYO (to Morgan):
> Shut up, you.

MORGAN (to Marie):
> Don't answer him.

Coyo takes a step toward Morgan, threateningly.

MORGAN (to Coyo):
> That's right. Slap me.]⁵⁴

RENARD:
> Come, come, Captain. This is not a brawl. We merely wish to get to the bottom of this affair.

[MORGAN:
> You won't do it by slapping Americans. That's bad luck.

RENARD:

> An American who interferes with the police of a foreign government is already in bad luck. That will do now.][55] If we need to question you further, you will be available at the hotel?

MORGAN:

> I'm not likely to go anywhere as long as you have my money and my passport both.

RENARD:

> Your passport will be returned to you. As for the money, if it is yours, that will arrange itself in good time.

MORGAN:

> Maybe I'd better see the American consul and get him to help you arrange it.

RENARD:

> That is your privilege. By the way, what are your sympathies?

MORGAN:

> Minding my own business.

RENARD:

> May I suggest—?

[MORGAN:

> And I don't need any advice about continuing to do it either. (To Marie.) Come on. Let's get out of here.][56]

Morgan and Marie exit.

DISSOLVE TO:

22. EXT. NARROW STREET   A FEW MINUTES LATER
[Sound of music from little bistro in basement. Morgan and Marie come around corner. Marie stops and looks into cafe.

MARIE:

> I could use a drink.

MORGAN:
>So could I.][57]

They exit.

23.　INT. BISTRO
Place crowded with Martiniquais and sailors. Couples dancing in small space surrounded by tables. Morgan and Marie enter and make their way to bar in rear.

[BARTENDER (in French):
>What are you going to have?

Morgan, putting hand in pocket, grins and shakes his head.

MORGAN:
>Just looking around.

MARIE:
>No money?

MORGAN:
>Those cops cleaned me out.

MARIE:
>Guess we'll have to wait till we get back to the hotel.

MORGAN:
>They're closed up tight.

MARIE:
>I forgot.

She turns to survey room, putting arms on bar.

MORGAN:
>Picking out somebody?

MARIE:
>This has been a pretty large day for me. I really need a drink. (As Morgan looks at her.) You don't mind, do you?

MORGAN (taking out cigarette):
    No. Go ahead.][58]

Marie, putting hand on his shoulder, pushes him back a little so she can look at other end of room, then walks out, taking cigarette from Morgan as she passes. Morgan, taking out another cigarette, watches her as she strolls among the tables. Several men give her the eye, but she pays no attention to them, until she passes a handsome young French naval ensign, giving a light to a friend. Marie, stooping, lights cigarette from extended match and continues on her way to dance floor. Young ensign, looking after her, rises with a grin at his companion and joins Marie. He asks her to dance. Marie looks him over, then accepts, and as they dance away she looks at Morgan over her partner's shoulder. Morgan, lighting cigarette, walks toward door. As he exits, we

DISSOLVE TO:

24.   INT. MORGAN'S SITTING ROOM   HALF AN HOUR LATER
Morgan, opening door, looks at Marie, who stands in hall with a bottle under her arm.

MARIE:
    Hello.

[MORGAN:
    Hello.][59]

He walks back and sits down at table. Marie, closing door, leans back against it and looks at him.

MARIE:
    You're sore, aren't you?

MORGAN:
    Why should I be?

MARIE (coming over):
    I didn't behave very well, did I?

MORGAN:
> You did all right. You got a bottle, didn't you?

MARIE (starting to open bottle):
> You're sore, aren't you?

MORGAN:
> Look. Get this straight. I don't give a—

MARIE:
> I know. You don't give a whoop what I do. But when I do it, you get sore. (Smiles.) You told me to, you know.

MORGAN:
> I told you?

MARIE:
> You said go ahead, didn't you?

[MORGAN:
> You were pretty good at it, too.][60]

MARIE:
> Thanks. (Goes to wall cupboard, returns with two glasses.) Would you rather I wouldn't?

MORGAN:
> Wouldn't what?

MARIE (pouring drinks):
> Do things like that.

MORGAN:
> Why ask me?

MARIE:
> I'd like to know.

[MORGAN (picking up drink):
> Of all the screwy dames—

MARIE:
> All right. I won't do it anymore.][61]

MORGAN:
>   Look, I didn't ask you—

[MARIE:
>   Don't worry. I'm not giving up anything I care about. It's like shooting fish in a barrel anyway.

MORGAN:
>   What?

MARIE:
>   These men— (Laughs.) They're all a bunch of— (Laughs again.) I'm a fine one to talk. The pot calling the kettle black.

She picks up glass and walks out door.][62]

25.   INT. HALLWAY
Marie crosses hall, unlocks door of her room, and exits.
>   DISSOLVE TO:

26.   INT. MARIE'S BEDROOM   A LITTLE LATER
Marie sitting at dressing table, brushing her hair. She has changed to negligee. She hears somebody opening door in sitting room.

MARIE:
>   Who is it?

[MORGAN'S VOICE:
>   Me.

MARIE:
>   What's on your mind?

27.   INT. MARIE'S SITTING ROOM
Morgan, closing door, takes bottle out from under arm.

MORGAN:
>   I brought your bottle over.

MARIE'S VOICE:
>   Thanks.

Morgan, setting bottle on table, looks around room. There are several framed snapshots on walls. Morgan goes and looks at a couple of them. In one, Marie, wearing a bathing suit, stands beside a shapely brunette who wears bathing suit marked Miss Miami. In the other, Marie stands beside another shapely blonde who wears bathing suit marked Miss Palm Beach. On the other walls hang snaps taken by professional photographers on the beach at Rio, Buenos Aires, Trinidad, etc. Marie and an Argentine girl sitting in a wheelchair. Marie sitting under an umbrella, with a handsome young escort.

28.   INT. MARIE'S BEDROOM

Marie, leaning back in chair and looking through doorway, sees what Morgan is doing.

MARIE:
    There's a scrapbook on the table.

Morgan picks it up, looking through album as he comes through doorway.

MORGAN (looking at clippings):
    You've been in quite a few of these contests.

MARIE (nodding):
    Always a runner-up.

Morgan walks over and looks down at her, studying her with a thoughtful eye.

MORGAN:
    What are you going to do, Slim?

MARIE:
    I was just going to ask you the same question, Steve.

MORGAN:
    How long have you been away from home?

MARIE (brushing her hair):
    This is about the time for it, isn't it?

MORGAN:
> What?

MARIE:
> The story of my life. Where shall I begin?

MORGAN (sitting down on bed):
> I've got a pretty fair idea already.

MARIE:
> Who told you?

MORGAN:
> You did.

MARIE:
> Go on.

MORGAN:
> That slap in the face you took.

MARIE:
> What about it?

MORGAN:
> You hardly blinked an eye. That takes a lot of prac-
> tice. Yeah, I know a lot about you, Slim.

MARIE:
> Hm-m. Next time I get slapped I better do something
> about it.

Morgan, rising, picks up bottle of perfume from dressing
table, smells stopper.

MARIE:
> Remind you of somebody, Steve?

MORGAN (putting bottle down):
> A little.

Marie, picking up bottle, puts some of the perfume behind her ears, touching stopper to her throat.

MORGAN (drawing a deep breath):
> It's nice.

He sits down on bed and looks at her with a frank, appreciative eye.

MARIE (after a moment):
> I'm tired, Steve. Think I'll turn in.

MORGAN (rising):
> Not a bad idea.

He exits into sitting room.

MARIE:
> Take the bottle along if you want.

MORGAN'S VOICE (in sitting room):
> I'll just take a nightcap.][63]

DISSOLVE TO:

29. INT. MORGAN'S SITTING ROOM   TEN MINUTES LATER
Morgan, sitting at table, is finishing drink. There is a knock at door and Marie enters in doorway.

[MARIE:
> Steve.

MORGAN:
> I thought you were going to bed.

MARIE:
> Are you going to see the American consul in the morning?

MORGAN:
> Sure.

MARIE (coming in):
> Think it'll do any good?

MORGAN:
> Not for now.

Marie, sitting down on couch, starts to take off her slipper.

MARIE:

> Who was the girl, Steve?

MORGAN:

> What girl?

MARIE:

> The one who left you with such pleasant memories. You don't think much of women, do you, Steve? (Morgan doesn't answer, and Marie starts to remove stockings.) She must have been quite a gal. I guess we're both in the same boat—only I don't feel so bad about it.

She takes some bills out of foot of stocking and goes over to Morgan.

MARIE:

> You can use this, can't you? (Holding out bills.) Here.

Morgan looks at money and shakes his head.

MORGAN:

> Thanks just the same.

MARIE:

> I thought they cleaned you out?

MORGAN:

> I thought you said you were broke?

MARIE:

> Oh, I always try to keep enough to be independent of certain situations. Sure you can't use this?

MORGAN:

> You need it more than I do.

Marie, looking at him, turns and walks over to door, where she pushes up transom.

MARIE (lowering her voice as she returns):
Going to take that de Gaullist job?

MORGAN:
I don't know. Depends.

MARIE:
We flew over Devil's Island. Doesn't look like such a high-class resort.

MORGAN:
That's what I hear.

MARIE:
I wouldn't take a chance on it for fifty dollars.

MORGAN:
You'll be taking a chance on it for nothing if you don't keep your nose out of it.

He walks over to door and pulls down transom again. Marie, watching him, smiles.

MARIE (studying him):
You don't like to take favors, do you?

MORGAN:
Not any better than I like doing them. (Lighting cigarette.) Anything else you'd like to know? I'm not much for keeping photos—or scrapbooks.

MARIE:
You're not very hard to figure, Steve—only at times. Sometimes I know exactly what you're going to say—most of the time. The other times— (sitting down in his lap) the other times, you're just a stinker.

MORGAN:
What's all this for?

MARIE:
Well, somebody has to make the first move.

She kisses him.

MORGAN:
> Why did you do that?

MARIE:
> I've been wondering whether I'd like it.

MORGAN:
> What's the decision?

MARIE:
> I don't know yet.

She kisses him again, and this time Morgan puts his arms around her and returns the kiss.

MARIE (rising):
> I thought you wouldn't take anything from anybody?

MORGAN:
> That's different.

MARIE (holding up money):
> Changed your mind about this, too?

MORGAN:
> No.

MARIE:
> I can't figure it.

MORGAN:
> What?

MARIE (looking at money):
> This belongs to me—so do my lips. I don't see any difference.

MORGAN:
> Who was the fellow?

MARIE:
> What fellow?

MORGAN:

> The one that left you with such a pleasant viewpoint.
> You don't think much of men, do you? He must have
> been quite a guy.

MARIE:

> We live and learn—but slow.

She puts money away, walks over, and picks up footgear,
starting toward door.

MORGAN (grinning):

> You're sore, aren't you?

MARIE (leaning against door):

> I've been sore ever since I met you. One look and
> you had me placed. You didn't see me take Johnson's
> wallet, but you knew I had it. I brought that bottle
> up here to make you feel cheap. But I haven't made
> a dent in you. I'm the one who feels cheap. I've never
> felt so cheap in my life.

MORGAN:

> What did I do?

MARIE (ironical, bitter):

> Nothing. That's the whole trouble. What's more, you
> don't have to do anything. Not a thing. Oh, maybe
> just whistle. (Opening hall door.) You know how to
> whistle, don't you, Steve? You just put your lips to-
> gether and blow.

She smiles and walks out, closing door behind her. As
Morgan looks after her, we][64]

FADE OUT

FADE IN

30.   EXT. NEGRO CABIN IN OUTSKIRTS

FORT DE FRANCE   NEXT MORNING

Little colored boy sitting on oxcart in front of cabin. He
sees automobile coming around bend in road. He looks
toward cabin and pretends to call chickens.

COLORED BOY:
> Chick—chick—chick—

It is a signal to his mother, who opens door of cabin and looks out [as automobile stops in front. It is a French command car, and it contains four armed sailors.

SAILOR (in French):
> Did you see two white men pass on this road?

COLORED WOMAN (in French):
> Not today.

SAILOR (in French, to boy):
> And you?

Boy shakes his head. Sailors exit in car. Mother smiles at boy and closes door of cabin.][65]

31.   INT. CABIN
Negro woman closing door. We see Beauclerc lying on cot, his rudely bandaged right leg resting on pillow. Mrs. Beauclerc sits on edge of bed, fanning away flies above her husband's face. Gerard standing nearby. Morgan turning from window in relief. Gerard wipes forehead and throat with handkerchief.

[BEAUCLERC (to Morgan):
> Yesterday you very definitely refused to have anything to do with us. Why have you changed your mind?

MORGAN:
> Yesterday I had eight hundred and twenty-five dollars in sight. Today—thanks to you and your Vichy friends—fifty dollars is fifty dollars.

MRS. BEAUCLERC:
> I wouldn't trust him.

MORGAN (without resentment):
> I usually do what I'm paid to do.

Gerard silently nods head to Beauclerc behind Morgan's back.

BEAUCLERC:

I'm sure of that, Captain Morgan.

MORGAN:

Where is this place you want me to take you to?

GERARD:

It is the little islet of Anguilla—about forty kilometers on the way to Guadeloupe.

MORGAN:

I know where it is. (To Beauclerc.) Who you running out there?

BEAUCLERC:

Nobody. We want you to pick up two people there and bring them here.

MORGAN:

I can't land anybody after dark. The port closes at sunset now. They'd nail us all.

GERARD:

We've arranged that. A bateau will meet you outside the breakwater and take them off. Then you can wait till daylight to come on.

MORGAN:

Okay. You be in that bateau. (To Beauclerc.) Where'll these people be?

BEAUCLERC:

I'll show you when we get there.

MORGAN:

You're not going with that leg.

MRS. BEAUCLERC:

Of course not. He can't put his weight on it.

MORGAN:

You'd only be in the way.

BEAUCLERC (making gesture of resignation):

You come along the lee shore of Anguilla from the south. They'll be watching for you, and when you put on your running lights, they'll answer it. You'll see two flashlights—one held above the other.

MORGAN:

There's a little jetty in there, isn't there?

GERARD:

That's where they'll be. The password is "Norlarie."

MORGAN:

"Norlarie." (To Beauclerc.) Can you pay me now?

MRS. BEAUCLERC:

You see how much he trusts us?

Beauclerc takes out packet of paper francs and counts them into Morgan's hand.

GERARD:

Harry, if you knew what this means to us—

BEAUCLERC:

Not only to us—but to France.

MORGAN (going over to light to recount money):

I don't want to know.

GERARD:

We won't forget it.

BEAUCLERC:

I knew you were on our side.

MORGAN:

Sure I am. I'm on any side that pays me. (Indicating Beauclerc's wounded leg.) Had a doctor look at that?

BEAUCLERC (shaking head):
> They know I'm wounded. They're watching all the doctors who are friendly to us.

MORGAN:
> Who told you to put this pillow under it?

MRS. BEAUCLERC:
> I did! What's wrong with it?

BEAUCLERC:
> It doesn't hurt so much that way.

MORGAN (removing pillow):
> You'll have to grin and take it. Unless you want gangrene to set in.

MRS. BEAUCLERC:
> Are you a doctor?

MORGAN:
> No. But I've handled quite a few gunshot wounds.

He starts out with Frenchy.

BEAUCLERC:
> Bon voyage!

MRS. BEAUCLERC (as they exit):
> Bon voyage to our money!][66]

> DISSOLVE TO:

32. INT. CAFE   AN HOUR LATER
[Morgan eating lunch. Gerard enters with pot of coffee. As he pours it into cup, Morgan sees Marie descending stairway. He waves to her.

MARIE (coming over):
> Hello, Frenchy.

GERARD (bowing):
> Mademoiselle!

He exits and Marie stops by Morgan's chair.

MARIE (shoving finger inside his collar):
How are you, Steve?

MORGAN (pulling out chair):
How'd you sleep?

MARIE (stretching luxuriously):
Wonderful!

Waitress enters as Marie sits down.

MARIE (to Morgan):
Can I start with a rum swizzle?

MORGAN:
Too early.

MARIE:
Just enough to fill an elephant's ear.

MORGAN (to waitress):
Bring her some breakfast, Rosalie.

ROSALIE (as she goes):
Yes, m'sieur.

MORGAN:
Could you get packed in time for the afternoon plane?

MARIE:
Why?

Morgan takes out envelope and gives it to her.

MORGAN:
There's a ticket to San Juan.

MARIE:
San Juan? What'll I do in Puerto Rico?

MORGAN:
Better town than this any day.

MARIE (after a moment):
Where did you make the raise?

MORGAN:
No fooling, Slim. This is a good place to be from.

MARIE:
So you took that job?

MORGAN:
I got the dough from Frenchy.

MARIE:
Funny, San Juan is just fifty-eight dollars as the crow flies.

Morgan finishes his coffee.

MORGAN (rising):
Drop me a card if you get stuck there.

MARIE:
Sure. X marks my room. Send fifty more.

MORGAN:
May stop by and pick you up on my way home. (Stoops and kisses her.) Keep your nose clean.

MARIE:
You do the same. (Draws his head down and kisses him.) Thanks, Steve.

MORGAN:
So long.

He rumples her hair and starts out toward front. Marie looks after him, her eyes slowly filling with tears.][67]

DISSOLVE TO:

FADE IN

33.   EXT. FORT DE FRANCE   DOCK   LATE THAT AFTERNOON
Morgan's ship, the *Queen Conch*, tied up. Morgan is working on engine. A plane passes overhead, the Pan Ameri-

can for Miami. Morgan looks up, watches it pass, believing that Marie is on it. Eddy enters on dock, longer, blearier, drunker than ever. He jumps down on deck and almost breaks in half.

EDDY:
> Hello, Harry. How's everything?

MORGAN:
> Fine. Didn't I tell you to stay at the hotel until I got back?

Eddy sits down in fishing chair and stretches out his legs.

EDDY:
> I knew you were going out.

MORGAN:
> Who told you?

[EDDY:
> You can't fool me, Harry. I can tell it just as plain.

MORGAN (coming out of engine hatch):
> Well, *you're* not going.]⁶⁸

EDDY:
> Can I have a little one, Harry? Just enough to fill a hen's ear?

MORGAN:
> Come on—get off.

[EDDY:
> You can't go without a mate.

MORGAN (coming aft):
> Do you think having a rummy on board makes any difference? (Jerking Eddy out of chair.) Get off of her. You're poison to me—]⁶⁹

EDDY:
> What's the matter, Harry? There's no sense getting plugged with me.

127

MORGAN:
Get off of her—

EDDY:
Aw, take it easy—

Morgan hits him on the face. Eddy sags down against dock, then, holding his face, he rises and climbs up onto dock.

EDDY:
I wouldn't do a thing like that to you, Harry.

MORGAN:
You're darn right you wouldn't. I'm not going to carry you. That's all.

EDDY:
Well, what did you have to hit me for?

MORGAN:
So you'd believe it.

EDDY:
You aren't treating me square.

MORGAN:
Who did you ever treat square, [you rummy?][70] You'd double-cross your own mother. You told me so yourself.

EDDY:
I was only kidding.

He starts to walk off down the dock looking longer than a day without breakfast. Then he turns and comes back.

[EDDY:
Say, Harry—will you let me take a couple of dollars?

MORGAN (handing him a bill):
Here.

EDDY (brightening):
>Okay. I always knew you were my pal. Harry, why don't you carry me?

MORGAN:
>You're bad luck.][71]

EDDY:
>You're just plugged. Never mind, old pal. You'll be glad to see me yet.

Morgan looks after Eddy as the latter walks off down the dock, then goes back into engine hatch.

>DISSOLVE TO:

34. EXT. QUEEN CONCH AT SEA   LATER THAT NIGHT
She is drifting in a heavy fog off islet where Morgan has a rendezvous. Morgan has just shut off motors and is throwing hook overboard.

35. INT. WHEELHOUSE
Morgan enters, opens locker, and takes out a twelve-gauge pump gun and a Winchester thirty-thirty and hangs them up in their cases right over the wheel where he can reach them. Taking pump gun out of case, he works her a few times, then fills her up with shells and pumps one in the barrel. Then he puts a shell in the barrel of the Winchester and fills up the magazine. He shoves Winchester back in the case. He hears something in the direction of the cabin. He takes thirty-eight Special out of waistband of trousers and walks forward.

36. EXT. DECK QUEEN CONCH
Morgan enters and stops as he sees cabin hatch is opening. He cocks six-shooter.

MORGAN:
>All right. Come on out.

Eddy cautiously sticks his head out of hatch.

[EDDY:
Don't shoot, Harry. It's only me.

MORGAN (putting gun away):
How did you get back on her?

EDDY:
Well, I walked up the street, bought a couple of bottles, and sneaked back in here when you were working on the engine.

Morgan grins in spite of himself.

MORGAN:
Come on out of there—and bring the bottles along.

EDDY (grinning):
I knew you would carry me, Harry.

MORGAN:
Carry you nothing. You're not even on the crew list. I have a good mind to make you jump overboard now.

EDDY (laughing):
You're an old joker, Harry. Us Key Westers ought to stick together when we are in trouble.

MORGAN:
How d'you know I'm in trouble?

EDDY:
You can't fool me. I always know.

MORGAN:
You with your mouth. Who's going to trust your mouth when you're drunk?

He walks into wheelhouse and Eddy follows him.

37.   INT. WHEELHOUSE
Morgan enters with Eddy.

EDDY:

I'm a good man, Harry. You just put me to the test and see what a good man I am.

MORGAN (sitting down on locker):
Give me those bottles.

Eddy reluctantly hands them over. One is open. Morgan takes a drink from it and puts it forward by the wheel. Eddy stands there and Morgan looks at him.

EDDY (looking around):
What's the matter, Harry? What are you looking at me like that for?

MORGAN:
Nothing. Just a joke that neither of us knows the answer to.

EDDY:
What joke?

MORGAN:
Whether you'll hold together or not.

EDDY (quickly):
I'm a good man. You know I am. (Suddenly sober.) Say—what's goin' on? What're we gonna do?

MORGAN:
I don't know, yet. Haven't got it all figured out, yet.

Takes another drink out of bottle. Stands looking at the fog on shore.

EDDY (after a moment):
Harry—

Morgan doesn't answer.

EDDY:
Why don't you ask me if I've got a mouth on me?

MORGAN (without turning his head):
> You've had enough for now. I'll give you one later on.

EDDY (wetting his lips):
> Can't I have just a little one now?

MORGAN:
> No. I don't want you to be rum-dumb—I want you to be rum-brave.

Then Eddy sees rifle and shotgun hanging over wheel.

EDDY:
> What the dickens is the matter?

MORGAN:
> Nothing.

EDDY:
> What's all the darn guns for?

MORGAN:
> In case we see a shark or something.

EDDY:
> A shark! At night? Look—what's goin' on here?

MORGAN (taking another drink):
> I always carry them on board to shoot birds that bother the baits, or sharks, when we are cruising along the keys.

EDDY:
> What's the matter, darn it, what's the matter?

MORGAN:
> Nothing. (Takes another drink.) We are going to do a little job. I'll tell you what to do when it's time.

EDDY (excited and happy):
> You couldn't have anybody better than me, Harry. I'm the man for anything.

Morgan looks at him—tall, lanky, and bleary—and he doesn't say anything.

EDDY (after a moment):
> Listen, Harry—would you give me just one? I don't want to get the shakes.

Morgan hands him the bottle.

MORGAN:
> I don't want you rum-brave until I tell you. Make it a short one.

He looks toward shore.]⁷²

38. INT. WHEELHOUSE QUEEN CONCH   OUTSIDE COVE
Morgan flashes on his running lights, then turns them off. There is an answering signal from shore—two lights—one held above the other. Morgan turns to Eddy, who sits on locker.

[EDDY (excitedly):
> Okay, Harry?

MORGAN:
> Get the hook aboard, you big brave man.]⁷³

Eddy goes forward and Morgan starts his motors. Then he goes forward.

39. [EXT. DECK OF QUEEN CONCH
Eddy is vainly trying to get anchor aboard. He's too weak to do much good. Morgan enters and gives him a hand.

MORGAN:
> Listen, we are going in to pick up two guys. You take the wheel when I tell you to and do what I tell you to. Come on. Get that hook up.

EDDY (as they get anchor on board):
> Harry, can I have one of those now?

MORGAN (starting back toward wheelhouse):
    I'll give you one in a minute.

EDDY:
    I'm a good man. You'll see.

MORGAN:
    You're a rummy.][74]

40. INT. WHEELHOUSE
    [Morgan enters with Eddy at his heels. He takes a drink
    from bottle and hands it to Eddy. As Eddy drinks, Mor-
    gan shoves in clutch and starts in toward shore.

MORGAN (jerks bottle from Eddy's mouth):
    Listen to me. When I give you the word, cut her and
    put the wheel over and let her drift stern first in to-
    ward the jetty. As soon as she comes around, put her
    in gear and keep your hand on the clutch. Two
    people are to come aboard. When I give you the
    word, hook her up quick, and get out of there. If
    more than two people try to board us, or anything
    happens to me, hook her up and head out to sea.
    You can hold the wheelhouse against them with the
    shotgun until you can make a deal, or at least find
    out what the score is.

EDDY:
    Alone? If anything happens to you? Then what do I
    do?

MORGAN:
    How do I know? You invited yourself on this trip. I
    didn't.

EDDY (trembling, but trying to pull himself together):
    All right, but you better give me another drink.

MORGAN (handing him the bottle):
    Here.

Eddy takes the bottle and drinks. Morgan snatches it away, strikes the cork in with his palm, and puts the bottle away.][75]

41. EXT. THE JETTY
The boat drifts up to the jetty, where three dim figures are waiting. They are Paul, Helene, and a guide.

GUIDE (in French):
Who's there?

[MORGAN:
"Norlarie."

GUIDE (in French):
Throw me your line.

MORGAN (catching hold of the jetty):
Never mind that. Put your people aboard.

GUIDE (to others, in French):
They have sent an American.

MORGAN (impatiently):
Come on. Come on.

Two of the dark figures reluctantly approach the boat. Helene starts to get down into it. She will have to jump, and hesitates. Morgan does not yet see that she is a woman. He holds out his hand. She takes it and jumps down into the boat. Only when he touches her hand does he realize she is a woman.

MORGAN (in surprise):
Say, what's this?

HELENE (in English):
Thank you.

MORGAN (to the guide):
They didn't say anything about a woman.

GUIDE (in French):
> I don't speak English. Here is Monsieur de Bursac.

MORGAN:
> All right, jump in.

Paul jumps down into the boat.

MORGAN (over his shoulder to Eddy):
> Hook her up. Let's get out of here.][76]

The boat starts to gather speed.

42.   GROUP SHOT
Morgan, Helene, and Paul at the stern. The boat is going fast.

[PAUL (in English):
> Permit me, Captain. My wife, Madame de Bursac. She is an American, too.

MORGAN:
> I don't care what she is. What did you want to bring your wife here for? What kind of a war are you guys fighting, lugging your wives around with you?

HELENE (bristling):
> What business is it of yours?

MORGAN:
> An American, huh? Well, nothing like a little cheese-cake for a touch of color. How come you didn't bring along a photographer?

PAUL (angrily):
> Who are you?

HELENE:
> Where is Beauclerc?

MORGAN:
> He got in a little trouble. Come into the wheelhouse. It's blowing up outside.

HELENE:
There'll be some more blowing up when we get to Fort de France, too. Of all the insolence!

PAUL (stiffly, to Morgan):
We will stay here. We will be quite comfortable, thank you.

MORGAN (as he goes forward):
Suit yourself.][77]

DISSOLVE TO:

43.   INT. WHEELHOUSE
Morgan is steering. Eddy dozing on seat. Morgan sees something ahead, reacts in alarm, cuts the switch. The SOUND of the engine STOPS. The boat drifts on.

[EDDY (sitting up):
What's wrong?

Morgan crouches over the wheel, tense, staring ahead into the darkness, Eddy beside him. As they listen, the SOUND of another boat, moving slow, comes from ahead.

EDDY:
Did you get a sight of it?

MORGAN:
I didn't have to. Don't you know that engine? It's the patrol boat.

As they listen tensely, the SOUND of the other engine STOPS. Morgan quickly takes the rifle from the rack on the bulkhead.][78]

EDDY:
Here! You can't fight those guys.

MORGAN (jacking a shell into the rifle):
What's the matter? This is where you ought to be telling me how good you are.

[EDDY (pulling himself together):
    All right. What do you want me to do?

MORGAN:
    Just what you did before. Put her in gear and be ready to pour the coal to her when I give you the word.

EDDY (trembling):
    Maybe I'd better have that other drink now.

MORGAN (about to exit):
    What other drink?

Morgan exits. Eddy stares ahead into the darkness, fumbling around for the bottle, trembling, frightened, but trying to hold himself together. He cannot find the bottle.][79]

44.   GROUP SHOT AT STERN
Paul and Helene have risen as Morgan enters with the rifle.

[PAUL:
    What is it?

MORGAN:
    It's the patrol ship.

PAUL:
    What shall we do?

MORGAN (staring into the darkness toward the invisible ship):
    Nothing. Get down below the gunwale and stay there.

PAUL (indicates the rifle):
    And you will try to resist with that? You'll get us all killed.

MORGAN:

> Look—will you get down there and shut up? Both of
> you. You just save France. Let me save my ship.][80]

Paul and Helene crouch below the gunwale. Morgan
crouches, staring into the darkness, the rifle ready. The
patrol boat's searchlight comes on, moves across the
water toward them, stops, swings back in the other direction, stops, then moves again across the water toward
them, drawing nearer and nearer until it picks up the
boat. As it does so, Paul springs up and stands on the
coaming with his arms raised above his head.

[PAUL (in French):

> We surrender. Don't—

Morgan knocks Paul down into the boat. Helene starts
toward Morgan with tigress fury.

HELENE:

> You big bully!

MORGAN (shoving her away):

> If you want to surrender, jump overboard. (To
> Eddy.) Hook her up.

The boat surges forward. Morgan fires at the searchlight,
misses, jacks another shell into the rifle. Paul tries to rise.
As he does so, a burst of fire comes from the patrol boat.
Paul is hit and cries out. Morgan shoots out the searchlight. As he turns to run to the wheel, he sees Paul
sprawled on the seat with Helene bending over him.

HELENE (in alarm):

> Paul! Are you hurt?

Morgan stoops to examine Paul's wound. He has been
shot in the right shoulder.

MORGAN:

> So that's how you're saving France—by surrendering
> to the first Vichy cop that yells "Stop" at you.

PAUL (weakly):
Please do as I say. It is for the best.

MORGAN (to Helene):
You see what happens when you lug women around?
(Pointing to Paul.) Get him off the seat. He's bleeding
all over my cushion.

HELENE:
What kind of a man are you—talking about your silly
cushion? Why don't you do something for him?

MORGAN (as he goes forward):
I haven't got time right now.][81]

DISSOLVE TO

45.   OFF SHORE   DAWN

The *Queen Conch* has stopped. Gerard and another man
pull up beside it in a bateau. Aboard the *Queen Conch*,
Paul lies on the floor of cockpit, a crude bandage around
his shoulder. Helene is beside him, looking wan and
dazed. [Morgan enters and catches painter.

MORGAN:
Hello, Frenchy.

GERARD (anxiously):
What happened?

MORGAN:
Your friend got shot up a little.

HELENE (rouses):
Who are these people?

MORGAN (to Helene):
This is Frenchy Gerard, the guy that hired me to
bring you here. (To Gerard.) All right, Frenchy. Take
them off.

HELENE:
I don't understand.

MORGAN:
This is all of it. The end of the line.

HELENE (looks about at the desolate shore):
Here? Like this? Aren't you going to take us any farther?

MORGAN:
This is as far as I go.

HELENE:
But you can't. You can't—

MORGAN (to Gerard):
Look. Get them out of my boat. And you better talk to them. If this is the sort of people you are hoping to save Martinique with, no wonder the Vichy cops run you ragged. (Over his shoulder to Eddy.) Come here.

Eddy enters, a little wobbly in the legs.

EDDY:
Hello, Frenchy.

MORGAN:
Give us a hand here.

Morgan, Eddy, and Gerard lift Paul into the bateau. Helene is dazed. She stumbles as she tries to follow Paul. Morgan catches her by the hand before she falls and helps her into the skiff. Gerard and the other oarsman row away.

MORGAN (to Eddy):
All right. Hook her up.

Eddy goes to the wheelhouse. The boat starts. Morgan turns away. He pauses, sniffs, as if he had suddenly smelled something, turns his head from side to side, sniffing, raises the hand with which he had helped Helene into the boat, sniffs at it, smells the faint scent which she had left, dips hand in water to wash it off.][82]

FADE OUT

FADE IN

46. INT. CAFE   LATER THAT MORNING

Place is practically deserted. Morgan, coming in with Eddy, pauses blankly as he sees Marie standing by piano, listening to Cricket rehearse a number with orchestra.

[MARIE (seeing him):
    Hello, Steve.

EDDY (turning to Morgan):
    I thought you said she pulled out?

MORGAN:
    Why didn't you take that plane?

MARIE:
    I decided to wait for you.

She puts hand in his pocket and takes out package of cigarettes.

MORGAN (angrily):
    I went to a lot of trouble to get you out of here.][83]

MARIE:
    That's why I didn't go.

[As Morgan looks at her, she takes some bills out of pocket.

MARIE:
    I got a refund on the ticket. Want me to keep it for you?

EDDY (seeing money):
    Listen, Harry. Could I—?

MORGAN:

> You've had enough to last you a week. (To Marie.) Don't buy him nothing but beer.

As he turns to go, Frenchy enters.

MORGAN:

> Have any trouble getting them ashore?

GERARD:

> No. But Madame refused to let us take them to that place in the country. She said it was too far. He would die before he got there.

MORGAN:

> What does she know?

GERARD:

> He is very badly wounded, Harry. Anybody can see that.][84]

MORGAN:

> I looked at it. The bullet hit the gunwale first and was practically spent. All you have to do is to get some-body to take it out. [(To Marie.) Had your breakfast?

MARIE (nodding):

> But I'll have a cup of coffee with you.

Morgan starts toward table in rear, but Frenchy follows him.][85]

GERARD:

> Couldn't you do it for us?

[MORGAN:

> Me? Listen, I'm hotter right now than any doctor. Don't you think they recognized my ship? Why, the minute I walk out of here they'll be right on my trail—

GERARD:

I thought about that. That's why I brought them here.

MORGAN (stopping in horror):
You what?

MARIE:
You brought them here?

MORGAN (pointing to big goldfish bowl):
Why didn't you stick them in that and be done with it?

GERARD:

I know it sounds crazy, but what could I do? If that man dies, our only hope of saving Martinique is gone.

MORGAN:

Listen, I don't owe you anything, Frenchy. I did what you paid me for, didn't I? I pay for everything I get around here, don't I? Ask her. (He gestures at old cashier behind grill;][86] turning on Marie.) You see what you got into by sticking around?

MARIE:
I'm willing to pull out any time you are.

[MORGAN (turning to cashier):
Make out our bills. (To Eddy.) Go upstairs and get our things packed.

EDDY:
Where we going?

MORGAN:
Never mind. Hurry up.

CASHIER (looking at ledger):
Your bill, Captain Morgan, being somewhat in arrears, amounts to six thousand three hundred and fifty-six francs.

MORGAN (to Marie):
> We haven't got half that, have we?

Marie shakes her head, whereupon the cashier smiles.

CASHIER:
> I think M'sieur Gerard will be glad to dismiss the whole matter if you will—

GERARD (eagerly):
> By all means.][87]

Morgan motions at Marie.

MORGAN:
> Throw her bill in with it?

GERARD:
> Sure thing.

MORGAN:
> All I have to do is to get the bullet out and put a dressing on it?

GERARD:
> That's all.

[MORGAN (to cashier):
> Put some water on to boil. I'll give you a probe to sterilize.

OLD CASHIER (as she exits):
> Voilà, mon capitaine.

MORGAN (starting toward stairway):
> I'll go up and get my kit.

MARIE:
> What can I do?

MORGAN:
> Go up and pack your things. (As she exits up stairs, he turns to Gerard.) Where are they?

GERARD (pointing to the floor):
Down in the wine cellar.

MORGAN:
You poor sap. That's the first place they'll look.

GERARD:
I know. We all crazy except you, Harry—and I think
you are a little crazy, too.

MORGAN (as he goes upstairs):
You said it.][88]

DISSOLVE TO:

47. INT. WINE CELLAR OF CAFE   A LITTLE LATER
Gerard and Morgan descending stairway. We can HEAR
Cricket at piano OVERHEAD. Morgan carries a ship's medical kit. Gerard, lighting a candle, leads him through aisle
in wine racks to far end of cellar. Here he pushes aside an
old sideboard, disclosing door. He opens door, motioning
Morgan to precede him.

48. INT. BEDROOM NO. 1   OLD SERVANT'S QUARTERS
The room is empty. Morgan looks around curiously as he
enters with Gerard.

[MORGAN:
What's this?

GERARD:
Some old servant's quarters.][89]

He leads Morgan through bathroom into another bedroom.

49. INT. BEDROOM NO. 2
Paul lying unconscious on cot. Helene sitting on chair
nearby, fanning him. She rises as Gerard enters with Morgan.

HELENE (recognizing Morgan):
What do you want?

[MORGAN:
    Hello, Cheesecake.

HELENE:
    Where's the doctor?

GERARD:
    Please be patient, madame. We will get one as soon
    as—

HELENE:
    Patient! You think I can sit here and watch my hus-
    band die—just because of a pack of cowardly—

MORGAN:
    Quit that yelling. (Starting to remove crude bandage
    from Paul's shoulder) He's not going to die.

HELENE (jerking him away from cot):
    Don't touch him—

GERARD:
    Really, madame, Harry is very good at this sort of
    thing—

HELENE (scornfully):
    I've seen a sample of his work—and I wouldn't let
    him touch my dog!

MORGAN:
    I stopped the bleeding, didn't I? That was more than
    you could do.

HELENE (almost beside herself; to Gerard):
    Once and for all, are you going to get a doctor or do
    you want me to go and do it?

MORGAN:
    Go ahead.

GERARD:
    Madame, I've told you it is impossible.

HELENE:

    All right—I'll show you how impossible it is.

She starts for door, and Gerard stops her.

GERARD (pleading with her):

    Please, madame. Control yourself. It will mean ruin—not only for us all—but for our cause.

HELENE (scornfully):

    The cause! The cause! That's all you think of. Paul is nothing to you. Well, he is to me, and if I haven't got something to say about this thing I'd like to know who has? Who put up the money for all this? Where would you be if it wasn't for me?

And she struggles like a madwoman to release herself from Gerard's grasp.

GERARD:

    Madame! Please—I beg you—

HELENE:

    Let me go! I'm an American citizen—and I'm not afraid of anybody!

MORGAN:

    Why don't you sing "The Star-Spangled Banner"? (To Gerard.) Let her go, Frenchy.

GERARD: (amazedly):

    Let her go? You know what it means if she appears on the street?

MORGAN:

    She won't go anywhere. She's just sounding off.

He pulls Gerard away from Helene, who stands there and stares at him infuriatedly.

MORGAN:

    You see?][90]

Helene suddenly hits him in the face. Morgan grins at her and introduces her to Marie, who has entered at this juncture with pan containing probe he gave cashier to sterilize.

[MORGAN:
> Miss Browning, this is Madame de Cheesecake. (Taking pan from Marie, he says to Helene.) Don't get tough with Slim. She's apt to slap you back.

MARIE (to Helene):
> Is there something I can do?

HELENE (icily):
> Don't ask me. Your friend seems to be in complete charge here.

MARIE (looking toward ceiling):
> Listen.

OVERHEAD we HEAR Cricket softly beginning to play plink-plink prelude.

MORGAN (opening medical kit):
> What is it?

MARIE:
> I told Cricket to play that if Renard came in.

Morgan looks at Helene.

MORGAN (lowering voice):
> That's the Gestapo. (Taking out can of ether and a packet of cotton, he hands it to Helene.) Get over there behind your husband's head, and if he comes to while I'm probing, pour some of that stuff on a hunk of cotton and give him a whiff of it to keep him quiet. (To Gerard.) Bring that lamp over here so I can see.

HELENE (unscrewing stopper from can):
> What is this?

MORGAN (preparing to go to work with probe):
    Ether. Be careful you don't get too many whiffs of it
    yourself, Cheesecake.

HELENE (brandishing can in a frenzy):
    If you call me that again, I'll throw this can clear
    through you!

GERARD (in alarm):
    Hush!

MORGAN:
    You better save it for Mr. Cheesecake.

As Helene glares at him, speechless with rage, Marie
reaches for can.

MARIE:
    I'll do it.

HELENE (haughtily):
    Are you a nurse?

MARIE:
    No. Are you?

HELENE:
    Yes. I took a course in Paris. That's why all this seems
    so horrible to me.

She goes and stands behind Paul, preparing to give ether
to him if he needs it. Morgan looks at her and motions to
Marie.

MORGAN:
    You better get out of here. You might not like this.

MARIE:
    I'll be all right.][91]

She picks up candle to give Morgan more light. Helene,
watching Morgan shove probe into wound, suddenly
keels over on the floor in a dead faint.

[MORGAN (seeing this):
　Look at our nurse.

MARIE (going to her aid):
　Oh, you poor thing.

MORGAN:
　Let her alone—and pick up that can—quick.

Marie obeys—but it is too late.

MARIE:
　It's all spilled.

MORGAN (in disgust):
　You dames! Pull Nursie away from it—and fan those
　ether fumes off me.

He continues to probe, and Paul, coming to, begins to
groan and writhe in agony. Gerard gazes fearfully at ceiling.

GERARD:
　You better stop.

MORGAN:
　I can't. (To Paul.) Take it easy. I'll be through in a
　minute. (To Gerard.) Put that lamp down. You and
　Slim'll have to hold him.

They obey, Marie gripping Paul's good arm, Gerard
clutching his legs. Paul's groans become louder and
louder. Helene dazedly sits up on floor.

MORGAN (to Marie):
　Put your hand over his mouth.

HELENE:
　Stop it. Stop it. Can't you see you're killing him?

MORGAN:
　It's your fault—spilling all the ether. See if you can
　find something for him to bite on. Then he won't
　make so much noise.

151

Helene looks toward ceiling, recalls Renard, rises, and goes around other side of bed. She evidently finds something for Paul to bite on, judging from muffled SOUND of his groans.

MORGAN (after a moment):
Here's the bullet.

He holds it up and Paul sinks back with a gasp of relief, his teeth relaxing their grip on the object Helene gave him to bite on. It was nothing less than the knuckle of the index finger of her own right hand, and blood is slowly welling up in the teeth marks.

MORGAN (seeing this):
Are you crazy?

HELENE:
It was my fault he was suffering so much. Why shouldn't I share it?

Marie, staring at Helene, makes a sudden rush for the bathroom, her hand clutching mouth.

MORGAN:
You dames! If it isn't one thing it's the other.

Then, as he starts to put bandage on Paul's wound, we
DISSOLVE TO:][92]

50.   [INT. CELLAR ROOM   THREE OR FOUR HOURS LATER
By candlelight Morgan, weary with a long vigil, sits by cot, watching Paul. On opposite side of cot Helene sits in a chair, watching Morgan. Latter, feeling Paul's forehead, takes hold of his wrist for a moment, then, blowing out candle and rising to feet, he stretches luxuriously in morning sunlight from dingy window.

MORGAN:
Guess I'll get some sleep.

HELENE:
Is he worse?

MORGAN (shaking head):
> No. Fever's all gone and his pulse is coming back strong.

HELENE (her face lighting up):
> He's going to be all right? Are you sure?

MORGAN:
> I'm no doctor—but he looks pretty good to me.

Helene suddenly breaks down—her eyes fill with tears—and she walks out of room.][93]

51.   INT. CELLAR
[Helene enters, sits down on chair, and sobs brokenly. Morgan enters and looks down at her.

MORGAN:
> You better get some sleep yourself. You've had a pretty tough time.

HELENE (broken and incoherent):
> I didn't want to come with Paul. But our people made me. They said no man was much good if he left somebody behind. The fear is too much. But I did my best to get out of it. I said I'd be in the way, but that wasn't it. I was simply afraid. More afraid to go than I was to stay. But Paul wouldn't leave without me. I thought he was very brave. But now I know he was afraid, too.

MORGAN:
> Well, he didn't invent it.][94]

[HELENE:
> But we have so much to do, and so little to do it with. You must tell these people what we are. It is only fair. You have risked everything to bring us here.

MORGAN:
> Not me. I got paid for what I did.

HELENE:
> You got no pay for saving Paul. And I tried so hard to stop you. I did my best. If I had something in my hands I would have killed you.

MORGAN (impatiently):
> Quit that baby talk. You aren't sorry at all. Nobody is. You're just sorry you made such a mug of yourself.

Helene stares at him for a moment, then smiles at him through her tears.

HELENE:
> You can't make me angry at you any more. I don't know why. You could do anything to me. I wouldn't care.

MORGAN (grinning at her):
> Of all the screwy dames— (After a moment.) What's your name?

HELENE:
> Helene. Yours is Harry, isn't it? Harry. I never knew anybody by that name.

MORGAN (holding out hand):
> Same here. Glad to meet you, Helene.

As she puts her hand in his, palm down, French fashion, somebody speaks behind them.

MARIE'S VOICE:
> You're supposed to kiss it.]⁹⁵

They turn and see Marie standing behind them with a tray of food in her hands.

[MARIE:
> I hate to break this up, but—

MORGAN:
> But what?

HELENE (in surprise):
Oh, hello.

MARIE:
Oh, *hello.* (To Morgan.) How's your patient? Or haven't you seen him lately?

MORGAN:
Lay off Helene. She's okay. (Nodding in Paul's direction.) So is he.

HELENE (to Marie):
I'm sorry I was so rude to you.

MARIE:
I'll get over it. (Setting down tray.) Here's some breakfast for you.

MORGAN (turning to go):
Listen, Helene, if anything goes wrong, don't be afraid to send for me.

HELENE:
I won't. Thanks.][96]

Morgan starts toward stairway. Marie looks at Helene. The two women measure each other. Then, without a word, Marie turns and follows Morgan. And as Helene looks after them, we

DISSOLVE TO:

51A.   INT. UPPER HALLWAY   A FEW MINUTES LATER
Morgan and Marie enter, but instead of going toward her own door Marie waits beside Morgan while he unlocks his door.

[MORGAN:
Why don't you go to bed?

MARIE:
I could use a drink.

MORGAN (opening door):
>   You're out of luck. Eddy finished that bottle.

He walks into room, and Marie follows him.

MARIE:
>   I didn't want one, anyway.][97]

51B.   INT. MORGAN'S SITTING ROOM
Morgan looking at Marie as she closes door.

[MORGAN:
>   Is there something you want to talk about?

MARIE:
>   No.

MORGAN (sitting down on couch):
>   Well, I wish you'd get it over with as soon as you
>   can. I'm dead for sleep.

MARIE:
>   So am I. (Kneels down and takes off his shoes.) That
>   feel better?

MORGAN:
>   Nope.

Marie, rising, starts toward bedroom.

MORGAN:
>   Where you going?

MARIE:
>   Run a tub for you.

MORGAN (rising):
>   No use. I'd only go to sleep in it.

MARIE (returning to him):
>   Isn't there something I can do for you, Steve?

MORGAN:
>   Yeah.

There is no mistaking his meaning, and Marie smiles at him.

MARIE (imitating Helene):
> You can't make me angry at you any more. I don't know why. You could do anything to me. I wouldn't care.

As Morgan looks at her she turns and starts toward door.

MORGAN:
> Wait a minute. (As she pauses he motions to her.) Come back here. (As Marie obeys.) Walk around me.

MARIE (puzzled):
> Huh?

MORGAN:
> Go ahead. Nobody's going to bite you.

Still puzzled, Marie slowly obeys. But by the time she has walked around him she isn't so puzzled.

MARIE:
> You're right, Harry. There's no strings tied to you. (Starting toward door.) I'm glad you brought it up.

MORGAN:
> It was getting me down.

He follows her to door, and as she opens it and goes out,][98] [Gerard hurriedly enters.

MORGAN (seeing Gerard):
> What's the matter?

GERARD:
> Renard's downstairs. He wants to see you.

Morgan shakes his head.

MORGAN:
> I'm too woozy to talk to him now. Tell him I'm in bed—see him in the morning.

GERARD:
>
> Harry, you better come down. I think he suspects something.

MORGAN:
>
> Sure he does. That's why I don't want to talk to him.

MARIE (entering from hall):
>
> Take a cold shower. You'll be all right. (Starting toward bathroom.) I'll fix it.

MORGAN:
>
> Okay. (To Gerard.) Go down and entertain him.

GERARD:
>
> Eddy's doing that already.

MORGAN (in alarm):
>
> Eddy! Holy mackerel! (Sitting down and putting on shoes.) Never mind the shower, Slim.

He jumps up and exits into hall, followed by Gerard and Marie:][99]

[51C. INT. UPPER HALLWAY

Morgan, coming out of room with Marie and Gerard, says to Marie:

MORGAN:
>
> See you later.

MARIE:
>
> I'm going with you.

MORGAN:
>
> No, you're not.

He shoves her toward door of her room. Key is in the lock. Morgan opens door, pushes Marie inside in spite of her protests, and, locking door, starts down hall with Gerard.][100]

52.   INT. CAFE

Eddy sitting at table with Renard and Coyo. Bodyguard stands behind Renard. Place is deserted except for early morning help getting things ready to open up for business.

[EDDY (taking a drink):
>He must have weighed nine hundred if he weighed a pound. You never saw such a marlin in your born days.

Morgan, entering on stairway with Gerard, hurriedly comes down to table.

RENARD (seeing Morgan):
>Good morning, Captain. Won't you join us?

MORGAN (as he sits down):
>I don't seem to have much choice.

GERARD:
>Anything I can get you gentlemen?

RENARD:
>Not now.][101] (To Eddy.) Continue, Mr. Eddy.

Gerard goes about his business.

EDDY (beaming):
>Did you hear that, Harry? He called me Mister. (To Renard.) [Well, sir, this fish was so big Harry and me could hardly budge him. We pumped on him till we was all wore out. (Taking another drink.) Long after dark we was still playing him. He must have weighed a thousand easy.

RENARD (turning to Morgan):
>I'm glad you arrived. Every time Mr. Eddy takes a drink this fabulous fish grows larger.][102] How did you finally manage to land such a leviathan?

[MORGAN (pouring self a drink):
  We had to cut him loose around eight o'clock.

RENARD:
  Why? Was he so big?

MORGAN:
  No.][103] We ran into a German submarine.

RENARD (startled):
  A German submarine?

MORGAN:
  Well, whatever it was, it turned a searchlight on us
  and opened fire. [So I didn't stick around to make
  any further inquiries.

Renard smiles admiringly.

RENARD:
  You are very shrewd, Captain Morgan. I don't think
  anybody could give a more logical explanation for refusing to obey the challenge of our patrol ship. Not
  to speak of shooting out their searchlight.

MORGAN:
  The patrol ship? Is that what it was? (Turning to
  Eddy.) You were right, after all.][104]

EDDY:
  I'm a good man in the dark. I always was.

[COYO:
  There's one thing very hard to understand.

MORGAN:
  What's that?

COYO:
  Why a professional fisherman goes fishing for his
  own amusement.

MORGAN:

I don't as a rule. But Johnson lost my heavy tackle, and I figured the fish that took it might be drowned if he couldn't get shut of it—so while I was trolling for the line I got hooked on to another one.

RENARD (looking at Coyo):

That seems reasonable. Quite reasonable. (Pouring drink.) Sorry to bother you, Captain.

MORGAN:

That's all right.

RENARD:

You are a very practical man, and I'm quite sure you have no special sympathies.

MORGAN:

That's right.][105]

[COYO:

There was only one possibility that might affect your judgment. (Pause.) Your financial condition.

MORGAN:

Why don't you do something about it?

RENARD:

That's one reason I came here. To rectify that mistake. (Taking large envelope out of pocket.) Here are the passports of yourself and mademoiselle. Eight hundred and twenty-five dollars in cash, representing your claim against the Johnson estate. And thirty-two dollars of your own money. (As Morgan stares at him, flabbergasted.) Will you see if it is correct and sign this receipt?

As Morgan hastily checks contents of envelope, Renard and Coyo rise to their feet.

MORGAN:

It's all here.

Coyo hands him fountain pen. Morgan signs receipt.

MORGAN:

Thanks a lot. There's just one thing.

RENARD (taking receipt):

You're quite free to do as you like. Stay or go. As you please.

So saying, he walks out, followed by his men. As they exit, Morgan picks up envelope and looks after them, deeply puzzled.][106] Frenchy enters from rear, beaming.

MORGAN:

Did you hear the same thing I did?

GERARD:

Most of it. [We did very well. It is clear they suspect nothing.

MORGAN (rising):

I'm not so sure of that.

He walks over and looks out crack in shade.

MORGAN:

That watchdog is still out there.

GERARD:

He always has been there. (Looking down at Eddy, who is dozing in chair.) That big fish of his was an inspiration. That and the German submarine.

EDDY (sitting up):

What fish?

GERARD:

I think it deserves a small libation.

MORGAN:

Wait till he sleeps this one off. (Pulling Eddy to his feet.) Go on back to the ship.

EDDY:
> Okay, Harry. (Turns to go, then stops.) Say, Frenchy.

GERARD:
> Yes, Eddy.

EDDY:
> Did you ever know a fellow by the name of Juggins?

GERARD:
> Juggins?

EDDY:
> Who?

Gerard stares at Eddy bewilderedly, and Morgan grins as we][107]

FADE OUT

FADE IN

53.   INT. CAFE   THAT EVENING
Place is crowded. [Cricket doing "Hong Kong Blues" number.][108] Marie, standing by piano, sees Morgan coming in entrance from sidewalk. He looks around room and goes to bar.

MORGAN (to bartender):
> Has Eddy been in?

BARTENDER (shaking head):
> I haven't seen him, Captain.

Morgan comes over to Marie.

[MORGAN:
> Hello, Slim. Are your things all packed?

MARIE (nodding):
> Have a good sleep?

MORGAN:
> Plenty. You look pretty good yourself. Seen Eddy around?

MARIE (shaking head):
Wasn't he down at the ship?

MORGAN:
No. Buy him something to eat if he comes in. I'll be
back in a little while.

MARIE:
Give her my love.

Morgan looks at her over shoulder as he exits behind
her.][109]

54.   INT. CELLAR ROOM
Paul is sitting up in bed. Helene is feeding him from tray
as Gerard looks on. They hear SOUND in other room and
Morgan enters.

MORGAN:
Hello, folks. (To Paul.) How you feeling?

PAUL:
Much better. [We are very grateful to you, Captain.

HELENE:
More than grateful.

MORGAN:
Forget it.

Morgan feels Paul's cheek and takes hold of his wrist.

MORGAN:
You're doing fine. You ought to be able to get out of
here tomorrow.

PAUL:
We were just discussing that. I hear you're going to
leave us.

MORGAN:
I haven't gone yet.

PAUL:
You look for trouble?

MORGAN:
I don't know what to look for. This guy Renard has got me guessing.

GERARD:
I think you're wrong, Harry. Believe me.

MORGAN:
I hope so. (Turning to go.) Well, folks, if I don't see you again—

GERARD (stopping him):
Harry, before you go—please give us some advice.

PAUL:
No—no. We have bothered Captain Morgan enough.

GERARD:
But he knows about these things—much more than we. I think he has even fished in those waters.

MORGAN:
Where's that?

GERARD:
Off Venezuela. Around Devil's Island. Didn't you tell me?

MORGAN:
I been around there. What about it?][110]

[PAUL:
It is a long story. We have no right to trouble you with it.

HELENE:
It is not a long story. We came here to free a man from Devil's Island—a man who can do more than any other to free this island. It is quite simple.

MORGAN:

Yeah. Sounds very simple.

GERARD:

We are going to steal the patrol ship.

MORGAN:

Is that a fact?

GERARD:

Everything else has been arranged. We are not planning a jail break at Devil's Island. Nothing so foolish.
There is a high Vichy official there who has agreed to
simplify the whole matter of the escape.

MORGAN:

For France?

GERARD:

No. For five thousand dollars. Our ship merely needs
to enter the mouth of the river. There a boat containing the prisoner and the high official will come out to
meet us. Then we will exchange the money for the—

MORGAN:

Wait a minute. Where is this money? Or are you
going to steal that, too?

PAUL (smiling):

No. That is one thing that we have. We brought that
with us.

GERARD:

What d'you think, Harry?

MORGAN:

Listen, Frenchy, let's don't get in an argument.

HELENE:

You don't think we have a chance?

MORGAN (frankly):
> I don't know what to think. I never heard anything so crazy in my life. In the first place, how are you going to steal the patrol ship?

GERARD:
> We thought you might suggest something.

MORGAN:
> I can't. I never stole a patrol ship.

HELENE:
> We'll manage it somehow.

PAUL (smiling):
> Helene is like you, captain. She is not afraid. I sometimes wonder why they chose me for this mission. As you know, I am not a brave man. The contrary, rather. I am always frightened.

MORGAN:
> Who isn't?

PAUL:
> Yet when you meet danger you never think of anything except how you will circumvent it. Obviously, the gestures of failure do not exist for you. While I— I think always—"Suppose I fail?"][111]

[MORGAN:
> Are you thinking that now?

PAUL:
> Yes.

MORGAN:
> I don't blame you. (Holding out hand.) So long—and lots of luck. You're sure going to need it.

PAUL:
> Same to you, Captain. And thanks.

MORGAN (turning to Helene):
> Good-by. (As they shake hands.) I wish there was something I could do for you people.

HELENE (smiling):
> There's one thing.

MORGAN:
> What's that?

HELENE:
> Send us back some cooler weather. (Opening dress at throat.) Is it always so warm here?

She picks up fan and starts to use it.

MORGAN (examining texture of her frock):
> You'll die in this kind of stuff.

HELENE:
> It's all I have with me.

MORGAN:
> I'll have Slim get you something lighter.

He walks out. There is a moment of silence, which is broken by Gerard.

GERARD (glumly):
> Well, here we are.

HELENE:
> Are all Americans like this? Have they no feeling, no pity?

PAUL:
> They are hard to arouse, but once it is done, their anger is terrible.

GERARD:
> Harry has no feeling for anyone—except Eddy.][112]
>
> > CUT TO:

55.   INT. CAFE
[Marie sitting at table near piano and doing card tricks for
Cricket and orchestra. Morgan, entering from behind bar,
comes over to table, looking around room for Eddy.

MARIE:
> He hasn't come in yet.

MORGAN (worried):
> I'll break his neck.

MARIE:
> Maybe he went up to your room.

MORGAN:
> Yeah. I'll go up and see.

Marie raises deck and riffles it in front of him.

MARIE:
> Decide on some card.

MORGAN:
> Okay. (Leaning over her and lowering voice as she
> shuffles cards.) Go out and buy Helene a couple of
> light dresses and things.

MARIE (taking card out of his pocket):
> Is this the card?

MORGAN (grinning):
> Huh! You're pretty good.

MARIE:
> Going to take her along with us?

MORGAN (startled):
> Say, that's not a bad idea.

He starts out toward rear, presumably to see if Eddy is up
in his quarters. Marie, picking up handbag, rises and
starts toward street entrance.

CRICKET:
Where you going?

MARIE (as she goes):
Down the street a ways.][113]

56.   INT. MORGAN'S SITTING ROOM
Door opens and Morgan enters. As he turns on light he
hears SOUND in bedroom. His face lights up.

[MORGAN:
That you, Eddy?

HELENE'S VOICE (in bedroom):
No. It's me.

Amazed, Morgan walks over to half-open door.

MORGAN:
What are you doing up here?

HELENE'S VOICE:
Frenchy brought me up the back way.

MORGAN:
What for?

HELENE'S VOICE:
I'd like to take a bath—if you don't mind?

MORGAN:
Why pick on me? Why didn't he put you in Slim's
place?

HELENE'S VOICE:
May I use your bathrobe?

MORGAN:
Help yourself.

He walks over to table, lights a cigarette. Helene enters
from bedroom, wearing his bathrobe.

HELENE:

I wanted to talk to you.

MORGAN:

It's no use. I wouldn't take that job if you offered me the whole five thousand.

HELENE:

We'll give you more than that when this island is free.

MORGAN:

I'm through working on the cuff. Once was enough. (Grins.) Now I'll make you a proposition.

HELENE:

I'd listen to anything.

MORGAN:

Slim and I are pulling out of here tonight. Why don't you come along with us?

HELENE (blankly):

What?

MORGAN:

You heard me.

HELENE:

You believe I would leave my husband?

MORGAN:

Nobody would blame you.

HELENE:

It's nice of you to feel sorry for me. I feel sorry for you, too.

MORGAN:

Why?

HELENE:

You look down so much upon Paul. You think you are so brave and that he is so weak. Well, I wouldn't have him any other way. I wouldn't have him like you if I could. I love him just the way he is, and I shall never leave him, no matter what happens.

MORGAN (grinning at her):
Never?

HELENE:
Never.

MORGAN (kissing her):
Never be too sure.][114]

As she draws back and stares at him there is a SOUND of running feet in hall. Then door is burst open and Marie breathlessly rushes in. [She carries paper-wrapped parcel in her hands.

MARIE (taking in tableau):
I hate to interrupt you two so much, but—

MORGAN:
But what?

MARIE:
Renard is on his way up here—

MORGAN (closing door):
Did he see you come up?

MARIE:
I don't think so.

Morgan points toward bedroom.

MORGAN:
Take her in there.

Marie grabs Helene's arm and starts toward bedroom.

MARIE (as she goes):
Better wipe off that rouge, Steve.

As they exit Morgan takes out handkerchief, wiping lips and going to hall door. He opens it and sees Renard approaching in hallway with Coyo and bodyguard.][115]

[MORGAN (affecting surprise):
    Hello, there.

RENARD:
    Hello, Captain.

MORGAN:
    You want to see me?

RENARD:
    Yes.

MORGAN:
    Let's go below. It's much cooler.

RENARD:
    Yes, but it is much more private here.

He walks in, his two henchmen bringing up the rear. Coyo closes door.

MORGAN:
    Well, what's on your mind?

Renard looks around, sniffs the air.

RENARD:
    Very nice perfume. Sorry if we interrupted you.

Morgan grins and turns toward bedroom.

MORGAN:
    Come on out, Slim.

In reply bedroom door opens and Marie enters.][116]

RENARD (seeing her):
    Well, now we are all here— [except Mr. Eddy.

MORGAN (after a moment):
    Humph! So that's where he is.

RENARD (seating himself):
> Yes. We picked him up shortly after he left here this morning.

MORGAN:
> What did he do?

RENARD:
> Nothing. But knowing your affection for him, we decided to make use of it.

MORGAN:
> Is that a fact?

He slowly starts toward Renard, but bodyguard blocks his path, putting hand under coat with a menacing gesture. Morgan pauses, and bodyguard, using free hand, motions Morgan to return to other side of table.

MORGAN:
> Don't you ever talk?

BODYGUARD:
> Not unless it is necessary.

RENARD:
> Please sit down over there, Captain.

He indicates chair on other side of table. Morgan, looking at bodyguard and measuring distance between them, thinks better of it and obeys Renard's injunction.

MORGAN (sitting down in chair):
> What are you going to do to Eddy?

RENARD:
> Well, your friend seems to be in a delicate condition, so instead of plying him with liquor and getting stories about a larger fish I have decided to withhold it for a while and see what happens.

MORGAN:
> You can't do that. You'll kill him.

RENARD:

> You should know.

MORGAN:

> He can't stand it. He'll go crackers.

RENARD:

> You can easily prevent it.

MORGAN:

> Yeah.

COYO (suddenly):

> Please put your hands on the table, Captain.][117]

Morgan looks at him, but makes no move to lift his hands, which are out of sight below level of table. Bodyguard starts forward, pulling revolver out from under coat. Morgan sees this, and as bodyguard aims weapon at him Morgan fires at him through compartment in table. Bodyguard, dropping gun and clutching stomach, falls face down on table. Marie screams at the shot, while Morgan, rising to his feet, gun in hand, throws it down on Renard and Coyo, both of whom sit as if paralyzed by the murderous suddenness of it all—until they both realize that Morgan is going to give them the same. For as the latter slowly rises to his feet, the hammer of the weapon also rises.

[RENARD:

> It won't do you any good to kill us. That won't save Mr. Eddy.

MARIE (getting up):

> That's right, Steve—

Morgan, trembling with ungovernable rage, shakes his head.

MORGAN:

> I don't care. They've pushed me around all I'm going to be pushed.

175

MARIE:
> Wait, Steve—

MORGAN:
> Don't get in front of them.

MARIE:
> Steve! Listen to me!

MORGAN (shoving her toward door):
> Go downstairs and tell Cricket to play real loud for a
> few minutes.

MARIE (in desperation):
> Steve! Why don't you try to make a deal with them?

MORGAN:
> Hurry up. Do what I tell you.

MARIE (turning to Renard):
> Look—there's a phone out in the hall—

RENARD (coolly):
> I know that, mademoiselle. But we have Mr. Eddy. If
> any deal is made, it will be made on our terms, not
> yours.

Morgan turns and looks at him.

MORGAN:
> Is that a fact?

He starts toward Renard, gun in hand. Renard slowly
rises to his feet. So does Coyo.

MORGAN:
> You're going to tell me what to do, huh?

RENARD:
> Yes.

MORGAN:
> I guess you fellows have whipped a lot of people
> with rubber hose, haven't you?

RENARD:
> Yes, Captain.

MORGAN:
> Did you ever whip anybody with a pistol?

RENARD:
> No, Captain.

MORGAN:
> You must try it sometime—

And using trigger guard like a brass knuckle, he hits Renard in the stomach. As the latter doubles up and reels against the wall, Coyo makes a leap at Morgan, who hits him in the jaw. As he goes down, Renard pulls himself erect.

MORGAN (socking him again):
> All right—let's see which one of you boys is the toughest.][118]

> DISSOLVE TO:

57. INT. UPPER HALLWAY A LITTLE LATER
[Coyo talking into wall telephone near doorway of Morgan's room. Morgan and Gerard watching him. Maybe Gerard is holding him up.

COYO:
> That's right. Let him go.

MORGAN (prompting him):
> We will explain later.

COYO (into phone):
> We will explain later.

As he hangs up, Marie sticks her head out of door.

MARIE:
> Renard's coming to.

Morgan, supporting Coyo, speaks to Gerard.

MORGAN:

Make him fill out those passes we found in his pocket.][119]

58.   INT. MORGAN'S SITTING ROOM

[Renard, dazedly lifting head from table, looks at Helene who has been pouring water from pitcher over his head. Morgan enters with Coyo, Gerard, and Marie, who closes door. Gerard puts passes in front of Renard and gives him fountain pen.

GERARD:

Fill in the names of Harry Morgan, Marie Browning, and— (turning to Morgan, who is tying Coyo to chair) what's Eddy's first name?

MORGAN:

Eddy. Eddy James.

GERARD (to Renard):

Eddy James.

MORGAN:

Make out one for Paul and Helene while you're at it.

GERARD:

That's a good idea. (To Renard.) Paul de Bursac and Helene de Bursac.

RENARD:

Who are these people?

MORGAN (coming over):

The two passengers I brought over from Anguilla. (As Renard stares at him, Morgan turns to Helene.) Go down and get your husband ready to travel.

HELENE:

Where are we going?

MORGAN:

Down to my ship for a starter.

HELENE (staring at him):
> You're going to do it?

MORGAN (tying Renard to chair):
> Not if you stand there gabbing all night.

HELENE (her eyes filling with tears):
> You'll never be sorry.

MORGAN (grinning):
> Never?

HELENE:
> Never.

She turns and goes out into hall, making exit to left to get over back way.

MARIE:
> Say, what is this? Where are you going?

MORGAN (gagging Renard):
> Get your bag out of your room. (To Gerard as Marie exits.) Give her a hand with it. And take along one of mine.

He points to two suitcases by door.

GERARD (indicating Renard and Coyo):
> What about them?

MORGAN:
> I'll talk to you about that downstairs.

GERARD:
> Okay, Harry. (Pausing by door.) Are you really going to take them to—?

He makes gesture toward south with head indicating Devil's Island.

MORGAN:
> Not if you can think of some better way.

Gerard smiles, tries to say something but chokes up, then goes and picks up both of Morgan's suitcases, looking at Morgan in dumb happiness as he starts out into hall.

MORGAN:
Don't strain yourself.

Gerard exits and Morgan carefully examines bonds and gags of his two captives.

MORGAN:
Well, boys, I guess that'll hold you for a while. (As Renard tries to say something through gag.) Be careful—you'll swallow it.

He turns and sees Marie standing in doorway, holding cigarette in her hand.

MORGAN:
All set?

MARIE:
Where are we going?

MORGAN (looking at Renard):
We're going to Devil's Island and get a man that'll set this place on fire. (To Marie.) Any objections?

MARIE:
What are you taking her for? What can she do?

MORGAN:
What can you do?

MARIE (after a moment):
Got a match?

Morgan, taking box out of table drawer, starts to toss it to her, pauses, opens box, and walks over to her, striking match and lighting her cigarette. As they stand there Eddy lurches up.][120]

EDDY (beaming):
Hello, Harry. How's everything?

[MORGAN:
    Fine. How are you?

EDDY:
    Fine. How are you?

MARIE:
    Fine. How are you?

Eddy looks at her and chuckles.

EDDY:
    Say, haven't I met this young lady before?][121]

MARIE:
    Was you ever bit by a dead bee?

EDDY (his face lighting up):
    Was you?

MARIE (nodding soberly):
    You've got to be careful of dead bees. If you step on
    them they can sting you just as bad as live ones.
    Expecially if they were kind of mad when they got
    killed. [I bet I've been bit a hundred times that way—

EDDY (delightedly):
    You have? (To Morgan.) You hear that, Harry? (To
    Marie.) Why don't you bite them back?][122]

MARIE:
    I would—only I haven't got a stinger—

Eddy looks at her a moment, rather puzzled.

[EDDY (feeling his forehead):
    I guess I better lay off for a while. I got a feeling I'm
    talking to myself. I never do that unless I'm pretty
    bad, do I, Harry?

MORGAN:
    That's right.

EDDY (feeling forehead and starting down hall):
    See you down at the ship.

MORGAN:

> Okay. (As Eddy exits, Morgan looks after him and says to Marie.) You keep that up and we'll have that guy on the wagon in no time.

MARIE:

> I'll do my best.

Morgan, taking key out of lock, prepares to go and waves to Renard and Coyo.

MORGAN:

> Good-by, gentlemen. (As they try to say something through gags.) Same to you—and many of them.

As he closes the door and locks it from outside, we][123]

CUT TO:

59.   INT. CAFE

[Gerard waiting by bar. He sees Morgan entering with Marie in rear and goes to meet them as they come down stairway.

GERARD:

> I sent your bags down to the ship.

MORGAN:

> What about Paul and Helene?

GERARD:

> I took them down there myself.

MORGAN (preparing to go):
> Well, Frenchy, I'll be seeing you—

GERARD:
> But, Harry—

MORGAN (to Marie):
> Wait for me on the sidewalk, Slim.

MARIE:
> So long, Frenchy.

Gerard nods at her mutely as she walks out.

MORGAN:
What is it, Frenchy?

GERARD:
Those fellows up there—what shall I do with them?

MORGAN:
That's up to you, old boy.

GERARD:
Me?

MORGAN:
You've got to do something. They know where we're going.

GERARD:
Who told them?

MORGAN:
I told Slim in front of them. Accidentally on purpose.

GERARD (after a moment):
You don't leave me much choice.

MORGAN:
It's time you fellows started on the offensive, Frenchy. No fooling. (As Gerard stares at him, Morgan indicates orchestra.) All you got to do is to tell Cricket and the boys to play real loud for a few minutes.

Gerard nods dumbly and Morgan walks out front door and joins Marie. Gerard looks after them for a moment, and as they exit he pulls self together, walks across to Cricket, and speaks to him. Cricket nods, understanding, turns to orchestra, tells them what to play, then, setting crescendo tempo, we hear the music roar out full blast and see Gerard returning across room to go and do what he has to do.

FADE OUT][124]

THE END

Notes to the Screenplay

1 In the film, the Foreword reads, "Martinique, in the summer of 1940, shortly after the fall of France." The title that follows is "Fort de France."

2 None of this action is in the film. Throughout the screenplay I have used brackets to indicate changes in the film; the corresponding material is supplied in the Notes.

3 To indicate that Morgan and the quartermaster have been through this exchange several times before, Hawks rewrote this scene so that Morgan answers each question before it is asked.

MORGAN: Good morning.

QUARTERMASTER: Good morning, Capitaine Morgan. What can I do for you today?

MORGAN: Same thing as yesterday.

QUARTERMASTER: You and your client wish to make a temporary exit from the port?

MORGAN: That is right.

QUARTERMASTER: Name?

MORGAN (laughing): Harry Morgan.

QUARTERMASTER: Nationality?

MORGAN: Eskimo.

QUARTERMASTER: What?

MORGAN: American.

QUARTERMASTER: Name of ship?

MORGAN: *Queen Conch*, Key West, Florida. We're going fishing the same as we've been doing every day for over two weeks. We'll be back tonight and I don't think we'll go more than thirty miles off shore.

QUARTERMASTER: Five francs, please. One more thing. You will go nowhere near the vicinity of territorial waters, St. Lucy, or La Dominique.

MORGAN: Is that a new order?

QUARTERMASTER: Yes. The decree was issued last night by His Excel-

lency, Admiral Robert, governor general of the French West Indies.

MORGAN: Oh! Good for him!

QUARTERMASTER: Why, any complaints?

MORGAN: No!

4   Eddy is asleep on the dock; Morgan douses him with a bucket of
seawater.

EDDY: Oh, hello, Harry. How's everything? That feels good. Did you
bring me a drink?

MORGAN: Horatio's bringin' it.

EDDY: You're my pal, Harry. I sure got 'em this mornin'.

MORGAN (laughing): You've got 'em every morning.

EDDY: Not last Thursday.

MORGAN: Oh, yeah. That's right, I forgot. You're right, Eddy. Oh,
here's Horatio. Give 'im a hand, will yuh?

5   HORATIO: Good morning, mon capitaine.

MORGAN: Good morning. Did you get the bait?

HORATIO: Yes, sir. Plenty of it. That guard took a bottle of our
beer.

6   EDDY: Harry, can I have—

MORGAN: Just one. [Enter Johnson, as described in script.]

JOHNSON: Good morning.

MORGAN: Good morning.

EDDY: Good morning, Mr. Johnson.

JOHNSON: Well, are we goin' out?

MORGAN: Well, that's up to you.

JOHNSON: What sort of a day'll it be?

MORGAN: Oh, I don't know. Just about like yesterday. Only better.

7   MORGAN: Yeah. Well, I'll need money for that.

This is a typical on-the-set line change. Hereafter, only the most
significant changes will be annotated.

8   MORGAN: Let 'er go! Watch it, Johnson! There's your strike! Put on
a little more drag. Not too much! You're gonna have to sock
him. He's gonna jump, anyway! All right, hit 'im again now!
Hit him three or four times! Stick it into him! Better get the
other teaser in.

9   MORGAN: No, he's not! Ease up on that drag! Quick! If he wants to
go, let 'im go!

JOHNSON: He's gone!

MORGAN: No, he's hooked good.

10 MORGAN: Reel 'im in!

JOHNSON: No. I'm sure he's gone.

MORGAN: I'll tell you when he's gone. Reel in fa—

11 Deleted.

12 JOHNSON: A dollar a day seems like an unnecessary expense to me.

MORGAN: He's necessary. Aren't you, Horatio?

HORATIO: I hope so!

EDDY: (Coughing.)

JOHNSON: Can't Eddy do it?

MORGAN: No, he can't.

EDDY: What's the matter?

MORGAN: He just lost a fish.

EDDY: Mr. Johnson, you're unlucky. Say, Harry, would it be all right if I, er—

MORGAN: In the icebox. Just take one.

EDDY: Thanks. Er—

13 JOHNSON: I was never bit by any kind of a bee.

EDDY: You sure?

JOHNSON: Yes, of course I'm sure.

14 Deleted.

15 MORGAN: Nothing. You just lost a rod and reel, that's all. You had the drag screwed down tight again and when the fish struck you couldn't hold it.

HORATIO: If you had the harness buckled down to the reel, that fish would have taken you along with him.

EDDY: You're just unlucky, Mr. Johnson. Now, maybe you're lucky with women. What do you say if we go out tonight?

16 JOHNSON: Fifteen!

MORGAN: You talk too much, Eddy.

EDDY: I know it, Harry.

MORGAN: Okay, forget it.

17 Again, the Pétain reference is deleted. As they leave the boat:

MORGAN: What about tomorrow?

JOHNSON: I don't think so. I, I'm fed up with this kind of fishing.

MORGAN: Well, I can see how you would be. Slack that off a little. You fish for sixteen days, hook into a couple o' fish that any good fisherman would give his life to tie into and lose 'em both.

EDDY: Er, Mr. Johnson, you're just unlucky. I never seen no one—

MORGAN: Shut up, Eddy!

JOHNSON: You said sixteen days. I only owe you for fifteen.

MORGAN: No. With today it's sixteen. And then there's the rod and reel.

JOHNSON: The tackle's your risk.

MORGAN: Not when you lose it the way you did.

JOHNSON: I've paid for the rent of it every day. The tackle's your risk, I tell yuh!

MORGAN: Look, if yuh hired a car and ran it over a cliff, you'd have to pay for it.

JOHNSON: Ah, that's different.

EDDY: Not if he was in it, Harry. That's a good one!

MORGAN: Yeah, that's good, Eddy. Now you lost the outfit through carelessness. It cost me two hundred and seventy-five. I won't charge you for the line because a fish that big could'a taken it all, anyway. And there's sixteen days at thirty-five a day, that's, er, five hundred and sixty. No, it's five hundred and sixty, Eddy. Now yuh got a little credit, so that'll be eight hundred and twenty-five altogether.

JOHNSON: Well—

MORGAN: That's what you owe me, and that's what I want.

JOHNSON: Well, I haven't got that much with me. I'll go to the bank in the morning. That be all right?

MORGAN: I guess it'll have to be.

JOHNSON: Well, let's go up and have a drink.

EDDY (laughing): That's a good idea.

MORGAN: You'd better stay here and lock up.

EDDY: Are you sure you don't—

MORGAN: No, Eddy.

JOHNSON: Look there! I thought everybody took their flag in after six o'clock.

MORGAN: Well, most of 'em do.

18　There are two civilians.

FIRST CIVILIAN: Suivez-le. ["Follow him."]

SECOND CIVILIAN: Entendu. ["Okay."]

19　FIRST CIVILIAN: Your names, please.

JOHNSON: Now look, we're Americans!

MORGAN: His name's Johnson. My name's Morgan. We're livin' over at the Marquis Hotel. That do yuh?

FIRST CIVILIAN: Merci beaucoup.

20　BARTENDER: Yes, sir?

MORGAN: What's yours?

JOHNSON: Bourbon.

MORGAN: Bourbon. And rum for me.

GERARD: Well, gentlemen, what luck today?

21 JOHNSON: Not me. I'm through. This is my last day.
GERARD: That's too bad.
MORGAN: Yeah.
JOHNSON: Here's to yuh! Well, I'm gonna clean up. Oh, that was eight hundred and, er—
MORGAN: —twenty-five.
JOHNSON: Eight twenty-five.
MORGAN: Uh-huh. Oh, Johnson!
JOHNSON: Yeah?
MORGAN: What time tomorrow morning?
JOHNSON: Oh, after I get to the bank. Say around ten-thirty, eleven o'clock.
MORGAN: I'll be waitin' for yuh.
GERARD: Any trouble, Harry?
MORGAN: No (laughing), no, Frenchy.
GERARD: Then you are free after today?
MORGAN: Yeah. Why?
GERARD: Er, there were some people in here today. They wanted to hire your boat.
22 MORGAN: Not a chance. Papa!
OLD MAN: Bon jour, monsieur.
CLERK: The key, monsieur.
MORGAN: Thank you.
GERARD: Please listen to me, Harry. They only want to use your boat for one night. They pay you well.
MORGAN: For what?
GERARD: Well—
MORGAN: I'd like to oblige you, Frenchy, but I can't afford to get mixed up in your local politics.
GERARD: I would not speak if it weren't important. I— Please, can I go with you to your room?
MORGAN: Sure. Come ahead.
23 MARIE: Anybody got a match?
24 MORGAN: Who's that?
GERARD: Oh, she came in this afternoon. The plane from the south.
MORGAN: Er, now look, Frenchy. Er, about that other thing. I know where you stand and what your sympathies are, and it's all right for you, but I don't want any part of it. They catch me foolin' around with you fellas and my goose'll be cooked.
GERARD: But—
MORGAN: Probably lose my boat, too. I ain't that interested.

GERARD: But they are coming to see you tonight.

MORGAN: Well, you better get word to them.

GERARD: Please—

MORGAN: Aw, they'd just be wastin' their time.

GERARD: Oh.

MORGAN: Sorry. I'll see yuh later.

25 Morgan lights a cigarette; he is sitting alone at a table. Marie leaves Johnson to stand by Cricket's piano and join him in "Am I Blue."

CRICKET: "Am I blue?
    Am I blue?
    Ain't these tears in my eyes tellin' you?
    Am I blue?
    You'd be, too,
    If each plan with your man done fell through.
    Was a time
    I was his only one,
    But now I'm the sad and lonely one,
    So lonely.
    Was I gay? 'til today—"

MARIE: (Humming.)

CRICKET: "Now he's gone and we're through,
    Am I blue?"
    Take over.
    "Was a time—"

MARIE: "I was his only one—"

CRICKET: "But now I'm—"

MARIE: "The sad and lonely one—"

CRICKET: "So lonely.
    Was I gay?"

MARIE: "Was I gay?"

CRICKET: "'til today—"

MARIE: "'til today—"

CRICKET: "Now she's gone and we're through, baby oh—"

MARIE AND CRICKET: "Am I blue?
    Am I blue?"

"AM I BLUE" © 1929 WARNER BROS. INC. Copyright Renewed. All Rights Reserved. Used by Permission.

GROUP (applauding, laughing): Bravo!

26 MORGAN: I didn't ask to see 'em. You better head 'em off.

27 MARIE: Hello.

MORGAN: Let's have it.

MARIE: What do you want?

MORGAN: Johnson's wallet.

MARIE: What?

MORGAN: Come on!

MARIE: What're you talking about? Say, mister, what's got into you? What do you think you're gonna do?

MORGAN: I'm gonna get that wallet, Slim.

MARIE: I'd rather you wouldn't call me Slim. I'm a little too skinny to take it kindly.

MORGAN: Quit the baby talk. Which is it?

MARIE: You know, Steve, I wouldn't put it past you. I didn't know you were a hotel detective.

28 MORGAN: Well, he's still my client. You ought to pick on somebody to steal from that doesn't owe me money.

MARIE: He dropped it and I picked it up.

29 MARIE: Besides, I need boat fare to get out of Martinique.

MORGAN: That's another good reason, but you'll have to get it from somebody else.

30 MARIE: Find anything?

MORGAN: Oh, about sixty odd dollars in cash and about fourteen hundred dollars in traveler's checks.

MARIE: Do you expect more?

MORGAN: That bird owed me eight hundred and twenty-five dollars. "I haven't got that much on me," he says. "I'll have to go to the bank and pay you off tomorrow," he says. And all the time he's got a reservation on a plane leaving tomorrow morning at daylight.

MARIE: So he was gonna skip out on you! Your client!

31 MORGAN: That's right. But if I hadn't stopped you, you'd'a gotten away with the whole works. After all, I am entitled to something. Don't you think so, Slim? What do you think's fair?

MARIE: I'll leave that to you.

MORGAN: Well, what would you say to—

32 MORGAN: Well!

GERARD: Please, Harry. I told them but they insisted on—

BEAUCLERC: It is not Gerard's fault, Mr. Morgan. Come in and close the door.

MORGAN: Well, you know, I told Frenchy I wasn't interested.

BEAUCLERC: I know. But close the door, please. I'm very sorry to intrude this way, Mr. Morgan, but this is a matter of great importance to us and we—

DE GAULLIST NO. 2: One moment.

MARIE: I'd better go. See yuh later.

MORGAN: Stick around. We're not through yet. It's all right to talk in front o' her, isn't it, Slim?

MARIE: Go ahead.

MORGAN: But it won't do you any good.

DE GAULLISTS: If you'd only listen—

MORGAN: It's no use. You boys are even takin' a chance coming here.

BEAUCLERC: We're not afraid.

MORGAN: Well, I am! I'm sorry, I can't do it and I won't do it.

33 DE GAULLIST NO. 2: It is more to us.

DE GAULLIST NO. 1: It is only a little voyage to a place about, er, forty kilometers from here.

34 DE GAULLIST NO. 2: That's all we have.

MORGAN: Well, boys, don't make me feel bad. I tell yuh true, I can't do it.

35 MORGAN: Yes, I know.

BEAUCLERC: Mr. Morgan, I thought all Americans were friendly to our side.

MORGAN: Well, that's right, they are. But you see there's a rumor going around that they put fellas on Devil's Island for doing what you're doing. I'm not that friendly to anybody.

BEAUCLERC: But they wouldn't do that to an American.

EDDY: Harry!

MORGAN: Do you really think that? Who's that?

EDDY: It's me, Harry.

MORGAN: It's all right.

36 MORGAN: Oh, hello, Eddy.

EDDY: Say, Harry, I wanted to talk to you about—

DE GAULLIST NO. 1: Mr. Morgan, could we continue—

EDDY: Who are these guys, Harry?

MORGAN: Eddy's a friend of mine.

EDDY: He was hangin' around the dock after yuh left.

BEAUCLERC: You've got a good memory for one who drinks.

37 EDDY: That's what Harry always says. But I ain't got no stinger!

DE GAULLIST NO. 1: Does he always talk so much?

MORGAN: Always. What do you want to see me about, Eddy?

EDDY: Er, oh, Harry, er—I guess I forgot.

MORGAN: That's all right. I'll, I'll see yuh down at the dock later on tonight.

EDDY: Say, Harry, could you— Thanks. You're all right. So long.

38 MORGAN: Sorry. Now look, boys, we could stay at this all night and the answer'd still be the same.

BEAUCLERC: Mr. Morgan—

MORGAN: I don't care who runs France or Martinique, or who wants to run it. You'll have to get somebody else. Come on, Slim. We still got some unfinished business.

MARIE: Good night.

MORGAN: Make yourselves at home, boys. Cigarettes on the table over there.

39 MORGAN: I want to see Johnson's face when you give it back to him.

MARIE: All right.

40 JOHNSON: I know. There's fourteen hundred dollars.

41 JOHNSON: Yeah. Sure.

MORGAN: Emil, yuh got a pen handy?

EMIL: Certainement, monsieur.

MORGAN: Eight hundred and twenty-five.

JOHNSON: Yeah.

42 MARIE: Say—

MORGAN: Stay where you are.

MARIE: I think I'm sitting on somebody's cigarette.

43 GERARD: Harry, this is awful.

MORGAN: Did they get 'em all?

GERARD: One got away at least. I think it was Beauclerc. Look, Harry, this is bad. But no one but me knows that you two saw them.

MORGAN: And Eddy, but he probably won't remember.

44 MORGAN: Frenchy, don't be a fool! Stay inside.

45 MORGAN: Cut it out, Cricket. He couldn't write any faster than he could duck. Another minute and these checks would have been good.

46 MORGAN: Who's that?

GERARD: Sûreté Nationale. ["National Police."]

MORGAN: Gestapo, huh?

GERARD: Uh-huh.

MORGAN: Lot of 'em, isn't there?

47 OFFICER: Yes, sir.

RENARD: Call attention.

MAN: Your attention, everyone!

RENARD: All this is regrettable, but there is no cause for alarm. We are only interested in those persons who have broken the rules

193

laid down for their behavior. We shall pick out certain individuals. Those we do not designate will leave immediately. This place will then remain closed for tonight. This man. You. You. And mademoiselle.

48 Deleted.

49 COYO: That is all. You may go.

RENARD: Have you got all of them?

DETECTIVE: No, sir. Beauclerc and Emil got away.

RENARD: How?

DETECTIVE: They jumped off the wagon and went up an alley.

RENARD: Search all the places you have on your list.

DETECTIVE: Yes, sir.

RENARD: Continue.

COYO: And you, Capitaine Morgan, did you know these men?

MORGAN: No, I didn't.

50 MORGAN: Because he owed me eight hundred and twenty-five dollars.

RENARD: So at least you had no reason to kill him, did you?

51 RENARD: Mademoiselle. That is all for you.

52 MARIE: I arrived by plane this afternoon.

53 COYO: Why?

MARIE: To buy a new—hat. Read the label. Maybe you'll believe me then.

54 MARIE: I was—

MORGAN: You don't have to answer that stuff.

COYO: Shut up, you!

MORGAN: Don't answer it.

COYO: I told you to shut up!

MORGAN: Go ahead. slap me.

55 MORGAN: Well, you'll never do it by slapping people around. That's bad luck.

RENARD: Well, we shall see.

56 MORGAN: I don't need any advice about continuing to do it, either!

RENARD: Good night, capitaine.

MORGAN: Let's get out o' this.

57 Morgan and Marie are walking down the street; by the end of the scene, they are outside the Zombie cafe.

MARIE: Say, I don't understand all this. After all, I just got here.

MORGAN: Well, you landed right in the middle of a small war.

MARIE: What's it all about?

MORGAN: The boys we just left joined with Vichy. You know what that is?

MARIE: Vaguely.

MORGAN (laughing): Well, they got the Navy behind 'em. I think you saw that carrier in the harbor.

MARIE: Yeah.

MORGAN: Well, the other fellas, the ones they were shootin' at, they're the Free French. You know what they are?

MARIE: It's not getting any clearer.

MORGAN (laughing): Well, anyway, most of the people on the island, the natives, are patriots. They're for De Gaulle, but so far they haven't been able to do much about it.

MARIE: Oh.

EDDY: Harry! (Enters.) Are we in trouble?

MORGAN: No, Eddy.

EDDY: Well, I seen them guys pick yuh up and I was a-scared—

MORGAN: Well, everything's all right. You go on back and get some sleep.

EDDY: I'd'a got yuh out, Harry. (Hiccoughing.) You know me.

MORGAN: Yeah, I know you, Eddy. You go on back to the boat.

EDDY: Say, Harry, could yuh—

MORGAN: No.

EDDY: But—

MORGAN: No more tonight, Eddy. Beat it.

MARIE: I could use a drink myself.

MORGAN: Well, we can get one in here.

58 BARTENDER: What do you wish to drink, sir?

MORGAN: What'll it— (Laughing.) Er, we're, er, we're just lookin' around.

MARIE: Change your mind?

MORGAN: No money. Those guys cleaned me out.

MARIE: I forgot, too. Maybe I can do something. This has been a long day, and I'm thirsty.

MORGAN: Picked him out yet?

MARIE: You don't mind, do you?

MORGAN: If you're thirsty, go ahead. If I get tired o' waiting, I'll be back at that hotel.

MARIE: All right.

59 MORGAN: Come on in.

60 MORGAN: Yeah, that's right. I, I guess I did. You were pretty good at it, too.

61 MORGAN: Well, of all the screwy—

MARIE: All right. All right. I won't do it any more.

62 MARIE: I know you didn't. Don't worry. I'm not giving up anything

195

I care about. It's like shooting fish in a barrel, anyway. Men like that. They're all a bunch of— I'm a fine one to talk. The pot calling a kettle.

MORGAN: How long have you been away from home?

MARIE: This is about the time for it, isn't it?

MORGAN: Time for what?

MARIE: The story of my life. Where do you want me to begin?

MORGAN: I got a pretty fair idea already.

MARIE: Who told you?

MORGAN: You did. That slap in the face you took.

MARIE: Yeah? What about it?

MORGAN: Well, yuh hardly blinked an eye. It takes a lot o' practice to be able to do that. Yeah, I know a lot about you, Slim.

MARIE: The next time I get slapped I'd better do something about it.

MORGAN: Hey, you forgot your drink.

MARIE: I don't want it.

MORGAN: Who's sore now?

MARIE: I am!

63 MORGAN: It's me.

MARIE: The door's unlocked.

MORGAN: Hey, you forgot your bottle.

MARIE: I said I didn't want it.

MORGAN: Hey, you are sore, aren't you? I asked you a question and you didn't answer me. I said you're sore, aren't you?

MARIE: Look. I'm tired and I wanta get some sleep.

MORGAN: That's not a bad idea. What made you so mad?

MARIE: I've been mad ever since I met you.

MORGAN: Most people are.

MARIE: One look and you made up your mind just what you wanted to think about me. You were— Oh, what's the use?

MORGAN: Well, go ahead. Keep on going.

MARIE: You don't know me, Steve. It doesn't work. I, I brought that bottle up here to make you feel cheap. That didn't work either. Instead, I'm the one who feels cheap. I've never felt that way before. I wanted— I thought that maybe— Go on, get out of here, will you, before I make a complete fool of myself?

MORGAN: How long have you been away from home, Slim?

MARIE: It's none of— About six months.

MORGAN: Goin' back?

MARIE: How?

MORGAN: What are you gonna do here?

MARIE: I don't know. Get a job, maybe.

MORGAN: Jobs are hard to get. I don't think you'd like it here anyway.

MARIE: Remind you of somebody, Steve?

MORGAN (muttering, laughing): This is brand new to me. I like it. Would you go back if you could?

MARIE: I'd walk, if it wasn't for all that water.

MORGAN: Yeah. Quit worryin', kid. You'll get back all right.

64   MORGAN: What the—

MARIE: Here's that bottle again.

MORGAN (laughing): Yeh. Well, it's gettin' to be quite a problem, isn't it? Do you want a drink?

MARIE: Nope.

MORGAN: I thought you were tired and goin' to bed.

MARIE: Yeh, I know. I thought so, too. You gave me something to think about. You said you might be able to help me.

MORGAN: That's right.

MARIE: Well, how can you do that if— Steve, you're gonna take that job with those men that were up here with Frenchy.

MORGAN: Yeah. If I can find what's left of 'em.

MARIE: I flew over Devil's Island. It doesn't look like such a high-class resort.

MORGAN: Yeh. That's what I heard.

MARIE: Well, I don't want to be the cause of—

MORGAN: Look. Don't you get the idea I'm doin' this just to help you. I need money, too.

MARIE: Won't Frenchy help you out without you having to do that?

MORGAN: I don't want his help.

MARIE: Don't do it, will you, Steve?

MORGAN: Look. Didn't you ask me—?

MARIE: Don't do it.

MORGAN: Why don't you take this bottle and go to bed?

MARIE (taking out money): Here. Can you use this?

MORGAN: I thought you said you were broke. You're good. You're awful good. "I'd walk home if it wasn't for all that water."

MARIE: Who was the girl, Steve?

MORGAN: Who was what girl?

MARIE: The one who left you with such a high opinion of women. She must have been quite a gal. You think I lied to you about this, don't you? Well, it just happens there's thirty-odd dollars here. Not enough for boat fare or any other kind of fare. It's just enough to be able to say no if I feel like it. And you can have it if you want it.

MORGAN: I'm sorry, Slim. But I still say you're awful good and I wouldn't—

MARIE: Oh, I forgot. You wouldn't take anything from anybody, would you?

MORGAN: That's right.

MARIE: You know, Steve, you're not very hard to figure. Only at times. Sometimes I know exactly what you're going to say. Most of the time. The other times— The other times you're just a stinker. (Kisses him.)

MORGAN: What'd you do that for?

MARIE: I've been wondering whether I'd like it.

MORGAN: What's the decision?

MARIE: I don't know yet. (They kiss.) It's even better when you help. Sure you won't change your mind about this?

MORGAN: Um-huh.

MARIE: This belongs to me and so do my lips. I don't see any difference.

MORGAN: Well I do.

MARIE: *Okay.* You know you don't have to act with me, Steve. You don't have to say anything, and you don't have to do anything. Not a thing. Oh, maybe, just whistle. You know how to whistle, don't you, Steve? You just put your lips together and blow. (She exits.)

MORGAN: (Whistles.)

65 Deleted.

66 Like the preceding scenes, this one reveals not so much rewriting as rearranging, with slight shifts in tone and emphasis.

COLORED WOMAN: It's all right. They have gone.

MORGAN: Go on.

BEAUCLERC: Well, you come along the lee shore of Anguilla from the south. About three kilometers from the point.

MORGAN: There's a little cove and a jetty, isn't there?

BEAUCLERC: You know it, then.

MORGAN: Um-huh. The signals been arranged?

BEAUCLERC: Yes. Emil can show you.

MORGAN: Emil's not gonna be there.

BEAUCLERC: Please, Mr. Morgan.

GERARD: Why?

MORGAN: I'm doin' this my way.

w, Harry, er, where we goin'? What're we gonna do?
tell you when the time comes. For now, get out some
tackle.

ren't you glad you came?

ere you are, Eddy, put this on. It's gettin' cold.
ll right, Harry. Say, what's goin' on? What's the matter?
othin'.
there is, too. Well, what's all the darn guns fer?
n case we run into a shark or somethin'.
ark? At night? (Laughing.) "Or somethin'"? What do you
"or somethin'"?
Watch your course, Eddy.
at's the matter?
We're goin' on a job. I'll tell you what to do when it's time.
ob? What kind of a job? What do you expect me to do?
Do you know how to handle one of these?
course I know how to handle one! Everybody knows how
andle a gun. All you do is work the lever and pull the trig-
You know I know that. (Mutters.) Foolish questions. Do I
w how to handle a gun! (Mutters.) What I gotta work a gun

: Oh, I just wondered if you could.
ou know I can. Harry, sometimes you act stupid. Just plain
pid. Sometimes I think you don't pay no attention to nothin'
ay. Sometime— Is it gonna be that bad, Harry?
N: I don't know yet. It all depends on how lucky we are.
Oh. That's why you didn't want to carry me. I knew there
as some other reason. You wasn't mad at me at all. You was
raid I'd get hurt! You was thinkin' o' me!
AN: Watch your course, Eddy.
laughing): I feel better now, Harry. I'll be all right. You'll see.
Vhat's the matter, Harry? What're you lookin' at me like that
r?
AN: (Laughing.)
What're you laughin' at?
AN: Just a joke that neither one of us knows the answer to.
: What joke?
AN: Whether you're gonna hold together or not. (Laughing.)

GERARD: But we have—
MORGAN: I'm goin' alone. What are the signals?
BEAUCLERC: You flash a light to the shore. They will answer it with
two lights. One held above the other. There will be two people
to bring back.
MORGAN: How will I know 'em?
BEAUCLERC: We've never seen them.
GERARD: We know the name of one only. Paul de Bursac.
MORGAN: Well, that's good enough. How about landing 'em back
here?
BEAUCLERC: Do you know Cape St. Pierre?
MORGAN: Uh-huh.
BEAUCLERC: A boat can meet you offshore there.
MORGAN: You be on that boat, Frenchy. I'll get out o' here around
noon. Supposedly fishing. With a little luck and no patrol
boats, I'll be back and off St. Pierre about midnight.
GERARD: U'mm.
MORGAN: I won't be burning any lights, so keep a sharp lookout.
BEAUCLERC: One thing, Mr. Morgan. Last night you very definitely
refused to have anything to do with us. Why have you changed
your mind?
MORGAN: I need the money now. Last night I didn't.
BEAUCLERC: If you knew what this means to us—
MORGAN: I don't want to know.
BEAUCLERC: I'm glad you're on our side.
MORGAN: I'm not. I'm gettin' paid. Oh, and, er, by the way, I'd like
that money now.
MRS. BEAUCLERC: Charles, if I were you I do not think that I would
trust Mr. Morgan.
MORGAN: Did you have a doctor look at his leg?
MRS. BEAUCLERC: No. They are watching all doctors who are friendly
to us.
MORGAN: Miss the bone?
MRS. BEAUCLERC: Well, as far as I can tell.
MORGAN: He's lucky. Who told you to put a pillow under it?
MRS. BEAUCLERC: Why not?
BEAUCLERC: It doesn't hurt so much that way.
MORGAN: Well, it'll have to hurt and you'll have to take it unless you
want to take a chance of gangrene setting in. All right, I'll take
that.
MRS. BEAUCLERC: Are you a doctor?

MORGAN: No. But I've handled quite a lot of gunshot wounds. You
  can trust me now.

GERARD: Good luck, Harry.

COLORED WOMAN: It's all right.

67   The revisions in this scene make it clear that most of Hoagy Carmichael's contributions were worked out on the set rather than in
  Faulkner's draft of the script. It's also interesting to see how Marie's
  drinking (the rum swizzles that are prominent in each draft of the
  script, and her play with Eddy's "just enough to fill a hen's ear") is
  written out, along with some of her ironic tone.

WAITRESS: More coffee, mademoiselle?

MARIE: Please. What is that you're playing?

CRICKET: Did you say something?

MARIE: Yeh. What is the name of that tune?

CRICKET: It hasn't got any name yet. I've just been foolin' around
  with the lyrics. They're not so hot, either. Would you like to
  hear it?

MARIE: Sure. (Hums.)

CRICKET: "I run to the telephone whenever it rings;
  I can't be alone, it's one of those things;
  I tell a star my little woes,
  Hang around at a bar till it's ready to close."
  So it goes. And that's about as far as it goes.

MARIE: I like it.

CRICKET: Yes. If I could get the right lyrics.

MORGAN: Good morning, Cricket.

CRICKET: 'Morning, Harry.

MARIE: Hello, Steve.

MORGAN: How'd you sleep?

MARIE: The best in a long time. Have some coffee?

MORGAN: No, thinks. I've had mine.

MARIE: You were up early. What were you doing?

MORGAN: I was gettin' you a ticket on the plane this afternoon. It
  leaves at four. Can you make it?

MARIE: Sure. You took that job, didn't you?

MORGAN: Uh-huh. Yuh see, I figured this way you wouldn't get
  your feet wet.

MARIE: Yeah, that's right.

MORGAN: Well, that's what you wanted, wasn't it?

MARIE: Sure. I just— You want me to go, don't you?

MORGAN: Yes, I want

MARIE: Okay, Steve.

MORGAN: Help her get

CRICKET: I sure will, Ha

MORGAN: Well, I'm goin
  won't see yuh agaiı

MARIE: Yeah. Do that. I'l
  find me.

MORGAN (laughing): Ma)
  long, Slim.

MARIE: So long, Steve. We

CRICKET: Maybe it's better

MARIE: I don't know.

CRICKET: You haven't know

MARIE: Yeah.

68   EDDY: Oh (laughing) yuh
  plain. Say, could I have

MORGAN: You're not goin'.

69   Deleted.

70   Deleted.

71   MORGAN: Say, Eddy—

EDDY: Huh. Thanks, Harry. I I
  yuh carry me?

MORGAN: Because I don't wanı

72   EDDY: It's only me, Harry, it's

MORGAN: How'd you get back

EDDY: Oh, I, I went up the stre
  I sneaked in up fo'ward wł
  I knew you'd carry me, Haı

MORGAN: Carry yuh, nothin'. If
  dump you overboard.

EDDY: Oh (laughing) you're an o
  together when we're in troub

MORGAN: How do you know I'm iı

EDDY: Oh, you can't fool me. I alwa
  Harry?

MORGAN: Eddy, what would you do

EDDY: Shot at me? With a gun? (La
  me?

MORGAN: If you're lucky, nobody!

EDDY: Er, no

MORGAN: I'I
  fishing

EDDY: Er—

MORGAN: A

EDDY: No!

MORGAN: I

EDDY: I'm

MORGAN: I

EDDY: Yes

MORGAN:

EDDY: A sl
  mean

MORGAN:

EDDY: Wl

MORGAN:

EDDY: A

MORGAN

EDDY: O
  to h
  ger
  kno
  for

MORGAI

EDDY: Y
  stu
  I s

MORGA

EDDY:
  w
  af

MORG

EDDY

V
  f

MOR(

EDDY

MOR(

EDDY

MOR

EDDY: Don't say that, Harry. I'm a good man! You know I am.

MORGAN: Yeah, I know you are, but you're goin' all over the ocean. Stay on your course.

EDDY: Oh, why do you always— Say, Harry, could I have just one? I don't want to get the shakes.

MORGAN: Well, make it a short one. I want you rum-brave, but I don't want you useless.

EDDY: Thanks, Harry.

73 Deleted.

74 Deleted.

75 EDDY: What's the matter, Harry? Who's that? What're we goin' to do?

MORGAN: We're gonna pick up a couple o' guys. Here's what I want you to do. Take this gun and get back there in the stern. If there's any trouble, start shootin', but don't shoot me.

EDDY: Yeah, but supposin' somethin' happens to you. What do I do then?

MORGAN: How do I know? You invited yourself on this trip. Not me. All right, get back there.

76 MORGAN: My name's Harry Morgan. Beauclerc sent me. Get that light out o' my face.

GUIDE: ["They've sent an American!"]

PAUL: What happened to Beauclerc?

MORGAN: Well, he ran into a little trouble. What's your name?

PAUL: De Bursac.

MORGAN: That's the name. It's all right, Eddy. Come on aboard. Hey, wait a minute. He didn't say anything about a woman.

PAUL: Permit me, captain. This is my wife, Madame de Bursac.

HELENE AND MORGAN: How do you do.

MORGAN: What do yuh want to bring a— Well, it's your funeral. All right, let's get out o' here.

GUIDE: Vos bagages, s'il vous plaît. ["Your bags, please."]

77 MORGAN: It's all right, Eddy. You can relax now. And don't unload. We're not home yet.

PAUL: Mr. Morgan—

MORGAN: If she gets cold, you can put her down in the cabin.

PAUL: Mr. Morgan, just who are you?

MORGAN: I own this boat. Beauclerc's paying me to get you people back to Martinique.

PAUL: You're not one of us.

MORGAN: No.

PAUL: You're not on our side.

MORGAN: Nope.

PAUL: I don't understand.

MORGAN: I don't understand what kind of a war you guys are fightin', luggin' your wives around with yuh. Don't you get enough of them at home?

PAUL: But I don't—

HELENE: Mr. Morgan! You say you're being paid for this.

MORGAN: That's right.

HELENE: Then I suggest you stop talking and take us to Martinique.

MORGAN: Well, that's where we're headin' right now.

78 EDDY: What's the matter, Harry?

MORGAN: Keep quiet. I thought I saw somethin' out there. Listen.

EDDY: (Hiccoughing.)

HELENE: What is it?

PAUL: I don't know.

MORGAN: Shut up! Hey, yuh hear that?

EDDY: I—is it the patrol boat?

MORGAN: Don't you know those engines? Sounds like she's off there. All right, stand by that wheel. Wait a minute! Gimme that gun.

79 EDDY: I can do it! Er, what do yuh want me to do?

MORGAN: Well, if we're lucky, nothing. If we're not, hook her up and get away from here fast.

80 PAUL: What does this mean, Mr. Morgan?

MORGAN: Trouble if they see us.

PAUL: What can we do?

MORGAN: You can't do anything. Just get down on the deck, flat, and stay there. Although I don't know what good it's gonna do yuh.

PAUL: You will try to resist them with that?

HELENE: Please don't.

MORGAN: Shut up, both of you! Get down on that deck, flat! You save France. I'm gonna save my boat. Hook her up, Eddy, and let's go.

81 PAUL: Don't shoot!

PATROL BOAT OFFICER: ["Fire!"]

HELENE: Paul!

MORGAN: Well, we got lucky again. Now you can ease her off and

put her on a hundred and sixty and then get that first-aid kit.
Well, that's not so bad. You wouldn't have gotten that if you
hadn't been so anxious to give up.

HELENE: Please, help me get him up on the seat.

MORGAN: Leave him where he is. I don't want him bleedin' all over
my cushion.

EDDY: Here yuh are, Harry.

MORGAN: Okay, Eddy. You can have a drink now.

EDDY: Thanks, Harry.

MORGAN: Here, help me off with his coat. Easy now, boy.

82 A *painter* is a hitching rope, usually at the bow.

MORGAN: All right, get ready. The men in that boat will take yuh on
from here.

HELENE: But, I don't understand.

MORGAN: A bunch of people spent a lot o' time figurin' this thing
out. They know more about it than we do. [Pause.] This is de
Bursac. She's the other guy I was supposed to pick up. His
wife.

GERARD: My name is Gerard.

PAUL: How do you do.

MORGAN: Easy with him. He's been shot up a little.

GERARD: Well, what happened?

MORGAN: We ran into a patrol boat. He'll tell you about it. I'll cruise
around a little and give you a chance to get ashore. Good luck.

GERARD: Thanks.

83 MARIE (singing and humming): "—how true,
    With a smile—
    . . . so rare"

CASHIER: Bon soir. ["Good evening."]

MORGAN: 'Evening, mamma.

MARIE: "Her complexion fair,
    A lady indeed beyond compare,
    Lo, how wonderful—"

EDDY: I thought you said she pulled out.

MORGAN: I thought she did.

MARIE: "She's an angel, too;
    By the stars above
    She's the one that I—"
    Hello, Steve.

MORGAN: I thought you were gonna put her on the plane.

CRICKET: Well, Harry, she said—
MORGAN: What's the matter, didn't it go?
MARIE: Yes, it went, but I decided not to.
MORGAN: Oh, you did? You know, I went to a lot o' trouble to get you out o' here.

84 From this point on, Frenchy/Gerard's speeches were labeled FRENCHY in the script. I have changed the name to GERARD for consistency; no changes have been made in the dialogue.

MORGAN: Yeah. You dames! A guy goes out and breaks his neck to— Well, I might have expected it.
MARIE: Steve! You're not sore, are you?
MORGAN: Look, it would be all right if I had any dough, but—
MARIE: I got a refund on that ticket. Here.
MORGAN: Yeah. That's gonna help a lot. You'd better hang on to it.
EDDY: Harry, we can use—
MORGAN: She'll buy it for you. Nothin' but beer for him, Slim.
MARIE: I'll remember. We'll be all right, Steve. I've got a job.
MORGAN: Doin' what?
MARIE: Frenchy seems to think I can sing.
MORGAN: Well, it's his place.
MARIE: Sometimes you make me so mad I could—
GERARD: Harry!
MORGAN: You could do what?
MARIE: I could—
GERARD: Harry, I need your help.
MORGAN: Well, what is it now?
GERARD: That—
MORGAN: That's all right. Go ahead.
GERARD: That man is very badly wounded, Harry.

85 Deleted.

86 MORGAN: Me? I'm hotter than any doctor right now. Don't you think they recognized my boat? They'll be on my tail any minute. All I gotta do is walk out o' here.
GERARD: You don't have to go out.
MORGAN: You didn't bring 'em here?
GERARD: In the cellar.
MORGAN: Why didn't yuh put 'em on the center table in a goldfish bowl and be done with it?
GERARD: We had to do something. They're watching every road out of town.

87   GERARD: Please, Harry, will you do it?

MORGAN: Not a chance, Frenchy.

CASHIER: Captain Morgan, your bill here at the hotel, being overdue, amounts to six thousand three hundred and fifty-six francs.

EDDY: Six!

MORGAN: Well, she's right, Eddy. Well, you really keep the books, don't you, mamma?

CASHIER: We will be glad to dismiss the whole matter if you will do this for us.

88   MORGAN (laughing): You know, you almost had me figured right, mamma, except for one thing. I'll still owe you that bill. Now look, Slim, up in my room you'll find a medical kit. It's gray, and about this big with the name of the boat on it. Bring it down to the cellar.

MARIE: Sure.

MORGAN: Oh, and Slim! Here's the key. Bring some hot water, too.

GERARD: This way, Harry.

EDDY: Harry! Harry! Can I help?

MORGAN: No, Eddy. You just stay out o' sight. But if you should run across the police, don't forget what I told yuh to tell 'em.

EDDY: Er, what was that, Harry?

MORGAN: Uh—just stay out o' sight, Eddy.

EDDY: I remember.

89   Deleted.

90   MORGAN: Well, I'll tell you, I was sort of invited. He asked me.

HELENE: You're not a doctor.

MORGAN: No.

HELENE: Where is the doctor?

GERARD: Please, be patient, madame.

HELENE: I have been patient. How do I know you know anything?

MORGAN: You don't.

HELENE: Wait a minute.

PAUL: (Moaning.)

MORGAN: How long has he been unconscious?

HELENE: Just a few minutes.

MORGAN: Say, now, look, um— Well, he's got some fever and his pulse is a little low. He'll be all right, though, as soon as we get the bullet out of him.

HELENE: You're not to touch him. Do you hear?

MORGAN: That's all right with me. I'm not gettin' paid.

GERARD: Please! She does not know what she's saying. She's not herself.

MORGAN: Who is she?

GERARD: Harry, you promised.

MORGAN: Look. You want to help your husband, don't you?

HELENE: Yes.

MORGAN: Then use your head. They can't get a doctor without givin' the whole show away. Besides, he's probably got as good a chance with me as anybody.

HELENE: I'm not gonna let you do it!

MORGAN: Why not? He's no different from anybody else. Just a little sicker, that's all. It means he's not worth so much. Now, look—

91 MORGAN: You can have another crack at me later on. Hello, Slim!

MARIE: Hello!

MORGAN: Miss Browning, Madame de Bursac. Don't get tough with Slim. She's apt to slap you back. That's what you said you'd do, wasn't it? Bring the water in here.

HELENE: Wait a minute, I—

MARIE: He's only trying to help you.

HELENE: Who are you?

MARIE: Nobody. Just another volunteer. Where do you want this water?

MORGAN: In that basin. Is it hot?

MARIE: Boiling.

MORGAN: All right, then pour some of this in it. And drop these in. You'd better get out o' here. You may not like this.

MARIE: I'll be all right.

MORGAN: All right. Then take this.

HELENE: What is it?

MORGAN: Chloroform. Get over there by your husband's head and if he comes to while I'm probing, pour some of that stuff on a hunk o' cotton and give him a whiff of it. Don't open it till I tell you to. Take out about four of those. Oh, George, bring that lamp a little closer so I can see what I'm doin'. That's good. All right, Slim. Hold that a minute.

PAUL: (Moaning.)

MORGAN: Easy, boy.

PAUL: (Moaning louder.)

MORGAN: Come on. Hurry up!

92 MORGAN: Well, that's fine! Don't worry about her. Pick up that can. Any of it left?

MARIE: I think there's enough.

MORGAN: No, wait a minute. I don't think we'll need it. He's out, too. Bring that light down a little lower. Frenchy, bring that basin over here. And fan some of those fumes away, will you, or we'll all be out. There yuh are, Frenchy. There's your bullet. I told you it was spent. It would have smashed the bone. All right, I don't need that. All right. You finish bandaging it up. Adhesive tape in the box. I gotta get Nursie out o' here or she never will come to.

93 In place of this scene, whose dialogue shows up later, Hawks has Morgan carry the unconscious Helene into the outer room.

MARIE: What are you trying to do, guess her weight?

MORGAN: She's heftier than you think. You'd better loosen her clothes.

MARIE: You've been doing all right. Uh, maybe you'd better look after her husband.

MORGAN: He's not gonna run out on me.

MARIE: Neither is she. Steve! Is it all right if I give her a little whiff of this?

MORGAN: (Laughing.)

94 PAUL: (Moaning.)

MORGAN: Oh, you're with us again. You were lucky. You passed out.

PAUL: What happened? I must—

MORGAN: We'll talk about that in the morning. See if you can get some sleep.

PAUL: Thanks.

[Some time later:]

MORGAN: Why did you ever come along with him on a trip like this?

HELENE: I loved him. Wanted to be with him.

MORGAN: That's a reason.

HELENE: There's another reason. They told me to come. Our people did. They said—they said no man was much good if he left someone behind in France for the Germans to find and hold.

MORGAN: Makes sense.

HELENE: I told them I'd only be in the way, that I could do no good, that I was afraid. But the worst of it is that it's been so hard for him to have me along, because I've made him that way, too. Now he's afraid.

MORGAN: Well, he didn't invent it.

HELENE: Invent what?

MORGAN: Being afraid.

HELENE: Thanks, Mr. Morgan.

95 Some time later:

MORGAN: Well, the fever's gone.

HELENE: Do you, do you—

MORGAN: I'm no doctor, but he looks pretty good to me. If he wakes up, give him another one of these pills.

[In the outer room:]

HELENE: Mr. Morgan. Mr. Morgan— I—

MORGAN: You're not going to faint again?

HELENE: No. I'm just having a, a hard time trying to say something.

MORGAN: Well, go ahead. Say it. I'm not gonna bite yuh.

HELENE: Well, if it hadn't been for you, Paul might have— I'm sorry for the way I've acted.

MORGAN: Aw, you're not sorry at all. You're just sorry you made a fool of yourself.

HELENE (laughing): I have, haven't I?

MORGAN: Uh-huh.

HELENE: You don't make me angry when you say that. I don't think I'll ever be angry again with anything you say.

MORGAN: Another screwy dame. Now, how can you—

96 MARIE: Hello. I hate to break this up, but I've brought some breakfast.

HELENE: Good morning.

MARIE: How's your patient?

MORGAN: Oh, he'll be all right—

MARIE: Or haven't you looked lately?

MORGAN: He'll be all right. I'll be back this evening. If you need me before then be sure to call me.

HELENE: I will.

MARIE: Yes. And I hope you have everything you need here. The eggs may be a little hard-boiled—

HELENE: Oh, that's all right. I like them that way.

MARIE: You're lucky. Isn't she?

97 MORGAN: I'm gonna get some sleep. I'll see you later.

MARIE: Thanks.

MORGAN: What do you want?

MARIE: I can use a match. Thanks. Now I need a cigarette.

98 MARIE: Here, I can do that.

MORGAN: No.

MARIE: Oh, come on, let me help.

MORGAN: Look, when I get ready to take my shoes off, I'll take 'em off myself.

MARIE: All right. Want something to eat?

MORGAN: No.

MARIE: Just a little breakfast?

MORGAN: All I want to do is get some sleep.

MARIE: It's a good idea. I can help you there.

MORGAN: Hey, now where you goin'?

MARIE: I'm going to fix you a nice hot bath. It'll make you—sleep better.

MORGAN: Look, Junior. I don't want you to take my shoes off. I don't want you to get me any breakfast. I don't want you to draw me a nice hot bath. I don't want you to—

MARIE: Isn't there anything I can do, Steve?

MORGAN: Yes. Get the—

MARIE: "You know, Mr. Morgan, you don't make me angry when you say that. I don't think I'll ever be angry again at anything you say." How'm I doing, Steve? Does it work the second time?

MORGAN: You've been wantin' to do somethin' for me, haven't yuh?

MARIE: Uh-huh.

MORGAN: Uh-huh. Walk around me. Well, go ahead, walk around me. Clear around.

MARIE: (Laughing.)

MORGAN: Yuh find anything?

MARIE: No. No, Steve. There are no strings tied to you—not yet. (They kiss.) Oh, I like that. Except, except for the beard. Why don't you shave and we'll (light slap) we'll try it again.

99 GERARD: Harry!

MORGAN: Oh, later, Frenchy.

GERARD: No, Harry, wait! Renard, the inspector, is downstairs. You'd better come down.

MORGAN: Oh, I can't do that. I gotta get a shave.

GERARD: He's got Eddy!

MORGAN: He's got—

GERARD: Eddy! He's giving him drinks and asking him questions.

MORGAN: I was afraid o' that. Good thing you didn't get me in that tub!

MARIE: Look out for those strings, Steve. You're liable to trip and break your neck.

GERARD: Strings? I didn't see any strings.

MARIE: They just don't show, Frenchy.

100   Deleted.

101   EDDY: You oughta seen that fish. It musta weighed nine hundred if
       it weighed a pound. It was the biggest marlin you ever seen in
       all your born days. You know, a marlin is a swordfish.

       RENARD: Good morning, capitaine.

       EDDY: Oh. Hello, Harry. How's everything?

       MORGAN: Fine.

       RENARD: Won't you join us?

       MORGAN: A little early for this kind of a party, isn't it?

102   EDDY: Say, you're all right. Was you ever bit by a dead bee—

       MORGAN: No, he never was, Eddy. Go on with what you were
       sayin'.

       EDDY: Oh, I was just tellin' 'im about the big one we hooked onto
       last night.

       MORGAN: Uh-huh.

       EDDY: Well, sir, that fish was so big that me and Harry could hardly
       budge 'im. We pumped on him until we was all wore out,
       didn't we, Harry?

       MORGAN: Right, Eddy.

       EDDY (laughing): I—it was after dark and we was still playin' 'im.
       He musta weighed at least a—a thousand easy.

       RENARD: Every time Mr. Eddy takes a drink this fabulous fish grows
       larger.

       MORGAN: He must have started with a pretty small one.

103   MORGAN: Well, we didn't. Didn't Eddy tell yuh?

104   MORGAN: I didn't stick around to find out.

       RENARD: I do not think—

       MORGAN: You know, you can't be too careful these days.

       RENARD: I do not think anybody could give a more logical explana-
       tion for refusing to obey the challenge of our patrol boat. Not
       to speak of shooting out their searchlight.

       MORGAN: Patrol boat?

       RENARD: Yes.

       MORGAN: Oh, that's what it was. You were right, Eddy.

105   MORGAN: You know, it's a funny thing; he kept sayin' it was a patrol
       boat all the time and I wouldn't believe him.

       COYO: There is one thing that is not—clear to me, Captain Morgan.

       MORGAN: Yeah? What's that?

       COYO: Why does a professional fisherman go fishing for his own
       amusement?

MORGAN: Well, uh— Hey, don't you ever ask any questions? Don't you ever talk? No, I, I guess you don't. What were you saying?

COYO: Does a professional fisherman go fishing for his own amusement?

MORGAN: Well, he does if he likes it. And we like it, don't we, Eddy?

EDDY: Yeah. You remember that night in Key West when we went—

RENARD: We do not seem to be getting anywhere.

EDDY: It was the Fourth of July and you sa—

RENARD: Mr. Eddy!

EDDY: I was only gonna tell him at Key West, the Fourth of July, three years ago, at eight o'clock! I got that in, Harry.

RENARD: What about your passenger?

MORGAN: It was seven o'clock, Eddy.

RENARD: What about your two passengers?

MORGAN: You oughtn't to burn up at him. You fed him the rum.

RENARD: What about your two passengers?

MORGAN: What passengers?

RENARD: The ones you brought over from Anguilla!

MORGAN: He was waitin' on the dock when we came in. How do yuh think I got 'em ashore, in my sleeves?

RENARD: You could have landed them a dozen places on our coast line.

MORGAN: That's right. I could've at that.

106 RENARD: Would five hundred dollars refresh your memory?

MORGAN: Oh, my memory's pretty good. For instance, I can remember that you're the guy who lifted my passport and all my money.

RENARD: Would your memory become any better if your passport and money were returned to you?

MORGAN: Does that include the eight hundred and twenty-five dollars Johnson owed me?

RENARD: Why not?

MORGAN: And the five hundred you just mentioned?

RENARD: You drive a hard bargain, Capitaine Morgan.

MORGAN: Well, that's no bargain. If these people are as important as you seem to think they are, they're gonna be pretty hard to find.

RENARD: Not for a man of your resourcefulness. Think it over and let me hear from you.

107 MORGAN: Bee-lips went away pretty mad. As soon as he cools off, though, he's gonna start thinkin'.

GERARD: He thinks now that you will turn them in.

MORGAN: Well, that's what you want him to think, isn't it?

GERARD: What will happen then?

MORGAN: He hasn't searched this hotel yet, has he?

GERARD: No, not yet.

MORGAN: Well, there's your answer. He doesn't want them. He wants the whole set-up.

GERARD: Then what shall we do?

MORGAN: It's not "we," it's "you," and you can't do anything until that fella downstairs gets strong enough to move. Until then, you're probably safe. Better get rid o' this.

GERARD: Yeah.

MORGAN: Oh, bring us some breakfast, will yuh, Frenchy?

GERARD: Sure. (Eddy mutters. Marie has come downstairs and joins them.)

MARIE: I thought you didn't want any breakfast.

MORGAN: I didn't, then. What were you sayin', Eddy?

EDDY: I, I've been figurin'. Them guys don't think that I'm wise, but they was tryin' to get me drunk. (Laughing.) They don't know me, do they, Harry? (Hiccoughing.)

MORGAN AND MARIE: (Laughing.)

EDDY: I think they're tryin' to find out somethin'. What do you suppose it is?

MORGAN: Well, don't you know?

EDDY: No. I ain't got no idea. (Hiccoughing.)

MORGAN: That's a good way to leave it. You know, you got the hiccoughs.

EDDY: Have I, Harry? (Hiccoughing.) Oh, yeah. I never noticed it.

MARIE: Don't you think you better take a drink of water?

EDDY: What, water?

MORGAN: That's a good idea, Slim.

EDDY: No. Oh, no, not that. (Hiccoughing.)

MARIE: It'll do you good.

EDDY: I'll be all right. (Hiccoughing.)

MORGAN: Hey, Eddy!

EDDY: Yeah, Harry? (Hiccoughing.)

MORGAN: Keep out o' sight and stay away from the police. They're not goin' to believe that story you told the second time.

EDDY: What story was that, Harry? (Hiccoughing.)

214

MORGAN: Er, keep out o' sight.

EDDY: (Hiccoughing.)

108   CRICKET: "It's the story of a very unfortunate colored man
Who got 'rested down in old Hong Kong.
He got twenty years' privilege taken away from him
When he kicked old Buddha's gong.
And now he's bobbin' the piano just to raise the price
Of a ticket to the land of the free;
Well, he say his home's in Frisco where they send the rice,
But it's really in Tennessee.
That's why he say,
'I need someone to love me,
Need somebody to carry me
Home to San Francisco
And bury my body there.
Oh, I need someone to lend me a fifty dollar bill
And then I'll leave Hong Kong far behind me
For happiness once again.
Won't someone believe
I've a yen to see that bay again;
But when I try to leave
Sweet loco man won't let me fly away.
I need someone to love me,
Need somebody to carry me
Home to San Francisco
And bury my body there.'"

109   MORGAN: Well!

MARIE: I'm going to work. Do you like it?

MORGAN: Well, you won't have to sing much in that outfit.

MARIE: You know, Steve, sometimes you make me—

MORGAN: That's why I do it. Haven't seen Eddy, have you?

MARIE: No, not since noon. Why?

MORGAN: He left the boat and he hasn't come back.

MARIE: Is, is there anything wrong?

MORGAN: I don't know. Say, don't look now, but over there by the door at the second table, there's a guy with a mustache. I think he's following me. Keep an eye on him, will yuh? I'm goin' downstairs.

CRICKET: Hey, Harry! Stick around a while. She's goin' to sing.

MORGAN: I'll be right back.

MARIE: Give her my love.

MORGAN: I'd give her my own if she had that on.

CRICKET: Here's the rest of the lyrics, Slim. How do yuh feel?

MARIE: Well, I could use a drink, Cricket.

CRICKET: Sure. Come on. Emil! What'll yuh have, Slim?

MARIE: Scotch and soda.

CRICKET: Same.

110 PAUL: I'm very grateful to you.

MORGAN: Aw, forget it. Let me have a look at this. Uh-huh. Well, there's no bleeding.

PAUL: No.

MORGAN: Does that hurt?

PAUL: Very little. My only trouble is when I'm eating. I'm awkward with my left hand.

MORGAN: Well, we'll see if we can't arrange to have you shot in the other arm next time. You won't need me any more. Frenchy, I'm pullin' out.

GERARD: When?

MORGAN: As soon as I find Eddy.

PAUL: Is your friend missing?

MORGAN: Yeah.

GERARD: What happened?

MORGAN: I don't know. He left the dock and hasn't been back since. He usually does what I tell him.

PAUL: I'm sorry if anything happened.

MORGAN: Well, I won't know that until I find him.

PAUL: Couldn't you leave him here?

MORGAN: I don't think Eddy'd like that. Now look, Frenchy, as soon as I'm gone, Renard's gonna move in and turn this place upside down, so you better start figurin' how and where you're gonna move him and quick!

PAUL: Wouldn't it be best if we went with you, captain?

MORGAN: Why do you want to go? I'm still tryin' to get out of the jam I got into bringin' yuh here. Just why'd you come here in the first place? I know why she came; she told me, but why did you?

216

111   PAUL: Did you ever hear of Pierre Villemars?

MORGAN: Pierre Villemars? Yeah. I read in a headline. He was quite a guy. The Vichy got him. He's dead, isn't he?

PAUL: No, no, no! He's on Devil's Island. They sent me here to get him, and to bring him back here to Martinique. He's a man whom people who are persecuted and oppressed will believe in and follow.

MORGAN: Well, just how are you gonna get him away?

PAUL: You don't think much of me, Captain Morgan. You are wondering why they have chosen me for this mission. I wonder, too. (Laughing.) As you know, I'm not a brave man. On the contrary, I'm always frightened. I wish I could borrow your nature for a while, captain. When you meet danger, you never think of anything except how you will circumvent it. The word "failure" does not even exist for you. While I, I think always "Suppose I fail?" And then I am frightened.

112   MORGAN: Yeah, I can easily see how it wouldn't take much courage to get a notorious patriot off Devil's Island, but, uh, just for professional reasons, I'd like to know how you're gonna do it.

PAUL: We will find a way. It might fail. And if it does and I am, I am still alive, I will try to pass on my information, my mission, to someone else. Perhaps to a better man, who does not fail. Because there is always someone else. That is the mistake the Germans always make with people they try to destroy. There will be always someone else.

MORGAN: Yeah.

PAUL: Originally, we planned to do everything from here. But then, because of my own clumsiness, it was impossible. And that's the reason we have to go with you.

MORGAN: Oh, I couldn't even get you on the dock. They got a man down there watching; there's one upstairs; they're all over the place. How would I get you through the streets?

PAUL: How will you go?

MORGAN: Well, they're watching me to find you. As long as I haven't got you along, I can at least get on the boat. There'll be a fog again and the tide'll turn a little after midnight. I can cut loose and drift out beyond the breakwater before I start my engines.

GERARD: But, Harry—

PAUL: Captain Morgan is right. This is not his fight yet. Some day I

217

hope it may be, because we could use him. You have done enough for us already. Gerard told me of your refusing Renard's offer to give us up.

MORGAN: How do you know I won't do it yet?

PAUL: There are many things a man will do, but betrayal for a price—is not one of yours.

MORGAN: Good luck.

PAUL: I hope you find your friend.

MORGAN: Thanks.

HELENE: Good-by. And—thanks!

MORGAN: Oh, uh, Frenchy, I got a few things I want to talk to you about before I blow.

GERARD: Well, then I'll be up in a little while, Harry.

113   Instead of doing card tricks or shopping for Helene, Marie is getting ready to sing.

MORGAN: Any sign of Eddy?

MARIE: Uh-uh. But your friend's still sitting at his table.

MORGAN: Yeh. I know.

MARIE: What's the matter, Steve?

MORGAN: I dunno. I got a hunch the whole thing's gonna blow up. It's too quiet.

MARIE: What are you gonna do?

MORGAN: We're gonna pull out o' here tonight. Soon as I find Eddy. We're leaving here for good. The three of us. Now wait a minute. I want you to know what you're gonna get into. It'll be rough. I'm broke. If we do get out of here, it'll be with a coupla hundred gallons of gas and a few francs. Just about enough to get us to Port au Prince, maybe.

MARIE: I've never been there.

MORGAN: I don't know when you'll get back home. Could be a long time.

MARIE: Could be forever. Or are you afraid of that? I'm hard to get, Steve. All you have to do is ask me.

MORGAN: How long will it take you to pack? There's a lot o' people around here; save it. We won't shove off till midnight. Go ahead and go to work.

CRICKET: You all set, Slim?

MARIE: Sure. Don't make it sad, Cricket. I don't feel that way.

CRICKET: You don't look that way either. Let's go. Top note, boys.

MARIE: "Maybe it happens this way;
       Maybe we really belong together

218

But after all,
How little we know.
Maybe it's just for a day;
Love is as changeable as the weather
And after all,
How little we know.
Who knows why an April breeze
Never remains?
Why stars in the trees
Hide when it rains?
Love comes along,
Casting a spell.
Will it sing you a song?
Will it say a farewell?
Who can tell?
Maybe you're meant to be mine;
Maybe I'm only supposed to stay in your arms awhile,
As *others* have done.
Is this what I've waited for?
Am I the one?
Oh, I hope in my heart that it's so
In spite of how little we know."

GERARD: Harry! Madame de Bursac wants to see you.

MORGAN: Now look, Frenchy, that's all over.

GERARD: She's up in your room.

MORGAN: She— Why did you—

GERARD: Please, Harry. That's all I will ask. Thanks, Harry.

114 MORGAN: Look, now you shouldn't have come up here. It's too much of a chance. I told you downstairs I can't take you.

HELENE: I know. I didn't come up for that. You've already done too much for us. But there's just one other favor I'd like to ask. I want you to take these. (Puts jewels in his hand.) They were my grandmother's, and her mother's before that. She gave them to me when I got married. They're all I've got left. I want you to take them out of here with you and save them till we can—

MORGAN: Suppose they get me before I get out?

HELENE: Then throw them overboard. At least they won't have them.

MORGAN: Suppose you never come for them?

HELENE: Then let it be a part payment for all you've done for us. Please. Won't you?

115 MARIE: Steve! Renard just came in. He's on his way up.

MORGAN: Did he see you?

MARIE: I don't think so.

MORGAN: All right. Now, here. You take these, and both you get in there (indicating bathroom, not bedroom) and keep quiet. Soon as I get rid of him, you take her back down to the cellar.

MARIE: All right, Steve.

116 RENARD: Good evening. May we come in?

MORGAN: Good evening. (As he's frisked.) No, I never carry 'em. What's on your mind?

RENARD: The whereabouts of the two people we are searching for.

MORGAN: Oh, you haven't found 'em yet?

RENARD: No. But since this morning through our sources we have learned their names: Monsieur and Madame de Bursac. That is correct, is it not?

MORGAN: How would I know that?

RENARD: Well, I thought, perhaps. Very nice perfume.

MORGAN: You like that, huh?

RENARD: Yes.

MORGAN: So do I. All right, Slim. Come out. You've, uh, met the boys.

MARIE: Good evening.

RENARD: Mademoiselle.

117 RENARD: Except your friend, Mr. Eddy, as he likes to be called.

MORGAN: So you got 'im.

RENARD: Yes. Now we lack only the two missing persons.

MORGAN: What are you gonna do with him?

RENARD: If you will not give us the information we want, perhaps he will. Before we made the mistake of giving him liquor; this time we will withhold it.

MORGAN: You know what that'll do to him?

RENARD: I think so.

MORGAN: He couldn't stand it. He'd crack up.

RENARD: You could easily prevent that.

MORGAN: Yeah, I can. Yuh got a cigarette? Can't you make him talk?

RENARD: When necessary.

MORGAN: You'll find some in that drawer, Slim.

RENARD: You could save Mr. Eddy a great deal of—er, shall we say, discomfort?

MARIE: Steve!

RENARD: And me a lot of time if you will tell us where these people are.

MORGAN: How much was it you were going to give me? More than what's mine already?

RENARD: I do not think now I will have to pay anybody anything.

MORGAN: You're probably right. I haven't got a match.

BODYGUARD: Don't go any—

118 MORGAN: All right, go on. Get 'em up. Go on. Go on, pull your guns. Go ahead. Go ahead. Get 'em out. Go ahead. Try it. You're gonna get it anyway.

RENARD: Harry, don't, don't—

MORGAN: You've been pushin' me around long enough. So you were gonna drive Eddy nuts. Pickin' on a poor old rummy that never— Slappin' girls around. That's right, go for it! Your boy needs company. (His gun hand shakes.) Look at that. Ain't that silly? That's how close you came. All right, Frenchy, get their guns. Here yuh are. Now get over on that couch. Go ahead, step over 'im. Sit down. All right, come on out. (Helene comes out.) That's one of 'em. The other one's down in the cellar. Frenchy, take her downstairs. Get some help. Have them both ready to leave on the boat. Then come back up here. Slim, you pack. We're shovin' off as soon as we get Eddy out.

MARIE: Okay, Steve.

RENARD: Just how do you think you—

MORGAN: Shut up! You want to know how I'm gonna get 'im out? That broke as easy as you will. There's a telephone out in the hall. You're gonna tell someone to let 'im go. Send him back up here. Oh, yes you are. One of you. I haven't forgotten you. You're both gonna take a beating till someone uses that phone. That means one of you's gonna take a beating for nothing. I don't care which one it is. I'll start with you.

119 It is Renard, not Coyo, on the phone.

RENARD: You will release him immediately.

MORGAN: Tell him you'll explain later.

RENARD: I will explain it later.

MORGAN: Tell 'im to send him back to the hotel and do nothing else till you get there.

221

RENARD: Send him back here to the hotel and do nothing until you hear from us.

MORGAN: All right—inside. You've got some harbor passes to fill out.

120 MORGAN: And now Paul and Madame de Bursac. I'll be right with you, Frenchy. They're all yours now.

MERCIER: Thanks, Mr. Morgan.

GERARD: They are all ready, Harry.

MORGAN: Here you are. These'll get 'em through the guard and on the boat.

GERARD: Where will you take them, Harry?

MORGAN: Well, maybe Devil's Island.

GERARD: What?

MORGAN: Might even get your friend Villemars off. That's what you wanted, wasn't it?

GERARD: Very much. Why, why are you doing this, Harry?

MORGAN (laughing): Well, I don't know. Maybe because I like you and maybe because I don't like them.

GERARD: I'm glad you are on our side, Harry. I'm glad—

MORGAN: No kissin', Frenchy.

GERARD: Oh. (Laughing.)

MORGAN: You know you'll have to take care of those guys in there.

GERARD: We will give you plenty of time!

MORGAN: If you let 'em go they'll come back here and burn this place down.

GERARD: Let them. It will be a very small fire. When Villemars comes back it will be our turn, then. We'll start a bigger one.

MORGAN: Meet you on the boat.

GUARD: One minute, please—

EDDY: Well, I—

MORGAN: That's all right. Let 'im through.

121 MORGAN: It's all right now.

EDDY: Say, you look glad to see me. You know, a funny thing—

MORGAN: Yeah, I know.

EDDY: I don't know what they wanted but they wouldn't even give me a—

MORGAN: I'll get you one down on the boat. We're leavin', Eddy. Ready, Slim?

MARIE: In a minute, Steve. Close that, will yuh?

EDDY: Say, what is this? She goin' with us?

MORGAN: Yeah, it looks like it.

EDDY: Aw, Harry, yuh mean— What's she got— Er, who are you?

122   EDDY: I feel like I was talkin' to myself.

MARIE: I bet I've been bit a hundred times that way.

EDDY: Why don't you bite 'em back?

123   EDDY: Oh. (Laughing.) I remember you. You're all right. She can come, Harry. It's okay with me. Now I'll have the two of you to take care of, won't I?

MORGAN: That's right, Eddy. You can begin by grabbin' these bags. Come on, Slim!

124   MARIE: Steve, do I have time to say good-by to Cricket?

MORGAN: Sure, go ahead.

MARIE: Cricket, I came to say good-by.

CRICKET: What?

MARIE: We're leaving now. Thanks for everything.

CRICKET: Hey, Slim. Are you still happy?

MARIE: What do you think?

Production Credits

Produced and directed by	Howard Hawks
Screenplay by	Jules Furthman
	and William Faulkner
Based on the novel by	Ernest Hemingway
Director of Photography	Sid Hickox, A.S.C.
Art Director	Charles Novi
Film Editor	Christian Nyby
Special effects by	Roy Davidson
	and Rex Wimpy, A.S.C.
Sound by	Oliver S. Garretson
Set decorations by	Casey Roberts
Technical Advisor	Louis Comien
Gowns by	Milo Anderson
Make-up Artist	Perc Westmore
"Am I Blue":	
Music by	Harry Akst
Lyrics by	Grant Drake
"Hong Kong Blues":	
Music and lyrics by	Hoagy Carmichael
"How Little We Know":	
Music by	Hoagy Carmichael
Lyrics by	Johnny Mercer
Musical Director	Leo F. Forbstein
Assistant Director	Jack Sullivan
Unit Manager	Chuck Hansen
Unit Publicist	Bill Rice

Released: October 1944
Running time: 100 minutes

Cast

Harry Morgan	Humphrey Bogart
Eddy	Walter Brennan
Marie Browning	Lauren Bacall
Helene de Bursac	Dolores Moran
Cricket	Hoagy Carmichael
Paul de Bursac	Walter Molnar
Lieutenant Coyo	Sheldon Leonard
Frenchy/Gerard	Marcel Dalio
Johnson	Walter Sande
Captain Renard	Dan Seymour
Renard's bodyguard	Aldo Nadi
Beauclerc	Paul Marion
Mrs. Beauclerc	Patricia Shay
Bartender	Pat West
Emil	Emmet Smith
Horatio	Sir Lancelot
Rosalie	Janette Grae
Quartermaster	Eugene Borden
Negro urchins	Elzie Emanuel
	Harold Garrison
Civilian	Pedro Regas
Headwaiter	Major Fred Farrell
Cashier	Adrienne d'Ambricourt
De Gaullists	Maurice Marsac
	Fred Dosch
	George Suzanne
	Louis Mercier
	Crane Whitley

Cast

Detective	Hal Kelly
Chef	Chef (Joseph) Milani
Naval Ensign	Ron Randell
Dancer	Audrey Armstrong
Cashier	Marguerite Sylva

This comprehensive cast list was compiled from the press book and from Paul Michael and others, eds., *The American Movies Reference Book* (Englewood Cliffs, N.J.: Prentice-Hall, 1969), p. 522.

Inventory

The following materials from the Warner library of the Wisconsin Center for Film and Theater Reserach were used by Kawin in preparing *To Have and Have Not* for the Wisconsin/Warner Bros. Screenplay Series:

Temporary, by Jules Furthman, October 14, 1943, with revisions to November 23, 1943, 208 pages.

Revised Temporary, by Furthman, December 30, 1943, with revisions to January 5, 1944, 111 pages, unfinished.

Final, by Furthman, January 22, 1944, with revisions to February 14, 1944, 151 pages.

Second Revised Final, by Furthman and William Faulkner, February 26, 1944, with revisions to April 22, 1944, 112 pages.

THE WHYS AND HOWS OF OIL & GAS INVESTMENT

By Lewis G. Mosburg, Jr.

First Printing: January, 1986
Oklahoma City, Oklahoma
UNITED STATES OF AMERICA
ISBN Number: 910649-22-7

ABOUT THE AUTHOR

Referred to by *Oil & Gas Investor* magazine as "the oil and gas investment maven" and "the man who tells investors to rebel," **Lewis G. Mosburg, Jr.** is one of America's most prolific speakers and writers on oil and gas, real estate and tax-sheltered investments.

Senior member of the Oklahoma City law firm of Mosburg, Sears, Kunzman & Bollinger, Inc., he is Vice Chairman of the Task Force for Oil and Gas Drilling Standards for the Financial Products Standards Board of The Institute of Certified Financial Planners. Mr. Mosburg has also served as Chairman of the Industry Advisory Committee to the North American Securities Administrators' Oil and Gas Interests Committee, as a member of the Direct Participation Committee of the National Association of Securities Dealers, Inc., the Oil and Gas and the Real Estate Advisory Committees to the California Department of Corporations, and was recently awarded his designation as a "Specialist in Real Estate Securities" (SRS) by the Real Estate Securities and Syndication Institute ("RESSI"), an affiliate of the National Association of Realtors, for his "extraordinary contributions to [the] industry." Mr. Mosburg is also the former General Counsel of the Oil Investment Institute.

In addition to his extensive public speaking, Mr. Mosburg presents in-house training programs for such organizations as Arthur Andersen & Company, the First National Bank of Boston, Amoco Production Company, and the National Association of Securities Dealers, Inc.

The author of over 50 books and audio and video cassette series, including Simon & Schuster's *Tax-Shelter Coloring Book* and Prentice-Hall's *Tax Shelter Desk Book,* Mr. Mosburg's most recent publications include *Investing in Oil, Private Placements in Oil Under SEC Regulation D, Financing Oil & Gas Deals, Economics of Oil and Gas Investment,* plus a book and audio cassette series presently under preparation on real estate investment and syndication.

ACKNOWLEDGMENTS AND DEDICATION

Let's face facts. Acknowledgments are for the birds. They admit the inevitable truth that there are many persons responsible for the preparation of any book; why not keep the credit in the author's corner (making sure that blame can still be spread if that becomes necessary)?

For that reason, no mention of all the hard work that Chris Mauldin, President of ETI, and Pamela Byrd-Mauldin, my long-time editor, put out in connection with this and my other books, in addition to somehow managing to remain my dear friends over the years. After all, what are publishers, editors, and dear friends for?

And, finally, the dedication:

- To the memories of my mother, Christina Jane Mosburg, and my father, Lewis G. Mosburg, Sr., for all they gave me on every level.

TABLE OF CONTENTS

FOREWORD

Properly understood, oil and gas is the most exciting investment opportunity around. The potential rewards exceed those which any other passive investment area, including real estate, has to offer. The downside risks traditionally associated with the "speculative" oil and gas search can also be greatly offset by an intelligent investment strategy. But since the risks of oil and gas are misunderstood, the oilman must offer you a much better deal to compensate for these "perceived" (or *mis*perceived!) dangers.

Oil and gas is often dismissed as a "tax shelter." And, certainly, there are many tax advantages (as well as some frequently-overlooked tax *disadvantages*) associated with investing in oil under our present tax laws. However, this investment area primarily offers you *an opportunity to make money*, enhanced with some "nice" tax overtones that are, to some extent, icing on the cake.

Even without these "tax incentives" traditionally provided the oil and gas industry, intelligent oil and gas investment can be extremely profitable. Even under the most harsh of "flat tax" proposals, the inevitable dry holes that must be drilled in any intelligent "mix" of potentially-profitable drilling "prospects" would remain deductible. (And a new-found realism now appears to have eliminated attacks on " 'productive-well' IDC's" as well.) So, under any set of tax laws, oil and gas offers a high degree of front-end deductibility, coupled with a true profit potential.

Oil and gas offers these opportunities, though, only when *properly understood*. To realize the benefits of oil and gas investment, it's necessary to develop that "intelligent investment strategy." And most oil and gas investors don't understand **why** this type of investment does (or doesn't) work—and **how** to make *intelligent* oil and gas investments.

Answering these questions is what **THE WHYS AND HOWS OF OIL & GAS INVESTMENT** is all about.

In **Chapter One, "An Introduction to Oil and Gas Investment,"** we'll discuss the *objectives* of investing in oil (making money); and explore both the *benefits* and *risks* of participating in the oil and gas search. (We didn't say oil and gas investment was risk free; we just said that these risks were misperceived, overemphasized, and could be alleviated—although not totally eliminated—by an intelligent investment strategy). The various *types* of oil and gas investment that are open to you will also be reviewed, as well as the relative advantages and disadvantages of each.

In **Chapter Two, "Oil and Taxes,"** you'll learn how current tax laws can be used to your advantage; certain tax pitfalls that you need to avoid; and how to modify your investment strategy to deal with "flat tax" changes.

In **Chapter Three, "Measuring Oil and Gas Investment Economics,"** we'll consider the return levels at which oil and gas will compete with—and significantly exceed—the returns you can expect from other investment areas. (Also scrutinized are certain "popular" types of oil deals which, when properly analyzed, offer you no better return, even on an after-tax basis, than you could get from paying your taxes and placing the remaining monies in a savings account.) We'll teach you how to convert an oilman's return projections into return levels that *you* can understand. And we'll see how diversified investment can reduce the admitted risks of oil and gas investment to acceptable levels, as well as determining what it takes to adequately diversify in oil.

In **Chapter Four**, one of the most misunderstood areas of oil and gas investment, **"Leveraged Investment in Oil and Gas,"** is explored. Is it simply a gimmick to entice the gullible, or does it offer *economic* (as well as tax) advantages? We'll attempt to determine if leveraged investment in oil is right for you; and, if it is, how do you *intelligently* invest on a leveraged basis?

Chapter Five, "Reaching an Intelligent Investment Decision," pulls everything together. Is oil a suitable investment vehicle for you? Or, perhaps better put, is your investment personality suitable for oil? (It isn't for everyone, including certain investors who can easily satisfy the suitability standards set by federal and state securities regulators.) Certain *preliminary investment considerations* are explored, such as investing well-by-well versus participating on a limited partnership basis, "public" versus "private" programs, and exploratory versus developmental drilling (to mention only a few), along with an "unheard-of" questioning of how much these factors should actually influence your investment decision. We'll talk about *analyzing the structure* of a proposed investment; *evaluating program management;* and *determining the potential profitability* of the various proposals you are considering, including the all-important analysis of "track record." We'll show you *how to be selective* in your investments, including some quick and dirty tests you can use to eliminate questionable "opportunities." (We'll even show you how to "Analyze Your Analyst," to be sure that the "expert" advice you are receiving from your broker or investment advisor is really all that expert!)

Chapter Six deals with a frequently ignored, but extremely important consideration: **Getting *Out* of Oil.** You'll see how to realize on your returns from successful ventures and how to cut your losses on those that have gone sour. We'll consider some ways in which your oil and gas investments can be used as a part of your estate planning. And then let's take a hard look at your rather considerable rights as an oil and gas investor, including those federal and state securities law protections that are available to you when your rights have been unconscionably—or sometimes merely technically—violated.

Finally, since many investors who are new to oil and gas frequently become confused by oil patch "jargon," Paulette Whitcomb and the **Oil & Gas Investor** magazine have kindly let us include their "A Glossary of Petrolese" in the **Appendix** to this book. And to make it easier to apply the lessons of **Chapter Five**, the **Appendix**—and this book—will close with an "Investment Decision Checklist."

Let's get on with it!

CHAPTER ONE
AN INTRODUCTION TO OIL AND GAS INVESTMENT

Why Should I Invest in Oil and Gas? Oil and gas offers investment opportunities which few other investments can match. Intelligently undertaken, the returns from oil should significantly exceed those which you could expect from other passive investments. And an oil and gas investment program can be tailored to fit your particular financial goals and needs.

You don't need to be a millionaire to participate in the rewards of this exciting investment area. And you can invest intelligently without having to retain a battery of high-priced experts and technical consultants to plot your investment strategy—although, as we'll see in **Chapter Five**, inexpensive expert advice is readily available which you may wish to tap. Nor do you have to be a *speculator* to realize handsome returns from an oil and gas investment program.

This doesn't mean that oil and gas investment is right for everyone or doesn't have its risks. In **Chapter Five,** we'll talk about the persons for whom this type of investment is—and is *not*—appropriate. And in this chapter, we'll consider both the advantages and pitfalls of participating in this most dynamic of industries.

But if your annual income has reached the fifty to sixty thousand dollar level, you'll find that an *intelligent* investment strategy can reduce the *perceived* risks of oil to levels far below that normally associated with "wildcatting"; and that intelligent oil and gas investment is not the gamble—or even the speculation—that you may have considered it to be.

And that's exactly what this book is about: *Intelligently* Investing in Oil!

The Purpose of Oil and Gas Investment. Far too many "tax-sheltered" investors have, often to their sorrow, forgotten an economic "basic": the purpose of investing is to MAKE MONEY!

If the objective of investing in oil were simply to reduce your taxes, there is a far easier way: just give your money to charity. An investment program which drills all non-productive wells ("dry holes") will certainly reduce your taxes—even under the most stringent of today's "tax reform" proposals. And one way of analyzing the results of such a "wipeout" investment is to remember that Uncle Sam bore half the loss.

But the other—and realistic—way of analyzing this dry hole adventure is that your "hard dollar" investment—the portion of your participation that was not offset by tax savings—was lost by *you*. And losing 50 cents on the dollar of your own money just to spite the government doesn't seem like much of an "investment."

Despite what you may have heard, most oil and gas investments don't result in a total loss of the dollars invested (except for the foolhardy investor who "experiments" by putting all of his money in a single well). (Those investors who do suffer such wipeout losses because of an inadequately diversified investment program seldom invest in oil and gas more than once!) But an equally important consideration, and one which many investors fail to understand, is that if your return from *productive* wells is *substandard*—if you never recover your original investment, or recover that investment too slowly—you still haven't realized a *reasonable* return from participating in the oil and gas search.

You may have heard that, with oil's admitted tax advantages, you are "making money in oil" if you simply recover one dollar of oil and gas production revenues for each dollar you invested. And you are receiving a return of a sort—about the same level of return that you could have realized from a savings account. (And that's *after* giving consideration to the tax advantages!) Which doesn't seem too handsome when you realize that the average "public" drilling program (an oil and gas limited partnership registered with the Securities and Exchange Commission) returns its investors, on an after-tax basis, the equivalent of a *20%* "Money Market" rate.

(We'll have more to say about return in **Chapter Three**, which deals with "Measuring Oil and Gas Investment Economics.")

That's not to say that oil and gas investment doesn't have significant tax advantages. (We'll discuss those in **Chapter Two**.) But even without oil's tax incentives, it would still represent an exciting—and risk-manageable—investment area. And all the tax advantages in the world won't turn an mediocre oil and gas proposal into an after-tax bonanza.

So your oil and gas investment strategy has to be aimed at **making money**, and not merely reducing your taxes. (Although we'll see how intelligent oil and gas investment can accomplish both!)

The Benefits of Oil and Gas Investment—Oil's Tax Advantages. The first feature of oil and gas investment to gain your attention may have been oil's admitted tax advantages.

From a tax standpoint, an "ideal" investment will involve expenditures which are *currently deductible* for federal income tax purposes (this will significantly cut both the cost of your investment, and its risk, on an after-tax basis), and revenues which are at least partially *sheltered from taxation* (this permits you to keep more of these dollars—again, after-tax).

Oil and gas qualifies in both these regards. First, *all of your costs associated with participating in dry holes will be currently deductible* as "Abandonment Losses." (While we don't like drilling dry holes, at least Uncle

Sam picks up half the loss.) More importantly, due to the "expense" nature of Intangible Drilling and Development Costs, *approximately 60% to 70% of the costs associated with productive ventures will also be currently deductible.*

As you receive revenues from these producing wells, *over 15% of your production dollars can be received tax free* as a result of the Percentage Depletion Allowance. And, in other instances, you may be able to *sell your interest in a well or program at Long Term Capital Gains rates,* or *exchange it for a marketable security, often on a tax-free basis.*[1]

(At this stage, we're only overviewing—and oversimplifying—the tax consequences of oil and gas investment. We'll get into a lot more detail in **Chapter Two.**)

While the tax advantages of oil are impressive, there are other "tax shelters" whose tax consequences are more impressive still. For instance, in real estate investment, you might be able to receive all of your cash flow for a number of years without paying *any* taxes on those distributed dollars; Long Term Capital Gains "conversion" is also more readily available in real estate. But oil and gas offers some special tax advantages that real estate—and other investment areas—do not.

In most tax-sheltered investments, high initial deductibility is created only through reliance on *leverage* — borrowing a substantial portion of the funds that will be used to conduct venture activities—or through reliance upon *"gray area" tax deductions*—aggressive tax positions that may, or may not, be sustained in the event of an audit. These same techniques are also used to increase the percentage of revenues which, it is claimed, can be received tax free. Unfortunately, these same techniques expose the investor to an increased likelihood of IRS audits—audits which often result in a disallowance of the claimed tax benefits; and to the *risks* of leverage. (As we'll be discussing in **Chapter Four,** leverage is a two-edged sword.). Furthermore, while the techniques improve the tax consequences of the investment (at least in the absence of an IRS attack), they frequently are "purchased" by reducing the economic potential of the investment.

Oil and gas is the only one of the so-called "tax shelters" whose tax benefits can be realized *without* reliance on leverage or questionable deductions, and without interfering with the legitimate economics of the venture!

(That's not to say that certain oil ventures don't rely upon tax positions which the IRS might challenge. We'll explore this further in **Chapter Two.** And, as you'll see below—and in greater detail in **Chapter Four**—

---

[1] What about the "flat tax"? We consider this in **Chapter Two.**

leverage, intelligently utilized, may prove a "plus" in your investment strategy. But in oil, using leverage, or taking a slightly more aggressive tax position is up to you, *not* a must in realizing significant tax benefits. And while some tax-structuring techniques can hurt the economics of your venture [see **Chapter Five**], the tax approaches we'll be talking about will make your oil and gas investment *more profitable*, rather than less profitable, on both a pre-tax and after-tax basis!)

There are other techniques you can legitimately use to increase the tax benefits of oil and gas. By "joint venturing" in oil with someone who is willing to bear that portion of venture costs which are not currently deductible—a technique referred to as "Functional Allocation"—*all* costs charged to your account are 100% deductible for federal income tax purposes. And the use of Leverage can raise the deductibility level—*as a percentage of your INITIAL cash investment*—to 200% to 500%.

As you'll see in later chapters, there is an economic price tag which must be paid if you wish to utilize Functional Allocation or Leverage to increase the deductibility of your expenditures. And that price tag may—or may not—be intelligent for you to pay. But, it's important to understand these techniques in plotting your overall investment strategy.

Finally, a "tax advantage" of oil and gas is that it is a truly economic investment area which doesn't have to rely upon tax benefits to have economic viability. The tax incentives which currently exist to encourage oil and gas exploration and development have been crucial in developing an *adequate* supply of domestic petroleum reserves. But as tax laws change, excellent investment opportunities remain—even though the country eventually will suffer due to insufficient domestic oil and gas reserves. This means that oil and gas is *much less vulnerable to changes in the tax laws* than other "tax-sheltered" investment areas.

—The Economic Potential of Oil and Gas. Even under "pre-flat tax" laws, no investment area exists where money can be made on the tax benefits alone. Properly understood, tax incentives merely *reduce the loss* on unprofitable ventures and *enhance the profitability* on those projects which possess intrinsic economic merit.

We've already mentioned that the inherent profitability of participation in the oil and gas search is the biggest "benefit" that oil and gas investment has to offer. Economic studies by a prestigious Wall Street investment banking firm—see **Figure One**— emphasize that the returns from oil and gas investment, even on a *pre-tax* basis, outstrip those available from other traditional investment areas such as housing, stocks and bonds. And analyses by two highly-respected firms have established that the returns to investors in SEC-registered "public" drilling programs have averaged in excess of an annual 20% "Money Market" rate, and, with selectivity, can exceed the return that a Certificate of Deposit paying *40% a year* would have provided![2]

These return figures are impressive. And they weren't doctored up by analysts who had been "bought and paid for" by the oil and gas industry. However, they do represent studies made prior to the enactment of the Economic Recovery Tax Act of 1981 ("ERTA"), which reduced the top federal income tax rate on "Ordinary Income" from 70% to 50%; prior to the Crude Oil Windfall Profit Tax, which imposes a special "excise tax" on domestically-produced crude oil; and prior to the precipitous drop in the price and demand for oil and natural gas, which commenced in 1982. And they don't reflect the implications, for *future* investments, of the possible enactment of a "flat tax."

So we have a question—and a legitimate one. Can we still say that oil and gas remains a potentially profitable investment area—and, particularly, *the* potentially most profitable investment area—in light of these changes in the tax laws, actual and contemplated, and in the economic conditions which govern today's oil and gas industry?

We'll have much more to say about these factors in **Chapter Three**. However, to summarize these present conditions impacting on oil and gas investment:

(1) *The Crude Oil Windfall Profit Tax no longer is a significant factor in analyzing current oil and gas investment.* Not only are the tax rates on the "Tier Three" oil which would be involved in today's investments relatively low; at present price levels, there is virtually no "windfall profit element" left to be taxed.[3]

(2) *Lower tax rates **increase the loss on unprofitable programs**, while **improving the return on profitable ones**.* If your purpose in oil is to find poor programs in which to invest, then you will be hurt by the fact that you are no longer being taxed at 70%. But if your investment objective is to find solid programs which offer good profit potential, your lower tax rate will let you keep more of your revenues on an after-tax basis.[4]

(3) *The drop in drilling costs since 1981, and the improvement in deal terms, has far more than offset the decline in the price of oil and gas.*

---

[2] See Stanger, "Drilling Fund Performance," **National Tax Shelter Digest** (December, 1982); King, "Oil and Gas Program Results: Simple Factors Make a Big Difference," **National Tax Shelter Digest** (March, 1983); King, "A Way to Get Rich Quick—Maybe," **National Tax Shelter Digest** (February, 1981).

[3] The Crude Oil Windfall Profit Tax is discussed in **Chapter Two**.

[4] Rate reductions below the present 50% level as a result of a "flat tax" would thus compensate for any loss of Percentage Depletion. See **Chapter Two**.

Last Ten Years	Return*	Last Five Years	Return*
1) Oil	22.9%	1) U.S. Stamps	26.6%
2) U.S. Coins	22.5%	2) Chinese Ceramics	23.7%
3) U.S. Stamps	21.9%	3) U.S. Coins	21.4%
4) Oriental Rugs	19.1%	4) Oil	21.2%
5) Gold	18.6%	5) Gold	17.3%
6) Chinese Ceramics	15.3%	6) Oriental Rugs	17.1%
7) Farmland	13.7%	7) Diamonds	13.7%
8) Silver	13.6%	8) Old Masters	13.7%
9) Diamonds	13.3%	9) Farmland	10.7%
10) Housing	9.9%	10) Housing	10.0%
11) Old Masters	9.0%	CPI	9.6%
CPI	8.6%	11) Stocks	7.7%
12) Stocks	3.9%	12) Silver	5.5%
13) Foreign Exchange	3.6%	13) Foreign Exchange	1.6%
14) Bonds	3.6%	14) Bonds	0.6%

*Compound annual rate of return

Last Year**	Return*	This Year***	Return*
1) Chinese Ceramics	36.5%	1) Bonds	11.4%
2) Stocks	25.3%	CPI	6.6%
3) Old Masters	22.9%		
4) U.S. Stamps	18.0%	2) Oil	6.3%
5) Oil	14.3%	3) Housing	3.4%
		4) Diamonds	0.0%
CPI	10.0%	5) Chinese Ceramics	-0.5%
6) Farmland	9.7%	6) Farmland	-0.9%
7) Housing	8.1%	7) Foreign Exchange	-1.9%
8) Diamonds	0.0%	8) U.S. Stamps	-3.0%
9) Oriental Rugs	-0.2%	9) Stocks	-10.5%
10) U.S. Coins	-8.0%	10) Oriental Rugs	-16.2%
11) Bonds	-9.6%	11) Old Masters	-22.0%
12) Gold	-13.9%	12) U.S. Coins	-27.8%
13) Foreign Exchange	-17.3%	13) Gold	-34.0%
14) Silver	-26.6%	14) Silver	-44.5%

** 6/80-6/81
***6/81-6/82

Source: Salomon Brothers Inc.

Source: "Ranking the Major Investment Vehicles," **Investor's Tax Shelter Report** (October; 1982) analyzing the results of a study by Salomon Brothers, Inc. Reprinted with permission.

FIGURE ONE: Comparative Rates of Return for Various Investment Types

Oil prices would have to drop below $15 a barrel before the profitability of today's search would fall below the *perceived* profitability of searching for oil in 1981, even if oil had remained at $40 a barrel.[5]

(4) *Enactment of a "flat tax" which eliminated the current deductibility of the costs of drilling productive wells ("Productive-Well IDCs") would require an adjustment in deal terms to reflect the change in tax laws.* However, the necessary adjustments can easily be quantified (see **Chapters Three** and **Five**); and many oil sponsors are *already* restructuring their deals to give you a better break in anticipation of the possible tax law changes.[6]

So if your investment objective is to make profitable investments while securing some added tax advantages along the way, and if you're willing to take a few minutes to learn how to invest *intelligently*, oil and gas is the investment area for you.

Most investors have been willing to admit that money can be made in oil and gas. But they've also associated oil and gas investment with a roller coaster ride of wild profits and even wilder losses. Most have also felt they lacked the expertise to select the *better* oil and gas opportunities. (And no one will deny that oil and gas investment offers its fair share of "dogs.")

Fortunately, as you'll see in **Chapter Three**, an intelligent *diversified* program will reduce the "peaks and valleys" of oil and gas to very manageable levels. And *selectivity* in oil and gas investment is much easier than you've probably imagined. (See **Chapter Five**.)

—**Ease of Analysis.** That's the next advantage of oil and gas investment. Believe it or not, oil and gas is the easiest of the investment areas to analyze—easier than real estate and easier than the stock market.

First, whether you want to invest ten thousand dollars, one hundred thousand dollars, or a million dollars a year, and whether you want to invest well-by-well or through a public or private limited partnership, there are hundreds of investment opportunities from which to choose.

Over 90% of the monies invested in limited partnerships are invested in oil and gas and real estate. Typically, about half of this investment is in oil

---

[5] Obviously, the unexpected decline in oil and gas prices adversely affected investors in partnerships formed in the late 1970s and early 1980s, where deals were being accepted by sponsors based upon erroneous price/demand assumptions. See "Oil & Gas Drilling Fund Performance Study," **The Stanger Report** (February, 1985). (Another reason for "time line" diversification. See **Chapter Three**.)

[6] This is a "no lose" situation for you as an investor. If the tax laws *are* changed, the improved deal terms have already compensated for the changes. But if the laws *aren't* changed, you've received a better deal—*plus* the same level of traditional tax benefits!

and gas. This means that there will be a *number of investment opportunities* to choose among, so that you can find one which is just right for your investment objectives, as well as one which you can check out to insure that the profit potential is truly there.

Secondly, there are *readily-available statistics* from which the performance of oil and gas investment in general, and the results to the investors of a particular program "sponsor," can be easily analyzed.

Finally, there are *well-established analytical techniques*—referred to as "due diligence"—through which the quality of a given program can be analyzed. And *qualified, independent consultants* are available to perform this analysis on your behalf.

In **Chapter Five**, we'll see just how easy it is for you to insure that such studies have been made on your behalf—and have been made properly!

—If Oil and Gas is All That Great, Why Does the Oilman Need Me? Oil and gas is a capital-intensive industry. All oil companies, large and small, are constantly looking for money to acquire additional exploration rights (referred to as "oil and gas leases"), to drill and test additional wells, and to install equipment on wells which appear capable of producing oil and gas in commercial quantities.[7]

The oil and gas industry tends to divide itself into two types of companies—a handful of industry giants, frequently referred to as the "Chase Group," which we'll call the "Majors," and thousands of smaller companies, referred to as "Independents."

Unlike most industries, which are controlled by a few large companies, the onshore domestic oil and gas search is dominated by the Independents. These Independents drill 90% of the wells, including the vast majority of the higher-risk "exploratory" wells which seek new discoveries of oil and gas, and are responsible for 75% of the dollars expended in the onshore search. The better Independents also tend to drill and operate wells more cheaply, and to be more effective oil finders, than the Majors.[8]

Both Majors and Independents spread their exploration dollars by joint venturing with other members of the oil and gas industry. The Majors secure the majority of their capital required to participate in this joint venturing through "internal generation of funds"—using the revenues from prior oil and gas discoveries to finance their ongoing oil and gas search.

---

[7] We'll discuss the mechanics of conducting the oil search below.

[8] These "better" Independents are usually run by oil and gas explorationists who were formerly employed—and trained—by the Majors.

Most Independents are newer companies and are growth-oriented. This means that their internally-generated funds, including the borrowing power which can be generated by pledging their oil and gas reserves in the ground, are quickly used up. To secure the capital necessary to engage in their typically aggressive search for new oil and gas reserves, most turn to an additional source of capital—outside investors.

Just as the oilman has a lot to offer you, you have a lot to offer the oilman. In addition to augmenting and spreading his capital, your investment dollars help him to *shift risk* by spending *your* dollars on the higher-risk aspects of the venture and through legitimate (and sometimes illegitimate) "promotion"—in other words, by having you bear a greater portion of venture costs than your share of venture revenues.

There is nothing wrong with the fact you are being promoted—so long as the promotional levels are not too high (more about this in **Chapter Five**) and the projects in which you participate have sufficient profit potential for you to bear that promotion without the project losing economic viability from your standpoint.

In the past, one of the advantages to the oilman of using outside investors as a capital source was that he could demand a higher promotional "spread"—a greater differential between cost share and revenue share— when he was dealing with outside investors than when he was "turning deals" within the industry. But informed (and properly represented) investors are currently able to cut just as good a deal with many high-quality oilmen as could an industry member.

As a matter of fact, some excellent oilfinders are now letting outside investors into their projects on *more* favorable terms than they will turn the projects within the industry. This is because you offer the oilman another advantage over dealing with an industry participant—you don't second guess him at every step of the way as to how the operation should be conducted. And many oilmen feel that this retention of control over the operations is just as important (and possibly more important) than the degree to which you are being promoted.[9]

This means that for smart oilmen and informed investors, there is a potential for a mutually-rewarding "partnership," under which each supplies something of true value to the other.

The Disadvantages and Risks of Oil and Gas Investment—In General. We never said that oil and gas investment was risk free; it's simply

---

[9] Remember, the men who head up that Independent often left a Major because they were tired of being second guessed!

that its risks are *misunderstood* and *overemphasized*. But any astute consideration of oil requires that you understand its risks, so you can structure a strategy which can greatly reduce those risks—and so you can be sure that oil and gas investment really is right for you.

The risks of oil fall into several categories:

(1) *The speculative nature of the oil and gas search*, which affects the oilman drilling for his own account just as much as it does you;

(2) Certain *unusual investment characteristics of oil*, not necessarily present in other investment areas, such as *delayed and unpredictable cash flow*; the need, in those oil ventures which offer the maximum profit potential, for *additional capital contributions* ("Assessments"); the fact that you will be *promoted* and that the venture will involve significant *conflicts of interest*; and—quite significant—that your role in the venture will be totally *passive* and will involve an *industry* which, to most investors, is *unfamiliar and confusing*;[10]

(3) *Tax DISADVANTAGES*, which must be understood and, if possible, eliminated or alleviated;

(4) *Risks of a PARTICULAR TYPE of oil and gas investment*, which we'll consider in a few moments when we talk about the different ways in which you can participate in oil and gas.

The offering document which the oilman submits to you when he solicits your participation in his venture will explain these risks, and many others, in nauseating detail.[11] All we're going to do here is highlight some of those risks which are most significant.

—The Speculative Nature of the Search for Petroleum—How the Oilman Finds and Produces Oil and Gas. Finding and producing oil and gas can—and has—been the source of many complete books.[12] However, let's spend just a moment considering the impact of the realities of the oil business on your investment decisions.

---

[10] It doesn't need to be confusing; that's one of the reasons for this book.

[11] Sometimes the oilman will attempt to intrigue you with his wonderful deal without "bothering" you with an offering document (or without a *complete* offering document). Run—don't walk—from these "opportunities." (See **Chapter Five**.)

[12] The premier non-technical book in this area is Norman J. Hyne's **Geology for Petroleum Exploration, Drilling and Production** (McGraw-Hill: 1983). Dr. Hyne has also prepared a brief "mini-book" which, in 30 minutes, will give you a layman's introduction to the oil and gas search. It's entitled **Finding and Producing Oil & Gas** (Energy Textbooks International, Inc.: 1985).

Oilmen don't find oil and gas, they find "traps"—places where oil and gas *may* have accumulated in commercial quantities.

Hydrocarbons were formed millions of years ago when a little-understood combination of heat, pressure, and the passage of time converted marine creatures buried in certain "sedimentary" rocks into oil and gas.

The oil and gas were not formed "in" the rocks, but in pore spaces *between* the rock particles. But the "source rocks" in which the hydrocarbons were formed did not contain sufficient pore space ("porosity") for commercial accumulations. Fortunately for the world's energy needs, these hydrocarbons then began to "migrate" to the surface of the earth.

Some of the oil and gas made it to the surface and were lost to us for all time through evaporation. In other instances, however, the migration of the hydrocarbons through the sedimentary channels to the surface was stopped by a "trap," where a high area in the sedimentary rock ran into an impermeable "cap rock." If the "reservoir rock" in which the oil and gas is now trapped contains sufficient porosity for large quantities of hydrocarbons to accumulate, and a sufficient interconnection from pore to pore so that the oil and gas can easily flow from one pore to another ("permeability"), conditions exist for a potentially attractive "discovery" of oil and gas.

Under present technology, the industry is unable to predict whether or not commercial accumulations of oil and gas *are* contained in an anticipated trap.[13] But through the "subsurface mapping" of information from wells previously drilled ("well control") and the use of various "geophysical" techniques such as "seismic" (measuring the echoes from sound waves sent into the ground), the geologist attempts to locate traps in areas where conditions are ripe for commercial oil and gas accumulation.

But look what can go wrong, even when the geologist is skilled at his job and has properly done his homework. We're dealing with very limited data in attempting to determine what went on, thousands of feet below the surface, millions of years ago. No oil or gas may ever have formed in the source rock; even if it did, it may not have been caught in the trap. There may not even be a trap; or it may not be located where we thought it was. The only way to find out is to drill a very expensive "exploratory well" to see whether or not we really have discovered a new oil or gas field.

(These uncertainties are why so many exploratory wells are non-productive—"dry holes"—either because there were *no* hydrocarbons present or

---

[13] There are certain "black box" techniques which their originators claim can actually find oil and gas, rather than traps. Some are questionable; others, while more reliable, tend to indicate the presence of *some* hydrocarbons, but not whether they are recoverable in commercial quantities.

there were *insufficient* hydrocarbons to justify the expensive "completion" and equipping of the well, which we'll discuss below.)

Even if a well is *productive*, this doesn't necessarily mean that it will prove *profitable*. If sufficient hydrocarbons are apparently present to justify completing and equipping the well, these steps will be taken even though the well will never "pay out"—return the costs of completing and equipping *plus* the costs of the original drilling.[14] And, as you'll see in **Chapter Three**, unless the well will return its cost ("pay out") several times over—*many* times over when our few exploratory "discoveries" must recoup not only their own costs but those of the numerous exploratory wells drilled which were not productive and/or commercial—your revenues received won't justify the dollars expended (much less the risk) in generating those revenues.

But why not let someone else take the risk of drilling exploratory wells, and simply limit our participation to the "exploitation" of the productive fields discovered by others? Even one out of three to one out of five "developmental wells"—wells drilled within a known oil and gas field—are non-productive.[15] And many developmental wells, particularly those which the oilman who discovered the oil and gas field is willing to turn over to others to drill, fall into the "productive but unprofitable" category of wells which will never return sufficient revenues quickly enough to justify their cost of drilling.[16]

Deciding *where* to drill is only one part of the risks involved in the oil and gas search. The conditions encountered *during the course of drilling and completing the well* can also be enough to increase the sales of tranquillizers to oilmen—*and* their investors.

First, once a "prospect has been originated" (the geologist has decided that a given area might contain an appropriate trap and thus be "prospective" for oil and gas), the right to explore must be secured from the landowner. This right of exploration is granted by a document referred to as an "oil and gas lease."[17]

---

[14] This is referred to as the doctrine of "sunk costs" or "yet-to-spend" economics: ignore the costs already spent and analyze whether the revenues now expected to be realized will justify the "yet-to-spend" completing and equipping costs.

[15] There are "sure thing" areas in which 90% to 100% of all wells drilled will be productive. However, the only *sure thing* about such wells is that very few of them are *profitable*. (See **Chapter Five**.)

[16] Keep in mind the distinction between: (i) the developmental wells which you drill to develop a productive exploratory prospect which YOU discovered, and (ii) developmental wells drilled on prospects discovered by SOMEONE ELSE, who is now willing to "turn" certain remaining developmental locations to you.

[17] The person granting the lease is referred to as the "lessor." The person securing the lease is referred to as the "lessee."

The landowner will be paid a cash consideration for granting the lease ("bonus"), plus additional compensation until a well is drilled ("delay rentals"). He will also receive a cost-free share of the oil and gas (or oil and gas sale proceeds) if hydrocarbons are produced ("royalty"). Also, the lease will be for a limited period of time, absent production; and if oil or gas is not discovered within this "primary term," the oilman's rights under the lease will terminate.

Often, the geologist who has "originated" the prospect idea won't have the money personally to put together the lease block, or the monies required to drill the well. If so, he will "turn" the prospect idea to someone else, again reserving a cost-free interest in production ("overriding royalty"). And the drilling party will frequently turn interests in the prospect to other oilmen—normally on a "promoted" basis—so that he has spread his cost and risk.[18]

Before the decision is made to drill, the oilman will prepare an estimate of well cost (an "AFE" or "Authority for Expenditure") and will compare this against the expected returns from the well, discounted to a "present worth" of the dollars and further adjusted to take into account the risks that the well will be non-productive or disappointing. If these *risk-adjusted* economics indicate an undiscounted return of from three to five to one if a developmental well is involved (a 3:1 to 5:1 "Return on Investment" or "ROI"), or a five to eight to one risk-adjusted return where exploratory drilling is involved, the decision will probably be a "go"—*if* the oilman can come up with the money to drill the well.[19] (See where you come in?)

Now the drilling engineer and wellsite geologist (both representing the company), and the "drilling contractor" (usually an independent contractor who will actually perform the drilling), take over. And all sorts of things can go wrong at this stage: the well can "blow out" as oil, gas or water enter the "wellbore" at abnormally high pressures, shooting to the surface; the sides of the well can collapse ("cave in"); fires can occur; corrosive or poisonous gasses can be encountered; equipment can jam or break off within the subsurface hole; the fluids ("drilling mud") which must be circulated within the wellbore for a variety of reasons while the well is being drilled may flow into surrounding rocks rather than remaining within the wellbore ("lost circulation"); or these fluids may destroy the productive capacity of the reservoir rock ("formation damage").

---

18 Notice that by the time the deal reaches *your* oilman, it may already have a number of "layers" of promotion tacked onto it. Notice also that your "working interest"—your cost-bearing share of the well—is considerably greater than your "revenue interest"—your share of well revenues.

19 In "sure thing" areas, the decision to drill may be based upon an expected 2:1 to 3:1 ROI—or lower if the promoter suspects his investor "mullets" don't understand oilpatch economics!

A good drilling engineer or drilling contractor will foresee and adquately prepare for most of these problems. But they can't foresee them all. And each problem that arises means, at best, extra time and money; and, at worst, a non-productive well.

Once the well has reached its objective ("total depth" or "TD"), the well must be evaluated. A number of "tests" are performed to determine the likely presence of hydrocarbons, including whether they are present in commercial quantities. Once this "casing point" has been reached (the testing is completed), a decision must be made as to whether or not to make the expensive "completion attempt" by lowering pipe ("casing") down the wellbore and cementing it to the sides of the well; blowing holes through this casing to permit the oil and gas to enter the wellbore ("perforation"); and performing various steps to stimulate the well so that it will produce faster ("fracing" and "acidizing"). If all goes well, production equipment, such as "christmas trees," pumps, "separators," and "stock tanks," are installed.

The mere fact that a well is "completed" does not necessarily mean that the completion attempt will prove successful or that the well will ever prove profitable. Thus, tens of thousands to millions of dollars may be legitimately spent on wells which still must be plugged and abandoned as "dry"; and many wells which initially flow in a fashion that leads the oilman controlling the well (the "operator") to order a new Mercedes very quickly cease to produce in paying quantities.

A final word about the oilfinding process. At various steps along the way, the oilman is required to estimate the oil and gas reserves that may lie under his "prospect." Obviously, such a determination must be made when a decision is being reached as to whether or not to drill a well; equally obviously, at this stage, the oilman has only a limited amount of "hard core" data on which to base that decision.

A similar determination must be made in deciding whether or not to complete and equip a well. Here, at least, the oilman has the information gained from drilling and testing the well. However, a scientific "guesstimate" is still involved.

After the well has been "put on stream" (production equipment has been installed and production has begun), the oilman must decide whether or not to drill additional wells on the prospect. At this stage, he will make a "volumetric" estimate of the recoverable reserves, based upon the porosity and permeability of the reservoir rock actually encountered in the well, plus experience in similar wells. However, volumetric estimates of reserves, though less of a guess than before, still tend significantly to overstate or understate the final recoverable reserves. (Guess which is more likely!)

After a well has been producing for a period of several years, reserves can be calculated on a "pressure decline" method. When properly performed by a qualified "reservoir engineer," this is a considerably more accurate method of estimating the recoverable *volume* of hydrocarbons. However, in estimating the profitability of the well, the oilman must still take into account *how rapidly* the reserves will be produced and *at what price* they can be sold—both a function of *demand*. And as we'll be discussing (and as you already know), these price/demand estimates can fool even the best of the experts.

—How Oil's Speculative Nature Affects You as an Investor. By now, it should be obvious that participating in the oil and gas search by the drilling of a single well is not merely a speculation—it's a *gamble*. Even if a developmental well is involved; even if you are participating in a "lease fund" which purchases leases for resale to other members of the oil and gas industry or a "completion fund" which merely shares in completion risks; and even if you are purchasing "proven" producing oil and gas reserves "in the ground," PARTICIPATING IN A ONE-SHOT OIL AND GAS INVESTMENT IS RISKY BUSINESS.

It should also be plain that, despite the speculative nature of the oil and gas business, a tremendous amount of *skill* is involved in the *intelligent* conduct of an oil and gas operation. Blindly choosing to invest with the first charismatic "promoter" who charms you with stories of "gushers" and tax benefits offers the royal road to bitter disappointment.

A key to intelligently investing in oil lies in remembering that the mere fact that a well is productive does not mean that it will prove profitable. Under the structuring of most oil deals, the oilman usually makes money *only* if a productive well is drilled. (See **Chapter Five**).[20] For this reason, few oilmen are intentionally going to drill a dry hole. But drill a *productive* well, and the oilman will often realize a handsome profit, even though your "reward," other than the return of a small portion of your cash, is non-existent.

So from a practical standpoint, your two major risks as an oil and gas investor—as long as you deal with someone who knows the oil and gas business and is good at what he does—are: (i) participating in the oil and gas search on an *undiversified basis*; or (ii) participating in *productive but unprofitable wells*.

On the other hand, as we'll discuss in greater detail before we leave the subject of the disadvantages and risks of oil and gas investment, if you will

---

[20] An exception to this can be wells drilled on a "turnkey" or fixed-price basis. See **Chapter Three**.

invest in oil on a **diversified** basis, and if you will be **selective** in choosing the persons with whom you invest, **the speculative nature of oil and gas will level out to manageable levels.**

—**The Other Risks of Oil and Gas Investment.** Besides the speculative nature of oil, we've mentioned that there are other risks of investing in oil and gas, such as oil's *unusual investment characteristics* (discussed in **Chapter Five**); the *tax pitfalls and tax disadvantages* that apply to oil and gas investment (discussed in **Chapter Two**); and the risks associated with *various types* of oil and gas investment (we'll discuss those below).

We'll leave these "other risks" until later in this book. But remember these points:

(1) *Oil and gas investment isn't right for everyone.* Early in **Chapter Five**, we'll help you determine if oil and gas is truly a suitable investment for you.

(2) *While conflicts of interest and being "promoted" are inherent in any investment, **excessive** promotion or **unreasonable** conflicts of interest (or conflicts of interest **unreasonably resolved**) can turn your investment into a disaster.* Later in **Chapter Five**, we'll show you how to spot these abusive proposals.

(3) *Oil's tax negatives must be taken into account in developing your investment strategy.* Often, the negatives can be reduced or eliminated. If not, they need to be taken into account in determining whether or not oil and gas investment really is suitable for your particular tax and financial picture. We'll get into all of that in **Chapter Two** and again in **Chapter Four**.

—**Living With and Managing the Risks of Oil.** Assuming that oil and gas is generally appropriate for your investment objectives, an *intelligent investment strategy* can reduce these risks to levels that are no greater than those of most "traditional" investments. And since the oilman must pay you a premium to attract investment dollars because of these *perceived* risks, this means that oil and gas offers the potential—indeed, the strong *probability*—of high rewards with only moderate (possibily relatively *low*) risk.

That isn't to say that oil and gas investment is *risk free*; no investment area is. Even a savings account has its risks. (Substandard return, for one.) But for an appropriate investor, an intelligent investment strategy will reduce those risks to levels you can live with.

Here are the steps in that intelligent investment strategy (the details will be discussed in later chapters):

(1) **Analyze how oil and gas fits into your overall financial and tax position and investment strategy.** (We'll get into that in **Chapter Five**). This will establish *your* suitability as an oil and gas investor.

(2) **Invest on a DIVERSIFIED basis**. In **Chapter Three**, we'll see just exactly what "diversified investment" means in oil and gas, and we'll determine whether diversification actually levels oil's speculative side.

(3) **Be SELECTIVE in choosing with whom, and in which programs, you invest**. The oilman who is managing your venture must be a *good oilfinder* who knows how to pick (or has access to) quality oil prospects; he must have *integrity* (some very good oilmen are much better at making money for themselves than they are at making money for you); he must be *properly staffed and properly financed*; and the deal he offers you must be *properly structured* (the prospect doesn't exist which can't be turned into a disaster for the investors if it's too highly promoted). And in **Chapter Five**, we'll show you EXACTLY how to make those determinations.

The Many Types of Oil and Gas Investment—In General. There are various ways of participating in the oil and gas search. One is to buy stock in various oil and gas companies, or in a particular company in which you have confidence.

There's nothing wrong with backing your belief in oil by this type of traditional investment. However, when you "participate" in the oil and gas search through the purchase of stock, you will make or lose money based on the *market-place reaction* to the oil and gas industry in general, and the companies whose stock you hold in particular. While your stock may provide predictable dividends and a liquid investment—characteristics which *direct participation* in oil and gas ventures doesn't offer—this won't be true if the stock of the company is closely held, or, as is often the case, if company revenues are being reinvested in ongoing activities. More importantly, unless the market reacts favorably to your company, you won't make any money, no matter how well your company is actually doing: there is no direct participation in the consequences of its activities.

The types of investments we're talking about are *"direct participation" investments*, where the consequences of the venture's activities flow directly through to you. Most people think of this as meaning that the *tax consequences* can be directly reflected on their own federal income tax returns; and this is certainly true. But of more significance, the *economic consequences*, including cash flow from operations, also directly flow through to your own pocket. For this reason, this type of investment might be best characterized as "joint venture financing"—you will be joint venturing with a member of the oil and gas industry in certain activities which he wants to undertake, and in which you wish to participate.

The flow-through of tax and economic consequences results from investing through a "pass through" ownership vehicle such as a co-ownership or limited partnership, rather than an "indirect ownership" vehicle such as a corporation.[21]

In deciding how you want to invest in oil, there are several other general choices for you to make besides this indirect/direct investment distinction. First, you need to choose between "direct" ownership as a co-tenant ("Fractional Interest" investment), and "indirect" ownership as a participant in a partnership (a "program" approach). Next, you need to decide whether you want to invest in a "public" program which has been registered with the Securities and Exchange Commission, or in a "private" offering which is properly exempt from SEC registration, usually under the Commission's "Regulation D."

The pros and cons of each of the approaches are discussed in **Chapter Five**.

—**"Drilling" Investments.** Traditionally, the most common method of investing in oil has been by participating in *drilling*—either on a "well-by-well" basis; through a "program" involving a single, designated ("specified") prospect; through a program which involves a group of diversified, though still designated, prospects; or through a "blind pool" or "blank check" partnership, in which the wells to be drilled are not designated, but left to the discretion of the general partner, subject to certain hopefully well-defined guidelines concerning the *types* of wells in which the partnership will participate.[22]

In an oil and gas drilling venture, you provide all or a part of the monies required to acquire the leases and drill, complete and equip oil and gas wells which seek to discover new oil and gas fields ("exploratory drilling") or develop existing fields ("developmental drilling"). (This is the "finding" process we've just discussed.)

Drilling ventures offer you the best use of the tax incentives available to the oil and gas industry, both as to tax treatment of expenditures and tax treatment of revenues.[23] They also offer the highest profit potential of any of the oil and gas investment areas. Drilling is also the most readily available oil and gas investment, and, *so long as you know what you're doing*, the easiest to analyze, due to the availability of extensive data and established "screening" techniques.

---

[21] The tax considerations involved in making sure that the benefits *do* directly flow through to you are discussed in **Chapter Two**.

[22] For the pros and cons of specified properties versus blind pool investment, see **Chapter Five**.

[23] See **Chapter Two**.

On the other hand, particularly on an undiversified basis, participating in drilling provides you maximum exposure to oil's risks: not only its speculative nature, but its delayed cash flow and assessments, and the confusion that has often existed concerning *how* to analyze an oil and gas proposal and *how* to intelligently invest in oil — a confusion that we hope will be significantly reduced for you after reading this book.

So if you can't afford to invest on a diversified basis; if early and predictable cash flow is one of your major investment objectives; or if you are not willing to take the time to learn how to invest on a selective basis, oil and gas drilling is *not* right for you.

—Production Purchase ("Income") Programs—In General.
Another popular way to participate in oil is to invest in a partnership which will purchase "proven" oil and gas properties—interests in wells which have already been drilled and are currently producing.

The *"income" program*, rather than drilling for, and establishing, an indeterminate quantity of hydrocarbons, acquires producing oil and gas properties drilled and developed by other parties by putting a price tag on the estimated future income stream from these "in-the-ground" oil and gas reserves. These properties must possess a sufficient production history for a petroleum reservoir engineer to calculate, with a relative level of comfort, the quantity of recoverable oil and gas reserves and the length of time which it will take to produce those reserves. Then, based upon various pricing assumptions, the engineer will calculate the estimated revenue stream by year and will discount these "future net revenues" to arrive at the "discounted present worth" of this revenue stream. Another discount for profit and risk— a "second haircut"—is then applied to arrive at the "present value" of the income stream.

The advantages of "income" program participation are that you will be acquiring a *relatively* stable and *relatively* predictable income stream: in other words, you are trading off a portion of oil's upside potential for reduced risk.[24] On the other hand, absent a reliance on leverage in acquiring the program properties[25], there is little chance of a "wipe out" (or any *major* impairment of your original capital investment) in an income program investment. Also, if oil and gas prices should increase at a faster rate than was assumed in estimating the future net revenues, or if the discount rate applied

---

[24] Many income programs contain a reinvestment feature which provides for an automatic reinvestment of a portion of your revenues—often the "return of capital" element—so that your "income stream," at least in theory, can continue at a predictable level indefinitely, rather than declining—and eventually terminating—when the reserves are depleted.

[25] The use of leverage in acquiring producing properties will be discussed below.

is too high as a result of a decline in the estimated inflation rate—both a possibility at the present time, particularly in view of the depressed condition of both prices and the industry in general—your "modest" return from an "income" program may prove to be quite spectacular.

Since income programs purchase reserves in the ground, rather than *drilling* for reserves, there is little front-end deductibility in an income program—your dollars are going for "capital" items, such as the reserves themselves and the equipment necessary to produce those reserves. Also, *Percentage* Depletion is not available to shelter the revenues from purchased properties, although *Cost* Depletion will be. However, while production purchase programs are not generally considered to be "tax shelters," depreciation of equipment provides some tax relief; and, since the majority of your subscription dollars *is* being spent for the acquisition of the reserves in the ground, Cost Depletion will shelter a far greater percentage of your production revenues in an income program than it would if a drilling venture were involved.[26]

The advantages of an "income" program are very real, particularly if you are one of those who feels that, in a few years, oil and gas prices will again be on the rise. (The desperate need of many members of the oil and gas industry, large and small, for ready cash is leading a number of companies to sell their in-the-ground reserves for what may prove to be "bargain basement" prices.) On the other hand, certain over-zealous advocates of income programs have characterized them as "bond" quality investments, with partially tax-sheltered revenues (true), a higher-than-average yield (often true), and virtually *no* downside risk (not so true). So just as it was necessary to look at the pros *and cons* of participating in drilling to arrive at an *intelligent* decision concerning its suitability as an investment area for you, it's equally necessary to understand the *downsides*—as well as the upsides—of income program investment.

First, let's consider some of the "generally" accepted disadvantages of an income program:

(1) *The tax characteristics are less favorable than in drilling.* Other than the ACRS amortization of the equipment, there are no tax "incentives" involved: the portion of your revenues returned tax free simply represents the return of your original capital investment.[27]

---

[26] These tax concepts are explored in **Chapter Two.**

[27] For the distinction between "artificial" and "economic reality" tax consequences, see **Chapter Two.**

(2) *Typically, there is a tremendous competition for attractive producing properties.*[28] Since less than 100% of your dollars are available for the purchase of those properties due to the front-end dilution which is typical of *any* limited partnership offering, your dollars are working at a competitive disadvantage. Also, your monies may have to "sit" while the general partner finds appropriate reserve acquisitions.[29] this hurts from a "time value" standpoint, can lead to some delays in that "rapid" cash flow, and can even cause a stampede to acquire *something*, even if the acquisition is not all that attractive.

Now, let's look at some less understood, but even more significant "truths":

(1) *You are acquiring a **commodity**, with all the risks that this entails.* While a qualified petroleum engineer can estimate, with considerable accuracy, the *volume* of reserves your company is acquiring (assuming a "mature" property which has been producing for a sufficient period of time to permit reserves to be calculated on a "pressure decline" rather than a "volumetric" basis), it's much more difficult to be totally comfortable in arriving at the *price* at which these reserves will sell or the *rapidity* with which they will be recovered.[30] This is the reason that investors in income programs formed in the early 1970s found that their "modest"-return investments in fact returned huge multiples on their money; this is also the reason that investors in the income programs of the late 1970s to earlier 1980s may be faced with little or no return on their investment—or even an impairment of their capital!

(2) *The realistic "target" returns of income programs—about 10% to 12%—are significantly lower than the returns that should be available through selective drilling program investment.*[31] If what we

---

[28] Here, an interesting distinction arises between the huge "public" income programs, which are able to compete for large reserve packages that small "private" partnerships can't touch, but aren't able to look at smaller acquisitions which might be more readily available at "fire sale" prices.

[29] Again, a distinction between the smaller private offerings, which typically designate their property or properties (the plus: they/you know what's to be acquired; the minus: less diversification and the costs of tying up the property, often months before it can be acquired) and the public programs, which are typically structured as "blind" (or partially blind) pools.

[30] How predictable are oil and gas prices? For a one-page "primer," see the "From the Editor" comments of Ron Cooper, entitled "A (Gulp) Consensus," in the February, 1985 **Oil & Gas Investor**.

[31] See "Returns to Expect From Newly Formed Oil & Gas Income Funds," **The Stanger Report** (February, 1984).

have—and will—discuss concerning diversification and the leveling of risk convinces you that drilling is not the "roll of the dice" you may have thought it to be, why settle for the poorer return?

Is this to say that income programs are unrewarding investments? Certainly not. As long as you understand their "commodity" nature—which can be a plus as well as a minus—participating in the acquisition of producing reserves can be a lower-risk method of participating in oil and gas, with a significant upside potential if prices increase. However, since an income program is looking for a significant multiple return, even after risk adjustment, income programs are even more susceptible to unexpected downturns in oil and gas prices or demand than is oil and gas drilling.

An interesting investment area? Yes. The equivalent of a high-yield, low-risk bond? No.

—The Impact of Leverage. The "creator" of the public income program was Petro-Lewis, which sponsored its first SEC-registered offering in 1970 and absolutely dominated the market until 1981.

Investors in early Petro-Lewis partnerships realized dramatic returns. In part, this was due to the unexpected level of the increase in oil and gas prices. Petro-Lewis investors in these early partnerships also benefited, however, from Petro-Lewis' borrowing policies: the partnerships were heavily leveraged, borrowing as much as two dollars in the form of "production loans," collateralized by the programs' reserves, for each dollar of equity capital invested. But these same borrowing policies created a disaster for investors in later partnerships—and for Petro-Lewis—when oil and gas prices and demand suffered their equally dramatic (and equally unexpected) collapse in the early 1980s.

Just as a bank will loan money against real estate, income-producing oil and gas properties can serve as collateral for loans which it is assumed can be retired by the properties' future income stream.[32] Once a well has been "on stream" for a sufficient period of time to permit the preparation of relatively reliable reserve evaluations, most "oil banks" will loan the owner of the reserves between 40% and 60% of his expected future net revenues, taking a lien on production revenues and the reserves in the ground.[33]

---

[32]Banks will not accept expected returns from wells *to be drilled* as collateral, irrespective of the geological merit of the prospect.

[33]As an additional protection to the lender, the loan will further be limited to an amount which should "pay out" from the production revenues within some specified period of time. (This period may vary from as short as three years to as long as eight years, depending upon the attitude of the banking community toward oil and gas lending at any particular time.)

There are pros and cons to leveraging in income programs. The obvious advantages are the ability to increase the amount of reserves acquired, as well as the percentage of dollars that are "going into the ground" (being used for property acquisition). Assuming that return levels exceed the cost of borrowing, your return, as a percentage of your cash investment, should also be enhanced. And that return can increase dramatically if prices rise to a higher level than was taken into account in estimating the future revenue stream.

The obvious disadvantage is that risk has been significantly increased: a further drop in oil or natural gas prices or demand, which, in a non-leveraged program, might simply reduce your return, could result in an actual impairment of capital in a leveraged program.

The "double-edged sword" aspects of leveraged investment are discussed in detail in **Chapter Four**. However, as mentioned above, participation in a successful drilling program should result in a multiple return of your invested dollars, so that modest declines in supply or demand could be withstood. Since income program investment simply involves purchasing a supposedly "established" income stream at a modest discount, the downside of leverage can prove much more serious in this type of investment than it might in a drilling venture.[34]

There aren't any rights or wrongs as to selecting an income program in which leverage is prohibited (or not expected to play any significant role) or one in which leverage will be utilized by the partnership in an aggressive fashion: it's simply a question of your investment objectives. If your reason for selecting an income program over oil and gas drilling is the *relative* predictability of the revenue stream and the *relative* safety of your capital, stay away from programs which intend to augment your cash contributions with additional borrowed funds.[35] But if you are interested in speculating on improved price and demand, a leveraged production purchase investment permits you to "gamble" on what will happen in this area without any significant gamble on the *volume* of reserves which your partnership will own.[36]

---

[34] Of course, this is one of the reasons for—and one of the protections of—the "second discounting" utilized to reduce the present *worth* of the estimated future net revenue to its present *value*.

[35] While many publicly-registered income programs still permit up to 50% borrowing, some either prohibit or drastically reduce any use of leverage in property acquisitions.

[36] Borrowing in SEC-registered income programs involves "project leverage"—the general partner is funding the acquisition of the properties in part through borrowing against their collateral value. Some private partnerships also provide an opportunity for "investment leverage"—a portion of your normal equity contribution is also borrowed, relying upon your personal letter of credit or surety bond as collateral for the loan, thus increasing both the potential rewards *and risks* of leverage. See **Chapter Four**.

—**"Combination" Programs.** Increasing attention is currently being focused on "combination" programs—partnerships which engage both in the purchase of producing oil and gas properties and in the drilling of wells.

Some combination programs primarily participate in new wells on previously undrilled locations on the partially-developed leases acquired by the partnership or in "in-fill" drilling—the drilling of additional wells *within* an existing drilling and spacing unit, where "increased density spacing" has now been ordered by the appropriate state conservation agency to permit a more rapid (or more effective) extraction of the already-proven oil and gas reserves. While under current law, the Intangible Drilling and Development Costs incurred in such drilling are still deductible for federal income tax purposes, you'll only be able to claim Cost (and not Percentage) Depletion on the production from the in-fill drilling, and may also be limited to Cost Depletion on any additional developmental drilling within the same reservoir from which the "proven" wells acquired by the partnership are also producing.[37]

Some combination programs, rather than simply drilling "exploitation wells" on the same productive leases which the partnerships are acquiring with their "income purchase" dollars, use the portion of their subscription proceeds committed to production purchase to reduce downside risk, and commit their drilling dollars to the higher-risk (and potentially higher-reward) drilling of wells on totally unrelated prospects.

Since, historically, income programs and drilling programs appeal to significantly differing investment objectives, combination offerings have had relatively little success in the market place.[38] But as investors have become more risk-averse, particularly as "flat tax" proposals indicate that, in the future, more "hard dollars" may be at risk and drilling dollars may no longer be currently deductible,[39] various techniques have been developed to reduce the risks of oil and gas drilling without totally eliminating oil's upside potential.

One commonly-touted method of reducing the risks of oil and gas drilling is to participate in programs which are drilling developmental wells in "sure thing" areas where 90% to 100% of the wells are "successful," i.e., completed as productive wells. Unfortunately, as discussed in **Chapter Five**,

---

[37] See **Chapter Two** for an examination of these tax consequences.

[38] Only about five percent of the monies invested in 1984 in SEC-registered oil and gas limited partnerships was invested in combination programs.

[39] The impact of certain proposed tax changes on the economics of oil and gas investment is discussed in **Chapter Three**.

such programs are seldom *profitable*. (Remember what we said above about productive but unprofitable wells?)

Another approach to reducing the risks of drilling is the "Zero Coupon Bond" program. In such partnerships, a portion of your agreed subscription is used to purchase a debt security which pays no interest until maturity, but whose value at that time will equal your subscription to the program.

The Zero Coupon Bond has the advantage of significantly reducing downside risk. (Of course, the same result could be accomplished by reducing your subscription to the program and purchasing your own equivalent security.) The disadvantage, other than the obvious one that only a portion of your money is going into the potentially higher return of oil and gas drilling, is that you have still lost the *use of your money* if additional revenues aren't generated by the drilling.

A combination program gives you less assurance that your capital will not be impaired: after all, the production revenues, even over time, may not equal the *full amount* of your subscription if the drilling activities of your partnership are unsuccessful; and you are still subject to price/demand decline risks even as to your production revenues. But under normal circumstances, the returns from an intelligent acquisition of producing properties should be higher than the interest factor on the Zero Coupon Bond; and you also will share in the upside of any unexpected *increases* in oil or gas price and demand. (There's no upside to a Zero Coupon Bond!) So for the investor who likes oil and gas, but wants some downside protection, combination programs offer some very real benefits.

—"Master" Limited Partnerships ("MLPs"). A current "hot button" on Wall Street is the Master Limited Partnership, or "MLP."[40]

Master Limited Partnerships are formed by offering to "roll up" (exchange) limited partnership interests in a number of existing partnerships for interests in a newly-formed "master" partnership, with the partnerships then being consolidated.[41] The interests in the new partnership are referred to as "depository receipts" or "units."

MLPs have some of the attributes of an income program and—in some instances—a drilling program. While some MLPs are self-liquidating, others distribute a portion of the cash flow from the producing properties

---

[40] For a detailed discussion of Master Limited Partnerships, see Sheehan, "Critical Mass," **Oil & Gas Investor** (June, 1984). See also "Oil & Gas Master Limited Partnerships," **The Stanger Register** (August, 1985); "Master Limited Partnerships," **The Stanger Report** (June, 1985); "Master Limited Partnerships Part Two: New Offerings," **The Stanger Report** (July, 1985).

[41] In some instances, an oil company will transfer certain of its assets to a partnership (a "roll out"), and offer interests in that partnership to outside investors.

developed by the acquired partnerships, and use the balance to acquire additional properties or to drill developmental or even exploratory wells.[42]

Even in "active" Master Limited Partnerships, a portion of the cash flow is distributed to the investors. (Since the MLP is a partnership, not a corporation, there is no double taxation of the revenues.)[43] Furthermore, Cost Depletion is available to shelter the distributions from taxation, in whole or in part; and any IDC or similar deductions generated by the activities of the partnership will flow through to the investors as well. And if the value of the partnership's assets grow as a result of its activities, the value of the depository receipt will also increase.[44]

The flow-through of tax benefits, and potential for income and growth, are all cited as advantages of the MLP. Also cited is the diversification provided the limited partners, due to the large number of properties involved. However, the main excitement over the Master Limited Partnership has been the liquidity of the partnership interests, since many of the MLPs have registered their units with one of the major stock exchanges.

The lack of liquidity for limited partnership interests has always been looked at as one of the disadvantages of oil and gas "program" investment.[45] Most sophisticated partnerships provide a "redemption" feature, pursuant to which investors are given an opportunity to sell their partnership interests to the general partner; some program sponsors also make periodic "exchange offers" through which the investor can exchange his partnership interests for stock of some corporation, normally that of the corporate general partner.[46] However, none of these "solutions" has proved a totally satisfactory answer to the liquidity problem. The Master Limited Partnership is thus being touted by some as the "perfect" method of participating in oil, either through an exchange of your existing partnership interests or by purchasing MLP units, either at the time of original issue or through the secondary market.

Before deciding to exchange your wife and children for units in a Master Limited Partnership, you need to understand that participating in an MLP has its problems as well. While the advantages of this approach to oil are very

---

[42] MLPs will also offer to acquire producing properties for unissued MLP units. Since this "contribution" of property to the MLP for an interest in that partnership is a tax-free transaction—see **Chapter Two**—it makes the MLP a more desirable purchaser.

[43] See **Chapter Two**.

[44] Remember, however, that the distribution of production revenues is depleting the original asset base.

[45] This "liquidity" issue is discussed in Lewis, "In Search of Liquidity," **Oil & Gas Investor** (December, 1983).

[46] Redemption and Exchange features are discussed in **Chapters Five** and **Six**.

real, the partnership will only fare well if it is run by quality management.[47] And even the best management won't necessarily overcome the inherent risks of either purchasing producing properties or drilling for oil, which we've just discussed. Furthermore, if there is any game-playing in the relative valuation of the interests being acquired, or if the market value of the units declines, you may find that your unit is less valuable than the limited partnership interest which you exchanged for it.[48] And even the benefits of liquidity—the Master Limited Partnership's most hailed attribute—may not be available in smaller MLPs if the general partner is unable to establish a trading market.

There are certain tax aspects of the Master Limited Partnership of which you should be aware. While Cost Depletion will be available to you, as well as the flow-through of the deductions and other tax benefits created by the partnership's activities, Percentage Depletion will not be available. Also, as a result of the Deficit Reduction Act of 1984, new exchanges of partnership interests for partnership interests can no longer be made on a tax-free basis.

—**Other Types of Oil and Gas Investment.** Participation in drilling ventures, the purchase of producing properties, or a combination of the two, represent the most popular methods of investing in oil: over 95% of the dollars invested in SEC-registered oil and gas investments in 1984 were invested in these three types of limited partnerships. The Master Limited Partnership is simply a continuation of these basic ways of sharing in oil's potential through drilling or the acquisition of "reserves in the ground." However, there are other ways of investing in oil and gas which you may wish to consider.

Completion Funds provide the money for equipping oil and gas wells once testing has been concluded and it's determined that the test results justify a "completion attempt." The Completion Partnership thus "gets a look at the bottom of the hole" before *its* dollars must be put at risk.

Don't get the idea that "there's no risk in completion."[49] Many wells, upon completion, prove productive but not profitable. And a number of completion attempts fail. But by avoiding the risks of *drilling*, a Completion Fund

---

47 To date, the MLP returns don't seem to be equalling the return levels of the "better" oil and gas drilling programs. Also, since most MLPs are issued, and traded, at prices higher than their underlying asset value, an inability on the part of the partnership to add to its assets on a profitable basis could have a most adverse impact on unit value.

48 Most MLP units are currently selling for less than their original issuance price.

49 If you have any doubt in this regard, read Ben Daviss' article, "Petroleum Primer—The Compleat Well" in the May, 1982 issue of **Oil & Gas Investor** magazine.

For a useful discussion of Completion Funds, also see Thompson, "Get a Piece of the Pipe," **Oil & Gas Investor** (March, 1983).

eliminates at least one of the most speculative aspects of the oil and gas search.

Since investors in a Completion Fund bear none of the costs of drilling, there are no deductions for Intangible Drilling and Development Costs—the most common method of creating high initial deductibility through oil and gas investment. However, amortization of equipment costs, normally utilizing the ACRS method, and claiming the Investment Tax Credit where available, will provide some tax benefits.[50] And through the use of Leverage, initial deductibility can be raised either to 100% of your initial cash investment, or even to "excess write-off" levels—with all the other consequences that leveraged investment also entails.[51]

As in a drilling program investment, the profitability of your investment in a Completion Fund will depend both on the speculative factors affecting *the search* for oil and gas (as contrasted with purchasing proven reserves) and the quality of the prospects in which your partnership is participating. (Although you've eliminated the pre-completion risks, participating in the costs of completing a series of mediocre wells has never made anyone—except the program sponsor—any money.) The structure of the venture—both as between you and your general partner and your partnership and those parties who are contributing the drilling dollars—will also have a major impact on partnership profitability. So, as in any oil-oriented venture, *diversification* and *selectivity* are the keys to profitable Completion Fund investment.

Investing in a *Lease Acquisition Fund* is another way of participating in the upside of oil and gas while eliminating *some* of oil's downside risks. Such partnerships acquire oil and gas leases, then "turn" (assign) them to other oilmen for the actual development of the leases, reserving an interest in any oil or gas produced from productive wells drilled on the leases.

Some Lease Acquisition Funds are "inventory" funds, which primarily acquire leases which the general partner intends to transfer within a relatively short period of time to an affiliated drilling program which he is also sponsoring. The sponsor benefits, since he isn't required to tie up his own limited capital in maintaining an expensive lease inventory. You benefit, since you have reduced (though not eliminated) the risk that the leases will never be resold and developed. But in reducing your risk, you have also eliminated your upside: the "inventory" funds usually resell the leases to the sponsor's drilling ventures at cost plus a mark up which equates only to an

---

[50] For a discussion of these tax consequences, see **Chapter Two**.

[51] See **Chapter Four**.

"interest allowance" on that original cost. While your partnership will be permitted to retain an interest in production as an additional consideration for having provided the necessary capital for leases, that interest will normally be relatively small—a one to three percent "overriding royalty interest."

Other Lease Acquisition Funds are structured as "trading" funds: leases are acquired by the partnership for resale to unaffiliated members of the oil and gas industry. The leases acquired by such partnerships often cover higher risk, higher reward exploratory or controlled exploratory prospects,[52] which may prove harder to "turn" and have a high likelihood of being non-productive even if drilled, but which offer a greater profit potential, both in the size of the production interest which can be reserved (and possibly the cash-on-cash profit paid by the assignee on the transfer of the leases) and the value of the reserved interest in production which will be realized if the leases can be turned and any resulting wells are productive.

In the typical Lease Acquisition Fund, you'll participate in the potential rewards of a successful drilling effort without sharing in the costs or risks of drillling or completing those wells.[53] However, just as in Completion Funds, this doesn't mean that your investment is risk free. Oil and gas leases give the lessee the right, *for a limited period of time*, to explore for oil and gas. If the leases selected by your general partner are not on high quality prospects, or, irrespective of the quality of the prospects, if a shortage of drilling capital makes it difficult to sell even high quality leases, you may be forced to resell your leases for far less than was paid for them. An even greater threat—you may watch your leases expire before they can be sold at *any* price. Furthermore, during the holding period before the leases can be resold, your Lease Fund must have the necessary capital reserves to pay periodic "delay rentals"

---

[52] The distinction between developmental, exploratory, and controlled exploratory prospects is discussed in **Chapter Five**.

[53] This is true if, as in most Lease Acquisition Funds, your reserved interest in production is a non-cost-bearing interest such as a Net Profits Interest, Overriding Royalty Interest, or Production Payment. On the other hand, some Lease Acquisition Funds permit the general partner to reserve a Carried Working Interest or Reversionary (Subordinated) Working Interest, which could share in *some* costs of drilling, completing, or reworking wells. Although this increases your upside potential even further, it also increases your risk.

As to the nature of these various interests which can be reserved when a lease is transferred to some other party for drilling, see Whitcomb, "A Glossary of Petrolese," **Oil & Gas Investor** (November, 1983), reproduced in the **Appendix** to this book. See also, "Options in Interests Assigned and Reserved Under the Farmout," contained in Mosburg (ed.), **Contracts Used in Oil & Gas Operations** (Energy Textbooks International, Inc.: 1985).

to the lessor or your leases will automatically terminate. (Thus, the greater potential risks of the "trading" fund.)[54]

The costs of evaluating and acquiring oil and gas leases are not currently deductible for federal income tax purposes and can be recovered only through Cost Depletion or as an Abandonment Loss if the leases terminate before they can be sold.[55] This means that participation in a Lease Acquisition Fund, absent leverage, creates virtually no currently deductible expenditures.[56] And there are also some special tax problems that arise when leases acquired by your partnership are disposed of.

A final type of oil and gas investment to consider is a *Royalty Fund.* These partnerships acquire the right to participate, on a cost free basis, in any oil and gas produced from wells drilled on a specified tract of land.

The "Non-Participating Royalty Interests" which such programs acquire create no obligation—or right—to drill wells on the lands to which the royalty interests pertain. Thus, unlike the Lease Acquisition Fund, you and your general partner will have less control over the development of the land. On the other hand, the majority of these royalty interests will have a perpetual duration, so if a well is *ever* drilled on the land, you will share in the production.[57]

The risk in a Royalty Fund is that wells may never be drilled on the lands to which your royalties pertain, or that the amount of production received when wells are drilled doesn't justify the price paid for the royalty. (Land and mineral owners usually insist on a relatively handsome consideration before parting with an interest in future production when that purchase is not coupled with the obligation to drill which a lease would impose if the

---

[54] The nature, risks and potential rewards of investing in leases are discussed in "Lease Acquisition Funds: Real Estate Deal, or Oil Play?", **Investor's Tax Shelter Report** (May, 1982), and Lenzini, "Mr. Landman, Bring Me a Dream," **Oil & Gas Investor** (May, 1981).

[55] See **Chapter Two**. As discussed in that chapter, this Cost Depletion recovery will normally be valueless to you if you are alternatively permitted, as an "Independent Producer," to claim Percentage Depletion.

[56] A "100% deductible" Lease Acquisition Fund can be created by heavy reliance on leverage—the interest expense on the loan equalling your initial cash contribution. (Note that this creates the same economic and tax considerations that are involved in any leveraged investment in oil and gas: see **Chapter Four**.)

[57] In some instances, the royalty will be limited to production pursuant to some existing lease (an "Overriding Royalty Interest"). Other times, your right to participate in production might terminate if the land isn't successfully developed for oil or gas purposes within some specified period of time (a "Term Royalty Interest").

Some of the royalties acquired by your partnership could relate to currently producing wells. If this is the case, you're engaging in a variation of an "income" investment.

interest were not to terminate.) Still, eliminating any necessity for participating in drilling or completion costs, and avoiding a termination of your rights if a well isn't drilled within a relatively short period of time, is a real advantage of Royalty Fund investment.

Each of the investment areas just discussed preserve much of the high profit potential of participating in the *search* for oil and gas without exposing you to certain of the risks of oil and gas *drilling*. However, each has its own peculiar risks. Furthermore, Completion Funds, Lease Acquisition Funds, and Royalty Funds are relatively new investment vehicles: this means that there is less experience to draw on regarding how such programs are working in practice, how the ventures should be structured, and the actual "track record" of investors in prior partnerships offered by this (or *any*) general partner. There will also be fewer of these partnerships for you to select among.

For an informed and discriminating investor, the relative newness of the investment areas may offer some very real opportunities—and some very real potential disasters. The bottom line? Investigation and selectivity are an *absolute must* before participating in such programs.

CHAPTER TWO
OIL AND TAXES

How Tax Laws Impact on Investment Return. As we discussed in **Chapter One**, the purpose of this book is to help you **make money** through oil and gas investment. But in determining whether or not you are "making money" from any kind of investment—and how much money you are (or aren't!) making—we have to consider the impact of federal income tax laws on investment return.

Tax laws affect investment profitability in two ways. First, and most obviously, they affect AFTER-TAX "income"—the only figure that counts— by determining how much of your *revenues* you're permitted to keep after Uncle Sam has taken his share. Second, they determine how much of the *cost* of your investment must come strictly from your own pocket and how much will be "paid for by Uncle Sam" through a reduction in taxes on your otherwise taxable revenues. In other words, in analyzing investment economics on an *after-tax* basis, you've got to look at both the tax treatment of your expenditures (that determines after-tax COST) and the tax treatment of your receipts from the venture (that determines after-tax INCOME) to arrive at after-tax profit—or loss!

There is one other factor that you must consider: the *time value of money*. The *timing* of expenditures and receipts always affect their true cost or value to us. And timing plays a particularly important role when we're factoring in the impact of the tax consequences of a venture.

("Time value" considerations will be examined in greater detail in **Chapter Three**, which deals with the economics of oil and gas investment.)

Normally under the tax laws, true economic gains and losses are also reported as such for tax purposes. However, if we can claim "cost" items more rapidly than they are incurred in economic reality, and if we can have the economic use of our revenues earlier than they must be reported for federal income tax purposes, we've profited from the "time value" use of the money.

The principle we've just highlighted is called "deferral." Often, someone will dismiss this advantage: "Oh, all you're doing is *deferring* the taxes." But deferral—and its time value consequences—is what most intelligent tax planning is all about.

(On the other hand, it's equally important not to confuse a "deferral" situation with a total elimination of a tax obligation. Deferral today means "phantom income" tomorrow: a tax liability on dollars that are non-existent in the current year. As discussed in **Chapter Four**, it can be an unpleasant to catastrophic error to confuse deferral with permanent tax savings.)

For accounting purposes, which, *generally speaking*, follow the economic realities of the transaction, expenditures fall into three categories. The first is dollars expended for an asset which will have a future useful life and which won't reduce in value over time (i.e., at least in theory, land). These *non-amortizable capital expenditures* can't be currently deducted (after all, you have acquired an asset that is going to be around for some time), nor can they be amortized (the asset is maintaining its value). But, when the asset is sold, your "gain on sale" is reduced by your "Basis" (capitalized cost) in the asset.

Dollars expended for an asset which has a future useful life but which will reduce in value over time (e.g., business equipment) are referred to as *amortizable capital expenditures.* Again, these dollars can't be currently expensed but must be capitalized as your Basis in the asset; however, since the asset is constantly reducing in value (again, at least in theory) as a result of wear and tear, obsolescence, or consumption, its cost is amortized over a period which (theoretically) approximates the useful life of the asset. (If the asset is sold in the meantime, or is destroyed, the asset's "Adjusted Basis"— the original capitalized cost, less amortization claimed to date—reduces the gain on sale or becomes currently deductible.)

Some expenditures are made for items which will have no future useful life (e.g., wages). These *expenses* are currently deductible for federal income tax purposes.

When revenues are received from a venture, your "income" or "gain" is the difference between those revenues less current expenses (or any sales proceeds) less unrecovered capitalized cost; a return of capital is not "income."

The tax code primarily consists of *"economic reality" tax consequences*: the tax treatment simply tracks the economic reality (and accounting treatment) of the deal. For instance, expenditures for items which have no future useful life can be "expensed" (currently deducted for federal income tax purposes), while the cost of assets which have a future useful life must be capitalized and amortized. And you pay a tax only on "income" and "gain," *not* on "return of capital" amounts.

On the other hand, our federal income tax code is also used to encourage the expenditure of capital in areas that are considered socially desirable, such as the development of housing, food, and energy. To accomplish this, the tax code creates *"artificial" tax consequences*: tax treatment which *does not* track the economic realities of the deal.

These artificial tax consequences fall into two categories: *tax incentives* and *tax negatives.*

Tax incentives can be created in one of two ways:

(1) *The AFTER-TAX COST of the venture can be artificially reduced by reducing the taxes payable on the "outside" income used to fund the venture.* (This can be done by artificially overstating the economic

cost of the venture—e.g., treating certain asset costs as currently deductible rather than amortizable expenditures; permitting an asset to be amortized more rapidly than its value is actually deteriorating); or by using the expenditures to create "tax credits" which can be used as a direct offset against normal taxes payable.)

(2) *The AFTER-TAX REVENUES of the venture can be artificially increased.* (This can be done by permitting a certain portion of the true economic profit or gain from the venture to be received tax-free; by taxing that profit or gain at a lower tax rate; or by deferring the tax until some date in the future while permitting you to have the economic use of the funds in the meantime.)

Tax negatives fall into various categories. Some are "tax pitfalls": negative tax consequences which will trap the unwary only if a deal is misstructured or certain inevitable tax consequences are not taken into account. Others, such as "phantom income," simply flow from "deferral" tax advantages claimed earlier, and simply must be taken into account in overall tax planning. However, some tax negatives represent actions by Congress to limit perceived abuses of the tax incentives it previously created by taking away a portion of those "abused" tax benefits.[1]

There are two key rules to remember in intelligently evaluating the impact of tax consequences on investment return:

(1) *No investment will "make it" (i.e., return an adequate profit) based upon the tax consequences alone.* However, the tax benefits can:

  (a) *Reduce the LOSS on an UNPROFITABLE venture;*[2]

  (b) *Increase the PROFIT on a SUCCESSFUL venture.*[3]

(2) *The tax consequences are simply ONE ELEMENT of the "bottom line" of the investment.* Thus, techniques which increase initial deductibility, such as Functional Allocation[4] and Leverage,[5] should be utilized if, but only if, they also improve investment *economics* on an after-tax basis.

---

[1] An example of this last type of tax negative is the Alternative Minimum Tax, discussed later in this Chapter.

[2] The after-tax exposure is limited to "hard dollar" costs—the portion of your investment which is not offset by tax savings. Also, a portion of your investment may be recouped through "undertaxed" revenues.

[3] "Internal Rate of Return" is automatically improved by reducing your investment base to the "hard dollar" cost of the investment. And, again, to the extent your revenues are "undertaxed," profitability is improved.

[4] See below.

[5] See **Chapter Four**.

Although the tax consequences of oil and gas investment don't automatically turn a mediocre investment opportunity into after-tax gold, they definitely affect investment return—both positively and negatively. Therefore, it's critical that you, as a prospective oil and gas investor, understand these tax implications to verify that the tax "positives" have been utilized to their fullest (consistent, again, with our "bottom line" principle) and have not been unnecessarily lost or endangered; that the tax negatives have been avoided or ameliorated (where possible), or at least taken into account in determining your investment strategy; and that both the tax positives and the tax negatives have been properly factored into your determination of the potential profitability of those investments you are seriously considering.

It's not the purpose of this book to serve as an exhaustive treatise on all the details of the tax code as it applies to oil and gas investment.[6] (That's the role of your attorney or accountant.) We have tried to highlight some of the tax code's key rules concerning oil and gas so that you and your advisors can determine if oil and gas investment really is right for you.

First we've outlined certain of the major tax incentives that the tax code presently provides for oil and gas exploration and development. (These are available to *anyone* engaged in the oil and gas search, from the Majors and Independents drilling with their own capital to you as an outside investor.) Then we explore these tax consequences in greater detail. Next, we look at some "special" rules—primarily "pitfall" in nature—which either apply uniquely to outside investors or which are more apt to arise when an oil venture is being financed with investor funds. And finally, we overview various "flat tax" proposals to see how the rules of the game *might* be changed in future years.[7]

An Overview of Oil's Tax Incentives. As we've just discussed, consideration of the tax consequences of any venture requires an analysis of the *tax treatment of expenditures* (this establishes after-tax cost) and the *tax treatment of revenues* (this determines after-tax income).

We've also seen that what we are looking for are "tax incentives": an artificial treatment of expenditures and/or revenues for tax purposes which

---

[6] For a much more complete discussion, see "Tax Consequences of Oil and Gas Investment," contained in Mosburg (ed.), **Techniques of Oil and Gas Tax-Shelter Financing** (Energy Textbooks International, Inc.: 1983, with 1985 Supplement); and "Tax Consequences of Oil and Gas Investment Under Existing and Proposed Tax Laws," contained in Mosburg (ed.) **Financing Oil and Gas Deals— 1986 Edition** (Energy Textbooks International, Inc.: 1986).

[7] In **Chapter Three**, we study the impact of the most stringent of these proposals to see what the impact would be on oil and gas investment economics under a "worst case" scenario. Then, in **Chapter Five**, an investment strategy is developed which should turn the *threat* of a flat tax to your advantage!

increases or accelerates tax deductions or tax credits, thus reducing the cost of the venture by reducing taxes payable on the cash necessary to fund that venture, or which "undertaxes" venture revenues.

Insofar as *expenditures* are concerned, if a dry hole is drilled which condemns the related prospect and the leases are released, ALL costs related to that prospect are immediately deductible for federal income tax purposes as "Abandonment Losses.[8] While we're not making any money off those dry holes, at least Uncle Sam is picking up on 50% of our loss. (Remember that "currently deductible" is the most favorable characterization of an expenditure for tax purposes.)

When a productive well is drilled, the costs of acquiring and evaluating the related leases and of equipping the well are not currently deductible.[9] However, the costs of *drilling the well*—referred to as "Intangible Drilling and Development Costs"[10]—*are* currently deductible. Since these "Intangibles" usually amount to between 60% and 70% of the costs of a productive prospect, this means that the lion's share of the costs incurred in even a successful oil and gas drilling venture will receive very favorable treatment under the tax code.

(This applies to *drilling ventures* only. Other types of oil and gas investments, such as Completion Funds, Lease Acquisition Funds, and Oil Income Programs—see **Chapter One**—will not provide this degree of initial deductibility.)

The 60% to 70% initial deductibility of the typical productive drilling venture can be increased by certain structuring techniques such as "special allocations," discussed below, or leverage, discussed in **Chapter Four**. But, as we've indicated, there's an economic price tag—possibly worth paying and possibly not—for securing these increased deductions. (For a more detailed explanation, see **Chapter Five**).

The tax code also provides favorable treatment for the *revenues* of an oil and gas venture. Unless you are acquiring "proven" oil and gas reserves, as you would in a production purchase program, over 15% of your otherwise taxable revenues from oil and gas production will be received tax-free under

---

[8] For this reason, we often say that "dry holes are 100% deductible. But, while *drilling costs* are deductible whether the well is productive or dry, the ability to claim the Abandonment Loss on Lease Costs is normally dependent upon a release of the leases.

[9] The tax treatment of Lease Costs and Equipment Costs on productive wells will be discussed below.

[10] That's quite a mouthful to say. Accordingly, Intangible Drilling and Development Costs are frequently referred to as "IDCs" or "Intangibles."

the Percentage Depletion allowance.[11] If you choose to sell your interest in a well or partnership, a portion of your taxable gain on sale may receive Long Term Capital Gains treatment.[12] In addition, there are "Exchange" opportunities where your interests in wells or partnerships could be exchanged on a tax-free basis, providing a possibly more liquid asset.[13]

Now, let's look at these tax consequences in a little greater detail.

Tax Treatment of Oil and Gas Expenditures—In General. For tax purposes, there are three major categories of costs incurred in assembling, evaluating, and developing an oil and gas prospect.[14] These are:

(1) Lease Costs;

(2) Equipment Costs; and

(3) Intangible Drilling and Development Costs.

Lease Costs include all expenditures relating to the acquisition or evaluation of a lease. Since the lease is an asset with a future useful life, such expenditures are not currently deductible: they must be capitalized to become the "Depletable Basis" in the lease.

Lease Costs are "recovered," for tax purposes, in one of three ways. If the lease is sold (or traded in a "taxable exchange"—see below), the unrecovered Depletable Basis reduces the taxable gain on the sale or exchange. If the lease terminates without any production, an "Abandonment Loss" equal to the unrecovered Depletable Basis can be claimed as a current deduction. But once production has been established, the Depletable Basis is recovered through Depletion—either amortizing the Depletable Basis over the life of production (Cost Depletion) or by claiming a statutorily-established percentage of the "gross income from the property" as an alternate Percentage Depletion allowance.[15]

The ability to claim Cost Depletion is extremely important in production purchase investments, since the entire acquisition price of the producing

---

[11] Where Percentage Depletion is not available, as in an income program, the "return of capital" portion of your production revenues will still be received tax-free through Cost Depletion. See below.

[12] This is subject to certain "Zero Basis" and "Recapture" pitfalls, discussed later in this Chapter.

[13] The subsequent resale of *that* asset could even avoid those Recapture problems: see below.

[14] There are other categories of cost incurred in connection with oil and gas ventures, such as expenditures for delay rentals, well operating costs, and the well operator's general administrative overhead. Most of these expenditures can be deducted for federal income tax purposes as ordinary and necessary Business Expenses. However, these expenditure categories are relatively insignificant when compared with the "big three."

[15] Both Cost and Percentage Depletion will be discussed in considerably greater detail when we look at the tax treatment of revenues later in this Chapter.

reserves (less the portion of the price properly allocable to the equipment on those leases) is treated as a Lease Cost. Thus in a typical income program, nearly half your production revenues may be received tax free as a result of Cost Depletion.[16] In a drilling venture, however, expenditures which must be treated as Lease Costs are valueless to you if you qualify, for tax purposes, as an "Independent Producer": you will be claiming Percentage Depletion, which is allowed irrespective of your Depletable Basis in the property.

(Fortunately in a drilling venture, Lease Costs generally average only five to ten percent of your overall expenditures.)

Equipment Costs are expenditures for tangible personal property.[17] Again, this is an asset with a future useful life, so these expenditures also must be capitalized for federal income tax purposes, becoming your "Depreciable Basis" in the equipment.

Equipment Costs are recovered, for tax purposes, through "depreciation" deductions—amortizing the Equipment Costs over a specified "recovery period."[18] However, the "recovery (amortization) period" used for tax purposes is normally shorter than the true useful life of the equipment. In addition, the amortization can be taken on an "accelerated" basis—more in the earlier years—which, under time value principles, make the deductions more valuable.[19] Expenditures may also qualify for the Investment Tax Credit, particularly where new equipment is being acquired.[20] Since these tax benefits can be claimed by an "Independent Producer *in addition to* Percentage Depletion, Equipment Cost expenditures, even though they must be capitalized, are still quite valuable, for tax purposes, to those engaged in the oil and gas search—much more valuable than Lease Costs.

---

[16] This result will still flow even under a flat tax: the "tax reform" proposals are attacking Percentage Depletion only, not Cost Depletion. Remember, though, that Cost Depletion shelters only the return of your *original capitalized investment* (an "economic reality" tax consequence): any true economic "profit" from the investment will still be taxed.

[17] Note that it's only the cost of the hardware itself that must be treated as an Equipment Cost. Costs of *installing* the equipment constitute IDCs. See below.

[18] In theory, they could also be recovered through a reduction of gain on sale if the equipment was sold before it had been fully depreciated, or as an Abandonment Loss if the equipment was "lost in the hole." However, since most oilmen use the "Mass Assets" method of accounting for Equipment Costs for tax purposes, depreciation is, in practice, usually the sole method of recovering this type of equipment expenditure.

[19] Under the current "Accelerated Cost Recovery System" (ACRS) method of amortization, the Equipment Costs are amortized over a five-year "recovery period," using a modified version of the 175% Declining Balance method of amortization.

[20] Under existing "ITC" rules, and subject to certain limitations, a tax credit equal to 10% of the cost of new equipment can be claimed as a direct offset against taxes payable.

(On a typical productive prospect, about 20% to 30% of your expenditures will represent Equipment Costs.)

Without question, though, the most valuable category of expenditures for tax purposes for Independent Producers are *Intangible Drilling and Development Costs.*

Under the tax code, Intangible Drilling and Development Costs are those costs which, in themselves:

(1) Have *no salvage value*; and

(2) Are necessary and incident to the *drilling* of wells or the *preparation of wells for production.*

(Another way of saying this: if it doesn't relate to a lease, and you can't kick it, it's an Intangible!)

As long as you own "operating rights,"[21] you can elect at your option to deduct rather than capitalize your Intangibles. And this is an election you—or your partnership—will always make.[22]

Figure Two illustrates the importance of this election concerning Intangibles: *your ability to expense rather than capitalize your Intangible Drilling and Development Costs cuts the AFTER-TAX cost of your well in half!*[23] And this reduction of the after-tax cost of even productive wells is the most important tax incentive provided the oil and gas industry under our tax code.

Until 1982, major oil companies and Independents were treated identically insofar as Intangible Drilling and Development Costs were concerned. However, the Tax Equity and Fiscal Responsibility Act of 1982 ("TEFRA") drew a dividing line between "Integrated Oil Companies" (corporations which also engage in petroleum retailing or refining) and "Independent Producers" (those engaged in the oil and gas search who are not also engaged in retailing or refining).[24]

Under TEFRA, Integrated Oil Companies were required to capitalize, rather than deduct, 15% of their Intangible Drilling and Development

---

[21] As long as you have the right to develop the land for mineral purposes and the responsibility to bear the costs of that development, you will be an owner of operating rights.

[22] Otherwise, the Intangibles would be capitalized partially as Lease Costs, to be recovered through Depletion, and partially as Equipment Costs, to be recovered through Depreciation.

[23] The impact of "flat tax" proposals which might eliminate the ability currently to deduct all of your IDCs is discussed later in this Chapter and in **Chapter Three**.

[24] The "Independent Producer" category actually was developed by the Tax Reduction Act of 1975 in connection with the partial repeal of Percentage Depletion: see below.

	IDC Expensed	IDC Capitalized
1. Well Costs	$100,000	$100,000
2. Tax Savings	[50,000]	-0-
3. After-Tax Cost of Well	$ 50,000	$100,000

*Assumes 50% Federal income tax bracket

FIGURE TWO: Ecónomic Impact of Deductibility of Intangibles

Costs.[25] And this capitalized portion was raised to 20% by the Deficit Reduction Act of 1984. However, if you're an Independent Producer—and remember, this is a question of whether or not you or your affiliates are also engaged in refining or retailing, not whether you're a "passive" investor[26]—you'll still be able to deduct 100% of your Intangible Drilling and Development Costs.[27]

—**Special Allocations.** Invariably when one oilman "turns" a drilling opportunity to another oilman, the second oilman is going to be "promoted"— he'll bear a greater portion of well costs than his revenue interest in that well. Similarly, when the oilman permits you, as an outside investor, to participate in his drilling ventures, he will "promote" you as well.

There is nothing wrong with the fact that you are being promoted[28]—*if* the promotional levels (including promotion retained by the parties from whom your promoter acquired his interest) aren't too high,[29] and the quality of the prospect is sufficiently strong to justify the promotion.[30] Some *types of promotion,* however, can create tax problems for you—UNLESS your venture is properly structured.

Generally speaking, if your share of venture costs is greater than your share of venture revenues, this "disproportionate allocation" will require you to recharacterize a portion of your expenditures for drilling and equipping the well—which should have been currently deductible or rapidly amortizable as Intangible Drilling and Development Costs or Equipment Costs—and treat these "excess" costs as Lease Costs, the *least favorable category* of expenditure for federal income tax purposes. In other words, to the degree that you've been "promoted," you'll lose the tax benefits that were created by the tax code to encourage you to take these very risks!

---

[25] The capitalized portion could be amortized over a 36-month period.

[26] This "Independent Producer" status is determined individually for each participant in a well or partnership. So as long as *you* aren't engaged, directly or through an affiliate, in retailing or refining, you'll still be able to deduct 100% of your portion of the Intangibles, even though your well operator or general partner would not qualify as an Independent Producer.

[27] Certain flat tax proposals also provide more favorable treatment on productive-well IDCs for Independent Producers than Integrated Oil Companies, reflecting the significance of the Independent in our onshore oil and gas search.

[28] As a matter of fact, be very suspicious if you're told that you are not being promoted or if the promotion appears to be unusually low. These "too good to be true" deals probably are!

[29] See **Chapter Five**.

[30] The economics of a "weak" prospect can be improved—or the negative impact of the loss of certain tax benefits lessened—by reducing the sponsor's promotion below normal promotional levels. The quality of the prospect must also be taken into account in determining whether or not a given "promote" is reasonable or unreasonable—which is why "structure analysis" is an inappropriate tool for making your *final* determination concerning the oil and gas ventures in which you should invest. See **Chapter Five**.

Note that this isn't always the case: the disproportionate allocation rule applies only if your "pre-payout working (cost-bearing) interest" is less than your share of pre-payout costs. To the extent that the landowner or the geologist who came up with the prospect idea has reserved a *cost-free* interest in production, such as a royalty or overriding royalty interest, or your sponsor has acquired his interest pursuant to a "conventional farmout," where the "farmor" (the person who turned the leases to your sponsor) has reserved a "reversionary interest"—one which will come into play only after the persons who have drilled the well have recouped those costs out of production—you can still deduct and/or amortize 100% of those costs.

A very common method for your sponsor to acquire drilling opportunities from other oilmen—or for investors to participate in drilling on a well-by-well basis—is on a "third-for-a-quarter" basis, under which you and your fellow investors will bear *33⅓%* of the costs of drilling and testing the well but will only be assigned a *25%* working interest. Under such an arrangement, absent careful structuring, 25% of the costs of drilling the well must be capitalized as a Lease Cost, rather than being deducted as an Intangible Drilling and Development Cost.[31]

Fortunately, there is a special way of avoiding these "disproportionate allocation" rules. Under the tax code, "special allocations"—allocations of deductions disproportionate to working interest ownership—are permitted *if the arrangement is properly structured as a "partnership" for tax purposes!* This means that if you invest as an investor in a "legal" partnership (e.g., a limited partnership), or if the venture is structured as a "tax partnership" (an arrangement that is treated as a partnership *only for tax purposes*), you won't be required to treat legitimate costs of drilling and equipping the well as "Lease Costs," even though you have been promoted.

Watch out for a Catch-22. There are also disadvantages in the use of the partnership structure, whether it's a legal or "tax" partnership. And if your partnership isn't carefully structured, those "special allocations" may not be honored. (Misstructure the deal sufficiently, and *none* of the tax benefits can be claimed by you on your own federal income tax return!)[32]

—Other Problem Areas Related To Expenditures. Problems concerning special allocations are one of the most serious tax pitfall areas that the oilman faces in structuring his drilling ventures. (It's a problem that is equally serious when the oilman is drilling with his own dollars.) But there

---

[31] For more on the "third-for-a-quarter" arrangement, see **Chapter Five**.

[32] Later in this Chapter we will discuss certain protective steps necessary to insure that the tax benefits you *thought* you could claim actually are available and can be claimed by *you* on your own federal income tax return.

are other potential dangers that also exist in analyzing the tax treatment of your expenditures. For instance, if you pay a fixed sum for the drilling of your well—a "turnkey" arrangement—will the full amount of that payment be deductible as an Intangible? If you pay for the well in the present year, but it's not drilled (or the drilling completed) till the following year, will the full amount of your "prepayment" be currently deductible? Are payments for "management fees" allowable as deductible items? Will certain of your expenditures create "Items of Tax Preference" which could reduce the net tax advantages of the venture?

All of these questions can arise in transactions between oil and gas industry members where no outside investors are participating in the wells. However, they tend to be most significant in investor-funded ventures. Accordingly, we address these questions later in this Chapter, when we consider "Special Problems for Investors."

Tax Treatment of Revenues—In General. The tax treatment of your revenues from an oil and gas venture will vary, based upon whether you hold your interest in the producing wells until the reserves are depleted ("production revenues") or dispose of your interest in those reserves while they are still "in the ground" by selling your interest in those producing wells (or your interest in the limited partnership which owns those producing wells).[33]

Most of your *production revenues* (see below) will be taxed as Ordinary Income; but a certain portion of those revenues can be received tax free, as a result of the Depletion Allowance.

If you *dispose of your reserves "in the ground,"* the tax treatment of those revenues will vary, based upon whether the transfer, for tax purposes, is characterized as a *Sale*, an *Exchange*, a *Sublease*, a *Sharing Arrangement*, or an *Exchange of Property for Services*. (Each of these will be briefly discussed below.)

—Production Revenues—The Depletion Allowance. Like all natural resources (with the possible exception of timber), oil and gas are "wasting assets"—as we use them, we also use them up. The basic concept of "depletion" is one of "economic reality": it isn't fair to treat the *gross revenues* from the production of a natural resource as "income" (as you would the dividends on a stock), since a portion of those revenues merely represent a return of your original capital investment in acquiring your interest in the reserves.[34]

---

[33] If your general partner decides to dispose of certain wells before the reserves have been depleted—a power he'll normally have under the limited partnership agreement—for tax purposes it's just as if *you* had sold an interest in those wells.

[34] Remember, we're only supposed to be taxed on income or gain, *not* on return of capital.

The usual, "economic reality" method of calculating your "Depletion Allowance" —the portion of your production revenues you'll receive tax free as a return of capital—is *"Cost Depletion,"* which permits you to amortize your capital investment in the natural resource over the life of production. And every member of the oil and gas industry who owns an "economic interest" in a mineral deposit can claim Cost Depletion.[35]

As an "economic reality" tax consequence, Cost Depletion is not threatened by tax code "reforms": under current tax laws, both major oil companies and "Independent Producers" can claim Cost Depletion, and the ability to claim Cost Depletion is not under attack under the flat tax proposals discussed later in this Chapter. However, while the ability to claim Cost Depletion is significant where an "income program" investment is involved,[36] so little of your dollars in a drilling program or completion fund are being spent on depletable Lease Costs that Cost Depletion shelters very few of your production revenues from taxation under these types of investments.

As we've learned, though, current tax laws also create "tax incentives" to encourage various socially-desirable activities—for example, developing a plentiful supply of domestic natural resources. For this reason, as to many minerals, an alternate way of calculating Depletion—referred to as *"Percentage Depletion"*—is created by the tax code.

Percentage Depletion permits you to receive a statutorily-established percentage of the "gross income from the property" free of tax.[37] And unlike Cost Depletion, *Percentage Depletion is not limited to your "Basis"—your capitalized Lease Costs—in your leases.* So while the amount of "Cost Depletion" dollars you can receive tax free is limited in a drilling venture and must be spread out over the life of production, there is no such limit on tax-free revenues under Percentage Depletion.

You can't claim both Cost and Percentage Depletion as to production from a given well: you're limited to the *greater* of the two.[38]

The rules concerning Percentage Depletion for the oil and gas industry were greatly modified between 1969 and 1975. As a result, the availability of

---

[35]An "economic interest" means that you've invested in the minerals "in place"; will be entitled to participate in income from the extraction of the minerals; and must look to that income from extraction as the *only source* for the return of your capital investment.

[36]Remember, in income (production purchase) programs, the major portion of your subscription proceeds will be expended on capitalized—but depletable—Lease Costs.

[37]For this reason, Percentage Depletion is also referred to as "Statutory Depletion."

[38]This determination is made separately, however, on an annual basis as to each separate "property" (basically, a lease-by-lease determination).

The ability to claim Percentage Depletion has historically been considered a major tax advantage.

Percentage Depletion for oil and gas production was repealed, with one important exception: Percentage Depletion could still be claimed by those who qualified as "Independent Producers or Royalty Owners."

We mentioned the dividing line between "Integrated Oil Companies" and "Independent Producers" when we talked about the ability to deduct Intangible Drilling and Development Costs.[39] Independent Producers (or Royalty Owners) are those persons owning economic interests in oil and gas who are not also engaged in refining or retailing of hydrocarbon products.[40] And such Independent Producers, as a general rule, can still claim a Percentage Depletion allowance equal to *15% of the "gross income" from a given property.*[41]

Obviously, if there is a "general rule" there are exceptions. And there are many complicated criteria under which Percentage Depletion might not be available or might be restricted in amount. Your chief worry, though, is something called the "proven property" exclusion: Percentage Depletion can't be claimed, even by an Independent Producer, if at the time he acquired his interest in the property, the property was already "proven."[42] For this reason, we're limited, in income programs, to claiming Cost Depletion. But in most drilling, lease fund, or completion ventures, Percentage Depletion should be available.[43]

—The Crude Oil Windfall Profit Tax. The taxation of production revenues was also affected by the enactment, in 1980, of a mislabelled *"Crude Oil Windfall Profit Tax."*

---

[39] The rules aren't quite identical. A taxpayer who could deduct 100% of his Intangibles because he wasn't a corporation (only corporate taxpayers are designated as Integrated Oil Companies) might not be able to claim Percentage Depletion if he were also engaged in petroleum refining or retailing.

[40] You can be a "little bit pregnant" through minor amounts of retailing or refining without losing Percentage Depletion. There are, however, very complicated "attribution" rules that can cause Independent Producer status to be lost. These are questions to take up with your own accountant or tax advisor.

[41] But you aren't taxed on "gross income": you're taxed on *net income.* This means that *something in excess* of 15% of your taxable income from production (gross income less operating costs) can be received tax free as a result of Percentage Depletion.

[42] In other words, the tax code wants to encourage us to search for oil and gas, not to purchase proven, in-the-ground reserves.

[43] There's considerable uncertainty as to exactly what's a "proven property" for purposes of this proven property exclusion. If a well were being drilled—or completed—in a "sure thing" area, it's possible that Percentage Depletion may not be available. But it's also present industry policy to claim Percentage Depletion as to all but "purchased" wells.

The Windfall Profit Tax is imposed upon the statutorily-defined "Windfall Profit element" that you receive from your production of "Crude Oil."[44] Basically, this Windfall Profit element is that portion of the "removal value" of your oil production which it's assumed you wouldn't have received unless oil prices had been deregulated.

The tax treatment under the Windfall Profit Tax varies, based upon the "Tier" (category) into which your crude oil falls for purposes of the tax. "Tier One oil" (basically "old" oil) and "Tier Two oil" (oil from low-producing "stripper" wells) are taxed at relatively high tax rates, with a much greater part of the "removal price" being considered a "windfall profit."[45] However, the tax rates are much more favorable, and the windfall profit element much lower, for "Tier Three 'new' oil," the category into which virtually all of your production from current ventures will fall.

At the current low tax rate for Tier Three oil—22½% until 1988—and with so little of your production revenues falling within the Windfall Profit element at today's price levels, the Crude Oil Windfall Profit Tax has little practical economic impact on current oil and gas deals.[46] But, if your sponsor's share of venture revenues is affecting *your* returns levels (e.g., as under a "net profits" arrangement or where "payout" is a factor—see **Chapter Five**), it's important that in defining that sharing arrangement, your revenues are calculated *net* of the Windfall Profit Tax.

—Tax Consequences of In-the-Ground Disposal of Reserves.[47] As indicated above, if you choose to dispose of your well or limited partnership interest before the reserves are depleted, the tax consequences of that transfer will vary, based upon how the transaction is characterized for federal income tax purposes.

Certain types of transfers—*Sharing Arrangements, Subleases*, and *Exchanges of Property for Services*—are primarily methods by which your venture will acquire, or dispose of, its interest in leases. Since these tax consequences will "flow through" to you, to be reported on your own tax

---

[44] "Crude Oil" is broadly defined for purposes of the tax: about the only thing that escapes is "dry gas."

[45] "Independent Producers" are taxed at a somewhat more favorable tax rate on Tier One and Tier Two oil.

[46] So who is the biggest loser when oil prices fall? Uncle Sam!

[47] Both the Windfall Profit Tax and the proven property exclusion for Percentage Depletion also indirectly affect your ability to "realize" on the results of a successful drilling venture by selling your interest in the in-the-ground reserves: since the tax treatment of the resulting production revenues may be less favorable to your transferee than the taxes payable if you had retained the reserves, the after-tax worth of those reserves will be diminished.

return—see below—they also affect the overall tax treatment of your venture.[48] But, at this point, we're principally concerned with what happens when you transfer *your* interest in a well or partnership; and these transfers will normally be taxed either as *Sales* or *Exchanges*.

These rules will apply whether you were selling or exchanging your interest in a well (or group of wells) or disposing of a limited partnership interest. They would also apply whether that sale or exchange was to an independent third party or to your sponsor pursuant to a "redemption offer" or an exchange offer (see **Chapter Six**). And if the sponsor of your limited partnership decides to accept a cash offer from some third party for a portion of the partnership's in-the-ground reserves, that would also constitute a "Sale" whose tax consequences would flow through to you as a member of the partnership.

A *"Sale"* occurs when you transfer your interest for *cash*. Under such a transaction, you are taxed on *the gain element only*—the difference between your Depletable Basis in your leases and your "amount realized" (the cash you're paid) on the Sale. Furthermore, at least in theory, you'll be taxed *at Long Term Capital Gains rates* if you've held your interest for over six months.

In an *Exchange*, you trade *property for property* rather than property for cash. But in most Exchanges, the tax treatment is the same: you are taxed on the "gain" element only and at Long Term Capital Gains rates if you've held your interest for over six months.

Your gain is easy to calculate in a Sale because your "amount realized" is the cash you're paid. In the Exchange, where you are paid in property, it's a little more complicated. Here, your "amount realized" is the fair market value of the property that you receive, as of the date you receive it.

Now, let's thicken the plot.

We've said that on both Sales and taxable Exchanges, you might be able to claim Long Term Capital Gains treatment. That's true—to the extent that some of that gain isn't subject to "Recapture" at Ordinary Income Tax rates.

Unfortunately, if productive wells have been drilled on your property—and if they haven't, you'll have little to sell or exchange—your prior Intangible Drilling and Development Costs on these productive properties will be

---

[48] "Sublease" characterization can also be extremely important in connection with a Lease Acquisition Fund investment.

subject to Recapture at Ordinary Income Tax rates.[49] And since, by the time you sell your interest, your Depletable Basis will probably be zero, your "gain on sale," for tax purposes, will be higher than you imagine—and primarily will be taxed at Ordinary Income Tax rates![50]

There is a method of avoiding most of this Recapture impact: to dispose of your interests in a *Tax-Free Exchange.*

There are various ways in which oilmen make non-taxable (tax-free) exchanges of oil and gas properties among themselves. However, when we're talking about you disposing of *your* interest in wells or limited partnerships on a non-taxable basis, we're primarily talking about your acceptance of an "Exchange Offer"—an opportunity for you to trade your existing interests for stock in a newly-formed corporation.

Not all Exchange Offers are tax-free in nature. And all must be carefully structured to insure a non-taxable result. But from a tax standpoint, *if* your sponsor—or some third party—does provide such an exchange opportunity, and *if* the offer is properly structured, you can acquire a security that may eventually have greater liquidity and possibly greater value than your well or limited partnership interests. And when you sell your interest in that stock, assuming the original exchange was tax free, you shouldn't trigger Recapture of your prior drilling deductions or Equipment Cost amortization.[51]

(Note that while the tax-free exchange has eliminated Recapture problems, your "zero basis" in your oil and gas interests will carry over to your stock, so that the *amount* of your taxable gain will remain relatively high.)

Special Pitfalls for Investors—In General. The tax treatment we've just discussed—including the "pitfalls" concerning disproportionate allocation, Recapture, and the like—apply just as much to the oilman drilling for

---

[49] Actually, it's only the "Excess Productive-Well IDCs" that are subject to Recapture (a calculation that *may* take into account greater Cost Depletion deductions that would have been available if you'd capitalized your Intangibles as Lease Costs.

In addition to Recapture of Excess Productive Well IDCs, prior amortization of Equipment Costs and certain prior "Section 1231" losses are also subject to Recapture. (You may also be required to restore certain Investment Tax Credits previously claimed.)

[50] Remember, it's the difference between your *Depletable Basis in your leases* and the amount realized, *not* your "hard dollar" cost, that's the taxable gain. (You've deducted your drilling costs, so they don't constitute a part of your Basis.) And, by now, that relatively low Depletable Basis will have been recovered through Depletion.

[51] That's the good news. However, for that exchange to operate in your favor from an *economic* standpoint, we're also assuming that a market for the stock you acquire does eventually develop, and that the stock has a realizable value equal to that of the well or partnership interests you gave up. See **Chapter Six.**

his own account as they do to you as an outside investor. There are, though, some problems that tend to take on the greatest practical significance when investors are funding a transaction.

Let's look at some of these.

—Will the Tax Benefits "Flow Through"? In **Chapter One** we saw that one method of participating in the oil and gas search is to purchase the stock of an oil and gas company. But, if your investment represents such an "indirect" participation in oil and gas, not only will the value of your stock depend upon market place reaction, but the tax consequences of oil will be "trapped" at the entity level.

A corporation is both a *legal* and a *taxable* entity. That means that the tax incentives which relate to oil will accrue to the benefit of the corporation and can't be reflected on your personal federal income tax return. It also means that there will be a double taxation of revenues: first, at the corporate level and, second, at your level as a shareholder when the monies are distributed to you as a taxable dividend. In other words, for tax purposes, a corporation is *not* a "flow through" vehicle.

There are several ways in which you can participate in oil through "pass through" methods which avoid double taxation of revenues and permit you to reflect oil's tax advantages on your own income tax return. The first is a "fractional interest" investment in which, for both state law and tax purposes, you are treated as being a "co-owner" with your fellow investors: that is, a co-tenancy.[52] The second is a *"tax" partnership*: under state law, a co-tenancy is created, but for *tax purposes only*, you're treated as being a member of a partnership. (Again, you've invested on a "fractional interest" basis.) The third is a *legal AND "tax" partnership:* you and your partners have formed a partnership for both tax and state law purposes.

Co-tenancy is a flow-through vehicle, which avoids double taxation of revenues or a trapping of tax benefits at the "legal entity" level; however, it doesn't provide limited liability or permit the use of "special allocations," discussed earlier in this Chapter. Forming a tax partnership gives the same flow-through advantages and also permits the use of special allocations; but it doesn't provide limited liability.[53] The legal partnership provides flow-through tax treatment, the ability to claim special allocations, and limited liability (assuming a limited partnership has been properly formed); both it

---

[52] The "fractional interest" versus "program" (limited partnership) approach was touched on in **Chapter One** and will be discussed in more detail in **Chapter Five**.

[53] Is the lack of *legal* limited liability a serious practical problem? See **Chapter Five**.

and the tax partnership, though, subject you to certain tax burdens that apply only to partnerships.[54]

The tax *disadvantages* of a partnership—"tax" or "legal"—are two-fold. First, while your partnership is not a "taxable entity," it is a "reporting entity": it must file an annual "Information Tax Return" with the IRS. Second, for your partnership's allocations of tax benefits and tax burdens among the partners to have validity for tax purposes, the allocations must have "substantial economic effect." And considerable confusion has been created as to what it takes for that "substantial economic effect" to exist as a result of certain 1983 proposals by the IRS—their "Partner's Distributive Share" Proposed Regulations.

The chief problem that exists concerning classification of your venture as a flow-through vehicle for tax purposes arises from a provision of the tax code which defines a "corporation," *for tax purposes*, as including "associations." These "Associations Taxable as Corporations" are the worst of all worlds: they provide none of the business advantages of a "legal" corporation, such as centralized management and limited liability; but for tax purposes, they have all the corporate disadvantages (double taxation of revenues and the trapping of the tax benefits at the artificial "corporate" level).

If the sponsor—and his tax advisor—know what they are doing, they will have structured your venture so that no "association" is created; and the venture, for tax purposes, will be treated as creating the type of flow-through vehicle (either co-tenancy or partnership) through which you wished to participate. But the rules can trap the unwary. So be sure that the sponsor's offering document contains an apparently reliable tax opinion which passes on the classification of your venture for tax purposes.[55] (It's also a good idea to have your own tax advisor review that opinion to get some independent assurance that the tax treatment, in this and other areas, will be as represented.)

—Turnkeys and Prepayments. Many drilling ventures provide for wells to be drilled on a "turnkey" basis—a fixed price to be paid for the drilling of the well, irrespective of the actual costs of the drilling.[56] Also, in

---

[54] The limited partnership also requires your name and the size of your investment to become a part of the public records.

[55] If the offering document doesn't contain a tax opinion (or agrees to make the underlying tax opinion available upon request), it's a danger signal that the sponsor doesn't know what he's doing in the tax area—or under federal and state securities laws. See **Chapter Five**.

[56] The stated reason for turnkey drilling is to limit cost overrun exposure. The true reason, if the well is being "turnkeyed" by the sponsor or one of its affiliates—or even the originator of the deal—is usually to disguise certain costs of buying into the deal as Intangibles rather than Lease Costs—and to permit the sponsor (or originator) to increase his front-end promotion.

many instances you may be permitted/required to pay for a well in the present year even though the drilling will not be completed (or even commenced) until the following year.

While properly structured turnkey or prepayment arrangements may increase your current tax benefits, they may not be too smart from an economic standpoint, even on an after-tax basis.[57] Certainly such arrangements make no sense if the venture has been improperly structured from a tax standpoint, so that the anticipated tax advantages will not in fact be available.

Deductions claimed for wells drilled on a turnkey basis will be allowed by the IRS *if* the turnkey price is not "excessive" (i.e., higher than the price an independent drilling contractor would have charged for drilling the well on a turnkey basis) and *if* there has been a proper allocation of the charges between IDCs and Equipment and Lease Costs (if applicable). Otherwise, the IRS will disallow the "excessive" portion of the turnkey (or the portion that was improperly allocated to Intangibles).[58]

Until recently, there was considerable confusion as to the circumstances under which payment could be made (and deductions taken) in the present year for drilling services that were not to be rendered until the following year. But, it's now clear that if the payment is a "true" payment and not merely a "deposit"; if a "business purpose" exists for the prepayment; and if the prepayment doesn't result in a "material distortion of income", the deductions will be allowed to cash-basis taxpayers in the year of payment *so long as certain additional requirements of the Deficit Reduction Act of 1984 are also satisfied.*

For a true "payment" rather than a deposit to exist, the payment must be made not later than December 31, with no right of refund and "no strings attached" (e.g., such as an escrow arrangement), to someone who takes on the contractual responsibility for the drilling of specified wells. However, the drilling need not be on a "turnkey" basis so long as any prepaid amounts over and above the actual cost of drilling the wells on a footage or daywork basis can only be applied to IDC costs on additional wells. Also, the "drilling contractor" doesn't have to be the person who actually drills the wells; and other wells can be substituted for those originally designated. (The IRS would

---

[57] This is particularly true where turnkeys to the sponsor or a sponsor affiliate are involved. See **Chapter Three**. The economic wisdom of properly structured prepayment arrangements primarily revolves around the quality of the prospects to be drilled and the reasonableness of the promotion. See **Chapter Five**.

[58] The IRS is most suspicious when the "drilling contractor" is the sponsor or one of its affiliates, particularly if that entity owns no rigs so that the actual drilling of the well must be subcontracted to some third party.

also require that the prepayments be required by contract and that "some well site work" have been performed in the year of the prepayment.)

A mere desire to reduce taxes in the current year is not enough to satisfy the "business purpose" test: there must be a "legitimate" business purpose, such as the drilling contractor's need for working capital or a desire to lock in a rate or price or to secure a more favorable rate or price. (An unrealistic "business purpose"—such as "insuring rig availability" when rigs are in excess supply—won't cut it. But it now appears that if there *is* a reasonable business purpose for the prepayment, there is no material distortion; and that *without* such a reasonable business purpose, a material distortion will almost inevitably arise.

The 1984 Act provides that "tax shelters" which use the cash method of accounting generally can't claim a deduction until "economic performance" has occurred—basically, the services have been rendered.[59] An exception exists, however, and the deduction will be allowed in the year of payment if economic performance occurs within 90 days after the close of the taxable year.[60] And as to the drilling of oil and gas wells, "economic performance" occurs when drilling is *commenced.* (This would seem, however, to require a "commencement" *in good faith,* followed by a diligent prosecution of the drilling.)

Even if your prepaid well is spudded by the following March 30, under the Deficit Reduction Act your prepaid deductions will be limited to your "cash basis."[61] While this is a complicated concept—see your own tax advisor—it basically means that borrowed amounts can't be included in "cash basis" *where the borrowings were "arranged" by the sponsor, a marketer, or any of their affiliates.* (Direct borrowings you arrange on your own are okay, so long as they aren't secured by the assets of the partnership.)[62] It would appear, though, that your entire "cash basis" could be allocated to the prepayments so that drilling costs actually incurred prior to year end could be "paid for" out of sponsor-arranged borrowings.

---

[59]"Tax shelter" is broadly defined to include virtually any type of arrangement which would be considered a "security" under federal or state securities laws, and would apparently include well-by-well deals in addition to partnerships. Note that this is *not* the same way in which "tax shelter" is defined for purposes of "tax shelter registration" under the 1984 Act—a problem we'll be discussing in a moment.

[60]Despite this unfortunate use of the word "after," the IRS interprets the provision to apply to wells spudded (though not completed) *before* year end as well as to wells spudded after December 31.

[61]"Cash basis" limitations apply only to prepayments; they aren't a further general "at risk" restriction. See **Chapter Four.**

[62]The use of leverage in oil and gas investment is discussed in **Chapter Four.**

—Organizational and Offering Costs and Management Fees.
"Organizational and Offering Costs"—costs of organizing and marketing the venture—are normally recharged to you and your fellow investors by the sponsor.[63] Such costs are not currently deductible but must be capitalized, with "Organizational Expenses" being amortized over a 60-month period.

("Organizational Expenses" are the expenses of *creating* (but not marketing) the partnership. There is no express amortization right under the tax code concerning the remaining "Syndication Fees.")

To avoid this capitalization requirement—which obviously makes the investment less attractive from a tax standpoint—sponsors frequently "waive" their right to reimbursement of the Organizational and Offering Costs but take a "Management Fee" out of the subscription proceeds which (surprise!) tends to equal these costs. (Management Fees may also be charged in lieu of a "mark up" on lease costs.)

You don't have to be a genius to realize that the sponsor is simply trying to disguise a non-deductible reimbursement of Organizational and Offering Costs as a deductible Management Fee. Neither does the IRS. For this reason, such payments are "high profile" on audit—and are usually disallowed. And even if the Management Fee isn't a disguised reimbursement of Organizational and Offering Costs or Lease Costs, its deductibility will still be disallowed if the "services" being performed are capital in nature or are to be performed in a subsequent year (this isn't an appropriate prepayment item) or if the payment is out-of-line with the value of the services being performed.

—The Alternative Minimum Tax. Congress doesn't like anyone using tax-sheltered investments to eliminate the need for paying *any* tax. For this reason, most provisions of the tax code which create artificial tax consequences are also designated "Items of Tax Preference."

The fact that a transaction generates Items of Tax Preference doesn't mean that its normally favorable tax treatment will be stripped away or that your U.S. citizenship will be revoked. It simply means that you'll now have to compute your tax liability in two separate ways: first, as you normally would, and second, after restoring your Items of Tax Preference, to see what your *Alternative Minimum Tax* would be if this "Alternative Minimum Taxable Income" were taxed at a 20% rate.[64] You then pay the *higher* of your tax calculated in the usual way and the Alternative Minimum Tax.

---

[63] As to necessary limitations on the reimbursement of Organizational and Offering Costs, see **Chapter Five**. The impact of such "front-end dilution" is discussed in **Chapter Three**.

[64] We're greatly simplifying this discussion of the Alternative Minimum Tax. For instance, before calculating the tax, you're permitted certain deductions and a statutory exemption.

"Excess" amounts of Productive-Well IDCs or Percentage Depletion deductions are treated as Items of Tax Preference.[65] But the value of these deductions or tax-free revenues won't necessarily be lost. This value, though, may be somewhat less than you originally assumed, to the extent you're required to pay any additional tax under the Alternative Minimum Tax calculation.

The fact that your oil and gas drilling or completion investment may create Items of Tax Preference doesn't necessarily mean that you'll have any additional tax liability as a result of the Alternative Minimum Tax, or that any such tax liability would be significant in amount. Even if there were some additional taxes payable, the quality of the venture might make this well worthwhile. But it is necessary that you consult with your own tax advisor— only he is aware of the totality of your financial transactions for the year that could go into the overall "AMT" calculation—to be sure that this particular investment is in fact appropriate under your overall financial plan.

—"Abusive" Tax-Sheltered Investments—In General. Some tax-sheltered investments involve projects having no economic merit and which use unintended "loopholes" in the tax laws and "aggressive" tax positions, along with heavy reliance on leverage, to assert astronomical tax benefits. (No revenues, just write-offs!)[66]

Prior to the early 1980s, the IRS' "arsenal" for dealing with abusive tax shelters was limited. Audit procedures were poor, particularly where partnership investments were involved, and penalties—besides investor "fraud"—amounted to little more than a slap on the wrist.

All that has changed in the 1980s. The IRS now has much more effective audit techniques; and the penalties that it can inflict on investors in—or the sponsors of—questionable tax shelters are quite formidable. Changes in the tax code have also restricted or eliminated the use of "gimmick" tax opinions[67] and "phony" debt in leveraged offerings.[68]

Most oil and gas investments—including most of today's leveraged investments—don't fall into the "abusive" category: the tax advantages of oil

---

[65] So are the excess of accelerated depreciation deductions on real property and leased personal property; "rapid write-offs" for R & D and mining; the "excluded" portion of your Long Term Capital Gains etc.

[66] Just because an investment utilizes leverage, or creates "excess write-offs"—deductions in excess of your initial cash contribution—doesn't mean that it's "abusive," even in the eyes of the IRS! See below and **Chapter Four**.

[67] See **Chapter Five**.

[68] See **Chapter Four**.

and gas are a legitimate and intentional result of the desire of Congress to encourage this socially-advantageous activity.

However, you will sometimes see an oil and gas offering that utilizes questionable tax positions to "enhance" your tax advantages to a far greater degree than Congress intended. When you do, run from that "opportunity." Your tax law exposure is such that those extra deductions simply aren't worth it. Furthermore, the "abusive" programs are usually far more abusive to you as an investor than they are to the IRS. The extra deductions are often "purchased" at the expense of the economics of the venture; and most oil and gas proposals that involve aggressive tax positions lacked economic merit in the first place. (As we'll see in **Chapter Four**, no matter what level of *initial* deductions are created, your "hard dollar" exposure *always* equals 50 cents on the dollar.) And an alarming number of the sponsors of such programs are the true "con artists" who don't intend to be around for long in any event.

Before leaving our discussion of abusive tax shelters, we do need to give more detailed consideration to one question: should you invest in an oil and gas program which may be required to be registered with the Internal Revenue Service as a "'potentially abusive' tax shelter?"

—Registration with the IRS as a "Tax Shelter." The Deficit Reduction Act of 1984 requires that all "tax shelters," as defined in the Act, register with the IRS and be assigned a "tax shelter identification number." Organizers and marketers are required to maintain lists of the investors in such "potentially abusive" investments, which are to be provided to the IRS upon request. And you must include the tax shelter identification number on any tax return you file which claims any tax benefit under one of these "registered" tax shelters.

The definition of "tax shelter" for purposes of this registration requirement is quite complicated, and doesn't track the definition of "tax shelter" under the Deficit Reduction Act's prepayment rules. For our purposes, let's simplify this by saying that, generally to be a "tax shelter" for IRS registration purposes, your investment must have the following characteristics:

(1) *The interests would constitute "securities" under federal or state securities laws.* (Your interests *would*, whether you're investing in a partnership or "well-by-well.")

(2) *It could be inferred that the "tax shelter ratio," in any one of the first five years of the venture, would be greater than two to one.*

Originally, it was assumed that the "tax shelter ratio" requirement would mean that only leveraged "excess write-off" investments had to register with the IRS; but that such registration would almost inevitably trigger a stringent audit.[69] "Tax shelter ratio," however, as defined in the Act and as interpreted by the IRS, is so broad that many direct participation investments that involve all-cash subscriptions are being registered to avoid the penalties that an inadvertent failure to register might create. And the IRS is making clear that it simply wants to insure that *no* potentially abusive investment escapes its net: the fact that an otherwise legitimate oil and gas venture must register as a "tax shelter" should not increase its likelihood of audit, even when the investment is made on a leveraged basis.[70]

—Other Potential Pitfalls. It's impossible in this book to consider every possible "tax pitfall" that can arise in an oil and gas investment. For instance, there are the special problems that *leveraged investment* in oil and gas can create under the tax code. (See **Chapter Four**.) Then, there is your *exposure on audit.* While this assumes the highest significance if your oil and gas investment—or *any* "tax shelter" in which you are participating in the same year—might be viewed as "abusive," a "high write-off" investment is more apt to trigger an audit, more likely to lead to time and expense in the IRS review of its tax consequences (and that's your personal expense, not that of your sponsor or fellow investors), and could lead to a discovery of other "questionable" tax positions you've taken in connection with non-related transactions.

You're also exposed to *changes in the tax laws.* Most Congressional changes in the tax code are prospective as to expenditures made prior to the enactment (or at least the introduction) of the proposed change. But the tax treatment of your revenues (e.g., Percentage Depletion or Long Term Capital Gains), or of future year expenditures (e.g., the deductibility of drilling future development wells), could be affected by changes in the tax code. And changes in administrative or judicial interpretation of the tax code may be applied on a retroactive basis. (This is another reason, as we'll see in **Chapters Three** and **Five**, to make sure that your investments make economic sense *aside from any artificial tax consequences.*)

But there is one aspect of tax law change that does require further thought. So, to close this Chapter, let's consider whether or not the proposed changes in our tax laws under the so-called "flat tax" have eliminated the need for—or the advisability of—oil and gas investment.

But What About a "Flat Tax?" The mid-1980s have seen a strong push toward "tax simplification" and a "flat tax"—a single tax rate to be applied

---

[69] The use of leverage in oil and gas investment, and the pros and cons of "excess write-offs," are discussed in **Chapter Four**.

[70] Many advisors are now concerned if they are told that a sponsor is *not* going to register his oil and gas venture as a "tax shelter"!

across the board irrespective of income level, to replace the current, highly complicated, "graduated" tax rates.

Early on, it became obvious that such "tax reform" was easier to applaud in the abstract than to apply in practice. There is major disagreement about what are "tax incentives" and what are the economic realities of a venture.[71] Some "sacred cows" are simply too sacred to touch.[72] And some "tax incentives" probably need to be retained, even though they do reflect artificial tax consequences, to continue to encourage activities that are admittedly in the national interest.

The difficulties involved in enacting a workable "flat tax" became obvious when each of the major flat-tax proposals emerged as "graduated" flat taxes: ones which still taxed various levels of income at differing rates and simply reduced the number of tax brackets.

It's impossible to say at the present time whether a flat tax will or will not be enacted; when it will be enacted (if indeed it does come to pass); or what form it will take, especially where oil and gas investment is concerned. Many investors, however, are shying away from oil and gas because of flat tax fears. And this is unfortunate, since, *properly understood*, the potential—or reality—of a flat tax can actually *improve your return* from oil and gas investment.

While it may be foolhardy to try to guess what form this "tax reform" may take,[73] intelligent oil and gas investment requires that the probabilities/possibilities of these tax law changes be factored into your investment strategy. So let's gaze into a crystal ball:[74]

(1) *There may still be SOME TAX LAW CHANGE before the end of 1985.* (Both political parties—possibly foolishly—have done too much "going on the record" in this regard.) If not, or if the changes are *totally* cosmetic, there should be legislation by 1987.

(2) *The tax law changes, IF ENACTED, wouldn't affect the deductibility of wells drilled in 1985.* However, the ability to claim Percentage Depletion in future years on the production from those wells could be affected. (In all probability, you would be permitted to deduct Intangible Drilling and Development Costs on future-year wells required

---

[71] For instance, is interest a legitimate deduction? What should be the period of time for amortizing buildings or business equipment? And should "dry hole" costs be currently deductible?

[72] For example, charitable contributions and interest deductions on a principal residence.

[73] Almost as foolhardy as trying to forecast changes in oil and natural gas prices!

[74] These pages have been programmed to self-destruct once new legislation is—or isn't—passed.

to fully develop prospects which you acquired and partially developed through current drilling period. There could, however, be some change in the rules concerning 1985 pre-payments.)

(3) *The current deductibility of dry hole costs should be preserved.*

(4) *Percentage Depletion will probably be eliminated, with the possible exception of production from stripper wells.*[75]

(5) *The biggest concern is the treatment of Productive-Well IDCs.* It presently appears that the current deductibility of these drilling costs—the most important tax feature of oil and gas drilling investments—will be preserved. If not, expect an ultra-fast amortization, at least for "Independent Producers."

If the rules concerning Productive-Well IDCs did change, there would be some impact on the economics of oil and gas investment—*assuming no change in deal structure!* The impact, though, would be relatively light; and, with the present "buyer's market" in the oil and gas investment area, sponsors could be expected to react—and *overreact*—to the need to attract you as an investor, despite the uninformed "fears" that are turning oil and gas investment into a "contrarian's dream."

So in **Chapter Three,** we'll put a pencil to the impact of the new tax laws on oil and gas investment under a "worst case" scenario. And in **Chapter Five,** we'll see how to turn these flat-tax fears to your advantage.

---

[75]As we'll see in **Chapter Three,** this isn't all that serious, in view of the lower tax rates. Also, Cost Depletion, which isn't under attack (remember, it's an "economic reality" allowance), will still be available—possibly on a more favorable "indexed for inflation" basis.

CHAPTER THREE
MEASURING OIL AND GAS INVESTMENT ECONOMICS

Why Worry About Economics? You wouldn't consider investing in a non-tax-shelter without considering your likelihood of profiting from that venture, and *how* the numbers stacked up compared to other opportunities available to you. In the past, even in tax-shelter areas such as real estate and cattle, the offering document always contained "projections," estimating the return to be realized (normally on an "internal rate of return" basis), assuming the venture performed as expected. (The return, invariably, was projected as phenomenal.)

Not so in oil and gas. Since the results of any given well or group of wells is speculative (see **Chapter One**), projections were generally looked at as meaningless—and potentially misleading.[1] Furthermore, "everyone" knew that if a well hit, your returns would be so rewarding that "economics" would take care of itself. (Besides that, with oil's tax advantages—see **Chapter Two** —who needed economics?)

And that was just the problem. As we've already seen, taxes *aren't* enough to convert a poor oil venture into a resounding economic success, even on an after-tax basis. The mere fact that a well is *productive* doesn't mean that it's *profitable*. And a few "big hits"—gratifying as they may be—won't necessarily compensate for a much longer string of dry holes. (We'll have more to say about this in **Chapter Five**.)

So evaluation of the *economics* of a proposed oil and gas investment was—and *is*—the key to its success. However, in the 1960s and 1970s, *no one* knew how to measure (or was measuring) the economics of this type of investment to convert the oilman's legitimate oil patch measurement standards into guidelines that a typical oil and gas investor could use to determine how well (or poorly) his investment return stacked up against other investment opportunities that were readily available to him. As a result:

(1) In the 70s and early 80s, many atrocious oil and gas investments flourished, since few investors (or their advisors) realized how poor these "opportunities" really were.

---

[1] Most state and federal securities agencies still consider the use of projections in oil and gas drilling ventures as highly questionable. **Chapter Six** will explain why that's of real concern to the legitimate oilman.

Is it really impossible to secure any useful guidance on the expected results of your oil and gas investments? We'll bring up this thorny topic later in this Chapter.

(2) Now most investors are shying away from outstanding proposals, since they don't realize how attractive *appropriate* oil and gas investments can be under today's conditions.[2]

In this Chapter, we'll first set return standards for oil and gas investment, and then see how likely it is that *intelligent* investment will deliver such levels of return. Next, we'll help you convert "oilman's return" into return levels that *you* can understand, and can convert into measurement bases which can be applied against the other investment opportunities you are considering. We'll determine whether or not diversification can level out the "peaks and valleys" that seem unavoidable in oil, and see exactly what constitutes such "diversification" where oil and gas drilling is involved. Finally, we'll factor in recent tax proposals to see what their impact might be on the profitability of oil and gas investment.

Setting an Appropriate Return Standard. We need a *return standard* for our oil and gas investment for various reasons. First, it will help us set a "minimum" required return: if we don't feel comfortable that oil can attain *this* standard, we should look for some other type of investment (even, as a last resort, paying our taxes and investing in Treasury Bills, Certificates of Deposit, or other "Money Market" instruments). Next, we'll establish a "target" level of return—one which we feel oil and gas can reasonably attain, if we simply use a little selectivity in choosing our oil and gas investments. (After all, why should you settle for an "attractive" level of return if selectivity could give you a *very* attractive return rate?)

(Note that we said our "target" needed to be *realistic*: one of the biggest mistakes an investor can make is to fall for the "siren song" of unscrupulous promoters, who offer "Easter Bunny" opportunities that common sense would tell you are clearly "too good to be true"!)[3]

Besides being *realistic*, our return standards must satisfy two additional criteria:

(1) The return must be stated on an *after-tax* basis: while, as we've seen, taxes won't "make" the deal, the tax consequences—both positive and negative—very definitely have an effect on investment return.

(2) Future revenues—and future expenditures—must be *discounted* to take into account the "time value of money."

---

[2] The "contrarian" opportunities presented by today's "buyer's market" in oil have been touched upon earlier, and will be discussed in greater detail later in this Chapter.

[3] The legitimate oilman's ventures often look anemic compared to these "spectacular" opportunities offered by the con man. But the con man can afford to make these promises: he doesn't intend to be around when they fail to materialize!

The "time value of money" concept was touched upon briefly in **Chapter Two**—there, in connection with its impact on the tax consequences of oil and gas investment. Basically, time value of money takes into account that the longer a liability can be put off, the less costly it will prove, since you will have the use of your money in the meantime (which means that this money can be making more money for you—often enough to pay off the eventual liability). Similarly, the quicker a benefit is received, the greater its value, since those dollars can now be put to work on your behalf (again, earning you money on your money).[4]

(Of course, the reverse is true as well. For instance, when an oilman tells you his venture should return you four to one on your money, ask him whether that's within two, or two hundred years!)

There is another factor we will need to take into account—whether the investment is made on an all-cash basis, without any use of borrowings, or whether leverage is to be utilized. This Chapter, though, is going to assume that your investment is all-cash; we won't get into leverage until **Chapter Four**.

As our *minimum return level*, let's set a *10% "internal rate of return."* (Internal rate of return, by definition, is an annual return rate, stated on an after-tax basis, and discounted for time. Thus, a 10% internal rate of return equates to a *20% "money market" rate* in a 50% federal income tax bracket; in other words, you'd require a Certificate of Deposit paying a taxable rate of 20% to equal this 10% "IRR.")

There are several reasons for using this 10% internal rate of return as our minimum return standard. First, it's a return rate that can be realized from one obvious alternative to oil and gas investment—investing in real estate.[5] It also bears some relation to the return levels which the recent "Treasury II" tax proposals assume are necessary to attract business capital.[6]

---

[4] For an excellent discussion of the time value of money as applied to tax-sheltered investments, see Krane, "A Dollar and Cents Analysis of Tax Sheltered Investments in an Inflationary Economy," **TAXES–The Tax Magazine** (December, 1980).

[5] The most recent study of the performance of SEC- registered real estate limited partnerships shows that such investments are returning an approximate 10% internal rate of return to their investors, assuming a 50% federal income tax bracket. See "The 1985 Investment Partnership Study: The Performance of Public Real Estate Limited Partnerships Formed Between 1971-1980" (Liquidity Fund: 1985); see also "Real Estate Performance Update," **The Stanger Report** (June, 1985).

[6] The May, 1985 "Reagan" tax reform proposals assume that business requires a 4% "real" (after-tax/after-inflation) rate of return, and also presuppose a 5% annual inflation rate. See "The President's Tax Proposals to the Congress for Fairness, Growth, and Simplicity," frequently referred to as "Treasury II."

And as mentioned in **Chapter One,** it's the *average* return currently being realized by investors in SEC-registered oil and gas drilling programs. (Why set a "minimum" return below that you could realize by throwing a dart at a list of the public drilling programs?)

But a "minimum" return standard is just that: the minimum below which we wouldn't even consider oil and gas as a possible investment vehicle. We hope we can do much better than this. So as our "target" return level, let's use a *20% internal rate of return.*

One reason we've selected this 20% IRR as our target is that we're talking about a return that equals a *40%* taxable "money market" rate—a *truly* attractive return level. (How many Certificates of Deposit—or other passive investments, including real estate—do you know that generate this level of return?) So this rate of return—if it's realistic to expect it can be realized from oil and gas investment—is certainly a step in the right direction as a method of compensating for the perceived risks of investing in oil. (And, as we'll see below, the *perception* of those risks is much greater than the reality.)

But a second reason for shooting for—and attaining (or exceeding!)—a 20% internal rate of return from oil and gas investment is that it is a return level which is *very easy to reach, SO LONG AS YOU INVEST WITH SELECTIVITY!* (We'll justify that statement a little later in this Chapter.) And why settle for less?

Can Oil and Gas Attain These Return Levels? Earlier in this Chapter, we said that it was critical that any return standards selected be *reasonable* return levels—in other words, ones which we felt *could* be achieved through our oil and gas investments, at least so long as we used a little selectivity.

A 10% internal rate of return doesn't sound all that hard to reach (although many uninformed or ill-advised oil and gas investors haven't even come close). But a 20% IRR starts to smack of that child-like belief in the Easter Bunny which we've been told to avoid. (This seems particularly true when we're also informed that this return level can be reached without taking the kinds of risk normally associated with oil and gas investment.) However, even this apparently high target return is easily attainable for the oil and gas investor who knows what he's doing.

Studies by the prestigious investment banking firm of Salomon Brothers have established that oil and gas has proven the most profitable of the major investment areas, even on a *pre-tax* basis.[7] (See **Chapter One.**) Furthermore, analyses by Robert A. Stanger & Co. and Investment Search, Inc., also

---

[7] See **Figure One**, contained in **Chapter One.**

cited in **Chapter One**, show that the *average* investor in SEC-registered drilling programs has realized a 10% internal rate of return. The results of the Stanger and Invesearch studies seem to bode well for investors who are satisfied with a 10% IRR.[8] However, they might seem to indicate that only with luck could you realize our target 20% return level. (And we're trying to *invest*—not gamble—in oil.) But the Investment Search studies also show that *20% of the sponsors of the public drilling programs—one out of five—have CONSISTENTLY delivered in excess of a 20% internal rate of return to their investors.*[9]

Historically then, investors who know how to invest selectively can realistically look forward to reaching or exceeding our target return levels. But what of recent changes in the tax laws, and in the economic conditions, facing the oil and gas industry? The top federal income tax bracket, which obviously affects the value of oil's tax advantages, has been reduced by the Economic Recovery Tax Act of 1981 from 70% to the present 50%—and may go lower. The demand for oil and natural gas has at least temporarily reversed the "insatiable need" pattern of the 1970s, creating an oil "glut" and a natural gas "bubble," with a resulting drop in both the demand, and the price paid, for these hydrocarbons. And the expected 1985 "turnaround" in oil and natural gas prices not only failed to materialize, oil prices have continued to decline and may go lower still.[10]

Finally, mislabelled tax "reform" proposals may eliminate—or significantly modify—some of oil's traditional tax advantages.[11]

In light of these changes—actual and anticipated—can we still say that oil and gas investment remains "the best game in town," one which still

---

[8] A Catch-22 is that investors who selected a drilling program offered by a large, established sponsor, or who relied upon the advice of major investment banking houses, fared much worse than this average. We'll have more to say about this in **Chapter Five**, where we'll also show you how to avoid this trap.

[9] If only 20% of the *partnerships* were reaching this return level, the figure would be less encouraging: it would be a question of whether you were lucky enough to participate in those particular undertakings. But since 20% of program *sponsors* are CONSISTENTLY attaining these levels of return, the question now becomes one of learning how to identify these one out of five superior performers. And such superior performers are easily identifiable, using the techniques we'll outline in **Chapter Five**.

[10] See "The Future of Oil Prices: The Perils of Prophecy" (Arthur Andersen & Co.-Cambridge Energy Research Associates: 1984). This joint study concludes that the most "certain" aspect of forecasting future oil prices is that such forecasting is *imprecise* in establishing a "single" case for oil prices: there is no way to develop a reliable, single case scenario that will tell us with any degree of certainty exactly what oil prices will be in the future.

[11] See **Chapter Two**.

offers you, as a passive investor, a strong likelihood of attaining our target return level?

First, let's look at the impact of a reduced tax rate.

One of the most common *misperceptions* concerning oil and gas investment is that such investment will prove profitable only for those in the higher federal income tax brackets. A high tax bracket primarily affects an investor's *ability to accept risk*. If I invest in an *unprofitable* well or program, *the higher my tax bracket the less money I LOSE*, since I have fewer "hard" dollars at stake. On the other hand, if I participate in a *profitable* well or program, *the higher my tax bracket the less money I MAKE*, since more of my profit goes to Uncle Sam. Thus, ERTA's lowering of the top federal income tax bracket from 70% to 50% made unprofitable investments even less profitable, but made profitable investments even more profitable. See **Figure Three**.[12]

(Doesn't that mean that you'd be even better off if "tax reform" reduced your top bracket to 35%? No, not really: as we'll see later in this Chapter, that drop in tax bracket would be offset by the loss of Percentage Depletion.)

But what about the drop in oil and natural gas prices? In 1981, oil was selling for $41 a barrel; in 1982, natural gas prices reached $11 an MCF. That's a far cry from today's prices.

True, today's prices are much lower. But, then, so are today's drilling costs, and the costs of equipment, supplies and services. And in today's "buyer's market," the terms on which your general partner can acquire leases from landowners or other members of the oil and gas industry are much more favorable—as are the terms on which he'll let you into his deals (if you're smart enough to know what to ask for!).[13] As a result, even at current oil and gas price levels, you should do *50% better* at today's lower costs and improved deal terms than you would have done at 1981 price levels (and 1981's higher costs and less favorable terms). *The price of oil would have to drop to below $15 a barrel for you to receive less than a 20% internal rate of return at present cost and deal term levels!*[14]

---

[12] Even more importantly, ERTA made *all* types of oil and gas investment more profitable for the former "maxi-tax" investor—the investor with a high income level the "earned" nature of which limited that investor's top tax bracket to 50%. See Mosburg, "ERTA Increases Both Risks and Rewards," **National Tax Shelter Digest** (March, 1982).

[13] We explain this change in deal terms in **Chapter Five**.

[14] See "The Economics of Oil and Gas Investment," contained in Mosburg (ed.), **Financing Oil and Gas Deals 1986 Edition** (Energy Textbooks International, Inc.: 1986). We'll be referring to this article as "Oil Investment Economics." (See also Mosburg and Fitzgerald, "When Do Investors 'Make Money' In Oil?," contained in Mosburg (ed.), **Techniques of Oil and Gas Tax-Shelter Financing** [Energy Textbooks International, Inc.: 1983, with 1985 Supplement].)

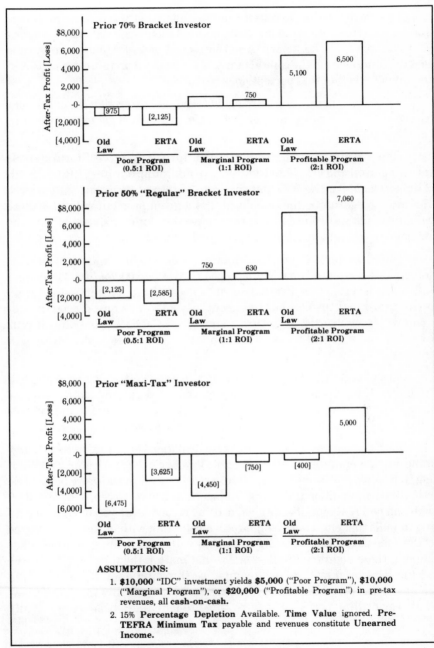

FIGURE THREE: Impact of ERTA's Rate Reductions.

So, contrary to the *perceived* effects, changes in the economic conditions and the tax rules affecting oil and gas investment have actually *improved* your chances to make money. And that's good news for you, since anyone seeking funding from the capital markets has to pay a premium for perceived conditions, whether that perception is real or not!

(Of course, there is one more *possible* change to consider: the enactment of certain "flat tax" proposals now before Congress. We'll get to those later in this Chapter.)

Converting the Oilman's Return Into a *Useable* Standard. So investing in oil and gas should deliver, at a minimum, our 10% IRR, and, with a little selectivity, the 20% internal rate of return that's our target level. However, to determine the likelihood that a given proposal will meet those return standards, we need to be able to convert "oilman's return" into the internal rate of return standard we've set for ourselves.

Unfortunately, when the oilman advises you how your well or partnership is doing (or tells you how a proposed investment *should* do), he doesn't talk about internal rate of return (or, if he does, it's often not presented in an accurate fashion). Instead, he talks about "payout"—how quickly your investment will be returned—or "return on investment" ("ROI"), the ratio of your expected undiscounted future net revenues to the monies you've invested in the deal.

Payout and ROI have one advantage: they're relatively easy to calculate from data the oilman must provide you under federal and state securities laws.[15] (We'll show you where to find that data, and how to use it, in **Chapter Five**.) They have, though, some real flaws as a useable standard for *you*.

Both payout and ROI are *pre-tax* calculations—and we need to determine our economics on an *after-tax* basis. Payout can be particularly misleading in a "program" investment, because most of your initial revenues will be reinvested in additional drilling, rather than being currently distributed. This can be a real plus, if additional drilling is successful: you'll be participating in wells that often have a high return potential, without the same degree of dry hole risk that's normally associated with such drilling. (On the other hand, if those additional wells—or, for that matter, the initial wells—never should have been drilled, you'll simply be throwing away those revenues.) However, this also means that, in a successful partnership involving a several-year drilling period, it may be three to four years before you actually

---

[15] Some oilmen won't furnish you that data in connection with a proposed investment, despite the fact that the securities laws say they must. What does that tell you about investing with such a promoter?

receive any significant distributions, and up to seven years until those distributions actually equal your original investment. (As a rule of thumb, a single-well investment should pay out in not less than two years—and hopefully much sooner, and a multi-well investment, which might include several non-productive wells, should pay out within not less than four years if all those wells were drilled in the first year of the program.[16]

Return on Investment, in addition to being a pre-tax figure, also hasn't been discounted for time.[17] So what we need is a method of converting that readily-ascertainable "ROI" figure into the one which will have more meaning for us: internal rate of return.

As a rule of thumb, if you are in the 50% federal income tax bracket,[18] and if you invest on an all-cash basis,[19] a return of $1.30 to $1.50, cash-on-cash, for each dollar you've invested, within ten years of the date of your investment, will equate to a 10% internal rate of return. (In other words, you invest $10,000, and receive back $13,000 to $15,000 within ten years from the date of your investment.) A ten-year cash-on-cash return of *two* dollars for each dollar invested will equal a 20% internal rate of return. ($20,000 over the ten-year period.)

We've illustrated these results—and their "money market equivalency" (what type of a Certificate of Deposit rate it would take to equal the oil and gas return)—in **Figure Four**.

In arriving at these conclusions, we've selected a typical "decline curve" for an oil well—the period of time over which our assumed revenues would be received. We've also factored in the tax consequences of the investment (e.g., the deductibility of the Intangible Drilling and Development Costs and the taxes payable on the revenues, assuming Percentage Depletion is available). We've also assumed that you were investing in a program which participated in drilling over several years, so that no revenues were distributed to you for 24 months. Then we've calculated the discount rate, *applied to the AFTER-*

---

[16] Doesn't that seven-year payout on a partnership which was drilling over a period of three to four years mean that your return has really suffered under time value of money principles? No, because your initial revenues *were* working for you by being reinvested in the additional drilling.

[17] Oilmen, for their own purposes, sometimes make a "DROI" (Discounted Return on Investment) calculation, where both revenues and costs are discounted for time before their ratio is calculated. However, for our purposes, this can be difficult to calculate from the *verifiable* data that will be readily available to you.

[18] Later in this Chapter, we'll give you some alternate standards if your tax bracket drops to 35% as a result of the enactment of "tax reform."

[19] As we indicated earlier, the rules will change if you decide to use leverage. See **Chapter Four**.

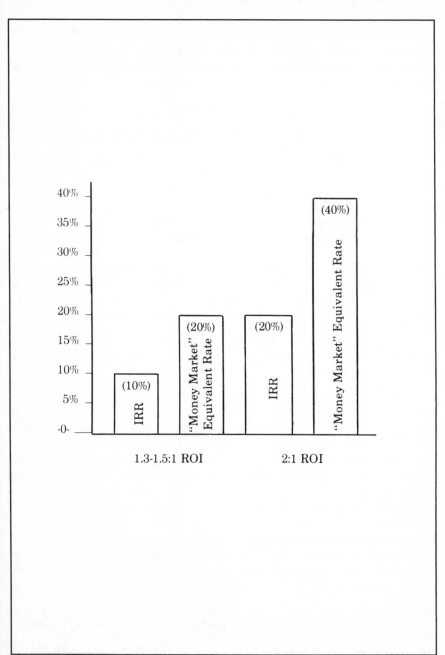

FIGURE FOUR: Oil and Gas "ROIs" Compared With Internal Rates of Return and "Money Market" Equivalencies: All-Cash Investor.

TAX figures, which would reduce the sum of the present worth of each year's net cash flow position to zero (the definition of internal rate of return).[20] **Figure Five** illustrates the calculation for a 1.36:1 ROI. **Figure Six** shows the calculation for a 2:1 ROI.

In developing these ROI guidelines for you, we're not trying to win the Nobel Prize for Accuracy in Economics. If the reserves depleted over ten years, rather than the eight years we've assumed, or distributions started at the end of the first year (or, better still, after six months) rather than at the end of the second year, the internal rate of return would change. What we *are* trying to do is help you develop a "gut feel" as to whether the returns from a given oil and gas investment represent a truly attractive return—one which you should actively pursue—or are no better (or even worse) than returns from other readily-available investments which involve little or no risk.

For instance, what about drilling in so-called "sure thing" areas? There are parts of the United States where virtually every well drilled will be a productive well, and the oilman brags about his "100% 'success ratio.'" Oh, sure, these aren't the "barn burners" that some oilmen occasionally hit, but at least the wells will "pay out."[21] And with the tax benefits—this oilman assures you—you'll still be receiving a very handsome return, with virtually no risk.

A great story—if you don't analyze the economics. Yes, you are making a profit on these sure thing wells (*IF they pay out*): *a 3% internal rate of return!* That's only a 6% "money market" rate—and you would have received that from a savings account. (Do you call this a 100% "success" ratio? I don't.[22])

There are certain factors, however, to which oil and gas investment return is very sensitive. You need to be aware of these in developing your investment strategy.

Oil and gas investment is very sensitive to the level of front-end deductibility. In a typical investment, your deductions in the first year will equal about 70% of your subscription, due to the "capital" nature of the Lease and Equipment Costs charged to your account.[23] However, if you invest on a "Functional Allocation" basis, where these capital expenditures are paid by

---

[20] This is a fairly simplified way of explaining the methodology used. If you'd like to look at a more complete explanation, see "Oil Investment Economics," cited in footnote 14, above.

[21] Have you noticed, though, how many of these wells which are "sure to pay out" never do?

[22] See why it's so important to know how to analyze the economics?

[23] See **Chapter Two**.

Present Worth at Assumed 1.36:1 Return*

YEAR	INITIAL CASH INVESTMENT (PRE-TAX)	PRE-TAX DISTRIBUTABLE REVENUES (UNDISCOUNTED)	TAX CONSEQUENCES TAX SAVINGS	(TAXES PAYABLE[1])	NET TAX IMPACT	NET CASH FLOW POSITION FOR YEAR	PRESENT WORTH AT PW$_{10}$ FOR YEAR	CUMULATIVE
0	(10,000.00)	0	5,000.00	0	5,000.00	(5,000.00)	(5,000.00)	(5,000.00)
1	0	0	0	0	0	0	0	(5,000.00)
2	0	680.00	0	(289.00)	(289.00)	391.00	322.97	(4,677.03)
3	0	2,992.00	0	(1,271.60)	(1,271.60)	1,720.40	1,292.02	(3,386.01)
4	0	2,856.00	0	(1,213.80)	(1,213.80)	1,642.20	1,121.62	(2,263.39)
5	0	2,448.00	0	(1,040.40)	(1,040.40)	1,407.60	874.12	(1,389.27)
6	0	2,448.00	0	(1,040.40)	(1,040.40)	1,407.60	793.89	(595.38)
7	0	1,360.00	0	(578.00)	(578.00)	782.00	401.17	(194.21)
8	0	340.00	0	(144.50)	(144.50)	195.50	91.30	(102.91)
9	0	340.00	0	(144.50)	(144.50)	195.50	82.89	(20.02)
10	0	136.00	0	(57.80)	(57.80)	78.20	30.18	10.16
	(10,000.00)	13,600.00					10.16	

(1) Assuming 50% bracket, disregarding Minimum Tax, and assuming 85% of revenues taxable.

*From *Study Guide, "Investing in Oil"*
Cassette Series, narrated by Lewis G. Mosburg, Jr.
(ETI Tapes, Inc.: 1982)

FIGURE FIVE: Present Worth (At PW[10]) For Assumed 1.36:1 Return: All-Cash Investor.

Present Worth of Assumed 2:1 Return*

YEAR	INITIAL CASH INVESTMENT (PRE-TAX)	PRE-TAX DISTRIBUTABLE REVENUES (UNDISCOUNTED)	TAX CONSEQUENCES			NET CASH FLOW POSITION FOR YEAR
			TAX SAVINGS	(TAXES PAYABLE[1])	NET TAX IMPACT	
0	(10,000.00)	0	5,000.00	0	5,000.00	(5,000.00)
1	0	0	0	0	0	0
2	0	1,000.00	0	(425.00)	(425.00)	575.00
3	0	4,400.00	0	(1,870.00)	(1,870.00)	2,530.00
4	0	4,200.00	0	(1,785.00)	(1,785.00)	2,415.00
5	0	3,600.00	0	(1,530.00)	(1,530.00)	2,070.00
6	0	3,600.00	0	(1,530.00)	(1,530.00)	2,070.00
7	0	2,000.00	0	(850.00)	(850.00)	1,150.00
8	0	500.00	0	(212.50)	(212.50)	287.50
9	0	500.00	0	(212.50)	(212.50)	287.50
10	0	200.00	0	(85.00)	(85.00)	115.00
	(10,000.00)	20,000.00				

	PRESENT WORTH	
	PW$_{20}$	
YEAR	FOR YEAR	CUMULATIVE
0	(5,000.00)	(5,000.00)
1	0	(5,000.00)
2	399.05	(4,600.95)
3	1,464.87	(3,136.08)
4	1,164.03	(1,972.05)
5	832.14	(1,139.91)
6	693.45	(446.46)
7	320.85	(125.61)
8	66.99	(58.62)
9	55.78	(2.84)
10	18.63	15.79
	15.79	

(1) Assuming 50% bracket,
    disregarding Minimum Tax
    and assuming 85% of
    revenues taxable.

*From *Study Guide, "Investing in Oil"*
Cassette Series, narrated by Lewis G. Mosburg, Jr.
(ETI Tapes, Inc.: 1982)

**FIGURE SIX: Present Worth (at PW[20]) For Assumed 2:1 Return:
All-Cash Investor.**

your general partner, you are charged only with currently deductible expenditures—and your return can significantly improve.[24] See **Figure Seven.**

(Does this mean that you should only invest on a Functional Allocation basis? No, because the Functional Allocation sponsor normally charges you a premium for agreeing to bear these Lease and Equipment Costs: he receives a larger share of "free" program revenues than does the non-Functional Allocation sponsor. So, in **Chapter Five**, we'll show you how to determine whether this premium is worth paying.)

Oil and gas investment return is also very sensitive to the date on which you begin to receive revenues. If possible distributions are being delayed to reinvest your share of well revenues in additional drilling, time value of money isn't working against you, as you are (hopefully) increasing your reserves. But if you participate in wells in a remote area where the production can't be marketed for a long period of time, or drill a series of "shut-in" gas wells for which there is no present market, it may be years before any revenues are generated and are available for reinvestment—or distribution. And, as **Figure Eight** illustrates, this delay in the receipt of cash flow—if it doesn't merely reflect a profitable reinvestment of otherwise distributable revenues—can have a devastating effect on investment return.

The single most IMPORTANT factor affecting your return, apart from dealing with a quality oil finder, is the degree of front-end dilution. Dollars that are charged to you for "front-end" items, such as front-end management fees, reimbursement for Organizational and Offering Costs, and the like, are not available for the conduct of operations—they're not "going into the ground." And this means that not all of your dollars are working for you.

A certain amount of front-end dilution is unavoidable in most program investments.[25] But, as **Figure Nine** illustrates, the degree of front-end dilution has a dramatic impact on the potential profitability of your oil and gas investment.

(This is the reason we warned you, in **Chapter Two**, that there are economic as well as tax snares in drilling wells on a "turnkey" basis. The "fixed fee" that the oil man charges for that "turnkeyed" well always represents a mark-up over expected actual cost—it's really a disguised form of front-end profit, and not monies that are truly "going into the ground." And even if that mark-up is no more than a modest 15%, this dilution plus a typical

---

[24] Functional Allocation was discussed in **Chapter Two**, and will be considered in greater detail in **Chapter Five**.

[25] In **Chapter Five**, we'll quantify what are acceptable and unacceptable levels of front-end dilution.

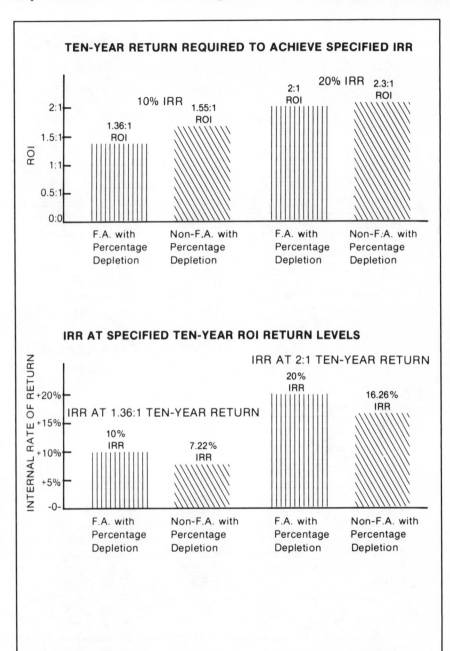

FIGURE SEVEN: Effect of Various Factors on Internal Rate of Return to All-Cash Investor.

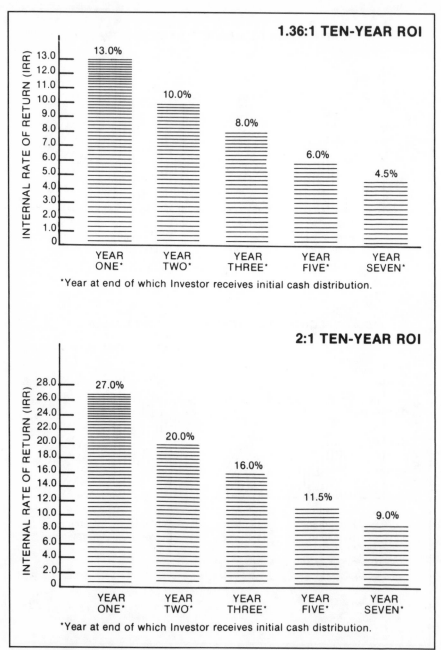

FIGURE EIGHT: Impact of Timing of Initial Cash Distributions to All-Cash Investor at Various Assumed Return Levels.

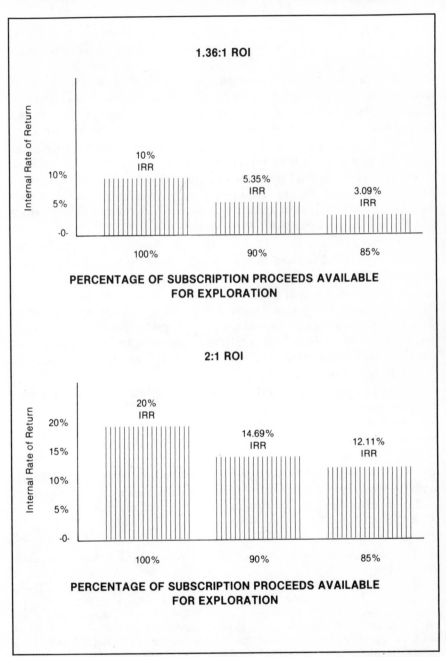

FIGURE NINE: Impact of Front-End Dilution on Return to All-Cash Investor.

charge of an additional 15% for Organizational and Offering Cost reimbursement would mean that *only 70% of your dollars were actually working for you.*)

The Impact of Diversification. In **Chapter One**, we examined the risks that are inherent in the search for oil and gas. And no matter how well the geologists and petroleum engineers do their job, investing all your money in the drilling of a single well is a gamble—and a gamble that few win.

(What if that single well is a developmental well, drilled within the limits of an established field, rather than an exploratory well? That can be riskier still. As we saw in **Chapter One**, "step out" developmental wells often are non-productive. And in "sure thing" areas, you won't lose *all* of your money, but it's usually equally sure that the well will never pay out—that's why the oilman preferred to let *you* drill that "sure thing".)[26]

We also promised you in **Chapter One** that we would show you how the risks of oil could be reduced to manageable levels through *diversification*. Now we'll try to live up to that promise.

Common sense would seem to tell you that, if instead of putting all your money in a single well you participated in a large number of wells, drilled on varying types of prospects located throughout the United States, the peaks and valleys of oil ought to level out. (If so, a "one shot" investment in oil and gas could still make sense.) Unfortunately, this is one time that "common sense" doesn't work out.

Figure Ten illustrates the results of participating in the separate partnerships sponsored by one of the largest public drilling program sponsors. Each of these partnerships participated in many wells in various geographical areas. As you can see, even that degree of "one-shot" diversification hasn't leveled out oil's risks.[27]

Now let's see what would have happened had you invested consistently with Company A for a three to five year period. As **Figure Eleven** shows, *no matter which three or five year period you'd selected, the results would have ALWAYS leveled out*!

---

[26] The choice between participating in exploratory and developmental drilling is examined in **Chapter Five**.

[27] However, recent studies have indicated that the results of a large, multi-prospect partnership may be *predictable* by a qualified "due diligence" expert. See Holmes *et al.*, "A New Method of Estimating Risk-Adjusted Reserves and Economic Potential of Exploratory Prospects," contained in Megill (ed), **Economics and the Explorer: AAPG Studies in Geology #19** (American Association of Petroleum Geologists: 1985). A simplified version of Mr. Holmes' conclusions is contained in Mosburg (ed.), **1985-1986 Real Estate and Oil & Gas Investment Symposium** (Energy Textbooks International, Inc.: 1985).

The significance of "due diligence" in oil and gas investment is discussed in **Chapter Six**.

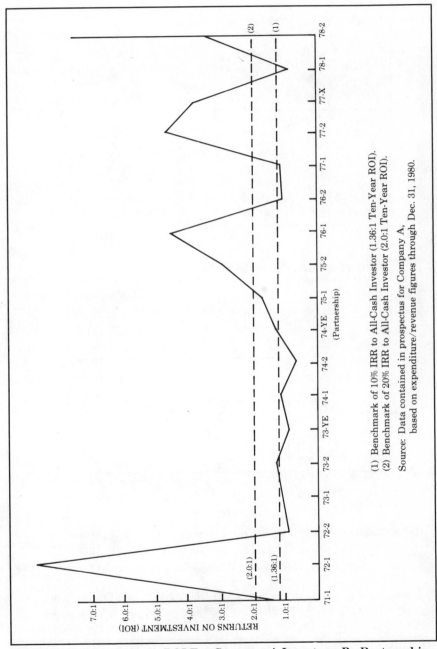

(1) Benchmark of 10% IRR to All-Cash Investor (1.36:1 Ten-Year ROI).
(2) Benchmark of 20% IRR to All-Cash Investor (2.0:1 Ten-Year ROI).

Source: Data contained in prospectus for Company A, based on expenditure/revenue figures through Dec. 31, 1980.

FIGURE TEN: Variance in ROI For Company A Investors; By Partnership.

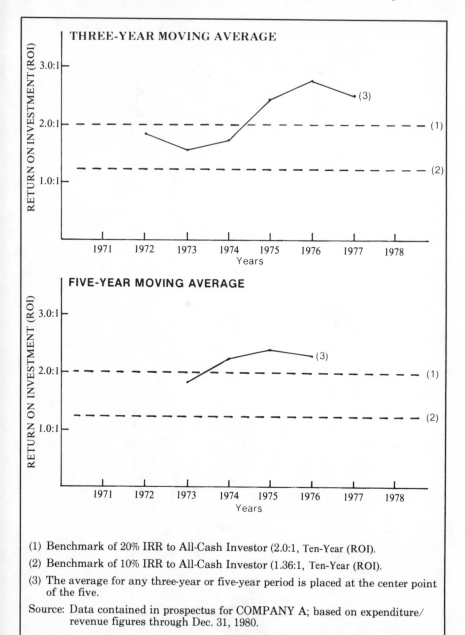

(1) Benchmark of 20% IRR to All-Cash Investor (2.0:1, Ten-Year (ROI).

(2) Benchmark of 10% IRR to All-Cash Investor (1.36:1, Ten-Year (ROI).

(3) The average for any three-year or five-year period is placed at the center point of the five.

Source: Data contained in prospectus for COMPANY A; based on expenditure/ revenue figures through Dec. 31, 1980.

FIGURE ELEVEN: Variance in ROI for Company A Investors: Three-Year and Five-Year Moving Averages.

Are we saying that it doesn't matter *which sponsor* you select to invest with, that the results will always be the same? Far from it! Three to five year consistent investment *with the same sponsor* will cause the results to level out to *that sponsor's normal performance level.* Some sponsors—like Company A—level out relatively well; others to mediocre levels, and others prove to be terrible. Thus, in **Figures Twelve** and **Thirteen** investors with "Brand X" and "Brand Y" have had a "leveling" experience that will probably lead them never to invest in oil and gas again! (See the need for selectivity?)

So diversification can level out the roller coaster effects of oil and gas investment—*if* you engage in "'time line' diversification": find a good oil man, and stick with him (if possible, participating in a little piece of each of his projects) over a three to five year period.

(By the way, this "leveling" through time-line diversification proves equally effective for the "wildest" of frontier wildcat programs as it does for the tamest of developmental partnerships.)

Understanding diversification will pay off for you in several ways:

(1) *Time-line diversification does level out oil's peaks and valleys,* reducing the actual risks to manageable levels.

(2) Since the PERCEIVED risks of oil and gas investment are much greater than the ACTUAL risks (assuming you invest on a diversified basis), *time-line diversification permits you to reduce those actual risks while receiving the "premium" return associated with high-risk investment.* (Remember what we noted earlier: someone going to the capital markets must pay for *perceived,* rather than *actual,* risk.)

(3) And since investor returns with any sponsor tend to level out over time, *a review of a sponsor's prior performance gives a strong indication of the results you can expect from future investment with that sponsor,* making oil and gas investment results much more predictable than they are generally assumed to be.[28]

But What About the "Flat Tax"? Much "conventional wisdom" has emerged on the impact of proposed tax law changes on the desirability and profitability of oil and gas investment. Some are saying that such investment would no longer be necessary; others say that the investments would no

---

[28] That isn't to say that this "track record" analysis gives an absolute guarantee as to future results. However, it can be a very useful tool in implementing our second key to intelligent oil and gas investment: selectivity. And in **Chapter Five**, you'll learn exactly how to analyze that track record from data readily available to you—as well as how to identify those situations in which "track record" may not tell the whole story.

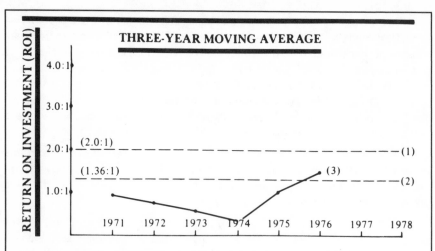

(1) Benchmark of 20% IRR to All-Cash Investor (2.0:1, Ten-Year ROI).

(2) Benchmark of 10% IRR to All-Cash Investor (1.36:1, Ten-Year ROI).

(3) The average for any three-year period is placed at the center point of the three.

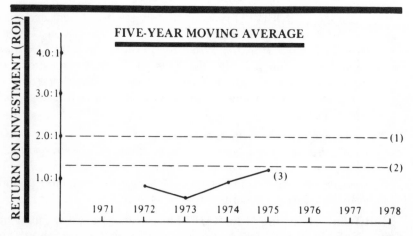

(1) Benchmark of 20% IRR to All-Cash Investor (2.0:1, Ten-Year ROI).

(2) Benchmark of 10% IRR to All-Cash Investor (1.36:1, Ten-Year ROI).

(3) The average for any five-year period is placed at center point of the five.

FIGURE TWELVE: Variation in ROI for "Brand X" Investors: Three-Year and Five-Year Moving Averages.

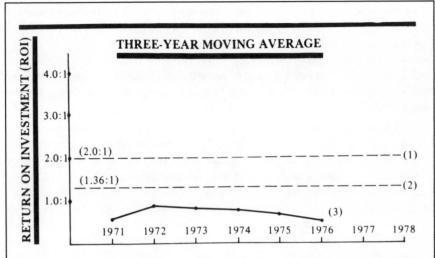

(1) Benchmark of 20% IRR to All-Cash Investor (2.0:1, Ten-Year ROI).

(2) Benchmark of 10% IRR to All-Cash Investor (1.36:1, Ten-Year ROI).

(3) The average for any three-year period is placed at the center point of the three.

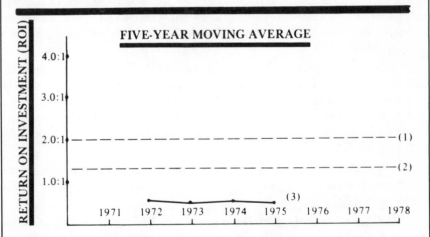

(1) Benchmark of 20% IRR to All-Cash Investor (2.0:1, Ten-Year ROI).

(2) Benchmark of 10% IRR to All-Cash Investor (1.36:1, Ten-Year ROI).

(3) The average for any five-year period is placed at center point of the five.

FIGURE THIRTEEN: Variation in ROI for "Brand Y" Investors: Three-Year and Five-Year Moving Averages.

longer be profitable if the "flat tax" were enacted. Still other savants assert that, under such a tax, the only intelligent way to participate in the oil and gas search is to select sponsors whose partnerships drill virtually no dry holes—and whose returns average three to four dollars for each of your dollars invested. You're also told to be sure that steady cash flow from those partnerships can be expected within 12 months from the date of your investment.

A word first about this last "suggestion." " 'Easter Bunny' Investing" has always been a plague that afflicts oil and gas investment. It would be marvelous to find programs that satisfy the criteria outlined by these sage advisors. And many sponsors declare (and many advisors claim) that this is exactly what they *will* accomplish, usually based upon highly-questionable analyses of *"future* net revenues." However, check the track records of any sponsors who raise money from passive investors. The 3:1 and 4:1 track records can be found—with *considerable* selectivity—but not among those sponsors drilling in "sure thing" areas.

Oil and gas is *not* an immediate cash flow game; it's an *accumulation of assets* endeavor. Money is made by accepting *intelligent levels of risk* and reducing that risk through diversification.[29] It requires making an initial investment to identify those prospects which are worthy of further development, followed by a several-year reinvestment of revenues to build additional reserves at much lower risk through that developmental drilling on prospects *whose profitability has been established by YOUR initial risk-taking.*

There is a significant distinction between "exploitation" developmental drilling on exploratory or higher-risk developmental prospects whose profitability has been established through risks taken by *you* and investing in a developmental program where even the initial drilling was to be "low risk." Again, ask yourself: if this is such a low-risk "sure thing," *why was the oilman willing to turn it to me?*

If you don't believe in the Easter Bunny, and you're questioning the existence of Santa Claus, you might take a long, hard look at claims of 3:1 to 4:1 (or even 2:1!) in "sure thing" areas.

Having reluctantly abandoned the Easter Bunny, we still must decide whether or not oil and gas will still have adequate profit potential if a "flat tax" is adopted.

(The term "flat tax" is now somewhat laughable, since the present tax reform proposals call for a "graduated" flat tax—what an anomaly!—with these three tax brackets in place of the present 14. The other labels of "fair"

---

[29] More about this in **Chapter Five**.

or "simple," though, seem equally absurd—have you seen just how "simple" these new rules would be?—so let's just stick with the original "flat tax" nomenclature.)[30]

"Tax shelters" will involve a greater degree of risk, and will offer a slightly reduced return even on profitable ventures, at a top tax rate of 35%, because of the greater "hard dollar" exposure and the increased after-tax investment base that arises from offsetting the tax advantages against 65-cent rather than 50-cent dollars. Also, the "money market equivalency" will drop, since those money market dollars would only be taxed at 35%, rather than 50%. But as you can see in **Figure Fourteen**, where we've compared the return from a 2:1 ten-year oil venture with and without initial deductibility, a profitable "tax shelter" is still much more profitable than the same venture without the initial deductibility.

At the present time, it's difficult to forecast when—if ever—any major "tax reform" legislation may be enacted. The current proposals—which were supposed to be "revenue neutral"—would, in fact, significantly increase the budget deficit. Furthermore, the compromises that are inevitable if any bill is to be passed would increase that deficit even further. And more and more Americans are beginning to realize that it is difficult to develop a tax code which is either "fair" or "simple"—and impossible to draft one which is both!

If major legislation is enacted, it now appears quite likely that Percentage Depletion would be eliminated or phased out. At a 35% tax rate, however, this would be comparatively irrelevant: a 35% tax on 100% of production revenues is virtually the same as a 50% tax on the dollars remaining after the 15% Percentage Depletion allowance has been deducted.[31] After the first frenzied cries to eliminate all past tax benefits, reason has apparently taken over; and even the most liberal members of Congress now seem to understand how important IDC deductibility is to the national economy and the national defense (as well as to the oil and gas industry!) Accordingly, your ability to currently deduct Intangible Drilling and Development Costs on productive wells as well as dry holes—oil's greatest tax advantage—no longer appears in jeopardy.

So long as IDCs remain currently deductible, the proposed tax law changes would have little effect on the internal rate of return from oil and gas

---

30 For a more detailed discussion of tax-sheltered investment and the flat tax, see "Flat Tax Fears in Real Estate and Oil & Gas," contained in Mosburg (ed.), **1985-1986 Real Estate and Oil & Gas Symposium** (Energy Textbooks International, Inc.: 1985).

31 As a matter of fact, oil would actually gain from this trade-off, since Cost Depletion would still be available. And if the President's "Treasury-II" proposals were enacted, the *indexing for inflation* of the Cost Depletion base could prove a major benefit, particularly for the "income" and "combination" programs discussed in **Chapter One**. However, watch out for the possibility of a soon-to-follow "temporary" surtax if the proposed "tax reform" is enacted!

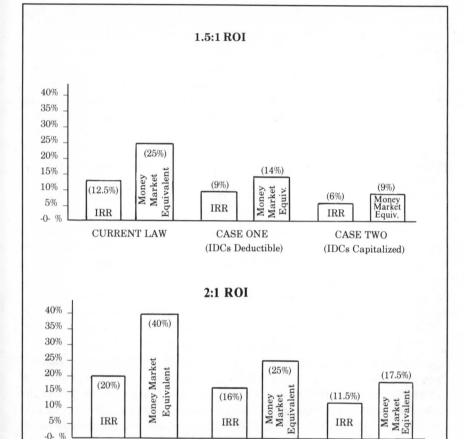

ASSUMPTIONS

(1) Investor is in 35% federal income tax bracket. Percentage Depletion is not available.

(2) Investor is charged only with Intangible Drilling and Development Costs (Functional Allocation program). All wells are productive.

(3) Case One: IDCs are currently deductible for federal income tax purposes.

(4) Case Two: IDCs are not currently deductible, and must be recovered through Cost Depletion.

FIGURE FOURTEEN: Significance of Deductibility of Drilling Costs at 35% Federal Income Tax Rate.

investment, even if Percentage Depletion were phased out: the ROI required to attain a 10% IRR would only rise from around 1.4:1 to 1.6:1, or from 2:1 to 2.3:1 to reach a 20% IRR.

But an unusual thing has occurred on the way to the Congressional circus, creating unprecedented opportunities for you as a "contrarian" investor who understands the true profit potential of oil and gas investment in today's market—with or without a "flat tax." Most investors don't realize how little oil would be affected by a flat tax. And in order to reach today's "tough" market, the better oilmen are restructuring their deals—improving deal terms *today* to match the kind of return that *would have been necessary* if IDC deductibility had been eliminated! (Remember what we said about those premiums that must be paid for *perceived* risk?)

With the levels of front-end dilution and sponsor promotion that have traditionally existed in the oil and gas industry—the same ones that provided better than a 20% internal rate of return to investors who knew how to be selective—it was still difficult for even an informed passive investor to average much better than a 2:1 to 2.5:1 ten-year ROI over any prolonged period of investment. "Oil patch insiders" who knew how to choose their oilman would normally average in the 3:1 to 4:1 range—but only because they were being let into these "oilmen's deals" on a much more favorable basis than was possible for the clients of brokerage houses and financial advisors.

Under current conditions, all that has changed. Reductions in front-end load and sponsor's promotion mean that today's selective investor can expect to realize returns in the 3:1 to 4:1 level. And even under a "flat tax," this equates to internal rates of return of 30% or better, and "money market equivalencies" in excess of a 40% annual rate—or IRR's and money market rates that go off the chart if tax laws remain unchanged!

So for the contrarian, this is the best of all times. If tax laws *do* change, today's better deal terms protect you—*more* than protect you. If the laws remain unchanged—or change, but without any elimination of IDC deductibility—you have the best of all worlds: significant tax benefits *plus* the type of investment "premium" that would have proved necessary if those tax advantages had been totally eliminated.

But those better deal terms aren't automatically going to come your way. Many oilmen are continuing to offer programs on the same "traditional" basis that was previously the rule. And you still won't make money by investing with a substandard oilfinder, irrespective of the structure of his program. So, in **Chapter Five**, we'll still need to concern ourselves with how to invest in oil on a *selective* basis.

CHAPTER FOUR
LEVERAGED INVESTMENT IN OIL AND GAS

An Introduction to Leveraged Oil and Gas Investment. A tremendous amount of confusion exists concerning the pros and cons of investing in oil and gas on a leveraged basis. Many experts assert that this type of investment is little more than a gimmick to attract the greedy and the gullible—a danger signal that there is no economic merit to the proposed investment. On the other hand, some investors assume—and a number of sponsors have asserted—that investing in oil on a leveraged basis, particularly in offerings which create "excess write-offs," guarantees investment success once the deductions reach or exceed the 200% level.[1]

Neither one of these bits of "folklore" is true. In fact, for an appropriate investor, leveraged oil and gas investment can prove an exceptionally rewarding method of participating in oil—actually enhancing investment return—*if, but only if, you understand how to PROPERLY utilize leverage.* (Unfortunately, in the past, few investors have possessed this understanding.)

Leveraged investment involves augmenting your initial cash contribution to the program with additional borrowed dollars. In some types of tax-sheltered investment, "project leverage" is involved: the partnership borrows a portion of the cost of acquiring its assets from conventional financing sources, pledging those assets as collateral for the loan.[2] But we'll be talking about "investment leverage" —where the investors borrow a portion of their customary equity contribution to the program.[3]

In this Chapter, we'll explore what leveraged oil and gas investment is all about—its pros, its cons, and its tax pitfalls—to help you decide whether this investment approach is right for you, and, if so, *how* to INTELLIGENTLY utilize leverage as a part of your oil and gas investment strategy.

The Lure of Excess Write-Offs. It's the "excess write-off" aspect of leveraged investment that first catches most investors' eyes. As illustrated in **Figures Fifteen** and **Sixteen**, once initial deductions rise to the 200% level, i.e., are twice the amount of your initial cash subscription, you are *initially* investing in the program cash-free, since your tax savings, in the 50% bracket, equal the amount of your initial cash subscription. Let those deductions rise to the 400% level, and you are creating an *initial* positive cash

---

[1] An "excess write-off" arises when your deductions exceed your initial cash investment in the program. *Such excess deductions can ONLY be created through the use of leverage.*

[2] Typical examples would be real estate, equipment, and "oil income" limited partnerships.

[3] While partnerships utilizing investment leverage have been the traditional "black sheep" of the leverage family, the "double-edged sword" aspect of leverage is equally applicable to project leverage. (See **Chapter One** for a discussion of some of the problems created by the use of investment leverage in "income" programs.)

1. Cash Subscription............ [$10,000]

2. Deductions.................... 20,000

3. Tax Savings 10,000
4. Less Subscriptions .... [10,000]
5. CASH-FLOW GAIN [LOSS] .... -0-

FIGURE FIFTEEN: Effect on Cash Position of 50% Bracket Investor of 200% Initial Deductibility.

1. Cash Subscription............. [$10,000]

2. Deductions...................... 40,000

3. Tax Savings 20,000

4. Less Subscription .... [10,000]

5. CASH-FLOW GAIN [LOSS] .. $10,000

FIGURE SIXTEEN: Effect on Cash Position of 50% Bracket Investor of 400% Initial Deductibility.

flow—the investment "puts cash in your pocket," because the tax savings exceed your original cash requirements. (But watch out for our constant emphasis of "initial" and "initially"!)

If these initial tax deductions represented permanent tax savings, then leveraged investment could guarantee investment success. Unfortunately, deductions generated through borrowed dollars create a *deferral* of tax liability only—you are simply "borrowing" tax savings from Uncle Sam (just as you borrowed the money which created those tax savings), and these deductions must eventually be restored.

The price tag for utilizing leverage is the creation of "phantom income"—an income tax liability on dollars which, in economic reality, aren't really yours, but for tax purposes are treated as your own taxable income. Why? Because when the loan which created the leverage is repaid, that portion of debt service which goes for the repayment of the principal is not deductible under the federal income tax structure.[4] This means that the dollars which you must earn to repay those borrowings will be taxed to you, even though you never see them, or see them only briefly on their way to your friendly banker. And even if the loan is foreclosed or forgiven, you are treated for tax purposes as having "constructively received" income equal to the "forgiven" portion of your debt.

This isn't to say that the deductions generated through borrowed dollars are useless to you—you've still had the "time value" use of those deductions in the meantime. But if you've treated those deductions as "permanent" in analyzing the economic merits of the venture—or if you haven't provided a source to pay the taxes due on that "phantom income"—problems can arise.

So let's emphasize several points before we go any further in our discussion of leveraged oil and gas investment:

(1) *Deductions in excess of your cash investment are **always** temporary in nature.* (There is no such thing as a "permanent" excess write-off.)

(2) *The use of leverage **always** creates phantom income.* (This is true even where the leverage is used merely to increase deductibility levels closer to the 100% level, as in an "income," "completion," or "lease" fund, without the creation of any excess write-offs.)[5]

---

[4] What about the interest payments? We'll talk about them later in this Chapter.

[5] Income, completion, and lease fund investments are outlined in **Chapter One**.

(3) *The leverage utilized in oil and gas investment **always** involves "recourse"—not "non-recourse" borrowing.*[6] And this personal liability is very real. (Just ask those who used letters of credit to secure borrowings from Penn Square Bank!)[7]

The Rise and Fall of "Non-Recourse" Oil and Gas Investment. Prior to the late 1970s, "excess write-off'" investments primarily depended upon the use of non-recourse loans to generate their high level of initial deductibility. The projects to be undertaken usually had little economic worth, particularly as structured: the "friendly lender" was usually the venture promoter (or an affiliate); and the loan merely financed the purchase of an asset, or the providing of services, at a highly inflated price. (That's the reason the affiliated lender could afford to loan on a non-recourse basis: he was simply lending a portion of the amount which the investors were being overcharged for the "privilege" of participating in the deal!)

In the '70s, oil had such investments: "non-recourse loan oil programs" in which wells were drilled on a turnkey basis, with 50% of the cost of the well being loaned to the investors on a non-recourse basis by the driller or one of his affiliates. In such programs, if the turnkey price was $100,000 (50% of which was provided through a non-recourse loan), the normal cost of the well would probably have been $50,000 (or less!). This also meant that, even if the arrangement survived an audit (or, as a result of "winning the tax audit lottery'" was *not audited*, the investor was still, at a maximum, receiving only $50,000 of "true action," i.e., only half of his money, at most, was actually going into the ground.

In theory, investors could make money from such investments through the time value of the excess write-offs, irrespective of the economic merits of the projects. In practice, however, these investments seldom proved profitable. And this, combined with the enactment by Congress of its "at-risk limitations on loss"—limiting an investor's tax benefits to the dollars for which he is

---

[6] In a "non-recourse loan," the lender looks only to the collateral for repayment of the borrowing. In a "recourse loan," you are personally liable on the debt.

[7] The "at-risk limitations on loss," considered later in this Chapter, require personal liability for deductions to exceed 100% of your cash contribution to the partnership. And even where the at-risk limitations would not apply (e.g., where you are only trying to raise deductibility to the 100% level), oil and gas lenders insist on personal liability on the part of the borrowers.

financially at risk—has significantly reduced investment in such "phony" tax shelters.[8]

The changes in tax laws, and in the attitude of the investors, hasn't signaled an end to the desire for excess write-offs. Instead, many investors now are prepared to accept a certain degree of increased risk—risk that in theory, but in theory only, the "non-recourse" nature of the previous lending had eliminated—in return for a combination of excess write-offs coupled with investments of true economic potential. And this has set the stage for an *intelligent* utilization of leverage.

Regrettably, there has been so little understanding of how leverage *can* be intelligently utilized in oil and gas investment that this "goal" has seldom been achieved. But—read on!

A Typical Scenario for Today's Leveraged Oil and Gas Investments—The Base Scenario. In the typical leveraged oil and gas program, you would be given various options on your method of subscription. First, you could subscribe on an all-cash basis.[9] Second, you could utilize a "built-in" leverage feature, through which you borrow a portion of your agreed subscription—anywhere from 30% to 90%—from a lending source arranged by the program sponsor; normally securing that borrowing through a letter of credit or investor surety bond.[10]

(What? Didn't letter of credit arrangements go the way of the dodo bird during the demise of Penn Square Bank? Far from it! And such arrangements can still make a lot of sense—*IF leveraged investment is truly right for you and IF you'll follow the guidelines we outline in this Chapter!)*[11]

---

[8] The at-risk limitations on loss, *which at the present time do not apply to real estate* (where non-recourse lending is a common, and legitimate, financing technique), will be discussed in more detail later in this Chapter.

To learn of other techniques currently being used to curb "abusive" tax shelters, see **Chapter Two**.

[9] This doesn't mean that you can't still utilize leverage through the "do-it-yourself" borrowing discussed later in this Chapter.

[10] The use of an investor surety bond as an alternative to a letter of credit has certain advantages, as we'll see below. However, as we'll also see, direct borrowing has advantages over both.

[11] In some instances, the sponsor may provide a third "built-in" alternative—*unsecured* borrowing through a source arranged by the sponsor for investors whose personal financial positions are strong enough to justify such loans. All of these "sponsored-arranged" borrowing options, though, are available only in "private" offerings—programs which are not required to be registered with the Securities and Exchange Commission, because of the limitations imposed on "public" programs (and "public" intrastate offerings) by Regulation T of the Federal Reserve Board. (These "Reg T" restrictions do not apply to "do-it-yourself" borrowing, where the sponsor is in no way involved in "arranging"—or paving the way—for the borrowing.)

Let's assume that you subscribe for a $25,000 "Unit" in XX Oil Company's 1986-1 Drilling Program. You elect to finance 80% of your subscription through a "letter of credit" option. You accordingly put up $5,000 of your own money, and borrow $20,000 from XX's bank, putting up a two-year irrevocable letter of credit from *your* bank as collateral for that borrowing. The full $25,000—your $5,000, plus the borrowed $20,000—is then paid into the partnership.

The amount of your letter of credit would usually equal 120% to 130% of the principal of the loan, to give the lending bank a "cushion" to cover accruing interest. In some programs, the letter of credit simply equals the amount of the loan principal; and the lending bank insists on a "reserve" to cover future interest. However, this alternative has quite an adverse effect on investment return.[12]

Since the general partner has received the full $25,000, he doesn't care whether you participate as an all-cash investor or utilize the leverage option. Also, note that only *you*—not the partnership, your fellow partners, or even the general partner or the assets of the partnership (other than *your* interest in those assets)—are liable on this loan; and only *you* will be charged with the debt service on the loan, including the interest obligation. (Or at least that's the way the loan *ought* to be structured!)

The partnership utilizes the full subscription proceeds—again, the amounts you and your fellow investor paid out of your own cash assets *and* the amount of your borrowings—to drill the partnership wells. If that drilling is successful, *in theory* the lending bank will replace the letter of credit loans with "production loans," accepting the reserves established by the drilling as collateral for the loans in lieu of the letters of credit; and your letter of credit will be released. You then— again, *in theory*—sit back and relax, while your share of the production revenues satisfy your debt service obligations.[13]

(Of course, if the drilling results are disappointing, you must pay off the balance of your loan obligation prior to the expiration of your letter of credit or face a "call" of the letter.)

Two important aspects of this method of investing need to be emphasized from the start:

---

[12] See "Oil Investment Economics," cited in footnote 13 of **Chapter Three**.

[13] Keep in mind that you are now in a "phantom income" position: your share of the production revenues will be taxed to you, even though the proceeds are normally going directly to the lending bank.

(1) Unlike the previous "non-recourse" leveraged oil programs, with their phony turnkeys, the full amount of your subscription is going into the ground: you are getting a full $25,000 worth of "action."[14]

(2) You are also "at risk" *in every sense of the word* for the *full amount of your subscription*—this is not a "paper" obligation!

—What About That Production Loan? Most investors who participated in "letter of credit" programs in the late 70s and early 80s assumed that their letters of credit would never be called. Sure, the confidential memorandum that accompanied that program warned them that a production loan *might* not be available and that there *might* be at least a partial call of their letters. Often, though, the investor was privately assured by the program sponsor (or by his own broker) that a production loan was sure to be available. And even without such assurances, most investors were certain that *their* letters of credit would never be called! (After all, at the time you invest, your enthusiasm for the program and the sponsor are at a fevered pitch.)

To insure that the letters would not be called as a result of a series of dry holes, many of these programs were set up to drill only in "sure thing" areas. (Many brokerage houses insisted on such a business plan.) But, then, no one was "putting a pencil" to the economics of such drilling—and the realities of production loans being available on such mediocre collateral in amounts sufficient to cover the letter-of-credit loan obligations.

The collapse of Penn Square Bank triggered the call of many letters of credit and an almost hysterical tightening of the availability of production loan credit. However, production lending practices are such that *only on an UNUSUALLY successful partnership* would a production loan have been available for the full amount of the "deferred" portion of the agreed subscription in any event.[15]

Furthermore, *accepting* a production loan, even if one is possible, may not be in your best interest. During the "drilling" phase of partnership operations, you are in a "tax positive" position: you are receiving tax benefits on dollars which you have borrowed, and a "riding" on Uncle Sam's dollars. Once production commences, you shift to a "tax negative" position as a result of your phantom income. So, from a dollars and cents standpoint, you are often better off to decline the production loan and immediately pay off the balance of your subscription loan.[16]

---

[14] Minus, of course, Organizational and Offering Costs or other front-end items.

[15] A study by Investment Search, Inc., estimates that the investors' return on investment needs to exceed 6:1 before such production loans would be possible. See "Leveraging Your Oil and Gas Investment," **Investor's Tax Shelter Report** (November, 1983).

[16] See "Oil Investment Economics," cited at footnote 14 of **Chapter Three**.

Leveraged oil and gas investment should thus be considered primarily as a financing technique which offers you more flexibility in your method of investing. It permits you to "stage" your contributions to the program *as you see fit*—in other words, it's an *installment* method of investing, rather than the "permanent" leverage found in real estate.

(In some instances, it will also provide the "permanent" leverage benefits. But, that's something we'll discuss further along in this Chapter.)

Avoiding the Tax Pitfalls of Leveraged Programs—In General. Even if leveraged investment is right for you—the true advantages and disadvantages are something we'll get into later in this Chapter—there are certain tax pitfalls that must be avoided at all costs.

The legitimate tax benefits of leverage are a key to its economic advantages. If these benefits are unnecessarily lost, then there is no reason to accept the "price tag" that leverage imposes. And there is such a price—you will be *economically at risk* for the full amount of your subscription, even when you aren't at risk for tax purposes. (It's also more costly to invest on a leveraged rather than on an all-cash basis—more about this below.)

Let's briefly list the special tax pitfalls in a leveraged oil and gas investment:[17]

(1) "At-Risk Limitations on Loss" and "Basis" Restrictions;

(2) Interest Restrictions;

(3) Phantom Income.

Remember that there are also special "cash basis" limitations that apply to prepayments; and that leveraged programs must almost invariably be registered as "tax shelters" with the Internal Revenue Service. (See **Chapter Two**.)

—At-Risk Limitations on Loss and Basis Restrictions. The games people play(ed) with non-recourse loans—usually "phony" in nature—to generate excess write-offs has been discussed earlier in this Chapter.

The at-risk limitations on loss seek to limit an investor's ability to claim tax benefits to the amount of his true economic exposure in the venture.[18] The concept, as originally enacted as a part of the Tax Reform Act of 1976,

---

[17] These pitfalls are, of course, in addition to those we discussed in **Chapter Two**, which are equally applicable to all-cash or leveraged investment. Our discussion of these special traps hits only the highlights; for a more complete consideration, see "Tax Consequences of Oil and Gas Investment Under Existing and Proposed Tax Laws," contained in Mosburg (ed.), **Financing Oil and Gas Deals—1986 Edition** (Energy Textbooks International, Inc.: 1986).

[18] Unfortunately, because of the technical nature of the rules, in a misstructured deal the investor can be economically at risk without being at risk for tax purposes.

contained enough loopholes that its provisions were fairly easy to evade. However, subsequent amendments to the tax code, culminating with the extension of the restrictions to tax benefits derived through the Investment Tax Credit, have put teeth into the at-risk rules. The limitations do not apply to all types of investment, even where tax benefits are a vital consideration. For instance, under current law (although not under the proposed Treasury II) they do not apply to investments in real estate. Likewise, they do not apply to investments by "regular business corporations" (i.e., corporations which are not S corporations or personal holding companies), although, again, Treasury II could create problems under its proposals concerning corporate loan interest as an Item of Tax Preference under the corporate Alternate Minimum Tax.

Under the at-risk limitations, a taxpayer is "at risk" (and his deductions and other tax benefits are effectively limited) only to the extent of his cash contributions to the venture, plus the amount of any loans on which he is *personally* and *primarily* liable. Even here, if the taxpayer is protected through "stop loss" or "guarantee" provisions, he isn't "at risk." Also, any such loan cannot come from anyone with any interest in the transaction, other than his interest as a secured creditor.

(Remember, we're greatly simplifying the at-risk rules.)

Aside from the care that obviously must be taken to insure that all of the technicalities of the at-risk rules have been complied with, several special problems need to be noted. First, it's critical, for economic as well as tax reasons, to be sure that the liability of the leveraged investors is several, not joint. (Remember also what we mentioned earlier concerning the inability of the creditor to reach any assets of the partnership, or to use partnership revenues, to satisfy any debt service requirements.) Second, general partner guarantees of the loan, even on a secondary liability basis, could create potential difficulties.[19] And, finally, the loan should be made *directly to you as the investor*. (You will then contribute those loan proceeds to the partnership as a part of the payment of your agreed subscription): a loan to the partnership *which is assumed by the investor*, even with personal and primary liability, would, in the opinion of the IRS, result in a lack of tax "basis" in the investor's partnership interest (an equally effective restriction on the investor's ability to claim tax benefits), even if you were "at risk" as to those amounts.[20]

—Interest Restrictions—"Investment Interest." The ability to deduct that portion of your debt service which is applied to the payment of

---

[19] See, e.g., *Raphan v. U.S.*, 55 AFTR 2d 85-1154 (Fed. Cir. 1985).

[20] See Technical Advice Memorandum 8404012.

interest certainly affects the economics of leveraged investment. However, if that payment were characterized as "investment interest," there would be definite limitations on its deductibility. (Under current law, your total annual investment interest deductions are limited to $10,000 plus an amount equal to your "investment income.")

Under both existing and proposed tax laws, interest paid on borrowed amounts would not be characterized as investment interest as long as you are "engaged in a trade or business." (Owning an interest in a well would qualify, even though you were not the well operator and knew little about the oil and gas business from a technical standpoint.) Under existing law, most partnership investors claim that it's the nature of the *partnership's* activities that determine the "trade or business status, so that limited partners in a leveraged drilling partnership would not be subject to the investment interest restrictions.[21] However, under Treasury II, any interest not incurred in connection with a "trade or business" of the taxpayer, including interest expense of limited partnerships in which the taxpayer is a limited partner and S corporations in which the taxpayer doesn't actively participate in management would be subject to investment interest restrictions.[22] (Quaere concerning interest on loans made *directly to the taxpayer* which were used to purchase limited partnership interests?)

—**Accrued Interest.** You'll be a "cash basis" taxpayer, entitled to claim deductions only when the related expense is actually paid. Often, a general partner won't get around to paying "year-end" interest on certain partnership loans until after the first of the year, or will permit interest to accrue. If this is the case, you won't get to claim the interest deduction until the interest is actually paid.

Accrued interest is both a tax and an economic negative.[23] Fortunately, in view of the "basis" problems discussed above, your loans will normally have been made directly to you, so that you can insure that interest is currently paid. However, avoid any loan arrangement in which the lender "kindly" permits you to defer any payment of interest until some date in the future.

---

[21] Quaere whether it makes a difference whether the loan was made to the partnership and assumed by the investor (which might create "basis" problems) or was made directly to the investor.

[22] The restrictions would be further tightened to reduce the annual deductible amount to *$5,000* plus net investment income; however, such income would include TAXABLE income from S corporations and limited partnerships.

[23] The economic negatives of permitting interest to accrue is discussed in "Oil Investment Economics," cited in footnote 14 of **Chapter Three.**

—**"Phantom" Income.** We discussed the concept—and realities—of phantom income earlier in this Chapter, and we've seen that phantom income is simply an unavoidable fact of life whenever leverage is utilized.

As we've already mentioned, since you've had the "time value" use of the "phantom deductions" the leverage creates, there is nothing wrong with the fact that a leveraged investment creates phantom income (unless your economic analysis assumed that these were "permanent" deductions), *so long as you've anticipated this eventuality and have set aside the cash (or have otherwise provided) for this eventual day of reckoning.*

In addition to setting up a sinking fund to cover this tax liability on "paper income," here are some tips you may want to think about:

(1) If your investment has utilized leverage merely as an "installment" feature—the approach we recommended above—your subscription loan should be paid off by the time your investment starts to generate significant revenues, so phantom income won't be a major problem.[24]

(2) If you haven't paid the balance of your subscription in installments, consider voluntarily paying off the balance of your subscription loan when the program starts to generate significant revenues. (Of course, you had to pay taxes on those dollars you used, to make the non-deductible portions of your debt reduction, but at least you staged it over a period of *your* choosing.)

(3) Try to invest in programs where the lending bank will agree to a "partial release of funds"—in other words, where a portion of your program revenues are paid over to you to provide cash to satisfy your tax obligation on the phantom income. (Most banks will agree to this so long as your letter of credit or surety bond remains in place as collateral for your loan until the debt is fully repaid.)[25]

Should *You* Invest on a Leveraged Basis?—The Pros and Cons of Leveraged Oil and Gas Investment. The high profiling of the "excess write-off" aspects of leverage have muddied consideration of whether or not leverage is right for a particular oil and gas investor.

A few preliminary observations. The decision to use—or not use—leverage is an individual one. Irrespective of financial suitability, leverage will be

---

[24] Again, that payment in itself must be made with non-deductible dollars. However, except on the most successful of programs, paying off the loan at the start of the "phantom income" period will be to your advantage. Again, see "Oil Investment Economics," cited at footnote 14 of **Chapter Three**.

[25] This approach doesn't hurt your investment return. See "Oil Investment Economics," *id.*

appropriate for some investors and not for others. For instance, if it would make you uncomfortable to invest on a leveraged basis, then leverage isn't for you, despite its admitted advantages. Even more importantly, leverage is NEVER appropriate unless, *in a worst case scenario,* you can pay off the borrowed amounts. (Of course, in the "recommended" installment leverage scenario, you do that automatically.)

Let's highlight the very real *advantages* of leverage:

(1) *Leverage makes it easier to invest.* For a relatively small initial cash contribution, you can secure a substantial participation. This flexibility in the timing of your personal cash contributions can prove a real advantage where you'd like to make a large investment, but would find this *temporarily* inconvenient.[26]

(2) *Leverage increases deductibility as a percentage of your initial cash contribution to the venture.* You can raise the tax benefits of a basically "capital" investment such as a lease, completion, or income venture, to the 100% (or higher) level; you can create "excess write-offs"; and, if that initial deductibility exceeds 200%, you have created an initial *positive cash flow*—in the year of investment, you have actually "put money into your pocket" through the mere fact of the investment.[27]

(3) Most importantly, *leverage **may** have a positive effect on venture economics.*[28]

Leverage also has some very real *disadvantages*:

(1) *You will be personally liable on the borrowing* IN EVERY SENSE OF THE WORD. Unlike the old non-recourse loan programs, or certain of today's "abusive" tax shelters where the "personal liability" exists on paper only, you will truly be liable—and exposed—for the full amount of your agreed subscription. If your deductions are to exceed the amount of your initial cash contribution, this is dictated by the at-risk rules. And even if no excess write-offs are created by your use of leverage, no financial institution will loan you money on an oil and gas project without insisting on personal liability. (And if the loan isn't coming from an independent financial institution, and the loan

---

[26] Unfortunately, sometimes this makes it *too easy* to invest on a leveraged basis, leading to a commitment which is significantly larger than you should have made to this particular deal. More about this later.

[27] Remember, however, that this is a temporary effect only: it will be offset in future years by the taxes payable on phantom income.

[28] We'll be discussing this in a moment.

is to be made on a non-recourse basis, you can be sure that your "borrowings" simply reflect the amount by which you are being overcharged to participate in the deal.)

(2) *You will be saddled with phantom income.* (Note that even our "installment" approach doesn't eliminate phantom income; it simply staggers it over the installment period.)

(3) *You will be required to make additional cash contributions over and above your initial cash payment.* This includes amounts that must be paid to satisfy the taxes on the phantom income; to cover the balance of your agreed subscription; and to pay your interest obligation on the loan. (True, it's possible that a production loan might be available to fund the balance of your agreed subscription. However, you are much better off currently paying interest costs out of your own funds rather than permitting that interest obligation to be deferred.)[29]

(4) Just as, in many instances, leverage helps venture economics, *leverage may have a negative effect on venture economics* in a given program.

—The Impact of Leverage on Investment Economics. The "excess write-off" aspects of leveraged oil and gas investment often have blinded investors to the most important issue: will the use of leverage help—or hurt—investment economics.

*If the AFTER-TAX cost of borrowing is **less** than the EXPECTED after-tax return from the investment, leverage is "positive"*: your return will be IMPROVED through the use of leverage.[30] On the other hand, *if the after-tax cost of borrowing **exceeds** the expected after-tax return from the investment, leverage is "negative"*: your return will be HURT if you use leverage.

As we discussed in **Chapter Three**, a "typical" oil and gas investment should produce an internal rate of return of 10%; and, with selectivity, you should be able to realize in excess of a 20% internal rate of return. Those are *after-tax* figures. And, since under present tax laws you are in a 50% federal income tax bracket and interest costs are deductible,[31] it's hard to imagine interest rates reaching the 20% to 40% levels required for leverage to have a

---

[29] See 'Oil Investment Economics,' cited at footnote 14 to **Chapter Three.**

[30] That's why leverage is used so frequently in real estate ventures, including "raw land" investments which have no front-end tax advantages.

[31] That's subject to the "investment interest" caveats we gave you earlier in this Chapter. And don't forget that under tax reform proposals, both your tax bracket (which determines the "value" of the ability to deduct an expenditure) and the very deductibility of partnership interest might change.

negative impact on investment economics—assuming you are being selective in your investments![32]

Remember, however, that we won't really know how the investment is going to perform, even on a well-planned, well-selected, well-executed venture, until the results of the drilling are in.[33] All the more reason to be sure that you don't invest more in any one venture than you can comfortably afford to lose, and that you use the diversification techniques—particularly "time-line" diversification—we discussed in **Chapter Three**, rather than *over-investing* in any one project, no matter how attractive. (Leveling out oil's peaks and valleys through time-line diversification is particularly important if you're going to invest on a leveraged basis.)

There is a little more to analyzing the impact of leverage on investment economics than the simple rules we've just stated. For instance, if your tax bracket drops to 35%, and interest is no longer deductible, the interest rates will have to be much lower to insure that investing on a leveraged basis will still improve your return. Also, in addition to the interest rate payable and the tax laws then in effect, the structure of the venture (e.g., what is first-year deductibility) and the structure of the loan (e.g., is there any disastrous "loan reserve") can also impact on whether the use of leverage will prove "positive" or "negative."[34] (Your advisor can help you determine this.)[35]

But now we might seem to be in a Catch-22. Earlier in this Chapter, we've suggested that you consider using "installment leverage"—treating leverage merely as a method of staging your contribution to the program. Doesn't this defeat the economic advantage that a permanent use of leverage would have provided?

As we've mentioned, the use of installment leverage has advantages of its own, even if you don't secure the economic advantages of "permanent" leverage. And that "permanent" advantage will be available only in those partnerships which are *highly successful*—which generate the 6:1 and higher return levels that will prove the exception rather than the rule, even when you invest with selectivity.

If you want to utilize the economic advantages of leverage to its fullest, as each installment falls due, determine how well your venture seems

---

[32] Can you see, now, just how "dumb" it was to invest on a leveraged basis in the previous "phony" leveraged arrangements, where the leverage was purchased by participating in projects which had no investment merit?

[33] See **Chapter One** concerning the risks of oil and gas investment.

[34] For a discussion of some of these other aspects of the financial impact of leverage, see "Oil Investment Economics," cited at footnote 14 of **Chapter Three**.

[35] The use of advisors is discussed in **Chapter Five**.

to be doing. If the partnership seems to be doing quite well—particularly during the "tax positive" period before significant revenues are generated, while you are still "riding" on the tax advantages provided by the borrowed dollars—you can consider borrowing the amount of that installment *from your own banker*. (These direct borrowings will also be made at a time, and in a manner, when you are less apt to be carried away by your earlier enthusiasm for the investment.) When you reach the "tax negative" period when you must bear the interest burden of your investment plus pay taxes on the "phantom income" that arises from investment revenues, you can determine whether the program is successful enough that the revenues will retire the loan within a reasonable period of time, or whether you should then commence your own orderly reduction of that debt.

One final point. Some investors (and some investment advisors) perceive leverage as being "good" or "bad," based upon the *degree of leverage* which you utilize. Under this theory, 50% leverage might help the investment, while 80% leverage would wreck investment economics.

From a "return" standpoint, leverage is either positive or negative. If leverage is positive—the expected return exceeds the cost of borrowing—the greater the degree of leverage, the greater the improvement of investment economics. If leverage is negative, all you have done by reducing the degree of leverage is to *reduce your loss* on an investment which should not have utilized leverage to any degree (and which probably shouldn't have been made at all, even on an all-cash basis).

(Remember, however, that while the degree of leverage used doesn't turn a good investment into a bad one, too high a reliance on leverage may lull you into investing more than you should be risking in this particular venture, no matter how good the HOPED-FOR return.)

Some of Your Alternatives in Investing on a Leveraged Basis. Since the demise of Penn Square Bank, some new alternatives have emerged that may make leveraged investment even more attractive.

We've already discussed one of your alternatives—to use *installment leverage*, rather than looking at leverage as a means of permanently avoiding additional cash contributions to the program.

Another of your alternatives is *"do-it-yourself" borrowing*—borrowing directly *from your own banker* rather than utilizing any "built-in" leverage feature contained in the program.

Do-it-yourself borrowing has several advantages. First, it almost invariably reduces the cost of borrowing. Even though those interest payments are deductible, this only means that Uncle Sam is paying half those interest costs; *you* are paying the balance. Since the improvement in return that arises from the use of leverage is based upon the amount by which that return exceeds the cost of borrowing the money, the lower the interest rate, the more leverage has worked in your favor.

Second, there are many attractive investment opportunities that won't have a built-in leverage feature.[36] In these programs, you can, if you choose, secure the advantages of leverage through direct borrowing.

Another method of leveraging is the *investor surety bond* approach.[37] In such programs, the use of a letter of credit as collateral for your borrowing is replaced by a surety bond from some recognized surety underwriter.

One advantage of the surety bond over the letter of credit is the reduced paperwork required: you simply submit an application, together with a personal balance sheet on your own form. (You should hear within a matter of a few days that your application has been accepted—assuming, of course, that you are "credit worthy"). This can be quite a contrast to the lengthy conferences with your own banker concerning the form of the letter of credit (and sometimes what a letter of credit is!), coupled with the all-too-frequent occasions when the letter of credit which your banker submits is not acceptable to the subscription lender. More importantly, the more reliable surety underwriters insist that a "due diligence" investigation of the program's bona fides and economic potential be conducted by an expert acceptable to the surety before they will agree to issue surety bonds in connection with the program. (This is to be contrasted with the letter of credit programs, where neither the bank issuing the subscription loan or the banks issuing the letters of credit require such due diligence.)[38] While this shouldn't be looked at as a "Good Housekeeping Seal of Approval" which eliminates the need for selectivity on your part, it is an added "plus" than can prove a real advantage.

Conclusion. Leveraged oil and gas investment isn't right for everyone. And it may not be right for you. But investing on a leveraged basis has some very real advantages—*if* you use *selectivity* in choosing those programs in which you participate, and *if* you understand *how* to utilize leverage intelligently as a part of your investment plan.

---

[36] "Built-in" leverage features are prohibited in public programs by Regulation T of the Federal Reserve Board. And some oil program sponsors aren't aware of the advantages that leverage can offer to the investors—or are afraid of the "taint" that leverage may suggest to those who associate it with the "phony leverage" investments.

[37] The surety bond approach to leveraged investment is discussed in detail in Klug, "Investor Surety Bonds: A New Approach to Leveraged Investments in Oil and Gas," contained in Mosburg (ed.), **Financing Oil & Gas Deals—1986 Edition** (Energy Textbooks International, Inc.: 1986).

[38] The importance of due diligence investigations is discussed in **Chapter Five**.

The *intelligent* use of leverage mandates that you understand what leverage can—and can't do for you. It normally won't prove to be "permanent" leverage in the oil and gas area: you must be prepared, in most programs, to pay the balance of your agreed subscription over some reasonable period of time, and to make interest payments currently out of your own pocket. It should never be utilized unless you are prepared, as needed, to pay in the balance of your subscription in cash. And the initial ease of investing on a leveraged basis should never lead you into committing more than makes economic sense to any single program, or to investing in a mediocre partnership simply because it contains a leverage feature.

Finally, if, emotionally, leverage troubles you, stay away from it.

Subject to these caveats, consider leverage: it may prove a highly useful tool in maximizing your return from oil and gas investment.

CHAPTER FIVE
REACHING AN INTELLIGENT INVESTMENT DECISION

Introduction. Now you understand virtually everything you need to know about oil and gas investment except the most important question: how do you make *intelligent* investment decisions?

Throughout this book, we've emphasized the need for *selectivity* in your oil and gas investments. And in this Chapter, we're going to learn exactly how *you* can be selective in choosing the particular programs in which to invest.

Most poor oil and gas investment experiences aren't the result of an investor being taken in by a fast-talking "swindler" selling some confidence scheme. The "con men" are relatively easy to spot. Instead, far more investors lose money in oil through participating with well-meaning but mediocre oilmen whose ventures simply won't generate superior returns.

We've already seen that the average oil and gas investment—at least in "public" (SEC-registered) drilling programs—is returning its participants a 10% internal rate of return.[1] That's not bad: as we saw in **Chapter Three**, it equates to a 20% annual Certificate of Deposit rate, assuming that you are in the 50% federal income tax bracket.

But if half of the investors in public drilling programs are realizing a 10% or higher internal rate of return,[2] the other half are realizing return levels that are lower than this "minimum" investment objective we set in **Chapter Three**. And there are a number of other investments whose returns could approach this 10% "IRR." Besides, why not go for the *20%* or higher internal rate of return—a *40%* annual certificate of deposit rate—which one out of five drilling program sponsors are returning to their investors?

So let's see how we can "Join the Twenty Percent": learn how to select the consistently "better performers" in oil and gas.

(By the way—in the **Appendix** to this book, you'll find an "Investment Decision Checklist" which will summarize the steps outlined in this Chapter which identify the road you need to follow to become a *selective* oil and gas investor.)

Preliminary Considerations—In General. Before choosing the particular programs in which to invest, there are certain preliminary matters which you should consider. These include your *basic suitability* as an oil and gas investor; the type of *investment vehicle* through which you should participate (e.g., well-by-well "fractional interest" versus limited partnership

---

[1] See **Chapter Three**.

[2] See **Chapter Three**.

participation); the choice between participating through a *"public"* (SEC-registered) *versus a "private" program*; and the *nature of the properties* which your partnership will acquire or develop (e.g., their location, degree of dry-hole risk, hydrocarbon objective, specified or unspecified, and questions of participating with a "deal maker," "deal taker," or "money manager").

(These questions are, of course, in addition to the issue of the *type* of oil and gas investment which you select (e.g., drilling, production purchase, lease acquisition or completion fund, etc.), which we discussed in **Chapter One**.)

—**General Suitability.** Oil and gas investment isn't right for everyone. While some of this "general suitability" determination turns on your *economic* suitability—we'll get to that in a minute—there are other factors which must be taken into account in determining oil's appropriateness for you—and your general suitability as an oil and gas investor.

For instance, there are the *psychological factors*. Some people aren't comfortable with oil due to their basic lack of familiarity with how the oil and gas industry—and oil and gas investment—works.[3] (Stocks and bonds, or even real estate, seem a lot less bewildering, although this perceived familiarity has lead many investors to "feel comfortable" with some very poor stock and real estate investments!) Others can't stand the "roller coaster" results from well to well, or partnership to partnership.[4]

So if you're not going to be happy investing in oil, even though you may be economically suitable, stay away from this area of investment.

Even if oil sounds great for you, there are a number of people for whom oil and gas is not right from an economic standpoint: if you lack general economic suitability, or oil and gas won't satisfy your particular financial objectives, oil is an investment area to avoid.

For instance, to invest in oil, you must be prepared to commit a minimum of $5,000 to $10,000—normally $10,000—to each venture in which you participate.[5] (Quality private programs will normally require a minimum commitment of $25,000 or more.) Unless you are making at least $80,000 to $100,000 a year—possibly a little less for an "oil income" investment—you simply can't afford to commit that much to a single venture. (This—plus the ability to accept risk—is why oil and gas investment is normally recommended only for persons in the higher federal income tax brackets.)

---

[3] You, too? See the books by Norman Hyne cited in note 12 of **Chapter One**.

[4] As we saw in **Chapter Three**, these peaks and valleys can be leveled out through diversified investment. However, we're talking about *psychological* factors, which often override what logic tells us.

[5] While there are some oil deals which accept smaller minimum investments, they usually are not the higher-quality opportunities.

The problems created by this "minimum subscription" requirement are heightened by the fact that intelligent oil and gas investment calls for you to have *"staying power"*—to make such investments on a "diversified" and on-going basis. As we saw in **Chapter Three**, you need to make similar commitments over a several-year period ("time-line" diversification). Further, it's preferable to spread your oil and gas investment among several oilmen. (And remember that *each* of their ventures will require a similar "minimum commitment.")

Your programs may also call for *assessments*—additional contributions of capital, normally for the drilling of additional wells.[6] While the vast majority of these assessments will be "optional"—your only penalty for failing to pay the "call" will be a reduced participation in the partnership or in the additional wells funded through the assessments—in many programs, it's only through participating in this additional "exploitation" drilling that superior return levels can be realized. Also, while such assessment calls normally represent "good news"—the results of the original drilling appear promising—there is no assurance that the additional drilling may not have disappointing results, eating up revenues that were generated by the original drilling.[7] And the "optional" nature of those assessments is somewhat illusory: not only do you need to participate in the additional drilling to realize significant returns in practice, only your general partner may know whether or not those additional wells really ought to be drilled.

So the financial commitment required to participate in an oil and gas venture—particularly oil and gas *drilling*—is substantial. And unlike an investment in the stock market or an existing, income-producing real estate property, there will normally be a *delay in the receipt of any cash flow* from even a successful oil and gas program. Besides the time delays involved in drilling your wells (or acquiring your producing properties) and negotiating the necessary marketing arrangements with production purchasers, the general partner's reinvestment of your revenues (or the pledge of those revenues) to finance additional drilling postpones any significant cash distributions—again, even assuming successful program results. (As a rule of thumb, in partnerships involving any exploratory or controlled exploratory drilling, *expect to wait at least two years* before you see any substantial distributable cash.)

---

[6] The need for assessments in oil and gas programs was touched upon in **Chapter One**, and will be discussed in greater detail later in this Chapter.

[7] A similar problem arises when the general partner funds the additional drilling through borrowings, pledging the reserves established by the original drilling as collateral—a power which most oil and gas limited partnership agreements grant to the general partner.

(And don't think you can offset this lack of quick cash flow by selling your interest if an emergency arises: like most tax-shelters, oil is an *illiquid* investment!)[8]

(But what about the liquidity provided by a "built-in" redemption feature? See **Chapter Six**.)

Finally, *don't attempt to invest in oil and gas unless you are willing to spend a certain amount of time developing—and implementing—an intelligent investment strategy*. The amount of time required for this is less than you probably imagine; and, as we'll be discussing, there are advisors available at very reasonable fees who can assist you in this process. But oil and gas investment is not for the person who likes to blindly invest on tips or the most recent comments in **The Wall Street Journal**.

If you can't take the time to analyze, DON'T TRY TO INVEST IN OIL!

—Choosing Your Investment Vehicle. First, forget all you've heard about general partnerships, "joint ventures," "S" corporations, and all those other "sophisticated" techniques. Aside from such considerations as the technical requirements concerning S corporations and the lack of limited liability in the other vehicles, oilmen—and the marketers of oil programs—like to offer the type of investment vehicle with which investors are most familiar—in other words, the *direct ownership* of "fractional interests" in wells, leases, or producing properties, or a *limited partnership*. So, except in the most sophisticated of "insider" deals, your choice will be between these two investment vehicles.

Reams have been written about the relative advantages of fractional interest versus limited partnership investment. Usually, these tomes emphasize the perceived lower promotional levels and front-end "load" in *quality* fractional interest offerings, as balanced against the limited liability and diversification provided by a limited partnership investment.

These arguments are really beside the point. "De facto" limited liability could be provided in fractional interest ventures through "turnkeys" (UGH!—see **Chapter Two**) coupled with an adequate program of insurance. Diversification can, and should be, secured by spreading your investment dollars among a number of wells. But, as to investment quality, the issue is not so much fractional interest versus limited partnership as the *structure of the deal* and the *oil-finding ability and integrity of the venture promoter*.

---

[8] It's also difficult to impossible to "realize" on the value of even a successful investment by pledging your interest to your friendly banker—interests of passive investors in oil and gas limited partnerships, or even individual wells, make lousy collateral!

Certainly some "oil patch insiders" have been able to participate in high-quality ventures on better terms than have *traditionally* existed in limited partnership offerings. (More about this later in this Chapter.) However, many supposedly "insider" deals are simply overpromoted offerings of low-quality prospects which are sold to the gullible, based upon representations that it is a real "ground floor" opportunity.

(Ask yourself: if this is really such a "sure thing," why is that fellow from Midland offering to sell it to *you*?)

It is difficult, in a "fractional interest" investment, to perform the due diligence investigation and on-going monitoring that is the key to successful oil and gas investment. (Again, more later.) The disclosure in such offerings is normally abysmal: not because the oilman, in many instances, is trying to mislead you, but because he feels—erroneously—that such offerings are not subject to federal and state securities laws, particularly their "full disclosure" requirements.[9] And while some of that disclosure may be "boiler plate," other portions, such as the entrepreneur's "track record," are critical to an intelligent investment decision.

Prior to the mid 1980's, many of the "better" oilmen avoided limited partnership offerings. But the industry's current—and desperate—need for capital, and the growing realization by oilmen that many of today's oil and gas investors know what they are doing and can be reliable partners, have lead many of the nation's best oil finders to turn to the limited partnership market as a source of capital. And many of these oilmen are letting their limited partnership investors participate *on the exact same terms on which an "industry insider"—or industry MEMBER—would be participating!* And, in such partnerships, you can secure all of the advantages of a diversified limited partnership, coupled with the advantages that have traditionally been associated with "industry insider" deals.[10]

So, unless you're convinced that you are a "true" industry insider, *and* can also afford to perform the "technical" due diligence and on-going monitoring that a well-structured limited partnership would provide—and can, as well, afford to spread your oil and gas investment budget over a large number of wells and prospects—you will normally be much better off investing in a quality limited partnership than hoping that the "honest" oil man who sold you a quarter interest in his well is as good (and will stay as good) as he thinks (or says!) he is.

---

[9] Your rights as an investor under the securities laws are discussed in **Chapter Six**.

[10] The levels of promotion, and degree of front-end dilution, that have traditionally separated the *true* insider deal from even the best of the limited partnership offerings will be discussed later in this Chapter.

(And if you are a fractional interest investor who has prided yourself on the fact that "you don't need to invest as a limited partner," at least consider the possibility of putting some of your dollars in one of today's "new breed" of limited partnerships.)

—"Public" versus "Private" Programs. Again, this "consideration" is a greatly overemphasized consideration.

"Folklore" says that most SEC-registered ventures are mediocre indeed; for those who can afford the "entry fee," the best (and also the worst) opportunities are to be found in the "private" programs (those offerings which are not required to be registered with the Securities and Exchange Commission as a result of the SEC's "private offering" exemption from securities registration, SEC "Regulation D."[11]

As mentioned above, some legitimate fractional interest sponsors do not comply with Regulation D, based upon the mistaken belief that the Regulation and/or the securities registration requirements do not apply to such offerings. Even where the sponsor is legitimate, this failure to comply with Regulation D does result in your not being provided with much of the information that is most valuable in arriving at an intelligent investment decision.

Certainly, the last part of that folklore—that many of today's worst "opportunities" are found in the unregistered programs—is true. However, until recently, the idea that the best of the privates would invariably outstrip the best of the publics—or that there was no such thing as a "good" SEC-registered program—had no foundation in fact.

As we've already discussed, the average public drilling program delivers a 10% internal rate of return for its investors, with returns in excess of a 20% IRR being the typical result for the higher-quality "one out of five." (And those one out of five sponsors can easily be identified with the techniques we'll show you in this Chapter!)

Whether you should invest as a public or private investor should turn on the *size of your investment*. Few sponsors of the "better" private programs will accept an investor for less than a $25,000 minimum commitment per partnership. (In normal times, when money is not so difficult to raise, that minimum subscription requirement climbs to $50,000.) So, if your investment funds are limited—and remember what we've said about diversification and the possibility of subsequent-year assessments—you are much better off investing in a high-quality public partnership than a mediocre private one.

---

[11] The securities registration requirements of the Securities Act of 1933, and the rights that an improper failure to register under that act give to you as an investor, are discussed in **Chapter Six**.

If the larger minimum commitment of the better private programs is not a problem for you, you may want to seriously consider private program investment. As discussed later in this Chapter, the flight of capital from oil and gas investment and the erroneous beliefs concerning what a "flat tax" would do to the profitability of such investment have lead many sponsors to structure deals for "private" investors on terms which would have been unheard of until recently. (To date, there has been no such pronounced change in the structure of public programs.) So, if one of these outstanding investment opportunities comes your way, and you are in the position to invest the larger amounts required for quality private program participation, take advantage of today's unusual opportunities.

But remember, even if you are a larger investor, the question is not "public versus private"—it's the quality of the venture.

—Nature of the Properties—In General. Determining the *type of properties* in which you should participate involves a number of considerations. First, are there any areas of the country which traditionally seem to provide better returns than others? Should you engage in frontier wildcatting, stick with close-in developmental drilling, or choose "controlled exploratory" opportunities? Should you insist that all properties be specified, or are there some advantages to a "blind pool" approach? Should your general partner be one who originates his own prospects—a "deal maker"—or are there times when participating with a "deal taker" or "money manager" may be in order? Is oil to be favored over gas, or vice versa? And are these decisions really that critical in arriving at your final investment decision?

Let's consider these one at a time.

—Hydrocarbon Objective. The oil and gas search is "directional": it can be directed toward the discovery of oil, gas, or a mixture of both.

Some analysts feel that oil will prove more profitable over the next few years due to a continuation of the "gas bubble"; others feel equally certain that the country's oversupply of natural gas (and the resulting decline in gas prices) is about to evaporate.[12] So, which set of analysts is right? And should your investment strategy emphasize oil over gas, gas over oil, or a combination of the two?

The "issue" we've just raised is one which shouldn't play any significant part in your investment decision. At today's oil prices, the selective investor will still realize handsome returns. Even if prices were to significantly decline, the returns from a well-structured, well-operated program would be

---

[12] See, as an example, Daviss, "Gas Slump: Foundation of Profit?," **Oil & Gas Investor** (May, 1983).

highly attractive. (See **Chapter Three**.) And while the gas market is weak in certain parts of the country, it remains strong in others; a good general partner will study market conditions just as carefully as he analyzes the geology of the prospect.

Some general partners' strength lies in testing or developing gas-oriented prospects; others are more at home with oil.[13] You shouldn't pressure an effective oil finder to move away from the type of drilling he knows best. Instead, your inquiry should be focused on *how well* he has conducted that prior search.

So, as a general rule, don't emphasize one hydrocarbon over another. Instead, base your investment decision on the skill that your general partner has exercised in profitably producing whatever mix of hydrocarbons *he* seems best able to find.

—Location of the Properties and Degree of Dry-Hole Risk—In General. We're considering these together because in many instances they are very interrelated.

First, there seems to be no area of the country which is particularly favored: you can do equally well—or poorly—in Oklahoma, Texas, or the Rocky Mountains. (Also, what do you mean by "Oklahoma"? The Sooner Trend, a low-risk, low-return "sure thing" area, or the Anadarko Basin, where the primary objectives are high-risk, high-return—maybe!—deep gas zones?)

However, there are certain areas which it seems smart to avoid—if you want to make money! These are the "sure thing" areas, such as Oklahoma's Sooner Trend, Texas' Spraberry, and most of the east and mid-east's Appalachian Basin, where virtually every well "hits" (but few pay out); and the ultra-high-risk areas, such as the Rocky Mountain Overthrust.

Why avoid these areas? This raises the issue of the degree of dry hole risk you should be willing to accept.

Frequently, you'll find such a discussion labelled "developmental versus exploratory drilling." But the spread of dry hole risk varies significantly, based upon the *type* of developmental or exploratory drilling involved.

"Developmental Drilling" covers a well drilled near proven production, where the proposed "drillsite" is believed to lie within the same geological "feature"—the trap which contains the oil or gas. In some "sure thing" areas,

---

[13] A review of the "Prior Activities" tables contained in your sponsor's offering document will show whether his prior experience is primarily in oil, in gas, or a combination of those hydrocarbons. It will also show *how effectively* that experience has been put to use. (Later in this chapter, we'll explain how to read those tables.)

virtually all of these wells will "hit" (prove productive); in others, as many as half of the geologically-justified wells will still be non-productive, even though they are "direct offsets" to producing wells.

"Exploratory Drilling" involves drilling outside a known, productive geological feature. The highest degree of dry-hole risk arises where such drilling is classified as "rank wildcatting"—either "frontier wildcatting," where wells are drilled in a "basin" where there is no existing commercial production, or "new field" exploratory drilling, where the wells seek to establish the existence of a previously-undiscovered field within a basin where other productive fields exist.

In between these two types of drilling lie "Stepout" Development—the drilling of wells to define the limits of a productive field—and "Controlled" Exploratory Drilling—the drilling of wells close to existing productive fields (or at least previous "shows" of oil or gas), where such drilling is justified by existing geological or geophysical data such as subsurface "control" or seismic.[14]

Drilling in "sure thing" areas never seems to pay off for the investor seeking a reasonable return (other than bragging at the country club that he's "just hit his 20th straight well"). Such wells seldom pay out **(Chapter Three** showed us the effects of this); where the wells do eventually return your investment, it is over so long a period of time and with so little additional upside potential that, under "time value" considerations, your return is substandard to non-existent. (You could have made a better return, with no greater risk, participating in an "income" program.)

In theory, drilling "rank wildcats" should be the most profitable way to search for oil and gas, assuming you possess the necessary "staying power" to participate in enough wells, over a long enough period of time, for diversification to work its magic. Unfortunately, in practice, the high incidence of cost overruns, one-well fields, and higher-than-expected dry hole ratios indicates that this simply is not the case: even *diversified* rank wildcatting seems to generate a lower rate of return than stepout or controlled exploratory drilling.

(Why is this true, since the oilman adjusts for risk before approving a prospect for drilling and requires a higher *risk-adjusted* ROI before okaying an exploratory prospect than he would if developmental drilling were involved?[15] Remember, the assumptions upon which those risk-adjusted economics were calculated were prepared by the geologist who developed the geological idea—and who wants to see that idea tested by drilling!

---

[14] For a further discussion, see **Chapter One**.

[15] Most companies require a minimum 2 to 4:1 *risk-adjusted* ROI for the "own account" drilling of developmental prospects and a 6 to 8:1 risk-adjusted ROI for exploratory prospects.

The superior returns seem to come to investors who accept a moderate degree of dry hole risk through participating in controlled exploratory or higher-risk, higher-return developmental drilling—but who control that risk by investing on a *diversified* basis.

Of the two—controlled exploratory or high-risk/high-return development—which is the better? It doesn't seem to make any difference, so long as the oilman who is conducting that drilling is good at what he does and has structured his program fairly.

So the rules concerning both location and "development versus exploratory" are two-fold:

(1) *Stay away from both "sure thing" and "rank wildcat" areas and drilling.*

(2) *Pick your oilman based not on his developmental or controlled exploratory orientation, but whether or not he seems to have a "track record of doing HIS PARTICULAR KIND OF DRILLING well!"*

(And if you want to reduce your "downside" risk, while still sharing in oil's "upside," consider the newer type of "Combination" Programs discussed in **Chapter One**.)

—"Easter Bunny" Investing. Recently, there has been considerable hoopla concerning the "new breed of oilman" who drills in "sure thing" areas while still averaging 2:1 returns for his investors—usually, so the story goes, due to the skill of his geologists or his use of some "proprietary" completion technique that permits extracting a greater percentage of the oil from the ground.

Surely, anyone would love to find a method of investing in oil which provides rapid and predictable cash flow, plus multiple returns within a reasonable period of time. (A 400% write-off to round off the package wouldn't be bad either!) But such "Easter Bunny" beliefs seem to come more from wishful thinking—particularly on the part of marketers who know that such programs would be easy to sell (and earn commissions on!)—than to be based upon actual, sustained performance.[16]

Little children are rewarded by Santa Claus or the Easter Bunny—and protected from the real world—through the kindness of loving parents. Most general partners aren't quite so benevolent.

—"Deal Maker," "Deal Taker," or "Money Manager?" A debate still rages over whether to invest only with those oilmen who originate the vast majority of their own prospects ("deal makers"); those who, after careful

---

[16] "But my general partner's *reserve reports* say...."

geological screening, accept deals from prospect originators ("deal takers") or those financially-oriented general partners who simply pick oilmen with whom they and their clients will invest, charging their investors a fee in the form of a portion of partnership profits or proceeds for this service ("money managers").

Logic would seem to dictate that participating with a money manager is foolhardy, with a deal taker a little better, and with a deal maker the best of all. But "logic" also said that rank wildcatting *should* be the most profitable way to invest in oil—but it isn't! (See above.)

Look at these considerations:

(1) A deal maker may be the originator of quality prospects—or of junk. He may let his non-industry investors participate on the same basis as industry partners (e.g., that "deal taker")—or may charge them a much higher level of promotion.

(2) A deal taker may be providing "value added" services by "cherry picking" the various prospects submitted for his consideration by the deal maker—or he may be taking anything that comes his way. He may structure his deal so that the *combined* promotion taken by him plus that of the prospect originator doesn't exceed normal levels—or he may "double dip," so that the combined promotion is totally unreasonable.[17]

(3) A money manager may play a valuable role in his screening and monitoring of a number of deal makers and/or deal takers to find the superior performers (and make sure they *remain* superior!) and in negotiating excellent arrangements for his partnership[18]—or he, as well, may double dip and merely go through the motions of screening and monitoring the oilmen with whom he deals.

If your general partner is good at the role which he has chosen to play, and performs that role conscientiously, and if the program is fairly structured, you'll make money whether a deal maker, a deal taker or a money manager is involved. Otherwise, stay away from the deal.

But how can *you* tell if the deal is fairly structured? If the general partner really is good at what he does, and if he is conscientious and caring? The answers to these questions will become clear when we discuss

---

17 "Reasonable" promotional levels are discussed later in this Chapter.

18 Many oilmen are still reluctant to deal directly with outside investors. The money manager–or deal taker–may be able to negotiate superior deal terms by bringing large amounts of money to the table–money which the deal maker can accept without having to take on the actual and perceived burdens of finding, and reporting to, a myriad of outside investors.

general structuring considerations, such as compensation, sharing arrangements, and conflicts of interest, and analyzing prior performance ("track record") and present potential.

One rule of thumb will help you quickly eliminate a number of substandard proposals. The offering document *should* disclose the "net revenue interest" of the partnership leases.[19] (Remember, this is before deduction of your general partner's own "carried" share of production.) *If that net revenue interest is less than 78% to 80%, it means that the combined existing promotional levels are too high.*

(In the 1977 through 1981 period, a 70 to 75% net revenue interest to the partnership was considered reasonable, assuming quality prospects. However, in today's "buyer's market," higher levels are readily attainable in most areas, even on high quality prospects—again, *if you'll be selective.)*

A word of caution in applying this standard. In some areas of the country—notably Southern Louisiana—potential rewards are so high that landowners demand higher royalty levels under their leases, and the net revenue interest to the partnership dips. Also, a given prospect originator may develop deals of such high quality that a lower net revenue interest would be justifiable. But don't accept the general partner's blithe explanations for the higher levels of pre-existing promotion without a little digging.

What if the offering document didn't disclose the net revenue interest (or the *expected* net revenue interest if a "blind pool" is involved)? Insist on the information—and ask yourself why it wasn't provided voluntarily in the first place.

What if you weren't even provided a thorough offering document? (Need you ask!)

—Specified versus Unspecified ("Blind Pool") Properties. In many programs, the majority (or all) of the wells to be drilled by the partnership are described in detail in the sponsor's offering document.[20] (This is particularly true in private offerings, and is almost universally the case if a "fractional interest" venture is involved.) On the other hand, the vast majority of public offerings, and a large number of private ones, are structured as

---

[19] "Net revenue interest" is the share of well production which your partnership, as a "working interest owner" (the owner of the cost-bearing operating rights which permit you to conduct drilling operations on the land), is entitled to receive. Thus, if a lease is acquired subject to a 12½% landowner's royalty, and assigned to your partnership subject to the reservation of an additional 12½% overriding royalty, your *working interest* would be 100%, while your *net revenue interest* would be only 75%.

[20] Programs in which only a portion of the properties are specified are colorfully referred to as " 'partially illuminated' pools."

"blind pools"—the sponsor does not advise you, in advance, of the exact location of the wells in which you will participate.

At first, it might appear foolhardy to participate in an offering in which the sponsor is given a "blank check" in choosing the drilling locations for which you are paying. However, the check isn't all that blank: the offering document should specify both the *type* of drilling in which you'll be engaged (e.g., the exploratory-developmental "mix"), and the *areas* where these wells will be located.[21] And with a proper combination of "due diligence" and "monitoring"—both discussed later in this Chapter—an expert retained to protect the interests of the investors can analyze the quality of the inventory of leases from which the sponsor will select the wells to be drilled by your partnership, and can make sure that the drilling locations selected from that inventory reflect the higher quality prospects and a proper drilling "mix."

The specified property offering permits you to analyze the geological and economic merit of the particular wells in which you'll participate. But exactly how meaningful is that to you, unless you're an "oil patch insider?"

The unspecified property offering gives the sponsor greater latitude and flexibility in selecting which prospects will be developed by the program. If he is unqualified or unprincipled, this gives him an even greater license to steal. (But why participate, under any circumstances, with such a sponsor?) If he knows what he's doing, it improves his ability to make himself—and *you*—the maximum profit by taking advantage of "targets of opportunity."

Analyzing the merits of a given prospect is beyond the abilities of most oil and gas investors—*and* their advisors. Determining whether or not the general partner is qualified is a task you can successfully undertake. (We'll show you how before this Chapter concludes.)

So, again, your attention should be focused on the abilities of the general partner, and the existence and quality of the due diligence review—not on the particular wells which the partnership will drill.

(Do, however, be suspicious of a private offering which is vague as to the location and nature of the wells to be drilled; which has been subjected to little, no, or "suspect" due diligence; or which is being offered by a sponsor who isn't able to demonstrate the availability of quality drilling opportunities sufficient to support the size of the program.)

---

[21] This disclosure of areas is virtually meaningless in a public program: as discussed above, the state of Oklahoma could involve such disparate drilling as the deep Anadarko Basin and the Sooner Trend. However, in a private offering, *there is no excuse for not pinpointing with consider-able specificity the areas and types of prospects to be emphasized by the program* (e.g., "the majority of the Program's wells will be drilled on Austin Chalk prospects located within the state of Texas ...").

Analyzing Partnership Quality—In General. The "preliminary considerations" we've just considered obviously will have some impact on your investment decision. However, as we've emphasized in the last few pages, most of them are far less important in arriving at your "go/no-go" conclusion than determining the *quality of the program.*

Answering this latter question involves two areas of inquiry:

(1) The quality of the program's *structure.*

(2) The quality of *management*, including both management's prior "track record," and the program's present profit potential.

You can't use *random selection* in choosing a program sponsor: only one out of five will deliver the superior returns to which you're entitled. You can't even rely upon *personally sizing up* the general partner. There are good, bad, and mediocre oil finders; but they have one thing in common: they're all charismatic. And you can't even rely upon the "established" reputation or size of the general partner, or the prestige of the "investment banking" firm (brokers to you) which is offering the program: the Stanger and Investment Search studies discussed in **Chapter Three** both emphasize that large, established sponsors tend toward substandard performance, particularly if the program is being sold through the larger brokerage houses.[22]

So let's look at several things we *can* do, starting with *structure analysis.*

—Analyzing Program Structure—In General. Structure analysis deals with the *terms of your arrangement* with the well operator or program sponsor. A fair structure won't turn garbage into gold, and some projects are so financially attractive that even a "poor" structure—one that would normally be considered "overloaded"—may be justified. However, the "terms of the deal" are extremely important in determining whether a project which admittedly has economic promise will not prove so promising from *your* standpoint.

There are a number of factors to consider in analyzing the structure of a proposed venture. The most important of these are:

(1) The *Sharing Arrangement*—how are costs to be borne and revenues split;

(2) *Compensation*—what will the operator or general partner or their affiliates be paid, over and above their share of well or partnership revenues, for providing necessary (or unnecessary!) services to the venture;

---

[22] This is *not* to say that all of the older, larger public drilling programs are poor performers.

(3) *Front-End Dilution*—how many dollars will be left to "go into the ground" (be available for the conduct of operations) after "front-end" items such as organizational and offering costs and up-front management fees have been deducted from the offering proceeds;

(4) *Conflicts of Interest* between management and the investors, and other practices which might reduce the likelihood of investor profit or increase the possibilities of investor loss;

(5) "Other" items such as *Assessment* policies and the presence or absence of a *"Liquidity Feature."*

—How Important *Is* Structure Analysis? Some "analysts" emphasize structure analysis to the exclusion of any other considerations in ranking investment proposals. And, clearly, analyzing the proposed terms of a deal is an important first step in the selectivity process. However, it's a *first step only*, not the basis for making your ultimate, final selection of those offerings in which to invest.

One of the main attractions of basing program selection on a review of the structure of the competing proposals is the ease with which such an evaluation can be performed. Several respected analysts have developed numerical "formulas" with which to grade offerings;[23] once the formula is understood, it can be used quickly to rank competing proposals.

This type of analysis does help eliminate patently-abusive offerings and "fine tune" your selection among obvious contenders.

An overly-abusive structure (e.g., a 30% front-end load or too heavy a "promote" in favor of the general partner) wrecks the economics (to *you*, not to the general partner) of what otherwise might have been a profitable project. It also shows that your sponsor is "dumb" (ill-advised as to the realities of the market place)—or thinks you are!

Despite the heavy reliance of many members of the financial community on structure analysis as the primary basis for their oil investment recommendations, there is a fatal flaw in using this analytical tool as the basis for your final investment decision. *Structure analysis doesn't tell you (or your advisor) anything about* **the quality of the prospects** *or* **the oil-finding ability and integrity of the general partner**. And, in the final analysis, it is these latter factors that will determine whether or not you receive a "fair run for your money" from your oil and gas investments.

There are certain structuring features which do have significant impact on your likelihood of making (or losing) money. We'll discuss each of them in

---

23 One such approach–the "Tower Formula"–is discussed in "Figuring a Fair Deal," **Oil and Gas Investor** (April, 1984). The publications of Robert A. Stanger & Co. and King Publishing Company also "rate" programs, based, at least in part, on such numerically-weighted analysis.

greater detail later in this Chapter. For now, let's simply highlight these "positive" features:

(1) *Limited Front-End Dilution*—the more of your dollars that are available for operations, the more profitable your investment will prove;[24]

(2) An *Unusually Favorable Sharing Arrangement* (unless it falls into the "too good to be true" category)—the smaller the sponsor's "promote" (free interest in program revenues), the better off you are (assuming quality prospects);

(3) A *"Democracy Rights" Feature*—to be discussed later in this Chapter, to give you the protection you need when you suspect your general partner is acting less than honorably;

(4) A *"Program Monitor" Feature*—so that someone who is "in your corner" can look over the general partner's shoulder to insure that the operations are being conducted prudently and fairly.

—Specific Structuring Considerations—Compensation and Sharing Arrangements—In General. We're considering these aspects of investment structure together because they are interrelated: they show what the general partner (or well operator) hopes to realize out of the deal.

(When we mention "the general partner" or "the well operator," we're also including their affiliates. From your standpoint, you don't care whether the general partner is gouging you directly, or has found some related entity to be the "gouger.")

Unlike real estate and agricultural syndications, where a major part of the syndicator's profit comes through "front-end load,"[25] there is little or no front-end load *in favor of the general partner* in the better-structured oil programs. Instead, the oilman seeks to profit by having you cover *all* (or the vast majority) of the costs of conducting the operation (including his own internal costs), and then to secure a promotional (cost-free) interest in the venture results.

In making this last statement, we've oversimplified. Some oil deals do include turnkey profits or lease mark-ups in favor of the general partner, or front-end management fees (although watch out if they are too high); and in many programs, the general partner will bear a portion of the costs of the operations (although his share of venture revenues will be greater than his

---

[24] See **Chapter Three**.

[25] Remember, if you purchase a piece of real estate, or a cow, at more than the actual cost to the syndicator, there is front-end profit—and front-end dilution! (The same is true when you drill wells on a "turnkey" basis.)

share of venture costs).[26] In the main, however, an oil and gas general partner expects to make his profit out of oil, not out of mark-ups or fees for services.

Doesn't that mean that the general partner can't profit unless you do? Unfortunately no, although some oil promoters will tell you this. While the general partner will profit *along with you*—the bigger your profit, the bigger his as well—his promotional interest insures that he'll make money even if you don't, or at least not lose *as much*—or any—money, even when the venture is a financial disaster from your standpoint.

The effect of the sponsor's promotional spread is illustrated in **Figure Seventeen**.[27] (We've also thrown in the impact of front-end dilution, to again emphasize the sensitivity of investment return to the percentage of dollars "going into the ground.")[28]

(Note also that not only does the sponsor's promotional spread virtually assure that he'll make money even if you don't, an *excessive* promotional spread virtually assures that *you WILL lose money!*)

—**Front-End Load.** As discussed in **Chapter Three**, oil and gas investment return is very sensitive to front-end dilution. (Refer back to **Figure Nine** of **Chapter Three**, as well as this Chapter's **Figure Seventeen**, if you have any questions concerning the accuracy of this statement.)

A *reasonable* level of front-end dilution for organizational and offering costs, management fees, "turnkey" profits, or the marking up of leases to their "fair market value" isn't a disqualifier. However, if the front-end items to be recharged to you exceed 12½% to 15%, this is a bad danger signal. First, from the standpoint of pure economics, too little of your money is "going into the ground." Second, most experienced (and legitimate) sponsors realize that brokerage houses and financial advisors turn first in an offering memorandum to the the "Application of Proceeds" section, to determine the percentage of subscription proceeds available for operations—and apply the 85% test as an absolute cutoff. If a general partner has structured a deal where "front-end" items, other than turnkey or lease mark-up profits, exceed 15%, he either doesn't understand today's market—or intends to raise his money primarily from "mullets" and "pigeons." In either case, this is a good program to avoid.

---

[26] In determining the level of promotion in a proposal, we look only at the general partner's "carried" (free) share of venture revenues. Thus, if the general partner is to receive 40% of partnership revenues, but is being charged with 20% of partnership costs, his *promotional interest* is 20%.

[27] This is one reason that public drilling program sponsors like large, multi-prospect *exploratory* partnerships: a few "big hits" generate significant revenues to the general partner under his cost-free interest, even though you lose money on the program as a whole.

[28] See **Chapter Three**.

| | "Own Account" Results | Limited Partnership Results | | |
		Aggregate	To Sponsor	To Investors
1. Dollars Available (1)	$1,000,000	$1,212,500	$ 212,500	$1,000,000
2. Organizational and Offering Costs (2)	-0-	[150,000]	-0-	[150,000]
3. Dollars Available for Operations	1,000,000	1,062,500	212,500	850,000
4. Revenues Generated (assumed at 300% of "3") (1)	3,000,000	3,187,500	1,275,000	1,912,500
5. ROI	3:1	2.63:1	6:1	1.91:1

(1) Assuming: (i) Sponsor expends $1,000,000 for "own account" drilling **versus** (ii) Investors subscribe $1,000,000, with **cost of operations** charged 20% to Sponsor, 80% to Investors, and revenues shared 40%/60% (20 Point promotional spread).

(2) Assumed at 15% of Investor subscriptions.

*From Mosburg, *Study Guide to "Investing in Oil"* Cassette Series

FIGURE SEVENTEEN: Impact of Sponsor's Promotion and Front-End Dilution on Investment Return.

Some front-end items, such as organizational and offering costs ("O & O") or fees paid to third parties, don't represent profit to the *sponsor*. However, where front-end dilution is concerned, you don't care who is benefiting from the payments: your dollars available for operations have still been unacceptably diluted. Also, while we are primarily concerned with front-end items to be recharged to *you*, excessive sales commissions and finders' fees are a danger signal, even if the sponsor is bearing the "excess" amounts. Generally speaking, "retail" sales commissions shouldn't exceed 10%, irrespective of who is being charged with the amounts. "Wholesaling" charges—amounts paid to those who coordinate the sponsor's sales effort—shouldn't run more than 3%, and normally should be borne by the sponsor, not recharged to you and your fellow investors. Sales compensation above those amounts are a danger signal that legitimate marketers—who won't sell deals for such excessive fees—were disenchanted with the quality of the offering. (In that case, you should be disenchanted as well.)

Traditionally, sponsors have been permitted to take *reasonable* turnkey profits (not to exceed 10% to 40% of estimated well costs), front-end management fees (not to exceed 10% of the proceeds of the offering), or lease mark-ups (not in excess of the current fair market value of the lease, as established by independent appraisal), in addition to the 15% maximum front-end dilution. However, such practices still dilute the amounts of money available for *true* conduct of operations—and thus adversely affect the program or well's profit potential.[29] Accordingly, you will be much better off investing in a quality program where no wells are turnkeyed *to the general partner or its affiliates*; where leases are transferred to the program at not more than the sponsor's "adjusted lease cost" (his original cost, plus interest, maintenance and evaluation costs, and "work-up" fees); and front-end management fees are waived in favor of on-going charges for "well supervision fees" and reimbursement of "general administrative overhead" ("GAO").

(Turnkey drilling by a *totally unaffiliated* independent drilling contractor isn't a "minus"; it's a plus. Many drilling contractors are so desperate for business in today's depressed industry that they will "lock in" a reasonable—and often substandard—price just to keep their rigs and crews busy.)

A final word concerning front-end dilution. In today's buyer's market, informed oil and gas sponsors realize that the way to that market is to offer investors a superior product, coupled with *unusually favorable* deal terms.

---

[29] Believe it or not, a quality sponsor is just as adversely affected by these practices as you are, since his profit—assuming he does his job well—is directly dependent upon the amount of monies available for operations. (Unfortunately, even most "informed" sponsors don't realize this—or don't have sufficient capital to directly pay front-end items out of their own pocket.)

Thus, "traditional" rules that the sponsor is to be reimbursed for *all* front-end items (other than wholesaling costs) are crumbling in the better-structured programs. Accordingly, later in this Chapter we'll show you how to identify quality programs in which the front-end dilution may be much less than the traditional 12½% to 15%.

—**Compensation and Cost Reimbursement.** As indicated above, most oil sponsors expect the program to carry the costs of conducting partnership operations, including reimbursement of the general partner or well operator's general administrative overhead and the costs of organizing the program and selling the units ("organizational and offering costs").[30]

As we've just mentioned, the "O & O" costs which are recharged to you and your fellow investors should be limited to not more than 15% of program subscriptions. (If you'll follow the "contrarian" investment strategy we will discuss later in this Chapter, your portion of these costs will be much less than this.)

Some sponsors make a point of "capping" the GAO: putting a limit on the amount of their general administrative overhead that can be recharged to the partnership. Since there are no "generally accepted accounting principles" as to how general administrative overhead is to be calculated, this "GAO cap" is relatively meaningless. (It's too easy to "recharacterize" a major portion of the costs as "direct" rather than "indirect," to avoid the limitation, or to utilize outside consultants to more expensively perform the services the sponsor should have been providing "in house.")

A tip: the sponsor with a quality in-house staff will have higher in-house costs—and may make you more money—than a poorly staffed but "low cost" operator. Your best test on the "reasonableness" of the sponsor's GAO charges is to analyze how investors have fared in his prior programs. If they have done well, the charges are well worth it. If they haven't done well, you don't want to invest with that sponsor, irrespective of the level of his general administrative overhead.[31]

The fact that the sponsor is providing various services to the program, directly or through his affiliates, may be a minus—or it may be a plus. Certainly, the charges for such services should be limited by a "competitive rates" test. (Below, we'll discuss whether they should be permitted at *any* cost level.)

---

[30] If the partnership's sharing arrangement requires the general partner to bear a portion of program costs—see below— the organizational and offering costs and GAO reimbursement may or may not be excluded from those costs in which the general partner is expected to share.

[31] This "track record" analysis is discussed below.

—**Sharing Arrangements.** The basis on which the general partner and his investors share in costs and revenues has a definite impact on the profitability of the investment. Certain sharing arrangements tend to create a greater commonality of interest between the sponsor and his investors. And if the sponsor's "promotional spread"—his free interest in program or well revenues—is too great, the venture is almost certain to self-destruct from your standpoint.

There are various ways in which costs and revenues can be split between the sponsor and the investors. Let's look at the most common arrangements:

(1) **Carried Interest.**[32] The sponsor bears none of the program costs, but receives an immediate share of the program revenues.[33]

(2) **Reversionary (Subordinated) Interest.** Investors pay all program costs and receive all revenues until a specified portion of their capital has been returned.[34]

(3) **Functional Allocation.**[35] Investors are charged with all "non-capital costs"—those costs which are currently deductible for federal income tax purposes—and the sponsor bears all "capital costs"—those costs which are not currently deductible. Revenues are divided either based upon fixed percentages or on some "flexible" basis.[36]

(4) **Promoted Interest (Disproportionate Sharing).** The sponsor bears a fixed percentage of *all* costs, and receives a disproportionately greater share of program revenues.[37]

---

[32] We're using these terms as they are defined in the financial community. Among oilmen, "carried interest" is used to define a totally different arrangement: the "third-for-a-quarter" sharing discussed below.

[33] E.g., costs are charged 100% to investors; revenues are credited 90% to the investors, 10% to the general partner. Note that for tax purposes, the general partner should be charged with at least 1% of program costs even in a "carried interest" arrangement. And some state securities administrators are requiring that the general partner bear at least 5% of program costs.

[34] E.g., costs are charged 100% to investors until a given well has attained "payout"; thereafter, revenues from that well are credited 70% to the investors and 30% to the general partner.

[35] Functional Allocation is sometimes referred to as a "Tangible/Non-Tangible" sharing arrangement.

[36] E.g., the sponsor bears the capital costs and is credited with 40% of program revenues; the investors bear the non-capital costs, including lease costs and costs of abandoned equipment on non-productive prospects, and are credited with 60% of program revenues. (In a flexible arrangement, the general partner's revenue share might be 25 percentage points higher than the ratio of the capital costs to total program costs.)

[37] E.g., costs are charged 25% to the general partner and 75% to the investors; revenues are credited 50%-50%.

(5) **"Combination" Arrangements.** The sponsor receives a carried interest during payout which will increase after payout.[38]

Traditionally, when an oilman was "turning" a deal to another oilman, or if an "industry insider" was purchasing an interest in a well, another arrangement—referred to in the industry as **"third-for-a-quarter"**—was used. Under this arrangement, the investor paid 33⅓% of his normal share of costs, and was assigned a 25% working interest.

(The big question, however, was third-for-a-quarter of *what*? In a "true" industry "third-for-a-quarter" arrangement, the promoted industry partner paid this disproportionate share of well costs only "to the casing point" [through the completion of testing]; thereafter, the costs of completing and equipping this initial well, and costs of all subsequent wells, were shared on a non-promoted basis. In some "third-for-a-quarter" arrangements, however, the promoter is "carried to the tanks" [bears no share of costs until production equipment has been installed]; and the promotion applies to each well drilled on the prospect, not just the initial well.)

Much—probably too much—has been written concerning the relative advantages or disadvantages of Functional Allocation over a Reversionary Interest approach, or a Carried Interest over Disproportionate Sharing. That kind of discussion is irrelevant: each arrangement has its advantages and disadvantages, and there is no "perfect" formula. (The better test, again, is to analyze track record and present profit potential.)[39] However, it's equally true that, whatever the arrangement, if *the sponsor's promotional interest is too great, it will be virtually impossible for you to make money.*

What levels of promotion were "too great?" As a rule of thumb, if the sponsor's "free" interest in production rose to 25%, there was little chance that the investors would profit over any significant number of wells, irrespective of the quality of the prospects or the oil-finding ability of the sponsor.[40] Furthermore, the sponsor's level of promotion also needed to take into account: (i) whether or not he is bearing any portion of program cost and risk; and (ii) intervening levels of promotion reserved by the persons from whom the prospects were acquired.

Levels of promotion that are above those generally reserved by legitimate sponsors of quality programs not only create the potential for an

---

[38] E.g., all costs are borne by the investors. Prior to payout ("BPO"), well revenues are credited 12½% to the general partner and 87½% to the investors. As each well pays out ("APO"), revenues from that well are credited 25% to the general partner and 75% to the investors.

[39] Don't worry, we will get to those in a moment!

[40] Remember, if the sponsor is paying 20% of program costs for 40% of program revenues, his "free" ("carried") interest is 20%.

economic disaster to the investors; they also signal that this may be a program offered by someone who only expects to deal with the unsuspecting—and gullible. Here are the promotional levels that have traditionally been deemed "acceptable," again assuming quality prospects and a high-caliber oilman:[41]

Type of Sharing Arrangement	Sponsor's Promotional Level
Carried Interest	10%-15%
Reversionary Interest	25%-33⅓% APO, on a *prospect-by-prospect* (**not** well-by-well) basis
Functional Allocation	"Spread" between estimated cost share and estimated revenue share shouldn't exceed 20%-25%
Disproportionate Sharing	Same as Functional Allocation
"Combination"	6.25%-12.5% BPO; 25%-40% APO on a *prospect-by-prospect* (**not** well-by-well) basis

In addition to these limitations on the sponsor's *direct* promotion, the Net Revenue Interest under leases *as acquired by the partnership* (i.e., before the sponsor's own promotion) traditionally was required to be not less than 70% to 75%, the variance depending upon the quality of the prospect; and the *investors'* Net Revenue Interest was required to be not less than 45%.[42]

—"Dangerous" Practices: Of Self-Dealing, Conflicts of Interest, and the Like. Every once in a while, you may read: "Avoid any program which contains a conflict of interest."

What a bunch of nonsense. *Every* oil and gas investment (or, for that matter, any type of investment) involves conflicts of interest. The sponsor's promotional interest is, itself, a conflict of interest. Most sponsors will be engaged in competing activities, both with other investor groups or for their own account. *Every partnership or well-by-well operation involves practices which, in the hands of an inept or unscrupulous operator, could cost you money.*

Take self-dealing. If the services provided by the sponsor are improperly performed, or are provided at an unreasonable price, this "conflict of interest" has operated to your detriment. On the other hand, if the sponsor provides

---

[41] Good news! Later in this Chapter we'll show you how you can get into equally quality drilling opportunities at *much lower* promotional levels.

[42] We say "required to be": in practice, very few investors—or their advisors—were making this kind of analysis. And do you notice that you're paying *100%* of well costs for *45%* of well revenues?

quality services (particularly at a time when the people who can perform those services may be in short supply), and his charges are reasonable, you have benefited from this "conflict."

So the question isn't whether or not there are conflicts of interest between you and the sponsor or well operator (there will be) or whether any conflicts will automatically be resolved in your favor (they won't be) but, *on balance, are you benefiting or being hurt by the sponsor's practices.*

The North American Securities Administrators Association ("NASAA"), the association of the 50 state securities administrators, have adopted certain "Guidelines for the Registration of Oil and Gas Programs."[43] Only "public" (SEC-registered) offerings are required by law to comply with these rules; however, business pressures require the sponsors of legitimate private partnerships to follow the spirit of these guidelines.[44]

Most of the "Restricted and Prohibited Transactions" dealt with by NASAA involve self-dealing. However, NASAA frowns upon certain other practices, such as other types of conflicts of interest (for instance, an unreasonable level of promotion) or commingling of funds.

Certain practices which are prohibited or drastically restricted in SEC-registered offerings aren't automatic disqualifiers in *quality* private placements. But how can *you* determine whether a given conflict should or should not be permitted, or has even been properly disclosed?[45]

First, your advisor—if he knows his job—can help you make this determination. (In just a moment we'll be talking about the advantages of expert counsel, and how to "analyze your analyst" to determine just how expert his advice is.) But there are certain tests that *you* can apply, without outside help, to see how serious the conflicts of interest are.

First, there are certain practices that should *never* be permitted: their presence in an offering is not only in itself a disqualification of that offering from further consideration, it also indicates that the sponsor is either so ill-informed, or considers you so gullible, that you wouldn't want to do business with him in any event. (After all, there may be other disqualifiers, not as

---

[43] These "NASAA Guidelines" are contained in Mosburg (ed.), **Financing Oil & Gas Deals— 1986 Edition** (Energy Textbooks International, Inc.: 1986), and in Mosburg (ed.), **Techniques of Oil & Gas Tax-Shelter Financing** (Energy Textbooks International, Inc.: 1983, with 1985 Supplement).

[44] Your rights—and the sponsor's obligations—under state and federal securities laws are discussed in **Chapter Six**.

[45] If it hasn't been properly disclosed, you will have a legal right under the securities laws to a return of your investment. See **Chapter Six**. However, that's of little comfort if your sponsor is now bankrupt or has "gone south" with your money.

readily apparent, which also taint the offering.)[46] These absolutely unacceptable conflicts include:

(1) Providing services at other than competitive rates;

(2) Unreasonable mark-ups on turnkey drilling, transfer of leases to the program, or any providing of goods;[47]

(3) Failure to assign you an interest in a reasonable number of surrounding drilling locations—preferably throughout the entire prospect—when you are "proving up" an area for the sponsor through the drilling of an exploratory, step-out, or "higher risk" developmental well;[48]

(4) The sale of properties *from* the partnership to the sponsor or any of his affiliates (other than an affiliated drilling or production program) except at the *higher* of cost or fair market value;[49]

(5) A reservation by the sponsor or his affiliates of any interests in production other than his share of partnership revenues,[50] or of *any* interest in production that doesn't bear its share of operating costs;[51]

(6) Loans by the sponsor *to* the program at interest rates that are higher than those being charged by independent lending sources (or at which the sponsor is himself borrowing); loans *by* the program to the sponsor under any circumstances; or any commingling of funds;

(7) A requirement in well-by-well offerings that completion costs be prepaid on a non-refundable basis before a completion decision has been reached.

There are other practices which are not absolute disqualifiers, but should indicate: "Proceed with Caution." These include:

---

[46] The ill-informed, or ill-advised, sponsor is probably inept in preserving your tax benefits as well. Or he may be promising the moon because he doesn't intend to be around long anyway.

[47] At a minimum, such practices should be supported by independent appraisal; turnkey rates shouldn't exceed the price at which drilling would have been performed on a turnkey basis by an independent drilling contractor.

[48] See above, and also **Chapter One**, concerning the degree of dry hole risk you should be willing to accept.

[49] Transfers to an "affiliated" partnership (one being organized by the same sponsor) should be on competitive terms.

[50] An exception: overrides or screening fees to consulting geologists, or the in-house technical staff, *so long as*: (i) the net revenue interest of the partnership's leases isn't reduced below the levels suggested in this Chapter; and (ii) the screener doesn't own any significant stock position in the sponsoring organization (e.g., in excess of 5%).

[51] Such "overriding royalty interests" permit the sponsor to drill and complete marginal or non-commercial wells on a profitable basis—to *him*!

(1) Turnkey drilling;[52]

(2) Mark-up of leases (other than to "adjusted lease cost");[53]

(3) A transfer of partnership properties (other than undeveloped leases) to the sponsor or any affiliate other than an affiliated partnership on *any* basis.

(And don't think you're adequately protected just because services are being provided at "competitive rates"—or even at "cost." "Competitive" is often hard to establish; so is the quality of the services being provided. Games can be played with "cost." In any event, the sponsor may be making a good living providing services or supplies to his partnerships; at a minimum, he's keeping his staff and facilities employed—and he may have found a "dumping ground" for some high-cost "dogs.")

Be wary of EXCESSIVE self-dealing or SIGNIFICANT variation from the spirit of the NASAA Guidelines.

However, there's a better method to "test" whether the sponsor's operating practices may get in the way of your making money. *Check the sponsor's "track record."* (We'll show you how in a moment.) If his prior investors are realizing excellent returns, it indicates that he isn't abusing the potential conflicts. If they aren't, it's immaterial whether he's abusing his powers or is a poor oil finder: if the investment will cost you money, you don't want to play whatever the reason.

(Of course, if the sponsor passes *this* test, we'll still need to insist on "due diligence" and "monitoring" to insure that his past performance is still indicative of his present potential. More of that in a moment.)

—In Search of Investor Protection: Of "Democracy Rights" and "Program Monitors"—In General. All of the "selectivity techniques" we're discussing help you determine whether or not, *at the time of your investment,* your program sponsor and his particular offering appear to be good bets. *But what if something goes wrong thereafter?*

Many deals sold during the "hysteria" period of 1977 through 1981 failed due to erroneous assumptions concerning price and demand. But many failed which were salvageable, despite the change in oil industry economics when "good" general partners went sour.

Structure and the to-be-discussed track record analysis and due diligence help you find *today's* quality deals. But what if your general partner develops a drinking problem? Goes through a divorce? Loses the enthusiasm

---

[52] We've indicated why elsewhere in the Chapter, as well as in **Chapters Two** and **Three**.

[53] I.e., interest and *reasonable* work-up fees.

that had lead to his prior spectacular performance? Gets into financial difficulties? Loses key employees? (The list is endless.)

(After all, an advantage—and a disadvantage—of investing with the "Independents" is that they are "one [or two] man shows." Not that they don't have their staffs—and often large, and important ones. However, it's usually those one or two key people that distinguish the "twenty percent"— the superior performers you are looking for—from the mediocre crowd.)

We need something to protect us when what should have been a good deal starts to go bad. That "something" can insure that the general partner or operator corrects the condition (after all, he doesn't want to lose control over his own operation)—or that a now tainted (and unsalvageable) oilman is replaced by a competent one.

What about the auditors? They play an important role in protecting us against improper charges, or embezzlement.[54] But it's not their job to pass upon many of the aspects of program operation that are critical to *your* making a profit.

So let's insist on two "after the investment" protections. First, someone in *our* corner, who looks over the sponsor's shoulder to insure that the earlier promise (and promises!) are honored. (We'll call him the "Program Monitor.") Second, some protections, similar to those given corporate minority share-holders, if our monitor determines that all is not well in Denmark.

—**Democracy Rights.** The NASAA Guidelines contain extensive "democracy rights" to protect the investor. Again, they are only required as a matter of law in public programs. However, legitimate (and informed) sponsors of private programs include them in their offerings as a matter of course.

The absence of the more significant of the NASAA democracy rights is a serious danger signal that you are dealing with an ill-informed—or illegitimate—sponsor.

It's not necessary that a private offering comply literally with the NASAA Guidelines.[55] However, it is critical that the *substance* of the "democracy right" protections be included in the venture agreement. These include:

(1) The right to *timely, complete and accurate reports.* These reports should include annual, *audited* and/or "reviewed" *financial information,*[56] including the costs charged and the revenues credited to the

---

54 For a discussion of the role of the auditor, see Sheehan, "To Err is Human, To Audit Divine," **Oil & Gas Investor** (July, 1984).

55 Public program sponsors have no choice.

56 Frequently, financial information prepared by independent certified public accountants on oil and gas limited partnerships must be "reviewed" rather than certified and/or audited.

investors; similar information concerning the sponsor's share of costs and revenues; compensation paid to the sponsor and his affiliates (and what they did to earn that compensation); and, after a two-year period, *reserve reports*, prepared by an *independent* and qualified petroleum reservoir engineer which include the *present value of YOUR interest in future net revenues*, not merely "reserves in the ground" of *undiscounted* future net revenues; and TIMELY *tax information*.[57]

(By the way, those reserve and present value reports should clearly distinguish between "proven" reserves [and, again, between proven *producing* reserves and those which are still "behind the pipe"] and "probable" and "possible" reserves. ["Probables" aren't always all that probable, and "possibles" frequently fail to materialize.])

(2) The right to a *list of the names and addresses of your fellow investors*, plus the ability of 10% "in interest" of the investors to *call a meeting of investors*.

(3) *Access to program records* (although your sponsor is given the right to keep certain "sensitive" information, such as well logs, confidential).

(4) Significant *voting rights*: a majority in interest of the investors should be able to remove the general partner and/or the well or program operator; cancel contracts with the sponsor or his affiliates; elect a successor to any removed parties (although frequently the sponsor must concur in the choice); and dissolve the program (again, frequently with the sponsor's concurrence).

—Program Monitoring: Your Investor "Safety Belt." But will these "rights" in fact prove meaningful? How do you know whether your sponsor is doing a good, mediocre, rotten or crooked job? How could you understand those program records—or even the financial information that you're receiving? Are the prospects that are being drilled, or the proven reserves that are being purchased, really all that spectacular? Could that well blowout have been prevented or not?

If your general partner or well operator is doing a good job, and we're merely caught up in the "speculative nature of oil," you don't want to remove

---

[57] For an excellent discussion of investor reporting, see "Investor Reports: What Should They Be Telling You?," **Investor's Tax Shelter Report** (March, 1983). This article is reproduced in **Financing Oil & Gas Deals—1986 Edition** (Energy Textbooks International, Inc.: 1986); **1985-1986 Real Estate and Oil & Gas Investment Symposium** (Energy Textbooks International, Inc.: 1985); and **Techniques of Oil & Gas Tax-Shelter Financing** (Energy Textbooks International, Inc.: 1983, with 1985 Supplement).

him.[58] If he has ceased to function effectively, he needs to "straighten up or ship out"! But if the sponsor *should* be removed, how can you and a group of equally inexperienced (oilwise) neophytes "choose" (or even *find*) a quality successor—or even cooperate in making the attempt?

Let's discuss the most important protection your program needs to contain: a "Program Monitor" feature.

The use of a "monitor" who would serve as an "ombudsman" for oil and gas investors was first suggested almost a decade ago,[59] but has only in recent years seemed to "catch on"—and here more with independent analysts rather than sponsors—or even brokerage houses.[60]

As we've indicated, the "Program Monitor" is an oil and gas professional—usually the consulting geologist or engineer who performed the initial due diligence on the sponsor (see below) who is on *your* side. He's qualified, objective, and independent; and his sole job is to insure that the "good" general partner or well operator remains that way. He'll be conducting periodic investigations and reviews, both scheduled and "sneak," to insure that only quality properties go into the program; that the qualified staff remains so; and that, generally, the sponsor performs as he represented he would. Since he's already performed the initial due diligence, he can conduct this "ongoing" due diligence at little cost to you. (Your financial advisor or broker should be requiring this anyway, as a part of the review of proposed new offerings by the sponsor.) Since he's an oil industry professional—and has already studied the sponsor's organization in connection with the first due diligence review—he'll be hard to fool, and quick to pick up on discrepancies. And since no operation is perfect, the tips he gives the operator on how to

---

[58]Remember the lesson of **Chapter One:** even the best planned oil venture may prove unprofitable—or disastrous.

[59]See Gracer and Sapperstein, "The Importance of Professional Monitoring of Oil and Gas Investment," **Investment Dealers' Digest** (July 4, 1978).

[60]Want to read what **Oil & Gas Investor** has to say about monitoring? See "Making Waves" (June, 1985) [reproduced in **Financing Oil & Gas Deals—1986 Edition** (Energy Textbooks International, Inc.: 1986), hereinafter referred to as **"Financing Oil & Gas Deals"**]; "A Diligent Monitor" (July, 1983) [reproduced in **1985-1986 Real Estate and Oil & Gas Investment Symposium** (Energy Textbooks International, Inc.: 1985), hereinafter referred to as **"Real Estate and Oil & Gas Symposium"**]; "Mosburg 'On the Record' " (**Oil & Gas Investor,** March and April, 1982), [reproduced in **Financing Oil & Gas Deals** and in **Techniques of Oil & Gas Tax-Shelter Financing** (Energy Textbooks International, Inc.: 1983, with 1985 Supplement), hereinafter referred to as "Tax-Shelter Financing"]. See also "The Incredible Sense of Program Monitoring," **Investor's Tax Shelter Report** (June, 1982); "Problems and Pitfalls in the 'Program Monitor' Concept," **Investor's Tax Shelter Report** (July/August, 1982); and "More Mousetraps in the 'Program Monitor' Concept," **Investor's Tax Shelter Report** (November, 1982) all reproduced in **Tax-Shelter Financing**.

conduct the operations more effectively on your behalf will more than pay for the costs of the "monitoring."

Of course, we're assuming that the monitor *is* qualified, that he *is* objective, and that he *is* independent. Later in this Chapter, we'll show you how to determine if the due diligence, the program monitoring, and the advice you are receiving from your "expert" counselor (by the way, we don't mean a lawyer) is as expert as it is supposed to be.

A parting word concerning "monitoring." *If your advisor recommends that you invest in ANY program that doesn't contain a "monitoring" feature, ask him why.* He'll find it hard to justify.

—Other Structuring Considerations: Of Assessments, "Liquidity" Features, and Insurance. A few words about some other structuring considerations.

What about *assessments*? Earlier in this Chapter, we mentioned the need to consider the likelihood that the sponsor might be required to call upon you (at least optionally) for additional cash contributions if the program's properties were to be fully developed.

No matter how carefully your oilman plans, except in "mature" areas—which frequently are lacking in profitability (see above)—"cost overruns" (the well cost exceeds original estimates) will occur.[61] The sponsor also can't determine how many wells will need to be completed (the completion phase has its share of cost overruns as well) or how many prospects will prove rewarding and require additional drilling. Rather than requiring you to contribute the maximum amount of cash that might be needed in the event of a very successful program, plus a large cost-overrun contingency factor, industry practice is to "assess" (require additional cash contributions) for amounts over and above original cost estimates.

Assessments for completion costs in well-by-well ventures, or for completion and other cost overruns in "program" investments, are usually "mandatory": you *must* pay the assessment if called. (Penalties for failing to pay are usually stiff, creating potential personal liability, or even forfeiture out of both future and *existing* wells—those for which you've already paid!)

Assessments for additional drilling are usually optional: you don't have to pay the assessment; but, if you don't, you're penalized by a reduction in your *overall* partnership interest or by being excluded from *any* participation in those optional wells (and possibly *all* future wells).[62]

---

[61] See **Chapter One** for some of the "speculative" conditions that can cause this to occur.

[62] Another alternative is to "carry" you subject to a penalty: you don't share in production from those "optional" wells until the participating parties have recovered their costs plus a premium—say 300%.

Some analysts—and most brokerage houses—are opposed to assessable programs.[63] (Brokers dislike assessments, since they are not permitted to charge commissions on such payments under state securities laws.) However, *to optimize your profit*, the program should contain *reasonable* assessment features: otherwise your program will not be able to fully exploit the opportunities created by its original drilling. While the undrilled locations could be "farmed out" (assigned) to another partnership or operator, with your program reserving a cost-free interest in production, you would lose a major portion of the upside potential at a *relatively* risk-free stage. (Remember, however, that geologically sound development wells may still be dry!)[64]

The assessment provisions must, however, be reasonable. The sponsor shouldn't expect you to give him a "blank check": assessments should be limited to not more than 10% to 15% of your original cash commitment for mandatory assessments, and not more than an amount equal to that original contribution for optional assessments. (By that time, any further drilling should be financible out of production loans.) Penalties should likewise be reasonable, particularly on optional assessments: a "penalty" of not more than 300%, exclusion from additional drilling, or a proportionate reduction in your interest in the overall program.

A word of caution: worry if penalties are *too* reasonable. You shouldn't invest in oil unless you are prepared to participate in this optional "exploitation" drilling. (That's where your greatest profits may result.) If the penalties amount to a mere slap on the wrist, other investors can go "non-consent"; you will be "carrying" them without adequate compensation for bearing their share of the risk. And if too many investors elect to follow this route, the program may be *forced* to turn away from some excellent developmental opportunities.

Most of today's better-structured programs contain various "liquidity" features: a "redemption" feature, under which the general partner periodically must offer to repurchase your interest in the program for cash, and, in some instances, an eventual "exchange" feature, where program interests are traded for stock (usually in the general partner's corporate entity or an affiliated "start up" corporation).

The "redemption" provision will be contained in your original venture agreement. It doesn't guarantee the return of any specified amount of money.

---

63 For a discussion, see "Assessments—Boon or Boondoggle?," **Investor's Tax Shelter Report** (May, 1982), and Lomasney, "The Importance of Assessments in Oil & Gas Drilling Programs," **Investment Dealers' Digest** (April 3, 1973), both reproduced in **Financing Oil and Gas Deals** and **Tax-Shelter Financing**, *op. cit.* n. 60.

64 See **Chapter One**.

(If it did, the "at risk" limitations on loss would be breached, causing a loss of anticipated deductions.)[65] However, the general partner will be required, normally after a two-year period (required to secure reliable reserve information), to offer to repurchase your interest based upon some percentage of its estimated "fair market value." (Be sure that the "fair market value" must be established by *independent* appraisal.)

The original offering can't contain a *guarantee* that an eventual stock exchange will be made: otherwise, in the opinion of the IRS, an "association taxable as a corporation" has been created.[66] However, a sponsor who has made a practice of making exchange offers in the past may well intend to do so in the future.[67]

The "liquidity" provided by these liquidity features may be illusory.[68] And there are disadvantages in accepting either type of offer. So we'll have more to say about these features in **Chapter Six**.

Adequate insurance to cover the liabilities and hazards of oilfield operations is a "must" in a properly-structured operation.[69] (The adequacy of insurance coverage is something that should be—and normally isn't—covered in the due diligence investigation.) However, there are certain new insurance features that are now available to give greater protection to investors.

The new insurance features are "errors and omissions" policies that protect investors against sponsor misdoings, including embezzlement. Another new type of insurance coverage are policies that would protect the *program* from loss if there were successful suits by other investors for violations of securities laws.[70] The premiums for such protection are quite low, and the protection provided is valuable. However, until investors (or their representatives) start *demanding* this kind of protection, it's not likely that the coverage will be voluntarily provided by the sponsor.

—Conclusions Concerning Structure Analysis. Structure analysis certainly has its place in the selectivity process. And, as discussed above, there are certain favorable structuring considerations that have a significant impact on program profitability and will affect your investment decision. But

---

[65] See **Chapter Two**.

[66] See **Chapter Two**.

[67] See **Chapter Two** for a discussion of the tax advantages of accepting a stock exchange offer over a cash redemption.

[68] For a discussion, see Lewis, "In Search of Liquidity," **Oil & Gas Investor** (December, 1983).

[69] See "Oilfield Armor," **Oil & Gas Investor** (June, 1983).

[70] For a discussion of these new policies, see "Oilfield Armor," *id.*

structure analysis doesn't answer the critical question: will this sponsor find oil profitably for *you*?

Another word of warning. Don't try for "too perfect" a deal. Even in today's "contrarian market," discussed at the close of this Chapter, the better oil finders—the ones with whom you want to invest—can always find investors, or simply turn their deals within the industry. They will turn away from proposals that don't offer them a reasonable opportunity for profit as well.

(And the oilman's willingness to accept a seriously substandard proposal may tell you something about his oil finding ability—or indicate the presence of hidden flaws in the proposal.)

—Sizing Up the Sponsor's Ability to Perform—In General. The key to selectivity in oil and gas investment is to analyze your sponsor's ability to perform—to determine whether he is (or isn't) a quality oil finder with the concern for his capital sources (that's *you*!) that marks him as one of the "twenty percent" who are superior performers.

In analyzing a sponsor's ability to perform, three questions must be answered:

(1) Management's *general experience, integrity and credentials*;

(2) Management's *"Track Record"* in performing for investors in prior programs;

(3) Management's *present potential*.

Let's look at each of these.

—The Sponsor's General Credentials. If you wanted to invest in real estate, would you select a syndicate that was staffed by geologists? Probably not. Yet, in the 1977-1981 "hysteria period," when the financial community was investing wildly in oil—normally in terrible deals—a large number of the subsequent poor performers were sponsored by former real estate syndicators with no experience whatsoever in oil.

My sponsor must be staffed with personnel who know oil. This experience can be provided by outside consultants, but finding oil profitably is tricky business. Invest with the pros.

Even the best oilfinder can't make you money if he's undercapitalized. Many of today's worst horror stories involve basically sound investments which went sour when the sponsor found himself in serious financial trouble. (See the need for program monitoring?) Your general partner or well operator must have sufficient *liquid* net worth to be able to help your program weather financial storms—and to be able to weather those storms himself.

So expertise, experience, and financial strength are a must in your sponsor. Unfortunately, it's easier to state the need for analyzing these factors than it is to perform the analysis. But as a first step, turn to the section in the offering document entitled "Management." (Remember, run from the proposals where you're not provided such information.)[71] If management consists of nothing but financial types, or former motion picture syndicators, you may need to look no further.[72] Then review the "Financial Information" that the offering document is required to disclose concerning the sponsor.

Unfortunately, all you can determine from the offering document are the *credentials* of management. An impressive string of important-sounding positions may merely indicate that your sponsor has been fired by some of the best oil companies in the United States. But if the sponsor and his organization don't even present the *appearance* of understanding oil, your inquiry is at an end. Adequate credentials are not enough. Not all oilmen are *good* oil finders. So now we need to go one step further: to evaluate the *economic potential* of the sponsor's offering.

—Evaluating Economic Potential—Analyzing "Track Record"—In General. It's difficult for anyone other than an oil industry professional to analyze the *present economic potential* of a sponsor's latest proposal. (Thus the need for "due diligence," which we'll be discussing in a moment.) However, the offering document contains plentiful information from which the sponsor's *prior performance*—his *"track record"*—can be reviewed. And this "track record" analysis is a "selectivity" step which you, personally, can perform.

How important is track record analysis? A smart promoter can play games with program structure; poor past performance is harder to disguise. Our analysis of the impact of "time line" diversification in **Chapter Three** showed that:

(1) *Poor performers tend to continue to perform poorly;*

(2) *Good performers tend to continue to deliver superior results.*

Of course, an outstanding prior track record doesn't prevent a subsequent loss of key personnel or the other condition changes that could affect the sponsor's *present* ability to perform. And a leopard can change its spots. But due diligence and monitoring will reveal changes in a sponsor's manner of operation that cast a cloud on his present potential. And that prior poor performer is frequently the same old leopard, masquerading in a new costume.

—But Can *You* Analyze "Track Record"? Track record is not all that hard to analyze—*if* you know where to look in the offering document for the necessary "input" data, and *if* you know how to use that data.

---

[71] **Chapter Six** will discuss the sponsor's obligation to make "full disclosure."

[72] Remember, though, that "management" also means any outside consultants or "program operators" with whom a "money manager" is dealing.

In the past, few investors (or investor representatives) have understood the use of the "Prior Activities" tables which, as a matter of law, must be provided potential investors in any proposed oil and gas offering, public or private.[73]

One method of analyzing past performance is to determine the *present value* of the *future net revenues* to the investors' account under the past programs. If those programs had adequate "democracy rights" provisions—and, if they didn't, by now you won't be considering investing with that type of sponsor—those figures must have been provided.

This is exactly what a "due diligence" consultant would (and will) review during the course of his due diligence investigation. But his review will be based upon his own independent verification of the reserves, and his own set of parameters as to future oil prices and demand, the appropriate discount factor to apply in reducing "future net revenues" to their present value, and the weight, if any, to be given "proven unproducing," "probable," and "possible" reserves. Since the sponsor can play his own games in providing those figures to his prior investors (or to you), and can select his own "independent" expert to arrive at those figures (or at least, within limits, set the rules under which those present value calculations will be made), it's not too wise to rely upon the sponsor's own optimistic estimates of the future performance of those programs.

(Sponsors have been known to look with rose colored glasses at reserve-based future performance estimates when they are trying to find investors for new programs, or to cajole prior investors to reinvest.)

The "Net Cash" and "Payout" tables which the sponsor *must* include in the "Prior Activities" section of his offering document are *cash-on-cash* data: totally non-subjective with no opportunity for "interpretation."[74] (The only way the sponsor can mask these figures is to lie about them, and that's a "go to jail" offense under the securities laws.)

(By the way, this information is just as necessary under the securities laws in well-by-well offerings as it is in limited partnership offerings, although most well operators don't realize this.)

The offering document will also contain certain information on the number of wells drilled in each past program; how many of these wells (gross

---

[73] See **Chapter Six**.

[74] Since federal and state securities laws give you an absolute right to the return of your money if this information isn't voluntarily provided to you—see **Chapter Six**—the absence of these tables from the offering document, or their presentation in a non-standard format should be a tip-off as to the results of those prior partnerships, and whether or not you wish to invest with that sponsor. (While a public program can't clear the SEC without including this data, you'd be surprised how many private offering documents don't include these cash-on-cash figures.)

and net) were completed as gas wells, how many as oil wells, and how many were dry. (This should be separately stated for exploratory and developmental wells.)

These "box score" tables show you how much diversification has existed in prior partnerships; the emphasis on oil versus gas; the degree of exploratory risk; and other interesting statistics. However, *a healthy completion ratio, attained by drilling in "sure thing" areas, should never be taken as an indication that these wells were profitable*: this can only be determined by analyzing the Payout or Net Cash tables. And don't be taken in by the sponsor's reference to his "success ratio."

In private programs the Payout and Net Cash tables may be supplemented by additional reserve, future net revenue, and present value information. This is useful data to have. However, be sure that the sponsor gives his assumptions as to oil and natural gas rates, and the discount rate that has been used to reduce the future net revenues to present value. (Be very cautious if only future net revenues, or reserves expressed in barrels of oil and MCFs of natural gas are given. And insure that the figures provided are for revenues/reserves to the *investors'* account.)

Back to the Net Cash and Payout tables. Sample "Investor Net Cash" information on "Company A" is contained in **Figure Eighteen**. (This is the data we used to analyze Company A's performance in **Chapter Three**.)

In **Chapter Three**, we saw the undiscounted, pre-tax, cash-on-cash "ROIs" required to equal both 10% and 20% internal rates of return. The Investor Net Cash table shows the cash subscribed by the investors, plus any additional assessments; total cash distributed; and cash distributions for the last three (or sometimes 12) months; all as of a specified date. *By projecting forward the latest 12-month (or annualized three-month) revenue figures, you can calculate a "ballpark" 10-year ROI result for each partnership. Then by a simple "averaging" process, you can determine the average results in a typical partnership.*[75]

You can also determine the *probability* that any given program will equal or exceed a specified ROI: *by plotting the ROIs, you can see how many have fallen below a given return standard and how many have exceeded that standard.*[76] And if you're experimenting with oil for the first time, and aren't feeling in a very speculative mood, you can look for sponsors with an excellent

---

[75] Sample calculations, and various more sophisticated methods of averaging, are set out in "The Economics of Oil and Gas Investment," contained in **Financing Oil & Gas Deals**, *op. cit.* n. 60. See also Mosburg and Fitzgerald, "When Do Investors 'Make Money' in Oil?," contained in **Tax-Shelter Financing**, *op. cit.* n. 60.

[76] Again, for sample calculations, see the articles cited in the previous footnote.

INVESTOR NET CASH

As of December 31, 1980

Drilling Program	Cash Subscribed and Assessed (1)	Total Cash Distributed To Investors (2)		
		Aggregate	Last 3 Months Ending 12/31/80	Month and Year Commenced
1. 1971-1 Program	$ 325,000	$ 313,950	$ 32,500	9/1972
2. 1972-1 Program	450,000	3,181,500	144,000	9/1973
3. 1972-2 Program	1,040,750	923,100	13,575	3/1974
4. 1973-1 Program	2,007,500	1,989,250	127,750	12/1974
5. 1973-2 Program	1,351,250	1,198,735	47,000	9/1975
6. 1973-YE Program	1,725,000	964,800	60,000	3/1977
7. 1974-1 Program	2,525,000	1,062,015	126,250	3/1977
8. 1974-2 Program	1,742,250	456,015	45,450	6/1977
9. 1974-YE Program	2,323,000	1,152,208	121,200	12/1975
10. 1975-1 Program	3,835,250	1,800,900	233,450	3/1978
11. 1975-2 Program	4,301,000	4,338,400	411,400	3/1977
12. 1976-1 Program	5,807,500	6,868,000	808,000	3/1978
13. 1976-2 Program	3,484,500	696,900	121,200	3/1979
14. 1977-1 Program	8,130,500	1,131,200	282,800	12/1979
15. 1977-2 Program	5,807,500	1,313,000	808,000	6/1980
16. 1977-X Program	5,807,500	1,313,000	707,000	6/1980
17. 1978-1 Program	13,938,000	1,212,000	363,600	12/1979
18. 1978-2 Program	9,292,000	1,292,800	969,600	6/1980
19. 1979-1 Program	18,239,000	--	--	--
20. 1979-2 Program	16,611,750	--	--	--
21. 1980-1 Program	20,200,000	--	--	--
22. 1980-2 Program	25,295,000	--	--	--
Totals	$154,239,250	$31,207,773	$ 5,422,775	

(1) Includes cash subscribed from Company A to the extent of its subscriptions to the Drilling Programs.

(2) No distributions represent a return of capital for Federal income tax purposes.

Amounts of long term capital gains are shown in Note 2 to the Investor Payout Table.

Source: Company A Prospectus, based on Revenues and Expenditures as of Dec. 31, 1980.

FIGURE 18: Company A "Prior Activities" Data

"Constancy Level": most of their programs seem to fall within acceptable levels.

("Constancy Level," however, normally has a price tag; less dramatic returns over any three to five year investment period. And don't let the Easter Bunny get to you: even sponsors with high Constancy Levels will have their occasional "bad" partnerships.)

Another tip: *pay attention to CHANGING TRENDS in the sponsor's track record.* If the sponsor's overall average performance is substandard, but the last five to 10 years have been excellent, the leopard may have truly changed his spots. (But don't get carried away with one or two years of "superior" performance—the oil business *is* speculative.) And an excellent aggregate track record may not mean too much if the sponsor's last few programs seem to be slipping—and there is an overall downward trend.

Will a purist cringe at this "simplistic" approach? Of course. Will it give you exact return figures? Certainly not. Will it give you useful "ballpark" figures to eliminate patently poor performers and identify those that seem worthy of further study? *Absolutely!*

By the way, your oilman is also required to provide *Sponsor* Net Cash and Payout figures. (Again, run if he hasn't done so voluntarily.) From these, you can determine, for the poorer performing partnerships, whether the sponsor's profit was modest to non-existent on those programs, or whether he was making a bundle while his investors were losing their shirts.

—**Going the Next Step: Expert Advice and "Due Diligence"—In General.** Track record analysis, which *you* can perform, discloses what the sponsor has done in the *past.* As such, it's very valuable: as we saw in **Chapter Three**, past performance tends to repeat itself in future programs.

Unfortunately, past performance doesn't always repeat itself. When we discussed "program monitoring," we saw how changed conditions can cast a cloud on a sponsor's ability to perform. And while our track record has given us a leg up on most oil and gas investors (and most investor representatives!), it's only an approximation of *actual* prior performance.

Can *you* accurately chart *present* profit potential? The answer to that question is "no." You not only lack the oil expertise, but it would also be far too expensive for you to send in the geologists, engineers and other technicians required to accurately evaluate the quality of the sponsor's technical staff, the quality of his inventory of leases or producing properties, and the value of the interests of his investors under prior partnerships. However, you can accomplish the same objective by pooling your dollars with those of other like-minded investors through the services of a qualified and conscientious advisor.

How can you tell if the advisor you select is qualified and conscientious? This part of the book will tell you how to "analyze your analyst."

—Do I Need An Advisor? The steps you've taken to analyze your sponsor's track record will help you select quality programs. However, an expert can insure that you are in "the best of the best." And for purposes of making the extremely profitable "contrarian" investments we'll be discussing at the close of this Chapter, that advisor can be a great help in negotiating the types of arrangements that are possible in today's environment—for one who knows what he's doing and has the bargaining power that one representing a large pool of capital can exert.

A quality advisor will coordinate a thorough due diligence investigation of the sponsor and his proposal; will have access to opportunities that would not otherwise have been available to you; and will be able to negotiate more advantageous arrangements on your behalf than you could have done acting alone. He'll work closely with your personal financial advisor to assure that the investments he recommends fit into your overall investment plan and financial and tax-planning strategy. And best of all: his services are *very* reasonable.

This "expert" you select may be a financial planner, an investment advisor, a broker, or a member of a bank advisory department. The key is that he thoroughly understand the ins and outs of oil and gas investment.

Unfortunately, not all financial planners, brokers, and the like fit in this category. Some don't claim to; others *claim to*, but do a very poor job of living up to their representations. (Some oilmen fall in the same category!)

In a moment, we'll tell you how to select a "quality" advisor. First, let's talk more about "due diligence."

—What Is a "Due Diligence" Review? It takes someone experienced in oil and gas exploration and development to determine whether another oilman is the quality performer he represents himself (and perhaps believes himself) to be. A qualified geological or engineering consultant—usually someone upon whom banks also heavily rely—can quickly tell whether the sponsor's staff is long on credentials but short on actual ability; whether the prospects selected for drilling by that staff are the high-quality opportunities investors need; and the myriad of other factors that need to be analyzed in determining the likelihood that you will profit from this investment.[77]

The objective of oil and gas investment is to MAKE MONEY.

---

[77] For a discussion of the scope of a due diligence investigation, see Holmes, "Technical Due Diligence Investigations of Oil and Gas Programs," contained in **Financing Oil & Gas Deals**, *op. cit.* n. 60. See also "A Diligent Monitor," **Oil & Gas Investor** (July, 1983), also reproduced in **Financing Oil & Gas Deals**, for an interview with Boulder due diligence and monitoring expert John Gustavson. (The Holmes article and Gustavson interview are also reproduced in **Real Estate and Oil & Gas Investment Symposium** and **Tax-Shelter Financing**, cited in the same footnote.

The only way to insure that this objective is attained is to insist on an adequate due diligence review, coupled with adequate program monitoring.

The benefits of a thorough due diligence review are immense. In a study recently published by the American Association of Petroleum Geologists, Denver due diligence expert Mike Holmes established that, in partnerships participating in at least 20 prospects, *the risk-adjusted economic results projected by the due diligence review, and the actual results, were within 10% for every partnership reviewed!*[78]

—"Analyzing Your Analyst!" Unfortunately, not all due diligence investigations are performed by "consultants" who are competent or objective.[79] Many "experts" who hold themselves out as "tax shelter analysts" are more interested in commissions than quality; and either: (i) don't perform (or commission the performance) of adequate—or *any*—due diligence; (ii) ignore the due diligence reports they receive; or (iii) insist on a "due diligence" which whitewashes those programs they wish to sell.[80]

It's easy to check out your analyst. (This method of "analyzing your analyst" will automatically verify the "quality" [or lack thereof] of his due diligence consultant). Just follow these guidelines:

(1) Ask to see the offering documents on the programs your potential advisor is currently recommending;

(2) Run the "track record' analysis" we've previously outlined on these programs;

(3) If the recommendations, in the main, reflect sponsors whose 10-year "ROI" to their investors equals or exceeds 2:1, you are apparently dealing with a "quality" advisor;

(4) If the majority of his recommendations didn't come close to our "target" 2:1 ROI—and look at the "contrarian" targets we recommend below—ask him: why was he recommending these programs? (Better still, seek a new advisor!)

---

[78] Holmes et al., "A New Method Of Estimating Risk-Adjusted Reserves and Economic Potential of Exploratory Prospects," contained in Megill (ed.), **Economics and the Explorer: AAPG Studies in Geology #19** (American Association of Petroleum Geologists: 1985), also reproduced in **Real Estate and Oil & Gas Investment Symposium**, *op. cit.* n. 60.

[79] We discussed the same problem earlier in this Chapter as to the non-conscientious, non-qualified, non-objective program monitor.

[80] Some due diligence investigations performed by *financially-oriented* consultants focus primarily on the structure of the program and an analysis of the sponsor's balance sheet. While this "structure/financially-oriented" analysis certainly has its value, your personal financial advisor could probably perform it for you at a greatly reduced cost. And if the review is not coupled with a "technical" review of management's abilities, prospect quality, and the like, it has missed the point of "technical" (economic) due diligence.

(While you're at it, ask him why he didn't insist on a program monitor feature.)

Investing as a "Contrarian." There has never been a better time to invest in oil and gas. Misperceptions concerning the risks of oil and the impact of price and demand declines, and "flat tax" fears, have left the industry desperate for capital. It's time for the contrarian investor to play "Let's make a deal."

Just as these times present tremendous opportunities for you, they represent a time of opportunity for the solid oil and gas operator, where participation in outstanding oil prospects can be secured at a fraction of the normal "dues." But to take advantage of these conditions, he requires capital.

The more experienced members of the oil and gas industry are willing to pay a handsome price if you will help them participate in what are possibly once-in-a-lifetime opportunities by providing the capital necessary to take advantage of those opportunities.

In **Chapter Three**, we mentioned that this added up to once-in-a-lifetime opportunities for you as well. The smarter oilmen are restructuring their deals to make them more attractive to *you*, so that they can secure this necessary capital despite today's market conditions. And look at the deal terms that are currently available—*if demanded*—as contrasted with previous "standard" arrangements:

Promotional Item:	Traditional	Recommended
Front-End Dilution:	15%	7½%-10%[81]
Sharing Arrangement:		
Carried Interest:	10%-15%	7.5%
Reversionary Interest:	25%-33⅓%	15%-25%
Functional Allocation:	20%-25% "spread"	15%-20% "spread"
Promoted Interest:	20%-25% "spread"	15%-20% "spread"

---

[81] This doesn't mean we think that brokers will be cutting their commissions on oil deals—not in this market! It means that the sponsor will now be bearing a portion of "direct" sales costs out of his own pocket, just as he should now be bearing *all* wholesaling costs personally.

Combination:	6.25%-12.5%	3.25%-6.25%
	BPO; 25%-40%	BPO; 15%-20%
	APO	APO
Net Revenue Interest:		
To Partnership:	70%-75%	78%-82%
To Investors:	45%	60%-65%

With these "new" program terms—and a quality oil finder—your Return on Investment should increase to 2.5:1 or better, a minimum 20% internal rate of return, even if tax laws change, and a spectacular return level if they do not!

But remember: just as you must insist on program monitoring if you're to receive this valuable protection, most oilmen won't give you these better deal terms unless you or your advisor *insist* on them. And the best deal terms in the world won't turn a mediocre prospect into a golden opportunity. (Thus the need for track record analysis and due diligence.)

(You'll find all of these suggestions, and the rest of the advice given in this Chapter, summarized in the **Investment Decision Checklist** contained in the **Appendix**.)

Finally, let your advisor know that you won't invest (through him) unless he exposes you to the quality opportunities that are available to today's contrarian. (If he won't listen, change advisors!) With his help and "pooled capital" negotiating power, you should find oil and gas investment a matchless opportunity.

CHAPTER SIX
GETTING *OUT* OF OIL

Introduction. It's never hard to get *into* oil. On every street corner there are promoters who are eager to sell you an interest in their well, or let you into their "private" limited partnership ("a very special deal, for real insiders only!").

Getting *out* of your oil and gas investment is another matter entirely.

In this closing Chapter, we'll explore (albeit quite briefly) what to do when your oil venture is successful; what to do if it's not so successful; what to do if you are audited; and what to do if you think you've been swindled.

We're not going to try to cover any of these subjects in any kind of detail. Each could be (and has been) the subject of extensive treatment elsewhere. (We will give you a few tips for further reading.) But, to round out this introduction to oil and gas investment, these are topics with which you need to be familiar.

What If I've Done Well?—In General. We hope this is the question you'll be asking; certainly, that's been the purpose of this book. But due to the speculative nature of the oil and gas business, certain of your partnerships will not do as well as others. (More about this in a moment.) And others should do spectacularly.

One "solution" for the successful partnership is simply to enjoy your success. Under present tax laws, Percentage Depletion will shelter a portion of your revenues from taxation; even if Percentage Depletion is repealed, the "return of capital" element of your production revenues, plus, possibly, an "inflation" factor, can be received tax free.[1]

But perhaps you'd prefer to liquidate your investment, preferably at Long Term Capital Gains rates. Most partnerships (although not most well-by-well deals) will contain a "Redemption Feature," under which the general partner is required, annually, to offer to repurchase your interest for cash.[2] Unfortunately, a major portion of that cash will be taxed at Ordinary Income tax rates, due to the "Recapture" and "Zero Basis" problems discussed in **Chapter Two**. By accepting an Exchange Offer—either one made by your general partner or some third party (possibly one of the Master Limited Partnerships mentioned in **Chapter One**), you can avoid most of the problems of Recapture, though not Zero Basis.

(Let us pre-warn you, however, that accepting a Redemption or Exchange Offer has certain disadvantages, too. We'll discuss them below.)

---

[1] See **Chapter Two**.

[2] See **Chapter Five**.

Finally, you can use your oil and gas interests as a part of your estate planning.

—Accepting a Redemption or Exchange Offer. As we just mentioned, and as was discussed in **Chapter Five**, most general partners are required, under their limited partnership agreements, to offer annually to repurchase your interests for cash. Furthermore, while there can be no "built-in" agreement that binds the general partner to exchange stock of his corporation for your limited partnership interests (to do so would potentially create an Association Taxable as a Corporation),[3] many general partners periodically do offer to "roll up" prior partnership interests for stock, or units in a Master Limited Partnership.[4]

There can be advantages in accepting a Redemption Offer. To the extent that the Redemption Price exceeds the amount of deductions previously claimed by you which are subject to recapture, such as your Productive-Well IDCs and the amortization of your Equipment Costs, the balance of the gain on the sale (if any) *will* be taxed at Long Term Capital Gains rates.[5] (This may all change, however, if current tax proposals are adopted.) And you will have exchanged an *illiquid* asset, the benefits of which would take seven to 50 years to fully realize, for the most liquid of all assets: cash.

There are certain disadvantages in accepting a Redemption Offer. First, in arriving at the "Present Worth" of your interests for purposes of the repurchase, the general partner will apply an initial discounting to your future net revenues to reduce those dollars to their "Present Value," and will then apply an additional discounting (referred to as the "second haircut") to arrive at the *risk-discounted* "Present Worth" of those dollars.

(The oilman isn't trying to take advantage of you as a naïve non-industry investor: this is the same approach used when one major oil company purchases reserves from another major.)

If you've followed the advice contained in **Chapter Five**, that determination of Present Value and Present Worth will be arrived at by "Independent Appraisal" by a qualified petroleum engineer. However, traditionally, this meant that by selling today you received an amount equal to approximately 50% of those estimated future net revenues. (Remember, of course, that you were receiving those dollars *today*—a time value benefit—and partially at Long Term Capital Gains rates.) With today's uncertainties concerning oil

---

[3] See **Chapter Two**.

[4] Master Limited Partnerships are discussed in **Chapter One**.

[5] See **Chapter Two**. If you have held your interests for less than five years, there may also be some ITC recapture.

and natural gas prices, and the number of "distressed properties" on the market, you may be lucky to receive 40% on the dollar—and the offer may be for substantially less.[6] (For this reason, be sure that the limited partnership agreement spells out the formula to be used in setting the Redemption Price.)

Except on the most successful of partnerships, that doesn't leave much of the Redemption Price to be taxed at Long Term Capital Gains rates.

Exchange Offers seek to give you a liquid asset as well—a tradeable stock or Master Limited Partnership unit—plus the upside potential of participation in an ongoing concern. If the partnership or corporation is well managed, that may work to your benefit. And while some of these Exchange Offers are *taxable*, many are made on a "tax-free" basis.

Tax-free exchanges are tricky: have your own tax advisor verify that the sponsor's tax counsel seems to know what he's doing. But if the exchange is properly made on a tax-free basis, you can then sell your stock (assuming there is a market) *without triggering recapture of Productive-Well IDCs or ACRS deductions.*[7] ("Unearned" ITC will still be subject to Recapture.)

The best of all worlds? Well, your "Exchange Value," if you accept an Exchange Offer, invariably is set at a much higher figure than your Redemption Price where the sponsor is repurchasing your interests for cash. In some instances, since the sponsor is buying with "paper," you will be paid a premium. However, since similar offers are being made to other unit holders, and you are simply acquiring a piece of that whole, you may find, when trading of the stock commences, that the "stated" value has been significantly overstated.

(And be sure that the Exchange Values have been set based upon a reliable Independent Appraisal, particularly of any interests being exchanged by the *sponsor*.)

If the necessary trading market in the stock or MLP units develops, and if the ongoing operations are conducted in such a fashion that your new security increases in value, you will have substituted an asset with liquidity (and collateral value) and potentially increasing value for an illiquid, static asset. However, if that liquidity doesn't develop, if the value drops, or management doesn't do its job, you have given up an illiquid asset which at least generated current, distributable cash flow for one which lacks both the liquidity and the distributable cash.

---

[6] The general partner additionally will reserve the right to suspend the Redemption Offer if more than 20% in interest of the limited partners request a redemption in any one year.

[7] As a result of the Deficit Reduction Act of 1984, exchange of limited partnership interests for depository receipts (units) in a MLP can no longer be made on a tax-free basis.

Finally, remember that these "Liquidity Features" don't give you an advance right to sell/exchange your interests for any pre-guaranteed price: the "value" will be based upon the results of your partnership's activities.

—Oil and Estate Planning. An interest in a successful well or oil and gas limited partnership can prove an excellent gift to provide income for a college education, the starting of a new marriage, or support for a parent. You've had the benefit of the deductions as an offset against *your* level of taxable income; your beneficiary will pay taxes on the income from the gifted asset, but at his lower tax rates.

(Sure beats your paying taxes on those dollars, and then making a non-deductible gift of those dollars to your loved one.)

You can even make use of a "Clifford Trust" to transfer the income for a period of time,[8] eventually regaining the property (and its income) without any loss of Percentage Depletion. (Percentage Depletion can also be claimed by your beneficiary if he or she is a "family member"—your wife or a minor child.)[9]

These income-producing assets will also prove a valuable portion of the estate upon your death. Percentage Depletion can still be claimed by your heirs or devisees. They are also permitted to "step up" the basis in the wells or partnership interests to their fair market value at the time of your death.[10]

There are many much more elaborate ways in which your oil and gas interests can be used as a part of your lifetime and estate planning.[11] However, whether your planning is simple or elaborate, *consult your personal financial and tax planner in developing any such strategies.*

What If I've Done Poorly? First off, face up to the fact that you've lost the money. There aren't any "magic" ways you can resurrect the dead to convert an oil venture that failed into some mystic tax success.

Oil *is* speculative. Not all of your wells or partnerships will work out. If you've invested on a leveraged basis (see **Chapter Four**), and did not utilize the "installment leverage" approach we recommended in that Chapter, you'll have to repay that loan with non-deductible dollars—a variation of the

---

[8] The beneficiary must be entitled to the income for at least 10 years, absent his earlier death.

[9] Percentage Depletion would not be available under other circumstances to the donee of a "proven property": see **Chapter Two**.

[10] The six-month alternate valuation date may be selected instead.

[11] For examples, see Crawford and Fohlich, "Estate and Gift Tax Planning for Oil and Gas Interests," **Oil & Gas Tax Quarterly** (September, 1982). See also Bienski and Lassila, "Lifetime Transfers: Oil and Gas Royalty Interests," **Oil & Gas Tax Quarterly** (September, 1984).

Phantom Income pitfall. (That's one reason we recommend the "installment leverage" technique.)

While your hard dollars (or most of them) now repose in a series of dry holes or marginal wells, you'll have two partial consolations—*if* you've followed the recommendations contained in **Chapter Five**:

(1) You didn't lose money by investing with a substandard or fraudulent performer;[12]

(2) You didn't invest more than you could afford to lose.

One of your biggest problems will arise if your program consists of wells which still need to be operated, where the sponsor has suffered financial setbacks or appears no longer to be functioning effectively. Due diligence should have foreseen this problem; and program monitoring should have caught and corrected the problem, or alerted you and your fellow investors before much harm was done. (Don't come bellyaching to us if you didn't insist on these protective features!)

If your general partner or well or program operator is no longer capable of functioning, the program monitor will notify you of this fact. (This is a major plus, in eliminating the uncertainty that plagues so many investors in programs which may—or may not—be suffering from mismanagement.) He can also serve as a rallying point, by alerting all concerned of the need for action; by recommending an adequate replacement; and by monitoring *that replacement* to insure that *he* performs properly.

And your democracy rights will give you the rights of access to the names and addresses of your fellow investors, and the removal, replacement, and contract cancellation rights that will prove critical if your sponsor goes sour.

What If I'm Audited? Absent a truly ill-informed or hostile auditing agent—which normally will not prove the case—your avoidance of "abusive" tax shelters will pay off now.[13] (Remember, even if you've utilized leverage—see **Chapter Four**—or have for other reasons invested in a program which is registered with the IRS as a "Tax Shelter," that shouldn't significantly increase your likelihood of audit, or make any audit an unduly traumatic experience.)[14]

Without being abusive, you may have claimed certain deductions which the IRS chooses to challenge.[15] (For a "laundry list," see the "pitfalls" section

---

12 Below, we discuss the steps to take if you feel you've been swindled.

13 See **Chapter Two**.

14 Again, see **Chapter Two**.

15 For years, prepayments were examples.

of **Chapter Two**.) Or the IRS may simply wish to review your return.[16] If this occurs, take the following protective steps:

(1) Immediately involve your attorney or accountant;[17]

(2) If the IRS does choose to challenge certain of your tax positions, discuss with your counselor whether to litigate or settle;

(3) Litigation has the advantage that the IRS has inadequate manpower and there is a massive backlog of cases before the Tax Court: it will be years before your matter is heard and you may well win;

(4) Litigation has the disadvantage that it's expensive: it may cost you more to "win" the dispute than to settle. So settling may be the more practical approach to take. (Remember, the IRS is just as eager to settle the matter as you are.)

What If I've Been Cheated?—In General. If you've been cheated—or *think* you've been cheated—you'll be thankful for insisting on a conscientious program monitor and adequate democracy rights. (You did, didn't you?)

It's often difficult for you as an investor to know whether you have been unfairly treated or not. It's also difficult to coordinate the actions needed to remove a less-than-reputable (as contrasted with a merely inefficient) general partner or operator. But for the same reasons that monitoring and democracy rights were important in dealing with this inefficient operator, they are critical where the sponsor may be a crook rather than an incompetent.

You'll have other weapons in your arsenal: your *contractual rights*; your sponsor's *fiduciary obligations*; and your *rights under federal and state securities laws*.

There are those who assert that a "truly sophisticated investor" will never sue his general partner. (It's usually the sponsor who is asserting this!) Don't you believe it. *You have every legal and moral right—and possibly a moral obligation—to take legal action against a sponsor who has betrayed your confidence.*

—Your Contractual Rights. The venture agreement will normally require the sponsor and his affiliates to take certain actions to protect your interests, and to refrain from other actions which could damage you. (We detailed some of these in **Chapter Five**.) Sometimes, these are a result of the

---

[16] The procedures for auditing the partnership are much more favorable for the IRS since the Tax Equity and Fiscal Responsibility Act of 1982.

[17] If you have any doubts concerning the wisdom of this statement, read "Tax Audits and Your Tax Shelter" from Swanson and Swanson, **Tax Shelters: A Guide for Investors and Their Advisors** (Dow Jones-Irwin: 1982).

federal and state securities laws; other times, of market pressures; and in some instances, they simply represent an effort on the part of the sponsor, at the time he was securing investors, to make his program more appealing than those of his competitors.

Whatever the source of these contractual rights, they are of real value to you. While they merely give you certain contractual remedies, and will usually not authorize the securities administrators "getting into the act," they normally have relatively long "statutes of limitation."

If the sponsor has violated the prohibitions, restrictions, or requirements of the venture contract, or you feel that the charging of costs and revenues, or the distribution of funds, is not in keeping with the venture agreement, insist that the contract be complied with or sue for damages.

(If you *don't know* whether your contractual rights are being respected, the venture agreement—or common law—will give you a right to have the affairs of the venture audited. You'll have the right to the appointment of a receiver if you feel the assets of the program are in danger.)

—Fiduciary Responsibilities and Liabilities for Negligent or Intentional Misconduct. Common law imposes a fiduciary responsibility on the sponsor of a tax-sheltered investment. While certain of the normal fiduciary obligations arguably can be modified by contract, there are others that cannot. The bottom line of this fiduciary responsibility: the sponsor and his affiliates owe you a duty of "utmost fair dealing."

Aside from fiduciary responsibility, if the sponsor conducts the venture in a negligent fashion, he may be liable to you and your fellow investors for any damages to your interests resulting from that negligence.

Normally, the venture agreement will contain a provision exonerating the sponsor from liability to the investors, except in cases of "gross negligence or willful or wanton misconduct." These "exoneration" provisions will usually be honored by the courts. However, in many instances, the sponsor and his affiliates cannot be exonerated from liability arising out of even "simple" negligence in the administration of the "internal affairs of the program" (as contrasted with negligence in the conduct of the program operations). And if the conduct does constitute gross negligence or willful or wanton misconduct, it is seldom that any "exoneration" provisions will protect the sponsor from liability to you and your fellow investors.

—Rights Under Federal and State Securities Laws. Oil and gas investments, no matter how structured, are "securities" under federal and state securities laws. This "security" characterization gives you a number of very powerful rights:

(1) You are entitled to receive a *complete offering document,* satisfying the "Full Disclosure" requirement that you be advised of every fact concerning the proposed venture which would be deemed "material" (i.e., might influence your investment decision). This Full Disclosure requirement applies equally to "public" and "private" offerings, including well-by-well offerings. *If you weren't provided with such a document, you have an ABSOLUTE RIGHT to get your money back.*

(2) Even if you were provided with an appropriate offering document which *did* meet the "Full Disclosure" requirements, *supplemental presentations* made to you cannot be characterized by any misrepresentations or material omissions which would violate the "Anti-Fraud" requirements of the securities laws. *A violation of this requirement also entitles you to a refund of your money.*

(3) The investment should either have been registered with the Securities and Exchange Commission and the applicable state securities agencies, or the complicated "conditions" necessary to claim an exemption from securities registration should have been satisfied by the sponsor. The fact that there were only a limited number of "sophisticated" investors provides no automatic exemption.

Again, if the offering was not registered, and the conditions of some applicable exemption were not met, *you have an absolute right to get your money back.* However, you must *act fast to claim this "Right of Rescission";* the statute of limitations applicable to "failures to register" requires that the action be brought within a shorter period than the limitations statutes that apply to your other rights.

(4) *As to the person selling you your interest:*

    (a) That person must be *registered as a broker-dealer.* (This applies equally to the sponsor, even if he's receiving no commissions in connection with the sale.)

    (b) The person selling you your interest in the program must *verify your suitability as an investor in this type of program.* (The sponsor, if he's not the one making the sale, has an independent duty of verification.) YOUR SUITABILITY STATUS IS NOT AUTOMATICALLY ESTABLISHED BY THE FACT THAT YOU SIGNED A "SUITABILITY LETTER" STATING THAT YOU WERE A FULLY-QUALIFIED, SUITABLE INVESTOR.

    (c) *Any finders fees or commissions,* including the persons to whom payable and the amounts, *must be disclosed to you,* whether they are to be recharged to you or not.

(d) Violation of any one of these rules will *probably* give you the right to a return of your money, at least under state securities laws.

In addition to your rights under the securities laws relating to actions of the sponsor, any professional brokerage house or investment advisor involved in the sale must comply with various provisions of the securities laws which apply to them. Irrespective of securities law liability, you are entitled to competent advice from such parties.

—Asserting Your Rights. If you "sit" on your rights, "statutes of limitation" may bar your ability to enforce your rights. Your initial reaction may be that you can't afford the costs that would be involved in such prolonged lawsuits. However, in many instances, merely letting the sponsor or other "interested parties" know that you are aware of your rights and intend to enforce them may bring you a return of your money. Furthermore, the statutes of limitation can be tolled, and the amount involved in any potential lawsuit raised to a level which will catch the attention of even the most blasé sponsor, by skilled utilization of the concepts of "Integration," plus your right to bring a "Class Action" on behalf of you and all other investors similarly situated; and any purported "waiver" of your rights which you may have signed in a weak moment, whether before or after your investment, is unenforceable under the securities laws.[18]

Most investors aren't aware of, or don't fully understand, their "investor rights." Others are reluctant to attempt to assert them, preferring to "lick their wounds in silence." However, when you have made a significant oil and gas investment, you should be prepared to assert your rights to their fullest. Many investors have found, to their delight, that a single trip to their lawyer's office, followed by a few letters or phone calls from their attorney, have yielded unexpected dividends.

Good luck in your oil and gas investment experience!

---

[18] This does not apply to a properly-prepared "rescission offer" which you have accepted, rejected or let lapse. *Never act, or fail to act, on such an offer without consulting your attorney.*

APPENDIX

Appendix

A GLOSSARY OF PETROLESE
By Paulette Whitcomb

You're looking over a prospectus, or on the phone with your operator, and you're suddenly confronted with spuds that aren't edible. TDs that never cross an end zone, and strippers that don't strip. You're a well-established professional, you hardly ever lose at Scrabble, you do the *Times* puzzle with a pen—but you've discovered a strange new language out there. You order an oilfield dictionary delivered by express mail only to find oilpatch terms explained in Petrolese. Or not listed at all.

Relax. With the above scenario in mind, we have prepared a glossary for you. In it are the words and phrases you are most likely to find in a prospectus and in communications from your operator. It is not the oilpatch in depth, for obvious space reasons; rather, it's a Berlitz course in Petrolese, both technical and financial. You'll not find the more abstruse geophysical terms, the names of the more specialized pieces of machinery, or financial terms that apply to investments other than petroleum. What you *will* find is the basic oilpatch main course. Helpful definitions that will keep you calm if, say, you learn of a delay in the drilling schedule because "the crew is fishing." No aperitifs, garnishes and desserts, just the basic meat and potatoes. Enjoy your meal.

AFE Authorization for expenditure, signed by the parties putting up the money to drill a well, stipulating they will bear the expenses of drilling. Generally has some built-in cost overruns.

Abandon To permanently plug a dry hole or well that no longer produces. See *Plug.*

Acidizing Acid is pumped downhole to help dissolve impediments to permeability. See *Stimulation Techniques.*

Air Drilling A form of rotary drilling that uses compressed air instead of mud. Used predominantly in shallow, low-pressure areas.

Allowable The amount of oil and/or gas a well is permitted by state authorities to produce. Not all states impose allowables.

Anticline An underground hill; rock strata form an arch under which oil and gas are frequently found.

Assessment Capital in addition to original subscription amount. If mandatory, investor is obligated to furnish it upon program manager's call; if

This article appeared originally in the November, 1983 issue of **Oil & Gas Investor.** It appears here with the permission of the author and publisher.

optional or voluntary, investor is not obligated to pay it, but will suffer penalty for noncompliance, usually loss of interest of as much as 300% and possibly more.

Associated Gas Occurs with oil in a reservoir either as free gas or in solution. Also known as *gas-cap gas;* a gas cap is an area of free gas above an oil zone. Gas occurring alone in a reservoir is *unassociated gas.*

Bcf One billion cubic feet of gas.

BOP Blowout preventer. Device(s) that can prevent a blowout if activated in time.

BS&W Basic sediment and water, that is, the foreign material that comes up with the oil and gas and must be separated *(treated)* from the oil and gas before they can be sold.

Back-In Interest Form of carried interest (see below) in which the latter converts to a regular working interest after payout, that is, after the carrying parties have recouped their costs, the carried party converts to a regular fractional working interest, paying its share of costs and receiving its share of revenues.

Barnburner Every investor's dream—a super producer that will propel one toward early retirement.

Barrel Equals 42 gallons. Oil was first marketed in whatever barrels were available; price was per barrel regardless of volume. In 1866, the 42-gallon herring barrel was made the universal standard container.

Basement Hard, igneous or metamorphic rock lying below sedimentary formations. Seldom contains petroleum.

Blind Pool Where the drilling program prospectus does not specify the drilling prospects.

Blowout A sudden, violent escape of oil and/or gas from a well caused by uncontrolled high pressure. Usually occurs when the well is being drilled.

Bonus, Lease Up-front payment to the mineral owner for entering into a lease. Additional payments made over the lifetime of the lease are referred to as *rentals.* Once production is established, the percentage of gross production proceeds received by the mineral owner is referred to as royalty (see below).

Cable-tool Drilling Age-old method employs a chisel-like bit that is raised and dropped to pound a hole in the earth. Still being used, primarily to drill shallow wells in eastern U.S.

Calculated Absolute Open Flow (CAOF) A theoretical figure of gas well's maximum producing capability per day. Usually based on results of a "four-point" test that involves four different choke sizes.

Carried Interest Where a party or parties have their expenses paid (in effect, are carried) by other parties up to a specified limit. A fairly standard industry deal is known as *third for a quarter,* in which an investor pays 1/3 of the expenses for 1/4 of the revenue. The promoter is thus "carried" for a quarter. The industry phrase *carried to casing* means the party or parties being carried have all costs paid by other parties through drilling and up to the point of setting production casing, i.e., completion. *Carried to the tanks* means carried up to the point of sale of the product; the carrying parties pay the total cost of the well, including surface production facilities.

Casing Sections of steel pipe set in a well to prevent the walls of the hole from caving in, to seal off fluids and permit production through selected perforations. *Through the casing:* When a well with good natural pressure flows without production tubing in the hole.

Casinghead Gas Gas that is produced along with oil from an oil well.

Choke An orifice installed in a pipeline at the well surface to control the rate of flow. Choke size, expressed in 64ths of an inch, is the diameter of the opening.

Christmas Tree Valves, gauges and chokes assembled at wellhead to control production.

Circulation, Lost When the mud (see below) does not recirculate to the surface because it is disappearing into a *thief zone,* a highly porous cavity. Such a zone must be immediately plugged with lost circulation materials (nut shells, sawdust, newspapers, cellophane, etc.), slurry or a chemical mix. Otherwise the well is at the mercy of any sudden high-pressure surge.

Compensatory Royalty Payment to the mineral owner(s) in case the operator fails to fully develop a lease.

Completion The process by which a well is brought to its final classification: dry hole or producer. A dry hole is completed by being plugged (see below). A well deemed to be commercially producible is completed by installing casing and production tubing downhole and surface production equipment.

Condensate Hydrocarbons in the gaseous state that become liquid as they leave the reservoir. Also known as *distillate.*

Contract Carriage Provision that a pipeline transport a producer's gas to its buyer (a distribution company or an end-user), despite the pipeline's refusal to purchase the gas, providing the pipeline has spare carrying capacity.

Core A solid column of rock up to four inches in diameter taken from a formation for study by geologists.

Curtailment When a well is forced to produce less per day than specified in purchase contract.

Day Rate Drilling contract where the contractor charges a fixed rate per day, no matter how much (if any) footage is drilled. Day rates prevail in high-risk formations, such as the Overthrust, and during a boom, when drilling rigs and crews are hard to get.

Dedicated Reserves Natural gas supply under contract to a pipeline company.

Deliverability A well's tested ability to deliver, or produce. Often not the same as the well's allowable production.

Development Well Drilled in the proven territory of a field, for the purpose of completing the desired pattern of production. The likelihood of a development well being a producer is fairly high.

Directional Drilling Drilling at an angle rather than vertically. Its many uses include controlling a blowout; avoiding populated areas, parks and difficult terrain; and targeting many locations from one site, especially in offshore drilling.

Doodlebugger Oil explorationist who relies on unconventional aids, from tea leaves to chemical or electrical paraphernalia. Sometimes doodlebuggers strike oil. Term is also jokingly applied to seismologists.

Downstream Term applied to refining and marketing phases of the industry. *Upstream* activities are concerned with finding petroleum and producing it.

Drillstem Test A test through the drillpipe to determine if oil or gas is present in a certain formation; preliminary sampling before well is completed.

Dry Hole. Also *duster*. An unsuccessful well. It may have oil and gas shows and still not be commercially producible.

Dry Hole Costs A well's drilling expenses (excluding lease costs) up to the point of deciding whether or not to complete it for production. Refers to the fact that at that point the costs are the same whether the well is a dry hole or a future producer.

Dual or Multiple Completion Completing a well with simultaneous production from two or more formations at different depths. Saves drilling two wells but more complex process.

Exploratory Well Also *wildcat*. Generally, a well drilled in an unproven area. More precisely, a well drilled no less than one mile from known production. Term originated in early drilling days in Pennsylvania when wells were drilled within sight and sound of wildcats.

Farm-In, Farmout If Company A wishes to earn an interest in Company B's lands or leases, or to acquire assignment of the lease, it farms in by drilling one or more wells, or performing some other activity. Company B has farmed out the land or lease, and may retain a variety of interests. Terms of such agreements vary considerably. Companies with substantial land positions may wish to farm out in order to *prove up the acreage,* i.e., have it explored, evaluated.

Fault A break or fracture in the earth's crust that causes rock layers to shift.

Fault Trap Oil or gas in a porous section of rock is sealed off by a displaced, nonporous layer.

Fee Lands Private lands, that is, nonpublic. Public lands belong to or are controlled by the federal government or one of its branches, states, counties, cities, school systems, boards and commissions, and Indian reservations.

Field An area in which a number of wells produce from a reservoir. There may be several reservoirs at various depths in a single field.

Fishing Retrieving tool or pipe that has come loose downhole.

Flaring, Venting Flaring is burning of gas vented through a pipe or stack. A method of disposing of gas while the well is being completed, or afterwards, if there is no market or other use for it. Flaring is regulated by state agencies; regulations vary from state to state. Venting—letting unwanted gas escape unburned—is generally prohibited.

Flowing Well One that produces oil and/or gas through natural reservoir energy and doesn't require pumping.

Footage Rate Drilling contract where the contractor charges strictly on the basis of footage drilled, no matter how little or how much progress is made on a given day. Usually a much better deal for the investor.

Formation A bed or deposit over a specific area, composed of substantially the same kinds of rocks. Also referred to as an *horizon.*

Fracturing, Frac'ing, Frac Job Fluids pumped under extremely high pressure into a formation to create or enlarge fractures through which oil and gas can move. *Propping agents (proppant)* such as sand are sent down with fluids to hold the fractures open. See *Stimulation Techniques.*

Front End Costs Percentage of initial capital contribution paid by limited partners for organizational and offering costs, such as sales commissions, management fees, general and administrative overhead.

Functional Allocation Program structure in which limited partners pay intangible (non-capital) costs, and general partner pays tangible (capital) costs. (See below.)

Greenshoe Provision Increase of the initial offering of a partnership by a set amount, as a response to market demand, at the general partner's option.

Heads Up An oil company or individual who drills heads up does so without outside funds.

Intangible or Noncapital Costs Partnership costs deductible for federal income tax purposes, such as costs incurred in drilling, testing, completing and reworking wells—labor, contract drilling, drillsite preparation, fuel, repairs, hauling, supplies, drilling mud, among others. The determining factor is that the item not have salvage value.

Joint Venture Where two or more parties (generally oil companies, but not always) agree to cooperate on a project. Differs from a standard partnership in that the project has large-scale scope, and in that one party provides the funds and the other party (which generally serves as the operator) furnishes the industry expertise, the staff, sometimes the acreage and/or the seismic data. In a joint venture, costs and profits are shared proportionately. Each venturer retains control over its interest, including the right to sell it. Each venturer has unlimited liability as to its interest. The operator is required to report to the other venturers.

Kick A well is said to *take a kick* when the pressure encountered in a formation penetrated while drilling exceeds the pressure exerted by the column of drilling mud circulating through the hole. If uncontrolled, a kick can lead to a blowout.

Kill A Well To overcome a high-pressure surge by *loading the hole,* that is, adding weighting elements to the drilling mud.

Landman Individual, self-employed or oil company employee, who secures oil and gas leases, checks legal titles, and attempts to cure title defects. The link between explorationist and the drilling itself, the landman is the person the royalty-hungry mineral owner is happy to see come through the door. The species is said to have incredible tolerance for vast quantities of coffee. Also known as *lease hound.*

Lease Broker Individual engaged in obtaining leases for speculation or resale.

Lifting Costs Synonym for operating expenses, that is, those incurred in operating a lease and equipment on it to produce oil and gas. Drilling costs are not included.

Log(s) The three basic kinds of logs—electrical, radioactive and sonic—have several subtypes. Basically, the logging device is lowered into the wellbore and transmits signals to the surface. These are recorded on film and then used to make a log showing the recorded measurements. The latter are used to analyze the formation's porosity, fluid saturation and lithology. The log's *header* gives the log's type and date, the operator, well name, field (if any), county and state, spot location, temperature, type of fluid in the hole, etc. Many (but not all) states require logs to be filed with the regulatory agency; the filing of a log is always required by the federal government if the drillsite is on federal land.

Mcf One thousand cubic feet of gas. *MMcf* = one million cubic feet of gas.

Market-Out Gas purchase contract clause with many variations. Basically it allows purchaser, at his discretion, to stop paying original contract price and institute lower price, with the intent of maintaining marketability of the gas. Some contracts may allow the producer to be released from the contract if he refuses the lower price; some contracts allow him, if he finds a buyer willing to pay a higher price, to sell his gas upon payment of a transportation fee to the original contract party; other contracts offer other remedies.

Mineral Rights Ownership of minerals under a tract, which includes right to explore, drill and produce such minerals, or assign such right in the form of a lease to another party. Such ownership may or may not be severed from land surface ownership. *Title in fee simple* means all rights are held by one owner; the *fee in surface* owner does not hold mineral rights. *Minerals* is loosely used to refer to mineral ownership and even, incorrectly, to royalty ownership. A *mineral acre* is the full mineral interest under one acre of land.

Mud Fluid of varying weights and thicknesses used in rotary drilling, so called because the original drilling fluid was, indeed, mud. It circulates from its mixing pit down the drillstem, flows into the hole through drill bit openings, and flows back up the sides of the hole into the mud pit. Its purpose is to carry cuttings to the surface, lubricate the drill bit, stabilize the hole (thus preventing cave-ins) and, perhaps most importantly, control sub-surface pressure through its weight. (Formation pressures of 20,000 pounds per square inch have been encountered.

Mud Logging Also *hydrocarbon well logging*. Basic function is to detect and position with respect to depth all hydrocarbons accumulations in the borehole. This is done by analyzing the rock cuttings and the gases associated with the oil brought up from downhole by the drilling fluids. The cuttings are sifted out through a vibrating screen, the *shale shaker*. Gases are detected by aerating the mud, thus breaking loose hydrocarbon molecules. Gas is then brought into a total-gas detector and chromatograph, which gives the quantity of total gas as well as its composition, such as ethane, methane, propane, etc. The well log analyst (or mud logger) then collects the cutting and gas data and drafts a time-versus-depth log on which all accumulated information is shown graphically.

Net Profits Interests As the name implies, a share of the fluids remaining after royalties and operating expenses have been paid. Like the overriding royalty (see below), it is carved out of the working interests and continues for the life of the lease.

Nonoperating Interest Such owners are without operating rights; they bear no part of the drilling or production costs and have no control over these activities.

Offset Well Typically refers to well drilled near the discovery well. Its purpose is to define the reservoir. Term also refers to the kind of well drilled on one tract of land to prevent oil and gas from draining to an adjoining tract where a well is being drilled or is already producing.

Oil or Production Payment A fractional share of production, free of costs of production, terminating when a specified dollar amount or volume of production is reached.

Operating Interest. Also *working interest, leasehold interest.* The interest (1/32nd, 1/8th, 1/4th, etc.) in a mineral property evidenced by a lease or other form of contract, such as mineral deed. Working interest owners have the right to conduct activities on the property (though the management of operations is assigned to one party—see *Operator*); they bear all costs and receive all revenues after taxes and royalties are paid.

Operator The party holding all or a fraction of the operating, or working, rights in a property or lease and designated as manager of operations, such as exploration, drilling, production. If the operator is a contractor, the term used is *contract operator.*

Overriding Royalty (ORRI) A different animal from standard royalty in that it is payable to someone other than mineral owner, often as landman's or geologist's incentive and/or reward. Carved out of operating interests, it pays its owner a share of gross production free of exploration, drilling and production costs.

Payoff When a well's production begins to bring in revenues. Incorrectly used interchangeably with payout.

Payout The amount of time it takes to recover the capital investment made on a well or drilling program. One of the yardsticks of profitability, it is a more complex yardstick than it appears to be at first glance.

Perforations Series of holes in casing and cement through which oil and gas flow from formation into wellbore and up to surface. Holes are usually made with a shaped explosive charge.

Permeability A measure of how easily fluids may flow through pore spaces; expressed in *millidarcies*. A tight rock, sand or formation will have low permeability and, thus, low capacity to produce. Wells in these zones usually require fracturing or other stimulation.

Plug To fill a hole with cement and/or mud as required by state regulations in abandoning a well.

Pool See *Reservoir*.

Porosity Pore space in rock enables it to hold fluids; measured in percentages from near zero to 35%.

Possible Reserves Production is presumed possible through geological interference of a strongly speculative nature.

Primary Recovery Production from a reservoir, through flowing or pumping wells, because of the existence of natural energy within the reservoir. Recovers 10% to 35% of the oil and gas in place.

Probable Reserves Not proved but presumed capable of production because of geological interference, that is, proximity to proved reserves in the same reservoir and experience in the same kind of reservoir.

Production Platform An immobile, offshore structure from which wells are drilled and/or produced. In general, wildcat wells are drilled from floating vessels (semisubmersible rigs and drillships) or from jackups, whose legs rest on the ocean floor; development wells are usually drilled from platforms.

Production Test Determines daily rate of oil, gas and water production from potential pay zone. Meaningful test after permanent production equiment has been installed. *IP* = initial potential determined by a production test.

Prospect A lease or group of leases on which an operator intends to drill.

Proved Behind-Pipe Reserves Recoverable by recompleting existing wells.

Proved Developed Reserves Recoverable from existing wells with existing facilities from open, producing pay zones.

Proved Undeveloped Reserves Recoverable through new wells on undrilled acreage, deepening existing wells, or secondary recovery methods, such as waterfloods.

Pumping Well One that does not flow naturally and requires a pump to bring oil and/or gas to the surface.

Recompletion To rework a well so that it produces from a different formation, either shallower or deeper than original completion.

Reduced Takes When purchaser takes (buys) a lesser quantity than stated in original purchase contract. Usually a negotiated reduction in exchange for some concession, perhaps on price or contract terms.

Reef A buildup of limestone formed by skeletal remains of marine organisms. It often makes an excellent reservoir for petroleum.

Regulatory Agencies Most states have an oil and gas commission to regulate the industry. Their names and responsibilities vary; one of the busiest is the Texas Railroad Commission, which guides operations in that heavily drilled state. Operators typically are required to apply for permits and file reports for all phases of drilling through transporting and refining. Regulations can cover the spacing of wells, amount of oil and gas that can be produced, as well as procedures for plugging and abandoning. Reports are required for spudding, depth, testing, completion or recompletion. In some states some operators may request their reports be kept confidential (see *tight hole)* for a certain period.

Relief Well A well drilled to a high-pressure formation to control a blowout.

Reserves Estimated amount of oil and gas in a given reservoir capable of being profitably recovered, assuming current costs, prices and technology. Not to be confused with *oil and gas in place,* which is the total amount of petroleum in the earth regardless of whether or not it can be technologically and/or commercially recovered. *Recovery* is a function not only of technology, but of the marketplace.

Reservoir A single accumulation of oil and/or gas trapped in a rock body. Also called *horizon.*

Reservoir Energy The natural forces that cause petroleum to move toward producing wells. Reservoirs are classified by the types of energy present. The principal mechanisms are: solution gas drive; gas cap drive (free gas expansion); water drive; gravity drainage; expansion of reservoir oil above its bubble point. The usual situation is what has been termed a combination drive.

Rotary Drilling Widely used modern method employs a rotating bit to cut through rock formations and drilling mud to remove cuttings. (See *Mud.)* Faster and more efficient than cable tool drilling.

Royalty Share of gross production proceeds from a property received by its mineral owner(s), free of exploration, drilling and production costs. Typically 1/8th to 1/6th of production, but may be other, higher fractions. Royalty payments take precedence over all other payments from lease revenues. Payment also may be in kind.

Scout This ferret-eyed individual observes and reports on competitors' leasing and drilling activities.

Secondary Recovery To supplement the natural reservoir drive, water or gas is injected into reservoir to force additional oil to the producing wells. Waterflooding is the most common secondary technique.

Seismic Survey Gathering information on underground strata in a specific area, onshore or offshore, by recording and analyzing shock waves artificially produced and reflected from subsurface rocks. *Shooting* = seismic survey.

Shoot A Well An explosive charge, say, nitroglycerine, is electrically set off downhole to crack open a tight formation. Not, as one might think, the act of a frustrated investor. See *Stimulation Techniques.*

Shut In To close the valves at the wellhead so the well stops flowing or producing. A shut-in well may be waiting for a pipeline connection, for a sweetening plant to be built, or for the market to improve.

Shut-In Royalty Payable to the mineral owner(s) if production is shut in, its purpose is to hold the lease till production actually begins.

Sour Gas Contains hydrogen sulfide. A *sweetening plant* must remove the H_2S before the gas can be sold.

Spud To start the drilling of a well.

Stepout Well Also *extension well.* Drilled a "step out" from proved territory of a field to determine the producing formation's boundaries.

Stimulation Techniques Many completed wells require additional treatment before oil and gas can be produced.

Stratigraphic Test A hole drilled only to gather information about rock strata in a certain area—the general character of the rocks, their porosity and permeability.

Stratigraphic Trap Hydrocarbons are retained in a porous section of rock by surrounding nonporous layers.

Stripper A well that yields 10 or fewer barrels of oil per day. A *gas stripper* is a designated gas well that produces no more than 60,000 cubic feet of gas a day during a 90-day production period and no more than one barrel of oil along with the gas.

Structural Trap A deformation in earth's layers of rock halts passage of petroleum.

Swab Test Fluids are lifted, or swabbed, to the surface with a cup-shaped rubber device. Fluids are measured to suggest well's potential.

Tcf Trillion cubic feet of gas.

TD Total depth drilled. A well is not always completed at its TD; the producing horizon may be up hole.

Take-or-Pay Gas purchase contract clause establishing amount a purchaser must either buy and take into its line, or pay for while actually taking possession later.

Tangible or Capital Costs Partnership costs required to be capitalized for federal income tax purposes (and recovered through depreciation and depletion), such as expenses for lease acquisition and related geological and/or geophysical work; all tangible equipment, purchased or leased, for drilling, completion and production. Expenses related to dry holes or leases abandoned without production are generally considered noncapital costs.

Tertiary Recovery Involves complex, exotic methods such as steam, chemicals, gases or heat. Total recovery by primary, secondary and tertiary methods may be as high as 75% of reservoir's oil and gas.

Tight Hole Drilling and completion information is not publicly released by the operator. Frequently secrecy is maintained so an operator may acquire surrounding acreage before news of a discovery drives up the price. Tight holes are rumor mills.

Toolpusher A foreman or supervisor in charge of one or more drilling rigs.

Tripping Pulling the drillpipe from the hole to change the bit and running drillpipe and new bit back in the hole. On deep wells, *round trips* or *a trip* may take 24 hours, that is, three eight-hour shifts.

Turnkey Drilling contract where the contractor, for a fixed amount, furnishes all labor, materials and equipment, and does all the work necessary to drill a well, to casing point or to completion, so all owner has to do is "turn the key." Generally used in areas where drilling problems are minimal and predictable, and costs fairly uniform.

Wildcat See *Exploratory Well.*

Workover To clean out or work on a well in order to restore or increase production.

Zone An indefinite term, but generally a specific interval of rock strata. Generally used interchangeably with formation.

INVESTMENT DECISION CHECKLIST
By Lewis G. Mosburg, Jr.

PRELIMINARY CONSIDERATIONS

General Suitability:

- Psychological Suitability
- "Staying Power": ability to deal with:
    - Assessments
    - " 'Time-Line' Diversification"
- Delayed Cash Flow
- Minimum Subscription Requirement ($5,000-$10,000)

Investment Vehicle: select diversified limited partnership unless can *personally*:

- Analyze
- Monitor
- Diversify

Public versus Private Offering:

- Don't invest privately unless can afford minimum subscription *per partnership* of $25,000 ($12,500 well-by-well)
- Base choice on quality of management (see below), *not* public versus private

Nature of Properties:

- **Location and Degree of Dry-Hole Risk:**
    - Select blend of Controlled Exploratory and Higher-Risk/Higher-Return Developmental
    - Avoid "frontier wildcat" and "sure-thing" areas
    - Consider "balanced" program of producing properties and high-quality drilling (permits acceptance of greater drilling risk)
- **Specified versus Unspecified ("Blind Pool"):** unspecified gives greater flexibility to sponsor to make *everyone* more money, *if*:
    - *Type* of drilling fully disclosed
    - Adequate due diligence and monitoring

- Lease "Net Revenue Interest" requirements (see below)

STRUCTURE ANALYSIS

In General:

- *Not* as useful a criterion as "Management Analysis" (see below)
- *Positive Structure Features*:
    - Limited front-end dilution
    - More favorable sharing arrangement (see below)
    - "Investor protection" features: *Democracy Rights* and *Program Monitoring*

Sharing Arrangement:

In General:

- Today's conditions permit negotiation of better deals (for investor) when:
    - Sponsor *acquires property*
    - Sponsor *assigns property* to investors/partnership
- *Don't go for "overkill"*
- Insure that sponsor's own promotion isn't merely "the tip of the iceberg"
- **"Traditional" versus Recommended Levels of Promotion and Lease Net Revenue Interest:**

Promotional Item:	Traditional	Recommended
Front-End Dilution:	15%	7½-10%
Sharing Arrangement:		
Carried Interest:	10%-15%	7.5%
Reversionary Interest:	25%-33⅓%	15%-25%
Functional Allocation:	20%-25% "spread"	15%-20% "spread"
Promoted Interest:	20%-25% "spread"	15%-20% "spread"

Item:	Traditional	Recommended
Sharing Arrangement (con't.):		
Combination:	6.25%-12.5% BPO; 25%-40% APO	3.25%-6.25% BPO; 15%-20% APO
Net Revenue Interest:		
To Partnership:	70%-75%	78%-82%
To Investors:	45%	60%-65%

Compensation For Services and Conflicts of Interest:

- **In General:**
    - Sponsor will be reimbursed for:
        - *Organizational & Offering Costs* (not to exceed 15% [7.5% preferred]), including *direct sales commissions* (not to exceed 10%), but *not* "wholesaling costs"
        - *Direct costs* of program
        - *General Administrative Overhead* (*don't* "cap")
    - Services should be provided at not more than competitive rates
    - Conflicts of interest will *always* be present (and not always resolved in investors' favor)
- *Generally avoid*:
    - "Mark-ups" on leases or any transfer of goods (other than to "adjusted" [time value] cost)
    - Turnkey drilling (if turnkeyed to other than an unaffiliated, independent drilling contractor)
    - Unreasonable "proving up" of acreage retained by sponsor
    - Sale of program properties to sponsor or affiliate *on any basis*, except sale to affiliated program at *higher* of cost or fair market value
    - Reservation by sponsor or any affiliate (except "screening" personnel) of *any* interest in production outside the program, or of overriding royalty interests whether within or outside the program
    - Loans *by* sponsor to program at unreasonable interest rates, or loans *to* sponsor by program on any basis
    - Non-refundable prepayment of completion costs before completion decision reached

- **Other Structure Features**
  - **Assessments:**
    - Generally, a "plus"
    - Must be limited to not more than 10% for mandatory assessments and 100% for optional assessments
  - **Liquidity Features:**
    - Redemption and Exchange features generally a "plus"
    - Should be based upon Independent Appraisal
  - **Insurance:**
    - Adequate insurance a must
    - "Investor protection" policies a "plus"

ANALYZING PROFIT POTENTIAL

In General:
- Analyze management's "credentials" to insure *appearance* of adequate experience level ("in-house" or retained)
- Analyze net worth

"Track Record" Analysis: Analyze Net Cash/Payout Tables to determine:
- "Average" 10-year "ROI" (should be in excess of 2:1— preferably 2.5:1 or higher)
- Per-partnership probability and Constancy Level

Present Potential:
- **In General:** Insist on:
  - Thorough due diligence
  - "Program Monitor" feature
  - "Analyze Your Analyst": verify quality of proposed advisor/adequacy of due diligence by:
  - Reviewing "track record" of presently-recommended programs
  - Whether or not advisor is insisting on inclusion of positive-for-investor features (e.g., reduced levels of promotion and front-end dilution, "program monitor" feature, etc.)